COLONIAL ROOTS OF MODERN BRAZIL

Colonial Roots of Modern Brazil

PAPERS OF THE NEWBERRY LIBRARY
CONFERENCE

Edited by Dauril Alden

UNIVERSITY OF CALIFORNIA PRESS
BERKELEY, LOS ANGELES, LONDON 1973

University of California Press
Berkeley and Los Angeles, California
University of California Press, Ltd.
London, England

Copyright © 1973, by
The Regents of the University of California

ISBN: 0–520–02140–1
Library of Congress Catalog Card Number: 78–174458
Printed in the United States of America
Designed by Dave Comstock

Dedicated to the memory of
FREDERICK ARTHUR HOLDEN HALL 1915–1972
A scholar and a friend to scholarship

Contents

Maps and Graphs

Preface

Since the first International Colloquium on Luso-Brazilian Studies was held in Washington, D.C., in 1950, a number of scholarly meetings in the United States have considered *inter alia* the history of colonial Brazil, but the Newberry Conference (November 21–22, 1969) was the first to be devoted exclusively to that subject. Plans for such a conference were first discussed at a breakfast organized by Professor Lewis Hanke in Cambridge, Massachusetts, during the 1966 Luso-Brazilian Colloquium. On that occasion, several scholars indicated the desirability of such a conference, and Dr. Lawrence W. Towner, Director and Librarian of The Newberry Library in Chicago, the premier research center in the United States for the study of Luso-Brazilian history, expressed a strong interest in holding the conference at his institution. Early in 1967 a planning committee was formed, consisting of the late Dr. Howard F. Cline, then Director of the Hispanic Foundation of the Library of Congress, and Professors Hanke, Stuart B. Schwartz, Engel Sluiter, Stanley J. Stein, and Dauril Alden (chairman).

After considering various suggestions, some of which had to be rejected because of limitations of funds, the committee decided that the conference ought to bring together young, established, and senior Brazilianists who were particularly interested in Brazil's colonial experience. The planners hoped that the meeting would stimulate in the United States scholarly interest in research on Brazil's colonial past and that the papers written for the conference would be of interest to both Brazilianists and other students of Latin America. Although financial restrictions made it impossible to invite as many scholars from the United States and abroad as the committee wished, efforts were made to include a few eminent Brazilianists from abroad. The meeting was intended primarily for historians, but the committee decided to invite specialists in other fields whose work was particularly relevant to that of historians of colonial Brazil.

Instead of seeking papers from well-known Brazilianists, the committee chose to tap the talents of a promising group of young

Brazilianists who had recently engaged in archival work for their dissertations but had not had an opportunity to present their findings to a scholarly audience. In order to place their contributions within a broad historical perspective, the committee commissioned a leading historian to review the status of scholarship concerning the history of colonial Brazil. Senior scholars also were asked to chair the four working sessions, and other well-known Brazilianists, including several foreign scholars, were invited to serve as discussants. The task of recording informal remarks on the papers during the working sessions was entrusted to a number of advanced graduate students and recent recipients of the doctorate.

The model for the Newberry meeting was the successful conference on seventeenth-century English America held at the Institute of Early American History in 1957.[1] Before the conference began, copies of all papers, except the address to the banquet, were circulated to all participants, including invited guests. At the beginning of each of the two segments of the working sessions, the authors were given a few moments to summarize their major findings; next, discussants focused attention on particular issues raised by the papers; a general discussion followed.[2]

The Newberry Conference was attended by about forty scholars led by Charles R. Boxer, a distinguished student of the Portuguese empire, who served as our evening speaker. The working sessions were chaired by Professors Manoel Cardozo (Director of the Oliveira Lima Library, the Catholic University of America), Bailey W. Diffie (formerly of the City University of New York), Charles E. Nowell (University of Illinois), and Robert C. Smith (Department of Art History, University of Pennsylvania). The discussants were Professor E. Bradford Burns (University of California, Los Angeles), Dr. José António Gonsalves de Mello (Director, Instituto de Ciências Humanas, Universidade Federal de Pernambuco), Fr. Mathias C. Kiemen (former Director, the Academy of American Franciscan History and former editor of *The Americas*), Professora Eulália

---

1. See James Morton Smith, ed. *Seventeenth-century America: Essays in Colonial History* (Chapel Hill, 1959).

2. The authors were expected to revise their papers after the meeting in the light of both the prepared and the informal remarks of participants; therefore it was decided not to publish such comments. In the months since the meeting nearly all of the papers have been substantially rewritten, and some have been enriched by the results of further research and refinements in research techniques.

Maria Lahmeyer Lobo (University of South Carolina), Professor
Frédéric Mauro (Université de Paris-Nanterre), and Professors Rich-
ard M. Morse (Yale University), Stanley J. Stein (Princeton Uni-
versity) and Hilgard O'Reilly Sternberg (Department of Geography,
University of California, Berkeley). The recorders included Dr.
Tarcísio Beal (United States Department of State), Miss Judith
Collins (University of Florida), Mr. and Mrs. Sheridan T. Grippen
(New York University), Mrs. Elizabeth Anne Kuznesof (University
of California, Berkeley), Miss Catherine Lugar (State University of
New York, Stony Brook), Professor Robert Mattoon (University
of Michigan), Professor Ann Pescatello (Washington University),
and Professor Sharon Wyatt (Wisconsin State University-River
Falls).

The affiliations of the essayists are indicated in the Table of
Contents.[3] With one exception, each had received his doctorate
within the three years preceding the conference. Each has received
fellowships that have enabled him to conduct extensive research in
the archives of both Portugal and Brazil. The planning committee
did not ask the contributors to shape their material in accordance
with the usual artifical general theme; each author was encouraged
to prepare a paper on a subject he considered particularly significant
and generally neglected or misunderstood. Some of the essays in this
volume represent themes that in different form appeared originally
in dissertations; others are based on research unrelated to the author's dissertation topic.

Whatever may have been lost by the absence of thematic unity
among these seven essays has been more than offset by the impressive contributions made by the papers. Professor Boxer surveyed
the state of the historiography of colonial Brazil in 1950; here he
reviews the literature two decades later, indicating where some gaps
have been closed and others remain. Professor Frank Dutra casts
new light on the significant but little studied rivalry between the
private donataries of Pernambuco and agents of the Crown in Bahia,
Lisbon, and Madrid during a period of increasing centralization of
royal authority. In his richly researched essay Professor Stuart
Schwartz demonstrates the important economic role played by the

3. Two of the essays contributed to the conference—"Colonial Brazil—
Coastal Enclave" by John Vogt (University of Georgia) and "Gomes Freire de
Andrada, Martinho de Mendonça and the Capitation Tax" by Robert White
(University of Massachusetts, Amherst)—will be published elsewhere.

hitherto largely overlooked independent small sugar growers (*lav-radores de cana*) in the captaincy of Bahia during the seventeenth and early eighteenth centuries. The revisionist essay by Professor Colin MacLachlan assigns a crucial role to the state in shifting the basis of Indian labor in the Amazon during the eighteenth century away from slavery and missionary paternalism toward a free market labor system. Inspired by well-known price studies undertaken by scholars in Europe and the United States, Professor Harold B. Johnson Jr. has painstakingly exploited previously neglected institutional archives in Rio de Janeiro to produce a pioneer study of the movements of prices and wages in Brazil's second capital during the late colonial and early national periods; he then compares his findings with those of the Latin American scholar Ruggiero Romano. The complex interplay between rival Spanish and Portuguese "freelances" and state agents during the eighteenth century that resulted in the winning of "the Brazilian West" for Portugal and ultimately for Brazil is the theme of Professor David M. Davidson's impressively researched essay. Last, Professor Kenneth R. Maxwell carefully assesses the internal and external political and economic factors that persuaded the Brazilian elite to reject republicanism and to support a continuation of monarchical government during the turbulent 1790s.

The co-sponsors of the Newberry Conference were The Newberry Library itself and the Conference on Latin American History, which contributed funds from its Ford Foundation grant. At a critical juncture the São Paulo-Illinois Partners of the Alliance program generously financed the travel of Professor Gonsalves de Mello. Throughout the preparations for the conference, Lawrence W. Towner assisted the planning committee in many ways, and during the meeting he and his charming wife Rachel gave a memorable banquet for the participants. Several members of Dr. Towner's capable staff, particularly Mr. Holden Hall, Dr. John Tedeschi, and Mr. James M. Wells, performed exceptional and indispensable tasks that greatly contributed to the success of the meeting. As chairman of the meeting and editor of the papers collected in this volume, I also wish to acknowledge the assistance of my ebullient fellow planner, Stuart B. Schwartz.

Among the invited guests of the conference was the ever-popular Dr. Ruth Lapham Butler, former Curator of the Newberry's Edward E. Ayer Collection (which contains a splendid array of colonial *brasiliana*) and William B. Greenlee Collection of Portuguese History and Literature. It is lamentable that the late Mr. Greenlee, founder of the collection which bears his name, could not have been present at this unique scholarly gathering; for one feels certain that he would have been pleased by the impressive convocation of Brazilianists in the comfortable second floor Fellows' Lounge of the Library and that, if he had had the opportunity to witness the lively discussions and to read the enlightening essays that follow, he would have been confident of the future of research by scholars in the United States on Brazil's colonial past.

All illustrative material for this volume was prepared by Mrs. Alice Alden except for that in Professor Johnson's essay. In the editorial preparation of these papers I have been ably assisted by Messrs. James Wells and the late Holden Hall whose sudden and untimely death deprived Brazilianists of a warm, exceedingly conscientious, ever supportive friend. It is fitting that this volume is dedicated to his memory.

D.A.

Abbreviations[*]

ABP—Arquivo Público da Bahia.
ABNRJ—*Anais da Biblioteca Nacional*, Rio de Janeiro, 1876—.
AGI—Archivo General de Indias, Sevilla.
AGS—Archivo General de Simancas.
AHI—Arquivo Histórico do Itamaraty, Rio de Janeiro.
AHU—Arquivo Histórico Ultramarino, Lisbon.
AMP—*Anais do Museu Paulista*, São Paulo, 1922—.
ANRJ—Arquivo Nacional, Rio de Janeiro.
ANTT—Arquivo Nacional da Tôrre do Tombo, Lisbon.
BAPP—Biblioteca e Arquivo Público do Pará, Bélem do Pará.
BNL/CP—Biblioteca Nacional, Lisbon. Coleção Pombalina.
BNL/FG—Biblioteca Nacional, Lisbon. Fundo Geral.
BNRJ—Biblioteca Nacional, Rio de Janeiro.
DH—Biblioteca Nacional, Rio de Janeiro. *Documentos históricos*, 1928—.
DI—Arquivo do Estado de São Paulo. *Publicação official de documentos interessantes para a história e customes de São Paulo*, 1895—.
HAHR—*Hispanic American Historical Review*, 1918—.
HCJB—*História da companhia de Jesús no Brasil*, by Serafim Leite, S.J., 10 vols. Lisbon-Rio de Janeiro, 1938–1950.
HCP—*História da colonização portuguesa do Brasil*, ed. Carlos Malheiro Dias, 3 vols. Lisbon, 1924–1926.
IHGB—Instituto Histórico e Geográfico Brasileiro. Rio de Janeiro.
IHGB/CU—The Arquivo Ultramarino collection of transcripts in the IHGB.
RAPM—*Revista do Arquivo Público Mineiro*, Belo Horizonte, 1896—.
RIHGB—*Revista do Instituto Histórico e Geográfico Brasileiro*, Rio de Janeiro, 1839—.

* Where two or more authors have used the same archives and the same manuscript and printed collections of sources or multivolume secondary works, citations have been abbreviated in accordance with this master list. Where only one author has used particular archives or manuscript or published collections, the citation is given *in extenso* the first time cited and thereafter in the abbreviated form indicated in the initial citation.

THE PAST IN
PRESENT PERSPECTIVE

MAP 1

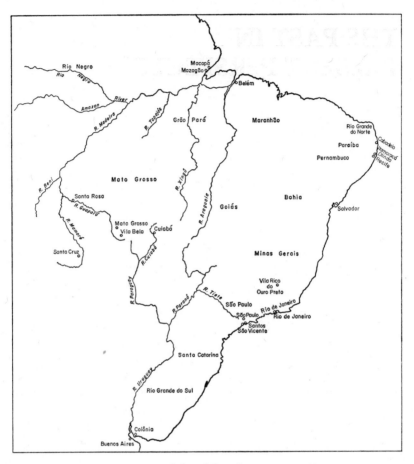

Colonial Brazil

CHARLES R. BOXER:

Some Reflections on the Historiography of Colonial Brazil, 1950-1970

In some brief remarks on the history of Colonial Brazil in a paper presented to the first International Colloquium on Luso-Brazilian Studies held in Washington, D.C., in October 1950, I quoted approvingly the late Professor Clarence Haring's observation in his (still indispensable) *The Spanish Empire in America*: "The present state of research into the colonial annals of Spanish America does not permit of an adequate, systematic description of society based upon solid documentation." I then observed that the same could be said, *mutatis mutandis*, of the history of the Portuguese colonial empire on three continents from the fifteenth to the nineteenth centuries.[1] Despite the great progress which has been made in both these fields in the past twenty years, there are still wide gaps in our knowledge of colonial Brazil. To fill them, we need both well-documented monographs on specific subjects and up-to-date works of synthesis. The latter necessarily depend on the existence of the former to be really satisfactory; but in order to get well-oriented and well-documented monographs, we need some general works which ask the right questions and suggest what lines of research would be both fruitful and useful—in other words, what worthwhile fields of historical research are still untilled or still inadequately exploited.

Admittedly, neither Portugal nor Brazil can produce the wealth of archival documentation possessed by the major Spanish and Spanish-American archives, such as those at Simancas, Seville, Madrid, and Mexico City. But there are some archives in Old and in New Lusitania, such as the Tôrre do Tombo and the Arquivo Histórico Ultramarino at Lisbon, and the archives of Minas Gerais at Belo Horizonte, which are richly provided with original material, if not

---

1. "Some Considerations on Portuguese Colonial Historiography," on pp. 169–180 of Vanderbilt University, ed., *Proceedings of the International Colloquium on Luso-Brazilian Studies, Washington, D.C., 1950* (Nashville, 1953). The remarks on Brazil are on pp. 176–178.

always with adequate catalogues. Moreover, there are numerous regional, local, municipal, and ecclesiastical archives, to say nothing of private archives, whose exploitation requires a substantial body of research workers, apart from those present at the Newberry Conference, to whose active, resourceful and successful efforts I shall only allude briefly. However, it is only fair to say here and now, that although much remains to be done, these pioneers have blazed the trail and, like the *bandeirantes* of old, have made things easier for those who come after them. In this connection, I should also like to pay tribute to the *Revista de História* of São Paulo, now in its twenty-first year, which has rendered such signal service not only to students of history in Brazil, but to historians on both sides of the Atlantic.

Reverting to the suggestions which I made to the Colloquium in 1950, I shall take in turn some of the points which I made then (*op. cit.*, pp. 176–177), and see how far we have progressed since then. I adverted in 1950 to the need to exploit some of the infrequently used regional archives of Brazil, such as those at Belém do Pará and at Belo Horizonte. This is now being done, as is evidenced by the works of several scholars to whom I shall have occasion to refer later. I have not myself worked in the archives of São João d'El Rei and Goiás, but those who have tell me there is plenty of rewarding material there. Doubtless this is true of several other regional and local archives. In this connection it would be useful to have a more detailed guide to the material in the Brazilian archives than Robert Levine's useful pioneer work, *Brazil: Field Research Guide in the Social Sciences* (School of International Affairs, Institute of Latin-American Studies, Columbia University, New York, 1966). More specifically, it would be useful to have a listing of all the archives' locations, hours of opening and closing, and state of cataloguing, with some indication of the material they contain. The recently published *Guia do Arquivo do Estado da Bahia* (Salvador, n. d., but 1968–1969 by the look of it) sets a useful precedent with its valuable survey of the colonial documentation, pp. 41–51.

Archival material in the U.S.A. should not be overlooked. For instance, anyone working on the critical years of Brazilian independence, 1822–1827, would do well to consult the voluminous papers of Sir Charles Stuart for the period of 1 January 1825 to 31 December 1826, which are now in the Lilly Library, Indiana University. They are complemented in part by the papers of a Portuguese politician covering a longer period in the first quarter of the nineteenth century, which form part of the George Boehrer Collection in the library of the University of Kansas. Copies of some of these documents may be in the archives of London and Lisbon, respectively (this is certainly true of Stuart's official correspondence with Canning), but the originals are now in the American Mid-West where one would not, at first blush, think of looking for them.

I observed in 1950 that there was no full-length and adequately documented biography of any of the leading governors of Colonial Brazil, comparable to Arthur Scott Aiton's *Antonio de Mendoza, First Viceroy of New Spain* (1927), or to Roberto Levillier's three-volume *Don Francisco de Toledo, Supremo Organizador del Perú* (1935–42). We now have Dauril Alden's masterly work on the Marquis of Lavradio, which portrays the man and his work firmly and expertly in the context of his time, thus greatly enhancing our knowledge of eighteenth-century Brazil.[2] We all look forward to the forthcoming biography of Francisco Barreto by José Antônio Gonsalves de Mello, whose superb two-volume study of João Fernandes Vieira is required reading for all students of seventeenth-century Brazil, and whose knowledge of the Ilíada Pernambucana is unrivalled. In 1950 I suggested a biography of Dom Pedro de Almeida Portugal (1688–1756), third Count of Assumar and successively Marquis of Castel-Novo and of Alorna, who was governor of Minas Gerais in 1717–1721, and Viceroy of India in 1744–1750. Assumar has recently found a biographer in Manuel Artur Norton, *Dom Pedro Miguel de Almeida Portugal*, (Lisboa, Agência Geral do Ultramar, 1967). This book, though well documented and extremely interesting on the viceroyalty of India, is weak on the governorship of Minas Gerais, for which it relies largely on such obsolete secondary works as Diogo de Vasconcelos' *História Antiga de Minas Gerais* and João Francisco Rocha Pombo's *História do Brasil*. An aspiring researcher might well direct his attention to another eighteenth-century fidalgo, Vasco Fernandes César de Menezes, Count of Sabugosa (1673–1741), Viceroy of India in 1712–1717, and of Brazil in 1720–1735. Both he and Assumar were *estrangeirados*; and if Assumar was more "enlightened" in some respects than Sabugosa,

2. Cf. the reviews of Alden's *Royal Government in Colonial Brazil* (University of California Press, 1968) in *The Times Literary Supplement* of 26 June 1969, and in *The Journal of Latin-American Studies*, I (Cambridge, Eng., 1969), 195–197.

the latter wielded a more pungent pen and never hesitated to write frankly to his royal master. Apart from whatever private papers his descendants may have (and I have reason to believe there are some), I have seen enough of his official correspondence in the archives at Lisbon and Bahia to affirm that he is worthy of another Alden.

Viceroys and governors were not, of course, the only *poderosos da terra* in colonial Brazil. Well-documented biographies are needed of such figures as the famous (or infamous, according to Assumar) *emboaba*, Manuel Nunes Viana (c.16??–1735); the Bahiano cattle-baron, João Peixoto Viegas (another wielder of a pungent pen); and the *sertanista*, Domingos Afonso Sertão, all of whom played a role in the urban life of Bahia as they did in the development of the *sertão*. The documentation may not be sufficient for a study in depth of the life and times of one man, but there is probably enough un-exploited material available for the social history of a particular family, such as the late Wanderley Pinho's *História de um engenho do Recôncavo, 1552–1944* (1946), and Lycurgo Santos Filho's *Uma comunidade rural do Brasil antigo: Aspectos da vida patriarcal no sertão da Bahia nos séculos XVIII e XIX* (1956), as John Russell-Wood has pointed out.

In this "century of the common man," I would not venture to suggest that biographical studies should be limited to the poderosos da terra and their families; but documentary material about the lives of the poor and lowly (which were often nasty, brutish, and short) must be hard to find, apart from the fact that the average *vil lavrador* and *vil mecânico* were illiterate. But sufficient archival material for a biography of some member of the middle class—a merchant, a government official, or an entrepreneur—may be available either in the voluminous records of the Inquisition at Lisbon, or in the archives of the Santa Casa de Misericórdia or the Third (Tertiary) Orders, which sometimes contain the papers of an accused person, or of a benefactor or debtor. In this connection, José Antônio Gonsalves de Mello, with whose fine monograph on *Antônio Fernandes de Matos, 1671–1701* (Recife, 1957) most students of colonial Brazil are probably familiar, is working on the papers and account-books of another prominent *mascate*, which are preserved in the archives of the Third Order of St. Francis at Recife. I do not know whether the Luso-Brazilian notarial archives contain biographical material on the scale of that which Ruth Pike was able to use for her splendid study of the Genoese at Seville. But I would hazard a guess that this potential source has not yet been adequately charted for the sixteenth to eighteenth centuries, let alone exploited.

In my 1950 paper, I made a plea for the historical study of regions which were then relatively neglected in comparison with the attention devoted to São Paulo, Pernambuco, Rio de Janeiro, and Bahia. Some of these gaps are now being filled. One such gap has been closed by David M. Davidson's recently completed (Yale, 1970) dissertation "Rivers & Empire: the Madeira Route and the Incorporation of the Brazilian Far West, 1737–1808." Whatever the shortcomings of Sebastião José de Carvalho e Melo and his brother Francisco Xavier de Mendonça Furtado, "that sinister pair," as Mr. Davidson has so aptly christened them, certainly left for posterity an enormous mass of documentation. This is likely to provide material for generations of Ph.D. students, although they may find the task of winnowing the wheat from the chaff rather wearying at times. From what I have seen of the archives of Minas Gerais, I think that Gomes Freire de Andrada also left behind him much manuscript material of the period 1733–1763, which has not yet been fully exploited, despite the attention devoted to that peregrinating martinet by Jaime Cortesão and others. This suspicion is considerably strengthened by a perusal of Robert White's interesting paper.

The hope I expressed in 1950 that Fr. Serafim Leite, S.J's., truly monumental history of the Jesuits in Brazil would be followed by comparable histories of the other religious orders working in the Land of the True Cross has not been fulfilled, although perhaps there is not sufficient archival documentation available in some instances. We have had, however, some useful and scholarly contributions to such a history, including those by Fr. Mathias Kiemen, O.F.M., Fr. Basílio Röwer, O.F.M., and Fr. Venâncio Willeke, O.F.M.[3] "A connected history of the activities of the Inquisition's emissaries in Brazil," which I ventured to describe as an obvious *desideratum* in 1950, has not yet appeared; but a major advance was made with the publication of Arnold Wiznitzer's carefully researched and meticulously documented history of *The Jews in Colonial Brazil* (Columbia

3. Mathias C. Kiemen, O.F.M., *The Indian Policy of Portugal in the Amazon Region, 1614–1693* (Washington, D.C., 1954); Basílio Röwer, O.F.M., *Os Franciscanos no sul do Brasil durante o século XVIII* (Petrópolis, 1954); Venâncio Willeke, O.F.M., *A Província Franciscana de Santo António do Brasil através das suas estatísticas* (Lisboa, 1966), to cite only one example of the works by each of these authors.

University Press, 1960), undoubtedly the definitive work on this aspect of the subject. I made the rather trite observation in 1950 that "in the fields of economic and institutional history, an enormous amount of research work remains to be done before any really adequate history can be published." Fortunately, it is in just these two fields that the most progress has been made in recent years. Apart from Dauril Alden's exhaustive analysis of the Pombaline fiscal reforms and their impact in his *Royal Government in Colonial Brazil*, we have John Russell-Wood's fascinating study in depth of the Misericórdia at Bahia, *Fidalgos and Philanthropists, 1550–1755* (1968), with its wealth of new information and new insights; Mlle. Andrée Mansuy's superb edition of Antonil's classic *Cultura e Opulência do Brasil por suas drogas e minas* (1711), which at last gives us an absolutely trustworthy text and a definitive annotation of this oft-quoted but hitherto inadequately edited work;[4] and Pierre Verger's massive *Flux et Reflux de la Traite des Nègres entre le Golfe de Bénin et Bahia de Todos os Santos du XVIIe au XIXe siècle* (Paris and The Hague, 1968) which covers a subject he is uniquely qualified to handle, having long been equally at home in Bahia, Dahomey, and Nigeria. Frédéric Mauro's *Le Portugal et l'Atlantique au XVIIe siècle, 1570–1670: Étude économique* (Paris, 1960), has deservedly become an indispensable *vade mecum* for anyone dealing with almost any aspect of seventeenth-century Brazil. Mauro has integrated the economic history of Brazil with that of Portugal, the Atlantic Islands, and West Africa more successfully than anyone else has yet done for the period in question, and his book serves in this and in other respects both as a guide and as a model.

Alice Canabrava's admirable monograph on *O Comércio português no Rio da Prata, 1580–1640* (1944) was already published when I compiled my 1950 paper, although by some oversight I failed to mention it; but Myriam Ellis's important contributions on the Colonial Brazilian salt gabelle, the provisioning of Minas Gerais, and the whale fishery (*O monopólio da sal no estado do Brasil, 1631–1801*, "Contribuição ao estudo do abastecimento das zonas mineradoras no século XVIII," and *Aspectos da pesca da baleia no Brasil colonial*), fall within our purview, having been published between

4. Andrée Mansuy, *André João Antonil. Cultura e Opulência do Brasil por suas drogas e minas: Texte de l'édition de 1711, traduction française et commentaire critique* (Paris, 1968).

1955 and 1959. There is no need to recall all the other works on colonial Brazilian economic and institutional history which have appeared in the last twenty years,[5] and I shall content myself with mention of a couple which are of particular interest to me owing to their connection with maritime history: Manuel Nunes Dias's well-documented if at times rather repetitive studies on the Pombaline trading companies for the Maranhão-Pará and Pernambuco-Paraíba,[6] and Roberto do Amaral Lapa's *A Bahia e a carreira da India* (Marília, 1966).

But if much has been done, much still remains to be done. The Brazil Company and its *junta* successor, which lasted in one form or another from 1649 to 1720, have not yet found the historian for whom I hoped in 1950. The pioneer work by Gustavo de Freitas, *A Companhia geral do comércio do Brasil, 1649–1720: Subsídios para a história econômica de Portugal e do Brasil* (São Paulo, 1951), is just what it claims to be, *subsídios*—contributions and material for a history of the Brazil Company—not the definitive history thereof. Invaluable as a guide to the unpublished documentation on the company in some Portuguese archives, de Freitas' monograph will serve as a corner stone (or as a launching pad, if a Space Age metaphor is preferred) for whoever decides to tackle such a history. Apart from the documents listed by Senhor de Freitas, much other relevant material doubtless exists. For instance, the Lilly Library at Indiana University possesses the original letter book of a Portuguese merchant (as yet unidentified), based at Lisbon, but with correspondents at Bahia, Pernambuco, Rio de Janeiro, Luanda, Madeira, Terceira, Venice, Hamburg, Rouen, and Amsterdam.[7] This codex contains copies of 349 letters written between 1646 and 1656— exactly the crisis years of the Luso-Dutch war in the Atlantic, when Portugal's survival hung in the balance, and when the convoys of the Brazil Company played their most vital part. Moreover, publication of this codex and its annotation by a competent economic historian (which I do not profess to be) might well prove as welcome to us as was Dona Virginia Rau's model edition of O *"Livro de*

5. Including the valuable series sponsored by the Instituto do Açúcar e do Álcool, *Documentos para a história do açúcar,* largely inspired by Dr. Gil de Methodio Maranhão.

6. Manuel Nunes Dias, "Fomento e mercantilismo: política económica portuguesa na baixada maranhense (1755–1778)," *V Colóquio internacional de estudos luso-brasileiros,* II (Coimbra, 1965), 17–97.

7. Lilly Library, call-mark, MS. 24861.

Rezão" de Antonio Coelho Guerreiro (Lisbon, 1956) for a slightly later period of the triangular trade between Portugal, Brazil, and Angola.

As a compulsive bibliophile, I hope I may be excused for mentioning that I have in my own library the original MS "Livro I de Viagens" of Gonçalo Xavier de Barros Alvim, a codex of some 477 folio pages which cover, in the form of shipboard journals from 1719 to 1738, the writer's services in the Brazil Fleets, including his naval service in the inconclusive Rio de la Plata campaigns of 1736–1737. I have not been able to locate the companion volume(s) (which presumably existed, as this one is numbered "Livro I"), which evidently cover his further services in the Brazil Fleets from 1738 to 1760, when he became garrison commander of Bahia. There, in 1761–1762, he served as one of the interim governors-general of Brazil, and there he died eleven years later. This codex, of which I hope to publish a summary catalogue one day, will be invaluable for anyone who wants to make a study of the eighteenth-century Brazil Fleets—a subject much neglected in comparison with the better known and more glamorous carracks and galleons of the *Carreira da Índia*.

It is welcome news that Dauril Alden is tackling the challenging topic of the economic activities of the Jesuits in colonial Brazil. It is equally satisfactory, but hardly surprising, to learn that he has found a mass of material which the Jesuit historians (understandably) have not exploited, since they were and are primarily concerned with other aspects of the sons of Loyola. Economic history is often inseparable from social history, especially nowadays; and in this connection I should like to suggest the desirability of a documented study of some aspect of the Luso-Brazilian tobacco industry and the tobacco trade. This suggestion applies both to its cultivation at Cachoeira and elsewhere, and to the functioning of the Crown tobacco monopoly, of which King Dom João V was so determined a supporter, as the foreign envoys at Lisbon during his long reign (1706–1750) had occasion to observe.[8]

No less interesting would be a study (or studies) of the Luso-Brazilian tax farmers or entrepreneurs, of the type so competently delineated by Dona Virgínia Rau in her essay on Manuel de Basto

8. Cf. the quotation from Lord Tyrawly, British envoy at Lisbon, in a dispatch of 1733, *apud* C.R. Boxer, *The Portuguese Seaborne Empire, 1415–1825* (London, 1969), p. 321.

Viana (1695–1760), "Um mercador Luso-Brasileiro do século XVIII," on pp. 103–116 of her *Estudos de história económica* (Lisbon, 1961), or of one of those tax farmers and merchant-princes, whom Pombal favoured so much, belonging to the da Cruz, the Bandeira, and the Quintella families. We get tantalizing glimpses of these tax farmers and merchant-princes in the *Recordaçoens* of Jacome Ratton (1810), but they lack adequate biographers. Pierre Verger has given us pen-portraits of several of the leading Luso-Brazilian, or Afro-Brazilian, slave traders of the early nineteenth century in his *Flux et Reflux*. It would be equally interesting to have more biographical information about the family and business relations of some of the earlier slave traders, especially the "New-Christian" merchants and entrepreneurs who farmed the West African slave contracts during the period of the "Sixty Years' Captivity," 1580–1640. This would, of course, necessitate archival work in Spain and Portugal rather than in Brazil, where little relevant material from those years has survived.

Students who are not attracted by Crown contractors, slave dealers, and other devotees of Mammon, will find new and (one hopes) more respectable avenues opened up for them by Stuart B. Schwartz's fruitful researches on the *desembargadores* and the *lavradores* of Bahia. His findings in these fields have come as an eye-opener to me, and I dare say to most people. He has conclusively shown that the Crown lawyers were a more important and a more interesting class, than I for one realised. So far as I am aware, he is also the first person to explore in depth the complicated and shifting relationship between the *senhores de engenho* and the *lavradores de cana* in the Recôncavo of Bahia. Clearly, similar studies for other regions of Brazil may prove equally rewarding.

Price history was something I never mentioned in my 1950 paper, and I must confess to an abysmal ignorance of this always important and nowadays fashionable subject. But, *in vino veritas*, I must also say that I found Mr. H. B. Johnson's modestly entitled "Preliminary Inquiry into Money, Prices, and Wages in Rio de Janeiro, 1763–1823," most fascinating reading and a veritable revelation. I hope that when he has done with Rio de Janeiro, he will turn his attention to some other region of Brazil, or to anywhere else in the old Portuguese seaborne empire for which the statistical material happens to be available.

Social history, which in 1950 seemed to be polarised between São

Paulo and Pernambuco, thanks to the well-documented works of
Afonso d'E. Taunay and Gilberto Freyre, respectively, is now no
longer so limited. Bahia, in particular, has come into its own with
the admirable works of Thales de Azevedo, *Povoamento da cidade
do Salvador* (São Paulo, 1955), Carlos Ott, *Formação e evolução
étnica da Cidade do Salvador* (2 vols., Salvador, 1955–1957), and
the previously mentioned works of J. Russell-Wood and Stuart B.
Schwartz. Minas Gerais has also inspired the authors of some excellent studies, such as Fritz Teixeira de Salles, *Associações religiosas no ciclo do Ouro* (2 vols., Belo Horizonte, 1963).

In my 1950 paper I mentioned the importance of Spanish and
Dutch sources for seventeenth-century Luso-Brazilian history, and
here again great progress has been made in the last twenty years.
In fact, I think that we could now declare a moratorium on the
so-called Dutch period in Brazil. José Honório Rodrigues, and, more
especially, José Antônio Gonsalves de Mello, have dealt or (in the
case of the latter) are now dealing with virtually everything that
needs revision or the light of day on this topic. A similar moratorium might, perhaps, be applied to the history of Luso-Spanish
rivalry in the Río de la Plata region, where a plethora of historians
on two continents has covered the field more than adequately. I
need only to refer to Luís Ferrand de Almeida's *A Diplomacia
portuguêsa e os limites meridionais do Brasil* (Coimbra, 1957), to
the late Jaime Cortesão's numerous publications on this subject,
and to the relevant chapters in Dauril Alden's latest book. Aspects
of this topic have also been well treated in several articles in the
Hispanic American Historical Review. However, if anyone is anxious
to dot a few *i*'s and to cross a few *t*'s of this well-worn theme, he
may find some new material in a collection of official papers and
unofficial correspondence in Spanish relating to the expedition of
Don Pedro de Cevallos in 1776–1777, in the Lilly Library, Indiana
University.[9]

Luso-Brazilian art history was relegated to a brief footnote in my
1950 paper, since the subject was treated in another section of the
first international colloquium on Luso-Brazilian studies. The debt
we owe to discriminating (and prolific) art historians like Robert C.
Smith, Joaquim de Sousa Leão Filho, Dom Clemente Maria da Silva-
Negra, O.S.B., and Germain Bazin is too obvious to need any elabo-

9. Lilly Library, Latin-American MSS, XM Collection.

ration from me, as is the loss which we have recently sustained with
the death of Dr. Rodrigo Melo Franco de Andrade, the tireless director of the *Patrimônio* for so many years. I therefore limit myself to
mentioning here a long-expected monograph by Francisco Curt
Lange, *La Musica en Villa Rica, Minas Gerais, Siglo XVIII* (Uni-
versidad de Chile, 1968), which is the interim fruit of his twenty-
two years of research in this field; an experience not without *dissa-
bores* and *contratempos*, but one which has revolutionized the
history of music in colonial Brazil. The medical history of colonial
Brazil received no mention in my 1950 paper, and I doubt whether
there was then any outstanding work on the subject. The situation
was completely altered in 1956 with the publication at Recife of
*Morão, Rosa e Pimenta: Notícia dos três primeiros livros em ver-
náculo sôbre a medicina no Brasil*, lavishly produced and eruditely
edited by Drs. Gilberto Osório de Andrade and Eustáquio Duarte.
Nevertheless, there is still plenty to do in this field, which is in-
separably connected with social history, as I have tried to show in
a recent article on the Luso-Brazilian surgeon, Luís Gomes Ferreira,
and his *Erário Mineral* of 1735 and 1755, in *The Indiana University
Bookman* (Number 10, November, 1969, pp. 49–70). A study of
the *Erário* by a qualified medical historian would form a major
contribution. As a *ponto de partida*, and as an example of what can
be done in the field of colonial Latin-American medical history, I
may instance *Morão, Rosa, e Pimenta*, and the numerous books and
articles by Dr. Francisco Guerra, M.D. Several of these, including
his succinct and fascinating paper on Aleixo de Abreu, author of
one of the earliest books on tropical medicine, are directly relevant to
Brazil.[10]

I conclude these brief and purely personal reflections on the historiography of colonial Brazil in the past twenty years, by suggesting
three projects which I would like to see undertaken by someone
younger and more competent than I:

1. A "popular" but substantial one-volume history of colonial
Brazil in English, to replace Robert Southey's still useful but inevitably outdated three-volume work of 1810–1819. This new his-

10. Francisco Guerra, "Aleixo de Abreu, 1568–1630, Author of the earliest
book on Tropical Medicine, describing Amoebiasis, Malaria, Typhoid Fever,
Scurvy, Yellow Fever, Dracontiasis, Trichuriasis, and Tungiasis in 1623," reprinted from the *Journal of Tropical Medicine and Hygiene*, LXXI (March,
1968), 55–69.

tory should not be the translation of an existing Brazilian work, admirable as some of these are, like the *História Geral da Civilização Brasileira*, edited by Sérgio Buarque de Holanda. The North American and British reading public has a different background from its Brazilian counterpart and needs a different approach. Many things that can be taken for granted in an educated Brazilian's knowledge of his own history, would be part of a *terra incognita* for the average North American or Briton. This caveat does not apply, of course, to works primarily intended for the specialist, such as Suzette Macedo's translation of Caio Prado Junior's *Formação do Brasil Contemporâneo: Colônia*, under the title *The Colonial Background of Modern Brazil* (University of California Press, 1968).

2. An album of Luso-Brazilian paleography on the lines of Agustín Millares Carlo & José Ignacio Mantecón, *Album de paleografía hispanoamericana de los siglos XVI & XVII* (3 vols., Mexico, D.F., 1955).

3. A definitive study of the life and work of that remarkable but strangely neglected publicist, the Franciscan friar José Mariano da Conceição Veloso. His numerous works, including the ten-volume *O Fazendeiro do Brazil* published between 1798 and 1806, reflect a determined if unfortunately abortive effort to improve and diversify the Brazilian economy by placing at the disposal of *fazendeiros* and entrepreneurs Portuguese translations of all the best French and English works on tropical agriculture, and on a wide range of other themes, from Roquefort cheese to metallurgy.[11] Parenthetically, we may recall that during Junot's occupation of Lisbon, Saint-Hilaire stole the drawings and manuscripts of Conceição Veloso and another distinguished Brazilian scientist and traveller, Alexandre Rodrigues Ferreira, and carried them off to Paris. In his ant-like industry and in his formidable output of published work of high quality, Conceição Veloso reminds me of the great Chilean historian and polymath, José Toribio Medina, and it is high time the Brazilian friar found a competent biographer.

No doubt there are other and better projects for research and publication; and there is indeed plenty of room in the realm of colonial Brazilian history. But of one thing I am sure. Whatever your choice may be, you will find a sojourn in The Newberry Library as profitable as it is pleasant. To a collection of Portuguese and Bra-

---

11. Cf. the list of his works in Rubens Borba de Moraes, comp., *Bibliographia Brasiliana* (2 vols., Amsterdam and Rio de Janeiro, 1958), II, 336–343.

zilian books which has few rivals in any working library, it adds a considerate and knowledgeable staff. All of us who are interested in Luso-Brazilian history have long owed The Newberry Library a debt of gratitude—a debt which has been further enhanced by its gracious hospitality to our Conference, for which we warmly thank the Director and his staff.

POLITICAL ASPECTS

FRANCIS A. DUTRA:

Centralization vs. Donatorial Privilege: Pernambuco, 1602-1630

"He made his public entrance under a canopy, bore the title of 'His Lordship', aspired to free himself from the authority of the governor [-general] and attempted to exempt himself from the jurisdiction and regulations under which his predecessors had served. . . . So absolute is his authority in that captaincy that not even the governor-general can enter it. . . . So great is his sovereignty that no one dares to antagonize him."[1] During the early 1620s these and similar charges were hurled at Matias de Albuquerque, governor and *capitão-mor* of Pernambuco and younger brother of the captaincy's lord-proprietor (*donatário*), by D. Luis de Sousa, Brazil's twelfth governor-general. Although similar complaints would be bandied about in Portuguese America for the remainder of the colonial period, as more and more governors and capitães-mores attempted to assert their independence from the Crown's chief officials in Bahia or (after 1763) Rio de Janeiro, the Albuquerque-Sousa charges were given a special flavor because Pernambuco was a proprietary colony trying to defend and expand its prerogatives at a time when the king and his governors-general were trying to exert greater control over all of Brazil.[2] The result was tension between the powers of centralization and of donatarial privilege. The stage was set for a series of bitter confrontations.

Perhaps it was inevitable that the extensive privileges and large tracts of land granted by D. João III to twelve lord-proprietors or donatários (between 1534 and 1536), in an attempt to colonize Brazil, would one day have to be restricted. In exchange for settling and defending these new territories at their own cost, the donatários received from the Portuguese Crown substantial administrative,

---

1. *Livro primeiro do govêrno do Brasil, 1607–1633* (Rio de Janeiro, 1958), pp. 341, 335–336.

2. For a discussion of some of the conflicts between governors of Brazil's captaincies and the governors-general and viceroys, see Dauril Alden, *Royal Government in Colonial Brazil* (Berkeley, 1968), pp. 35–43 and 447–472.

fiscal, and judicial prerogatives. Although within a short time the captaincies of Pernambuco and São Vicente became relatively prosperous, and Porto Seguro and Ilhéus managed to survive, eight other captaincies either were never exploited by their lord-proprietors or quickly failed because of Indian attacks.[3] In 1549, in order to combat an increasingly serious French threat and to establish supremacy over the Brazilian proprietary colonies, D. João III established at Bahia a centralized government for Portuguese America. Important limitations were placed on the Crown's overgenerous grants to the donatários, and the influence of the royal government's judiciary and treasury became more pervasive. Brazil's captaincies were now viewed as parts of a larger, total unit. With each renewal of donatarial charters (doações) occasioned by the death of a proprietor, the original rights were watered down. Symbolic of the changes was the statement repeated in each letter of appointment to the governorship of Brazil that the governor-general was to have full authority in the colony regardless of what individual letters patent said to the contrary.[4] Some donatários felt particularly threatened by the Crown's instructions that each captaincy be inspected by key royal officials, for one of the lord-proprietor's most cherished privileges was the king's promise never to send his corregedores into their territories.[5] As Duarte Coelho Pereira, the donatário of Pernambuco, wrote to D. João III on 24 November 1550: "All the people of this

3. The standard treatment of the early days of Brazil's captaincy system is found in HCP, III, 165–323. The carta de doação and the foral of Duarte Coelho, lord-proprietor of Pernambuco, have been reprinted many times. A Portuguese version is found in HCP, III, 309–313. For an English translation, see A Documentary History of Brazil, ed. E. Bradford Burns (New York, 1966), pp. 33–50. In addition to the usual obstacles to colonization (e.g., a new frontier situation, disease, Indian attacks, etc.), the Portuguese throughout the sixteenth and early seventeenth centuries encountered frequent harassment by the French who were also attempting to set up colonies in Brazil.

4. The disturbed reactions of Duarte Coelho to the inauguration of centralized government in Brazil are found in his letters to the king, dated 14 April 1549 and 24 November 1550, published in HCP, III, 318–321. A new reading of the donatário's Brazilian letters is found in Cartas de Duarte Coelho a El Rei, eds, José Antônio Gonsalves de Mello and Cleonir Xavier de Albuquerque (Recife, 1967). For modifications in the donatarial charters, see BNL/FG, cód. 7627, fols. 41–43v, 50, 52–53, 62, 63–63v. The governor-general's letter of appointment is printed in HCP, III, 318–321.

5. The Crown's grant to Pernambuco stated: "I [the king] consider it good and it pleases me that at no time may a magistrate or circuit court or any other courts enter in any way in the lands of the said captaincy to assume jurisdiction in it." Burns, A Documentary History of Brazil, p. 43.

Nova Lusitania were and are very much upset with these changes."[6]

Pernambuco was most notably affected by the institution of a central government in Brazil. For almost a century, from the arrival in 1535 of Duarte Coelho and his wife, D. Brites de Albuquerque, to the invasion by the Dutch in 1630, the Albuquerque Coelho family and its relatives presided over the most prosperous and populous privately controlled captaincy in Portuguese America.[7] Because of his exploits in the Far East and his other military and diplomatic services, Duarte had received the choicest grant of land in Brazil, territory characterized by fertile soil, a good port, previous settlement, and proximity to Portugal.[8] The first donatário of Pernambuco soon put his colony on the high road to order and prosperity by leading the fight against hostile Indians and French interlopers and by providing the blueprint for a stable agrarian society—the inspiration for Pernambuco's golden age between 1580 and 1630. Brazilwood had been the region's most important product before the era of the captaincies and during much of Duarte's lifetime, but it was gradually supplanted by sugar. In 1550, there were five *engenhos* or sugar mills in the colony and others in the planning stage.[9]

Though Duarte Coelho died in 1553, Pernambuco continued to prosper. By the 1570s the captaincy had two towns, Olinda and Iguaraçu, and a European population of 1,000. Many of the new arrivals soon were settled around the engenhos coming into existence on lands bitterly won from the Indians a few years earlier. At the time of Pêro de Magalhães Gandavo's visit (c. 1568–1571), there were twenty-three sugar mills, each producing, on the average, three thousand *arrôbas*, or ninety-six thousand pounds, of sugar annually.[10] A decade and a half later, according to the glowing reports of Padres Fernão Cardim and José de Anchieta and the Bahian

6. Duarte Coelho to king, Olinda, 24 November 1550 in *HCP*, III, 321.

7. During the Dutch occupation (1630–1654) Pernambuco was ravaged by guerrilla warfare. Although the captaincy began to recover during the latter part of the seventeenth century, in 1716 the adopted son of D. Maria Margarida de Castro e Albuquerque (daughter of the fourth donatário) surrendered to the Portuguese Crown all claims to Pernambuco in exchange for 80,000 cruzados and the title of Marquês de Valença. See Francisco Augusto Pereira da Costa, *Anais Pernambucanos*, 10 vols. (Recife, 1951–1966), IV, 351–352.

8. A good summary of Duarte Coelho's career in the Orient is found in I.A. Macgregor, "The Portuguese in Malaya," *Journal of the Malayan Branch of the Royal Asiatic Society*, XVIII (1955), 36–39.

9. Coelho to king, Olinda, 24 November 1550, in *HCP*, III, 321.

10. Pêro de Magalhães de Gandavo, *Tratado da província do Brasil*, ed. Emmanuel Pereira Filho (Rio de Janeiro, 1965), pp. 68–71.

landowner, Gabriel Soares de Sousa, the white population of Pernambuco had more than doubled and the number of sugar mills nearly trebled.[11]

Almost all who visited or wrote about sixteenth- and early seventeenth-century Pernambuco praised the richest sugar-producing region of Brazil whose busy port, Recife, was visited "each year by more ships from Portugal than any of the other captaincies" and whose bustling capital, Olinda, was described as a "little Lisbon."[12] As Gabriel Soares de Sousa remarked in 1587: "So prosperous is this captaincy that it contains more than one hundred men whose annual income ranges from one to five thousand *cruzados;* and there are even some incomes of eight and ten thousand cruzados. Many who arrive in this land completely inpoverished leave for Portugal wealthy."[13]

Despite Pernambuco's enviable economic situation, a series of crises seriously disrupted the life of the colony. Accusations of graft and corruption, echoed by *licenciado* Domingos de Abreu e Brito during his visit in 1591, and coupled with attacks by him on the privileges of the Pernambucan sugar lords, added to the worries of a captaincy still restless and insecure in the face of Indian wars, foreign threats, rapid economic growth, the extinction of the House of Avis, the ascendancy of the Spanish Habsburgs, and the absence of strong leadership by the lord-proprietor.[14] The "Padre de Ouro" episode, which was related to the greedy quest for new sugar lands and workers and the alleged mistreatment of the Indians, had involved several members of the Pernambucan establishment (including the second donatário) and had seriously divided the captaincy.[15]

11. Fernão Cardim, S.J., *Tratados da terra e gente do Brasil*, eds. Baptista Caetano, Capistrano de Abreu, and Rodolfo Garcia (2nd ed.; São Paulo, 1939), pp. 294–295; José de Anchieta, S.J., *Informações e fragmentos historicos* (Rio de Janeiro, 1886), p. 33; and Gabriel Soares de Sousa, *Tratado descriptivo do Brasil em 1587*, ed. Francisco Adolfo de Varnhagen (3rd ed.; São Paulo, 1938), p. 29.

12. For the above descriptions, see respectively Magalhães de Gandavo, *Tratado*, pp. 72–73, and Ambrósio Fernandes Brandão, *Diálogos das grandezas do Brasil*, ed. José Antônio Gonsalves de Mello (Recife, 1962), p. 28.

13. Soares de Sousa, *Tratado Descriptivo*, p. 29.

14. For Abreu e Brito's report, see *Um Inquérito à vida administrativa e economia de Angola e do Brasil em fins do século XVI*, ed. Alfredo de Albuquerque Felner (Coimbra, 1931), especially pp. 57–67. For other threats to the sugar lords, see Archivo Historico Nacional, Madrid, Estado (Portugal), lib. 81, fols. 244–245v.

15. A well-travelled cleric who had run afoul of the Inquisition several times

Further anxious moments were provided by Indian threats to Pernambuco's northern borders and to the colony's "satellites"—Itamaracá, Paraíba, and Rio Grande do Norte—where Pernambucan men and money were heavily invested, and by outsiders, such as French, English, and Dutch corsairs. Incidents like James Lancaster's seizure of Recife in 1595 kept Pernambuco in a continuous state of uneasiness. This edginess could be seen in the witch-hunting atmosphere accompanying the Inquisition's two-year visitation of Pernambuco and the neighboring captaincies to the north, beginning in 1593.[16] As a colonial historian of the United States commented on a similar period in Anglo-American history: "For a society in transition, uncertain of its aims and precepts, scapegoats become a substitute for purpose. A society that is confident of itself, its ends and its future, does not read into the views or practices of minority segments threats of dissolution."[17]

Many difficulties might have been avoided if Duarte Coelho's two sons and their successors had spent more of their time in Brazil than in Portugal and North Africa. But during the seventy-six years following the first donatário's death in 1554, only one of his suc-

in Portugal, Antônio de Gouveia—the legendary "Padre de Ouro"—was exiled to Pernambuco in 1567. Attracting the attention of the settlers by alchemy and of the Indians by magic, he soon became a celebrity and, to the Jesuits, a gadfly. At the same time he had friends in high places, including the Bishop of Brazil, Dom Pedro Leitão, and the second donatário himself—both of whom were most probably interested in the mines Gouveia was searching for and the Indians he was enslaving. For much the same reasons he was also supported by the settlers in Pernambuco. The Jesuits, however, soon accused Gouveia of practicing heresy, performing Judaic ceremonies, and insulting the Eucharist, along with such misdeeds against the Indians as sadistically murdering them or capturing and then personally whipping them and branding their faces. He was turned over to the Inquisition and shipped off to Portugal where it seems that nothing much came of the charges made against him in Brazil. Despite this, the "Padre de Ouro" was forced to remain in the prisons of the Inquisition in Lisbon, where he was last heard of in 1575. See Pereira da Costa, *Anais Pernambucanos*, I, 393–399 and *HCJB*, I, 480–484. Two *processos* of the Inquisition dealing with Gouveia were published by Pedro de Azevedo in *Arquivo Historico Portuguez* (Lisboa, 1905), III, 179–208 and 274–286.

16. Part of the Inquisition's investigations has been published. See Heitor Furtado de Mendoça, *Primeira visitação do santo officio às partes do Brasil: Denunciações de Pernambuco, 1593–1595* (São Paulo, 1929).

17. Clarence Ver Steeg, *The Formative Years, 1607–1763* (New York, 1964), p. 144. See also p. 133. Ver Steeg was referring to the anti-Catholic excesses in Maryland, the Salem witch hunts, Bacon's Rebellion in Virginia and Leisler's Revolt in New York—all of which occurred within several decades of each other and during a comparable stage of Anglo-American colonial development.

cessors resided in Pernambuco. The other two lord-proprietors were absentee landlords running the captaincy via substitutes (*loco-tenentes*), most of whom were relatives. Duarte Coelho de Albuquerque, the first donatário's elder son, was only in his teens when he inherited the captaincy and did not return to Brazil until 1560. Though he remained in Pernambuco for twelve years, his administration was not a successful one. Despite continuing enonomic prosperity and the savage destruction of Indian power in coastal Pernambuco, the second donatário faced one leadership crisis after another. The colony was having its growing pains and there was much dissension. It was soon evident that the younger Duarte did not have his father's ability to cope with the difficult problems of this troubled period.[18] His brother and successor, Jorge de Albuquerque Coelho, wounded in and disillusioned by the 1578 debacle in North Africa which ended in King Sebastian's death, did not set foot in Brazil during the two decades he served as donatário.[19] After Duarte Coelho de Albuquerque's return to Portugal in 1572, nearly half a century elapsed before a male member of the lord-proprietor's immediate family (i.e., the fourth donatário's younger brother) set foot in Pernambuco to run the captaincy. And it was not until late in 1631, almost thirty years after he had inherited the colony, that the lord-proprietor himself finally arrived.[20] By that late date most of Pernambuco was in Dutch hands, where it remained until 1654.

18. See Francis A. Dutra, "Matias de Albuquerque: A Seventeenth-Century *Capitão-Mor* of Pernambuco and Governor-General of Brazil," (Ph.D. diss., New York University, 1968), pp. 44–46 and 49–55.

19. For a brief biography of the third donatário of Pernambuco, see Francis A. Dutra, *Notas sôbre a vida e morte de Jorge de Albuquerque Coelho e a tutela de seus filhos* (Recife, 1970). Also cf. C.R. Boxer's three studies: "Jorge de Albuquerque Coelho," *Anais da Academia Portuguesa da História*, 2d ser. 15: 135–147; *Further Selections from the Tragic History of the Sea, 1559–1565* (Cambridge, England, 1968), pp. 12–21 and 108–157; and "Jorge d'Albuquerque: A Luso-Brazilian Hero of the Sea, 1539–1602," *Luso-Brazilian Review*, VI: 1 (1969), 3–17.

20. The fourth donatário, Duarte de Albuquerque Coelho, tried to land in his captaincy after participating in the restoration of Bahia in 1625, but high seas and bad weather prevented him from leaving ship. See Frei Vicente do Salvador, *Historia do Brasil, 1500–1627*, ed. Capistrano de Abreu, Rodolfo Garcia, and Frei Venâncio Wílleke, O.F.M. (5th ed.; São Paulo, 1965), p. 501. Three years later Duarte was scheduled to return to Brazil to prepare Pernambuco for a rumored Dutch invasion, but poor health prevented him from accepting the post, which ultimately went to his brother Matias. See consulta of the Council of State, 13 May 1628 in AGS, Estado (España), legajo 2646.

During these years of absenteeism or ineffective leadership by the Albuquerque Coelho family, a series of threats to donatarial prerogatives, Pernambucan autonomy, and the hegemony of the captaincy over much of the Brazilian Northeast was being posed by the Crown, and especially by the ropal authorities in Bahia. As mentioned earlier, the revisions of the doações in 1548–1549 instructed the governor-general and other high officials to inspect Brazil's captaincies.[21] During Duarte Coelho's lifetime, D. João III, in deference to the excellent colonizing efforts and leadership of the most successful of the donatários, had commanded Tomé de Sousa, Portuguese America's first governor-general, to exempt Pernambuco from the inspection required by his *regimento*. This dispensation rankled with the governor-general as well as with the Jesuit, Manuel da Nóbrega, both firm supporters of strong and centralized rule, and they promptly complained to the king. In a letter dated 18 July 1551, Tomé de Sousa stated: "I repeat again, Your Highness, that the captains of these parts merit many honors and rewards, most of all Duarte Coelho, concerning whom I have written extensively to Your Highness. But as Your Highness does not let me go to his captaincy, it seems to me a great disservice to God and your conscience and very prejudicial to your income."[22] Less than two months later, Padre Nóbrega echoed his friend's report: "Duarte Coelho and his wife are very virtuous. . . . However, he is already old, and there is much lacking for the good administration of justice; and because of this, the jurisdiction of all the coast ought to be that of Your Highness."[23]

After Duarte Coelho's death, however, the king had no qualms about suspending his earlier prohibition regarding the inspection of Pernambuco. Fortunately for the Albuquerque Coelho family, a chain of unexpected events prevented the governors-general from visiting the captaincy during the remainder of the sixteenth century. Indian threats to Bahia forced Duarte da Costa, Brazil's second governor-general, to turn back from his journey to Pernambuco in 1555. Continued dissension in the Brazilian capital probably dis-

21. Regimento of Tomé de Sousa in *HCP*, III, 347. However, Sousa's orders required him to go directly from Lisbon to Bahia. *Ibid.*, p. 345.
22. Sousa to king, Bahia, 18 July 1551 in *HCP*, III, 361–362.
23. Nóbrega to king, Pernambuco, 14 September 1551, in *Cartes do Brasil e mais escritos do P. Manuel da Nóbrega*, ed. Serafim Leite, S.J. (Coimbra, 1955), p. 99.

couraged him from any later attempts to leave Bahia.[24] The French
along with the Indians kept Mem de Sá, the next governor-general
(1558–1572), from making his assigned visit to Pernambuco. Rio de
Janeiro and the south of Brazil were the foci of attention for most
of his long term of office.[25] During the subsequent two decades Mem
de Sá's successors, despite, or perhaps because of, attempts at administrative reorganization in Brazil, failed to inspect the captaincy
of the Albuquerque Coelho family. D. Francisco de Sousa, the sev-
enth governor-general (1591-1602), one man who might have been
expected to visit Pernambuco because of his lengthy stay in Brazil,
never ventured that far northward. Most of his time was taken up
with threats of foreign attack and the search for mines to the south.
He inspected Espirito Santo, São Vicente, and São Paulo, not Pernambuco—though the latter was clearly the most important of all
the captaincies.[26]

The early seventeenth century brought an end to the "neglect"
by the governors-general of the Albuquerque Coelho family's captaincy. Between 1602 and 1617 all four men appointed to the governorship of Brazil landed in Pernambuco after the voyage from
Lisbon. Their inspections, however, went far beyond the Crown's
instructions and took on the character of a permanent stay, with
the governor-general spending a considerable part of his term of
office in the lord-proprietor's captaincy. Thus, the more-or-less-to-
be-expected process of erosion of donatarial authority, underway
since 1548 with royal pressure for greater centralization in Brazil,
accelerated sharply. The result was a crisis for the Albuquerque
Coelhos and a conflict with the governors-general and the *Relação*
or High Court which opened wounds that would take several generations to heal.

Despite loud complaints by the donatário and his relatives, the
governors-general and their allies easily won the early encounters.
Diogo Botelho arrived in Olinda, Pernambuco, on 1 April 1602 to
begin his term of office as governor-general of Brazil, and stayed a
year and a half in the Pernambucan capital before moving on to

24. Duarte da Costa to king, Bahia, 10 June 1555 in *HCP*, III, 377–379. For
domestic rivalries in Bahia, see *ibid.*, pp. 341–342.
25. Mem de Sá's administration is discussed in Francisco Adolfo de Varnhagen, *História geral do Brasil, antes de sua separação e independência de
Portugal* (7th integral ed.; São Paulo, 1962), I, especially pp. 299–313.
26. Frei Vicente, *História*, pp. 331–332 and 335–336.

Bahia.[27] He was followed by D. Diogo de Meneses e Sequeira who landed in Brazil in January of 1608 and, like Botelho, remained in Pernambuco instead of Bahia. It was not until early in December, after an eleven month "inspection" that he left for Brazil's capital.[28] But Meneses' sojourn in Pernambuco was only a whistle stop compared with the actions of his two successors. When Gaspar de Sousa arrived in Olinda on 18 December 1612, the French were in the process of strengthening their influence in northeastern Brazil. Making the "conquest" of Maranhão the key project of his administration—he had hopes of carving out a captaincy for himself in the new region—and using the excuse that the efficient direction of operations in northern Brazil demanded his presence in Pernambuco, Sousa spent more than three-and-a-half years, or almost his entire term of office, in the captaincy of the Albuquerque Coelhos.[29] Following the example of his seventeenth-century predecessors, D. Luis de Sousa also took power in Olinda (1 January 1617). Once settled in Pernambuco, he, too, found it hard to leave, and did not proceed to Bahia until early 1619.[30]

In the seventeen years between Diogo Botelho's arrival in 1602 and D. Luis de Sousa's departure in 1619, the four governors-general had spent eight years in Pernambuco and only nine in Brazil's capital. This innovation did not go unnoticed. During the first three decades of the seventeenth century, countless charges and countercharges were bandied about concerning the reasons for the governors-general's presence in the captaincy of the Albuquerque Coelho family.

27. Diogo Botelho's residence in Pernambuco is discussed in Francis A. Dutra, "A New Look into Diogo Botelho's Stay in Pernambuco, 1602–1603," *Luso-Brazilian Review*, IV:1 (1967), 27–34. See also "Correspondência de Diogo Botelho," *RIHGB*, 73:1, vii–258.

28. The best source for Diogo Meneses' visit to Pernambuco is the governor-general's own correspondence in *ABNRJ*, LVII (1935), 31–59.

29. For Gaspar de Sousa's lengthy stay in Pernambuco, see *ABNRJ*, XXVI (1904), 311–320; Guilherme [Barão de] Studart, *Documentos para a história do Brasil e especialmente a do Ceará* (4 vols.; Fortaleza, 1904–1921), I, II, *passim*; and the manuscript "Cartas del Rey aos Srs. Alvaro de Sousa e Gaspar de Sousa" in AHI.

30. For the extent of D. Luis de Sousa's residence, see the *prolegômenos* to Frei Vicente, *História*, pp. 383 and 385. The governor-general claimed that he remained only a little more than a year. *Livro primeiro*, p. 336. From all available evidence, however, it was closer to two years. A record of D. Luis' stay is also found in *AMP*, III: 2 (1927), *passim*.

The governors-general themselves pointed to their regimentos
to justify their stays. These instructions were, in the main, quite
similar. Most of the regimentos for the early seventeenth century
are missing, but an idea of the precise nature of the orders to the
governors-general can be gained by a review of several sections of
the 1588 instructions to Francisco Giraldes. Chapter twenty-five
states: "After you shall have become well informed regarding those
things that deal with the captaincy of Bahia and have provided what
is necessary for its safety and its good government and administration in matters of justice as well as my treasury, you shall arrange
to visit [i.e., inspect] the other captaincies of your governance,
bringing with you the High Treasurer [*provedor-mor*] and as many
officials and others as seem fitting to you." Chapter twenty-six of
the same regimento is quite explicit about which captaincies should
be inspected first; it states that the governor-general is "to go first
to those captaincies of which you [the governor] have information
that they have more necessity of being visited."[31] In light of these
instructions, the impropriety of the stays by the governors-general
in Pernambuco can be argued on three grounds: first, with the exception of Gaspar de Sousa and D. Luis de Sousa, the governors-
general had been ordered to go directly to Bahia; second, their
"inspections" had become semi-permanent residence; third, though
the regimento stated that all the captaincies were to be inspected,
only Pernambuco was being visited.[32]

The opponents of the sojourns of the governors-general in Pernambuco were bitter in their attacks. Ambrósio Fernandes Brandão,
the author of the *Diálogos das grandezas do Brasil* and a spokesman
for the donatários and sugar lords of Pernambuco and the surrounding area, was frankly critical of the presence of so many royal officials, and insinuated that the profit motive and not their prescribed
duties was luring the governors to Pernambuco. He sarcastically
questioned whether the governors-general "preferred to remain in
the captaincy of Pernambuco . . . because they can draw more
profit from it, or because it is nearer to Portugal."[33] Frei Vicente do

31. Giraldes' regimento is published in *RIHGB*, 67:1, 227.
32. For the instructions of Gaspar de Sousa and D. Luis de Sousa to visit
Pernambuco first, see respectively the consulta of the Conselho da India, 18
April 1614 in AHU, Bahia, Papéis Avulsos, caixa 1 and AGS, Sectarias Provinciales (Portugal), lib. 1516, fol. 11v. For the latter, cf. king to Luis de Sousa,
11 April, 1617, *AMP*, III:2, 37.
33. P. 31.

Salvador reported that some Brazilians were of the opinion that the riches of Pernambuco and the many opportunities for personal profit were the motivating forces behind the visit of Diogo Botelho.[34] Though Diogo de Meneses' stay was probably too short to arouse much opposition, the arrival of his two successors during the initial settlement of Maranhão (with its countless possibilities for profiteering) brought new misconduct charges. Besides undermining the influence of the donatário, the last two governors-general to reside in Pernambuco seemed to be taking away business from merchants living there. D. Luis de Sousa, in particular, was accused of favoring his protégés when naming contractors or purveyors for the North. He was also charged with assuming for himself the role of purveyor, and deriving excessive profits from merchandising for his favorites and himself.[35] In addition, the governors-general residing in Pernambuco were blamed for some of the unsavory deals being made regarding sugar grown in Paraíba and later shipped to Pernambuco to avoid taxes.[36] According to André Farto da Costa, the secretary of the junta sent to Brazil by the Crown to investigate certain irregularities in the collection of taxes, there was evidence that high officials—especially Gaspar de Sousa—had conspired with the sugar planters in annually defrauding the royal treasury of great sums of money.[37]

The interference of the governors-general in the captaincy's political and economic life also aroused the ire of the lord-proprietor, his relatives, and other Pernambucan leaders. As Frei Vicente do Salvador perceptively noted, the governors-general frequently failed to distinguish between the authority and jurisdiction of the governor-generalship of Brazil and that of the governorship of Pernam-

---

34. Frei Vicente, *História*, p. 337. At the same time, however, Frei Vicente emphasized that he thought Diogo Botelho probably stayed in Pernambuco in order to inspect the captaincy and fortifications which were to be under his jurisdiction.

35. For the above charges, see *Livro primeiro*, p. 409.

36. Brandão, *Diálogos das grandezas*, pp. 21–22.

37. "Requerimento de André Farto da Costa pedindo que se vejam uns apontamentos que deu no Conselho da Fazenda 'sobre os direitos dos asuq^{res} q̃ se sonegão' " [n.d., 1614?] and *anexo* along with Farto da Costa to king, Bahia, 15 June 1614, AHU, Bahia, Papéis Avulsos, caixa 1. As to be expected, Sousa protested his innocence to the king. See *ABNRJ*, XXVI; 316–317, 318. The governor-general later accused Farto da Costa of collecting monies for the Crown and not turning them over to the royal treasurer. See anexo to Capítulo de carta régia de 29 julho de 1617 in AHU, Bahia, Papéis Avulsos caixa 1.

buco.[38] Vasco de Sousa Pacheco, who succeeded Alexandre de Moura in 1615 as governor and capitão-mor of Pernambuco, became so exasperated with Gaspar de Sousa's interference that he sent his brother, a Franciscan friar, back to the Iberian peninsula with a petition to the king for a transfer to another post because "the governor [-general] did everything"; there was nothing that he, the capitão-mor, could do, so that he was quite bored and was wasting his time in Pernambuco.[39] Similar complaints were voiced against D. Luis de Sousa. Besides taking charge of the provisioning and colonizing of Maranhão, this governor-general, like his predecessor, tried to run Pernambuco as if it were Bahia. To many it appeared that D. Luis had united the duties and prerogatives of both posts. Resentment against this practice flared up when the governor-general tried to have his supporters and friends appointed to a number of sensitive positions in the captaincy of the Albuquerque Coelho family. When Vasco de Sousa Pacheco was transferred to Bahia, D. Luis de Sousa named the wealthy Pernambucan landowner, João Pais Barreto, capitão-mor until the king could select a replacement. The Crown's choice, Martim de Sousa de Sampaio, was captured by the Dutch and never arrived in Brazil. Therefore, Pais Barreto, collaborating closely with the governor-general, stayed on as capitão-mor.[40] But an outcry arose when Pais Barreto himself attempted to fill the post of *patrão da ribeira* and *juiz dos calafates* for the port of Recife, left vacant by the death of Tomé Mendes. Though in a letter to the king, D. Luis de Sousa defended the capitão-mor's actions, stating that Pais Barreto had intended to make the appointment "in the name of Your Majesty," Mendes having served "by the decree and pleasure of Your Majesty," a number of officials in Pernambuco did not agree.[41] Before long, the *ouvidor* of Pernambuco (an appointee of the donatário) and several members of the town council of Olinda—the most vocal being Cristóvão de Albuquerque, uncle

38. Frei Vicente, *História*, p. 425.

39. *Ibid.*, p. 421. Vasco de Sousa Pacheco was eventually given the post of capitão-mor of Bahia. See king to Luis de Sousa, São Lourenço, 18 July 1617 in *AMP*, III:2, 42. Also AGS, Guerra Antigua, leg. 905.

40. *Livro primeiro*, pp. 339–340. For Sousa de Sampaio's capture by the Dutch, see Manoel Severim de Faria, *História portugueza e de outras provincias do occidente desde o anno de 1610 até o de 1640* (Fortaleza, 1903), p. 21. Also consulta of the Council of the Treasury in Studart, *Documentos para a história do Brasil*, I, 307–308.

41. *Livro primeiro*, p. 340.

of the lord-proprietor—were loudly challenging Barreto's action.[42] Cristóvão de Albuquerque took exception to the practice by the governor-general of directly or indirectly (via the capitão-mor in this instance) appointing an official to a post which many Pernambucans felt was not subject to royal appointment. So heated were the protests of the donatário's uncle that he was arrested and imprisoned by the capitão-mor in a fortress fifty leagues from the captaincy.[43]

These incursions into what the donatários had considered their private preserve occurred at the worst possible moment for the Albuquerque Coelho family. In 1601, on the eve of Diogo Botelho's arrival in Pernambuco, Jorge de Albuquerque, the third donatário, died in Lisbon, leaving his ten-year-old son, Duarte de Albuquerque Coelho, to succeed him as lord-proprietor of a captaincy three thousand miles away.[44] To make matters worse, Pernambuco at the time was under the leadership of a capitão-mor, Manuel Mascarenhas Homen (1596–1603), who was repeatedly away from the captaincy, busily leading expeditions against the Indians and opening up new frontiers in northeastern Brazil.[45] This two-fold absenteeism left the door wide open for Diogo Botelho's entrance into Pernambucan politics, and gave both the enemies of the Pernambucan establishment and those in favor of centralization a chance to take matters into their own hands.

The Albuquerque Coelho family made a determined effort to maintain control. Fortunately for Duarte de Albuquerque Coelho, he had a protector in high places in the person of his uncle and legal guardian, Matias de Albuquerque, the former viceroy of India and councillor to the King.[46] Although the viceroy, a victim of court in-

42. Ibid.; for the ouvidor, see ANTT, Chancelaria de Filipe II, Doações, liv. 29, fl. 48. In a way, the reactions of the town council of Olinda and Cristóvão de Albuquerque were a bit surprising, since the former had seemingly been friendly with the governors-general during their stays in Pernambuco and, in 1603, the donatário's uncle was one of the town councillors who rallied to the support of Diogo Botelho. See RIHGB, 73:1, 28.

43. Livro primeiro, p. 340.

44. Dutra, "Matias de Albuquerque," pp. 77–80.

45. Frei Vicente, História, pp. 318–330 and 333–334. For Mascarenhas Homen's term of office, see Pereira da Costa, Anais Pernambucanos, II, 94.

46. Matias de Albuquerque, the viceroy of India, is not to be confused with his nephew, ward, and heir, Paulo de Albuquerque (younger son of Jorge de Albuquerque, the third donatário of Pernambuco) who changed his name to Matias after his uncle's death.

trigues, was occupied with the task of staying out of prison, he
did manage to engage tutors for his ward's education and attempted
to look after the young donatário's interests. Even though Duarte
had been named heir to his father's captaincy of Pernambuco, the
king allowed almost two years to lapse—until 2 July 1603—before
signing the patent for the new lord-proprietor. To protect his
nephew during this transitional period, Matias de Albuquerque
appealed to D. Filipe II, and on 6 February 1602 obtained for Duarte
the privilege of exercising for two years all the prerogatives listed
in his father's grant of Pernambuco, without formal papers being
signed by the monarch.[47] In the meantime, the former viceroy tried
to watch over both the administration and the revenues of Pernambuco. But because he was unable to be present in Brazil, he had the
same problems as his cousin Jorge maintaining discipline there.

Matias' supervision, however, did force the governor-general
and his allies to watch their step. When Diogo Botelho stayed on
in Pernambuco, there were protests in Brazil and in Portugal, resulting in two investigations (devassas) into the behavior of the
governor-general. The first took place in 1603 in Pernambuco and
was, in fact, nothing more than a thinly-veiled eulogy of the governor-general. But the second, held in Lisbon in the same year, was
unfavorable to Diogo Botelho. Presided over by licenciado Belchior
do Amaral, it was a dramatic reversal of the Pernambucan findings
and a damning indictment of the governor-general, containing a
recommendation that he be removed immediately from his post.
Though there is no direct evidence, at least the second of these investigations was probably undertaken at Matias de Albuquerque's
prompting.[48]

The advantages of having an important advocate to represent and
defend his interests were not long-term ones for young Duarte Albuquerque Coelho. On 4 March 1606 his uncle died, and soon after-
ward Matias' widow entered a convent.[49] After a bitter family
squabble over the custody of Jorge de Albuquerque's two sons, the

47. ANTT, Chancelaria de Filipe II, Privilégios, liv. 2, fl. 13; for Matias de
Albuquerque's care for his wards, see BNL/FG 1555, fol. 326 and AGS, Sect.
Prov., lib. 1465, fls. 175–181v.

48. For details of the two devassas, see Dutra, "Diogo Botelho," pp. 29–34.

49. For the date of Matias de Albuquerque's death, see ANTT, Chancelaria
de Filipe II, Doações, liv. 16, fol. 161v. For his widow's actions, see AGS, Sect.
Prov., lib. 1465, fols. 175–181v.

widow's brother, D. Lourenço de Sousa, the king's *aposentador-mor*, was appointed guardian for Pernambuco's fourth donatário.[50]

The fourteen years following his uncle's death (1606–1620) were difficult for Duarte de Albuquerque Coelho. He was forced to stand by almost helplessly while one governor-general after another interfered in his captaincy. At the same time D. Filipe II took advantage of the lord-proprietor's youth and inexperience to cut deeply into his donatarial prerogatives.

A serious problem for Duarte was the Crown's failure to allow him either to name his own capitão-mor and governor of Pernambuco or to submit a list of choices for the position, although the first three donatários, when absent from their captaincy, had, as a matter of course, named whom they wished to run Pernambuco.[51] But a definite change had occurred after Jorge de Albuquerque's death. In his last will and testament he mentioned that he was being permitted to submit a list of three choices for the post of capitão-mor and governor. The Crown would then choose from these nominations.[52] Whether this was a precautionary move on the part of Jorge to safeguard the family's interests while his heir was still a minor, or whether it was forced on him by the king, is uncertain. Evidence seems to substantiate the former conclusion. Happily for both parties, Alexandre de Moura, the man who was named to the governorship of Pernambuco in 1602 to serve "during the minority and absence of the said captain proprietor," was a choice agreeable to all.[53] However, when Moura's long term (twelve years—four times the usual tour of duty for a governor and capitão-mor) ended in 1615, Duarte de Albuquerque Coelho was rebuffed in his efforts to name a successor.

50. *Ibid.* (especially fol. 177) and ANTT, Chancelaria de Filipe II, Doações, liv. 18, fols. 194ᵛ–196. In the five years between the deaths of Jorge de Albuquerque and Matias de Albuquerque, Pernambuco had earned more than 60,000 cruzados for the fourth donatário.

51. As mentioned earlier, most of these loco-tenentes were relatives. For a list see Dutra, "Diogo Botelho," p. 29n. Since there is no record in the *chancelarias reais* of the Crown's making appointments to the position of governor and capitão-mor of Pernambuco, it seems that such assignments were solely in the hands of the donatários.

52. ANTT, Chancelaria de Filipe II, Doações, liv. 10, fols. 196v–197.

53. *Ibid.* For the Crown's attitude toward Alexandre de Moura, see king to viceroy, Aranda, 7 September 1610 in AGS, Sect. Prov., lib. 1503, fol. 65v; and king to viceroy, São Lourenço, 9 September 1614 in AGS, Sect. Prov., lib. 1511, fol. 172v.

When D. Filipe II, without consulting the lord-proprietor, appointed Vasco de Sousa Pacheco to succeed to the governorship of Pernambuco, Albuquerque challenged the Crown by seeking an injunction against the appointment of Sousa Pacheco on the grounds that the lord-proprietor had the right (as the king phrased it in a letter to his viceroy) "to propose persons from whom I [the king] will choose one to serve in his absence."[54] Although the lord-proprietor four years earlier had received confirmation of the donatarial prerogative of nominating men for the post of ouvidor in Pernambuco, the *Casa da Supplicação* overruled Duarte's plea, and Vasco de Sousa Pacheco became governor and capitão-mor of Pernambuco.[55] When Sousa Pacheco was transferred to a similar post in Bahia after serving a little more than two years in Pernambuco, the Crown continued to ignore the wishes of the donatário and named as capitão-mor, Martim de Sousa de Sampaio, who three years earlier had been promised the position as a reward for his services.[56] As mentioned earlier, Sousa de Sampaio and his family were captured by the Dutch and never arrived in Brazil. Taking advantage of the vacancy in Pernambuco, D. Luis de Sousa, the governor-general, gave the post to his friend, João Pais Barreto, who held it until Matias de Albuquerque, the donatário's brother, arrived in Brazil in May of 1620.[57] Though D. Filipe II seems to have been informally influenced by Duarte de Albuquerque Coelho in appointing Matias, it was not until 7 August 1627 that the Crown issued an *alvará* allowing Duarte, as a reward for his services in the recovery of Bahia from the Dutch in 1625, to submit a list of three choices for the office of capitão-mor.[58] In 1629 Francisco Coelho de Carvalho, the lord-proprietor's cousin, was named to

54. AGS, Sect. Prov., lib. 1511, fol. 282. For Sousa Pacheco's appointment, see *ibid.* and lib. 1512, fol. 79v.

55. AGS, Sect. Prov., lib. 1511, fol. 305v.

56. Sousa de Sampaio was rewarded with the "Capitania de Pernambuco por tempo de tres anos na vagante da pessoa que está prouido delle" on 19 October 1616. See AGS, Sect. Prov., lib. 1514, fol. 82v.

57. *Livro primeiro*, pp. 339–340. For the date of Albuquerque's arrival, see *ibid.*, pp. 304–305.

58. ANTT, Chancelaria de Filipe III, Doações, liv. 22, fol. 20v. In the meantime, the Crown appointed André Dias da Franca to succeed Matias de Albuquerque. AHU, Pernambuco, Papéis Avulsos, caixa 1. Joaquim Veríssimo Serrão, *Do Brasil filipino ao Brasil de 1640* (São Paulo, 1968), p. 203, is of the opinion that it was through the efforts of Diogo Luis de Oliveira that Dias da Franca was named capitão-mor of Pernambuco.

serve in Pernambuco.[59] His appointment, however, was a hollow victory for the Albuquerque Coelhos, for the next year the Dutch occupied their captaincy.

Paradoxically, although D. Filipe II prevented Duarte de Albuquerque Coelho from choosing Pernambuco's capitães-mores, he avoided tampering with other provisions of the donatário's patent. On 13 March 1607, the king gave D. Lourenço de Sousa, the lord-proprietor's guardian, authority to fill judicial posts in Pernambuco.[60] In 1610 when a dispute arose regarding D. Lourenço's actions in connection with the office of ouvidor in Pernambuco, D. Filipe supported the lord-proprietor's guardian.[61] The following year, on 11 November 1611, the monarch transferred the right to propose ouvidores for Pernambuco to twenty-year-old Duarte de Albuquerque Coelho.[62] Nine years later the donatário won a signal victory over both the governor-general and the chancellor of the Relação of Brazil concerning certain prerogatives of the ouvidor in Pernambuco[63] In fact, the same governor-general (D. Luis de Sousa) petitioned the king not to hold his *residência* in Pernambuco, claiming that de Sousa could not receive a fair hearing there since the capitão-mor and the donatary were his "sworn enemies" and completely controlled the captaincy's judicial and financial apparatus.[64]

In light of the refusal by D. Felipe II to allow Pernambuco's lord-proprietor to name his own substitute and the Crown's ambivalent attitude toward donatarial prerogatives, it is tempting to interpret the king's ineffective efforts to have the governors-general leave Pernambuco for Bahia as part of a plot to increase royal authority in Brazil's proprietary colonies by pruning away at the donatário's powers and privileges. But although D. Filipe II may have wished to benefit from his governor's interest in the captaincy of the Albuquerque Coelhos to achieve a more centralized and effective government in Brazil, there is no evidence that the Crown secretly encouraged the governors to visit Pernambuco for this purpose. In fact, the

59. AGS, Sect. Prov., lib. 1522, fols. 89 and 119–119v.

60. ANTT, Chancelaria de Filipe II, Doações, liv. 18, fls. 194v–196.

61. King to Viceroy, Madrid, 7 September 1610 in AGS, Sect. Prov., lib. 1503, fls, 71ᵛ–73.

62. ANTT, Chancelaria de Filipe II, Doações, liv. 29, fol. 48.

63. AGS, Sect. Prov., lib. 1517, fol. 34v.

64. These and similar ideas were expressed in a number of letters written by D. Luis after his return to Portugal. They are printed in *Livro primeiro*, pp. 333–344. See especially pp. 334–335.

king made several efforts to pry the governors-general away from Pernambuco, albeit for reasons that revealed no concern for the diminution of donatarial prerogatives.

The Crown was upset by the disobedience by the governors-general of royal orders and their neglect of Bahia. And many of those living in Brazil's capital seem to have been just as irritated as the king. It was claimed that Bahia was not being properly defended at a time when corsairs were raiding Portuguese shipping in the Atlantic with impunity and even making forays onto the Brazilian mainland. Furthermore, in the absence of the governor-general there was an abnormal amount of corruption and dissension in Bahia. Thus Bahians were pressuring the Crown to stop the absenteeism by the governors-general from the Brazilian capital.[65]

The failure of the Crown to punish the disobedient governors should not be taken as an indication of their innocence. The foreign menace (especially French and Dutch), put Brazil in a vulnerable position. There was a great fear of attack. The safety of Portuguese America was paramount in the king's mind. Thus he was forced to leave many abuses unpunished—especially in the upper echelons of Brazil's government. The fear of attack explains D. Filipe II's fore-bearance with his unresponsive governors-general. For example, on 9 November 1602, the Crown gave explicit orders that Diogo Botelho go immediately to Bahia, reminding him that any other action would be considered a disservice to the Crown and emphasizing that "in your regimento I ordered that you go directly to the city of Salvador da Bahia de Todos os Santos where the governors have always resided."[66] Yet despite the governor-general's further delay in Pernambuco and the recommendations of the king's councillor, Belchior do Amaral, that "Your Majesty ought to send another governor to that Province [Brazil] because Diogo Botelho was acting without proper authority," D. Filipe II allowed the governor-general to stay at his post.[67] Why? Because he did not want to jeopardize Brazil's security by changing governors at such a dangerous time. This concern of the Crown was still evident in 1607, when it ex-

65. José Justino de Andrade e Silva, *Collecção chronologica da legislação portuguesa*, 10 vols. (Lisbon, 1854–1859) (hereafter cited as *CCLP*), III, 5. See also the *requerimento* of André Farto da Costa (1614) in AHU, Bahia, Papeis Avulsos, caixa 1; and Frei Vicente, *História*, pp. 416–417.

66. Centro de Estudos Históricos Ultramarinos, *Documentação ultramarina portuguesa*, IV (Lisbon, 1966), 519.

67. BNL/CP, cod. 249, fol. 206v.

pressly directed Botelho to remain in Bahia until his successor, D. Diogo de Meneses, arrived, to insure that the capital city would have adequate leadership.[68]

Meneses' delay in Pernambuco did not go unnoticed by the king, who clearly was becoming angered by the failure of his governors-general to obey his orders to proceed to Bahia. In a letter to the Crown written in December of 1608, Meneses mentioned how D. Filipe had commanded him "to proceed to Bahia as soon as possible." Hurt that the king had questioned his actions and intentions, the governor wrote back that he had only been awaiting the proper winds, and emphasized that "the time which I spent here was only in the service of Your Majesty."[69]

Gaspar de Sousa's stay in Pernambuco, despite later disclaimers by the Iberian monarch, was D. Filipe II's own doing. But the Crown's orders that the governor-general visit Pernambuco before establishing himself in Bahia resulted from concern over the French presence in northern Brazil and not over the powers of the donatários. On 19 March 1614, the king wrote to the viceroy of Portugal regarding "the great harm that results, as experience has shown, when governors visit the captaincies of that State [Brazil]" and ordered that the governors "shall not do this without my express permission and that they always reside in the city of Salvador [Bahia]." The king concluded by inquiring under what orders Gaspar de Sousa was delaying so long in Pernambuco.[70]

To his surprise, D. Filipe II discovered that he himself had been directly responsible for Gaspar de Sousa's visit to Pernambuco. In answer to their monarch's query of 19 March 1614, the Portuguese Council of the Indies (Conselho da India), in a consulta dated 18 April 1614, informed the king that in Sousa's regimento the Crown had ordered the governor-general to "go directly from this city [Lisbon] to the fortress of Rio Grande and visit that captaincy along with those of Paraíba, Itamaracá, and Pernambuco and that after arriving in Bahia, he [the governor] should advise if it would be in Your Majesty's interest to go visit the other captaincies." Furthermore, the Council of the Indies reminded the king that they had sent him a draft of the regimento with a consulta on 18 June

68. Viceroy of Portugal to Diogo Botelho, Lisbon, 7 June 1607, in BA, 51-IX-29, fol. 34.
69. Meneses to king, Recife, 4 December 1608 in ABNRJ, LVII, 44.
70. AGS, Sect. Prov., lib. 1511, fol. 23v; also lib. 1510, fols. 4–4v.

1612 which D. Filipe had approved in a letter of 8 August the same
year. The reason why Gaspar de Sousa was being delayed in Pernambuco, the council reported, was that the governor-general had
been entrusted with the task of driving out the French from
Maranhão and completing the conquest of that region. Pernambuco
was simply a more convenient base for the job than Bahia. The council's suggestion: name other suitable persons and entrust them with
the task of dealing with northern Brazil, since the conquest of
Maranhão was being delayed and Sousa's presence was required
in Bahia.[71]

On 4 June 1614, the king wrote to his viceroy in Portugal that
"orders should be given to the said Gaspar de Sousa to go immediately to Bahia . . . and not stay any longer in Pernambuco." A little
more than a month later, on 16 July 1614, the command was repeated, and D. Filipe instructed his viceroy that "the order should
be given for the governor to go to Bahia in case he has not already
done so as I have already commanded many times previously." After
still another month's interval, a similar letter was sent by the king
to the governor-general. Despite these urgent messages to leave
Pernambuco for his official residence in Bahia, Gaspar de Sousa remained in the captaincy of Duarte de Albuquerque Coelho.[72] Whether Sousa ever received the king's instructions, or whether he simply
failed to obey them, is not known. At any rate, on 31 January 1615,
the eve of his departure for Bahia, the governor-general penned the
following note to the king: "You commanded that I go assist in
Bahia, and this being the first letter of Your Majesty that I received
dealing with the matter, I presume that you have sent me others in
which you have given similar orders. But these letters never arrived,
[probably having been] lost or robbed." And Sousa added: "Thus
Your Secretary is wrong in his supposition that I comported myself
badly in a matter of such importance and neglected the obedience
which I owe to Your Majesty and to Your Royal Orders."[73]

Despite the Crown's growing opposition to the stays in Pernambuco by the governors-general, the manifold problems of the conquest of Maranhão and Pará at times forced the King to hold in

71. The discussion in the above paragraph is based on the consulta of the
Conselho da India, 18 April 1614 in AHU, Bahia, Papéis Avulsos, caixa 1.
72. For a sampling of the royal correspondence to Gaspar de Sousa quoted
above, see AGS, Sect. Prov., lib. 1510, fols. 32 and 48v–49.
73. Sousa to king, 31 January 1615, ABNRJ, XXVI, 311.

abeyance his instructions for the officials to go directly to Bahia. Though D. Luis de Sousa's regimento has not been uncovered, it is clear that he, too, was commanded to spend a short time in Pernambuco to attend to matters dealing with Portuguese expansion into northern Brazil.[74] As the king informed the viceroy of Portugal on 1 February 1618: "I have ordered that ways and means be studied to settle and improve the lands which have recently been opened to us in Maranhão and Pará. And this was the principal reason why I commanded D. Luis de Sousa to reside some time in Pernambuco so that from there he could send the necessary help and provisions to the captains and soldiers who assist in these conquests."[75] Once settled in Pernambuco, however, D. Luis did not want to leave, although as early as 16 September and 8 October 1617, the king began hinting that it was time for the governor-general to depart.[76] As D. Filipe II wrote to his viceroy in Portugal on 1 February 1618: "Because of the problems regarding the said conquest [of Maranhão], a goodly amount of time has elapsed since the governors have served in the city of Salvador da Bahia de Todos os Santos— a place where their presence is very necessary for a number of reasons. Therefore, the capitão-mor of Pernambuco should be instructed to take charge of filling the needs of Maranhão . . . [and] thus D. Luis can go immediately to take up residence in Bahia as is necessary."[77] Although the language in the king's letters to his governor-general became more and more urgent, D. Luis continued to delay his departure. He finally reluctantly left Pernambuco early in 1619.[78]

On 21 February 1620, after almost two decades of ineffective efforts to have the governors-general reside in Brazil's capital, the Crown issued an alvará which stated in no uncertain terms that "the governors of the State of Brazil shall reside personally in the city of Salvador da Bahia de Todos os Santos or they will not earn a salary or have any jurisdiction whatsoever."[79] For the remaining years of donatarial rule in Pernambuco no more governors-general

74. King to Luis de Sousa, 11 April 1617, AMP, III:2, 37.

75. AGS, Sect. Prov., lib. 1516, fol. 11v.

76. E.g., king to Sousa, 16 September 1617 and 8 October 1617 in AMP, III:2, 46, 48 respectively.

77. AGS, Sect. Prov., lib. 1516, fols. 12–12v.

78. King to Sousa, 30 May 1618, 6 November 1618, and 16 February 1619 in AMP, III:2, 65, 78 and 89.

79. CCLP, III, 5.

resided in that captaincy. On 20 March 1620, less than a month after this alvará was issued, D. Filipe II appointed the fourth donatário's brother, Matias de Albuquerque, as governor and capitão-mor of Pernambuco.[80]

The question immediately arises whether there was a link between these two edicts. Was the word of a possible Dutch attack on Brazil the only reason for the young soldier's appointment to Pernambuco?[81] Did D. Filipe also feel that Albuquerque's presence in Pernambuco would keep his governors-general in Bahia where they were most needed? There is some evidence that a growing friendship between the donatário and the king, cemented by the lord-proprietor's marriage to the daughter of D. Diogo de Castro, a trusted and highly regarded member of the king's Council of State, might have prompted the king to realize that in light of the governors-general's disobedience, the Crown's interests might better be served by holding the line on encroachments upon the donatário's authority.[82] As Frei Vincente do Salvador, who was in Lisbon at that time, pointed out, Duarte de Albuquerque Coelho clearly believed that his brother's presence in Pernambuco would end lengthy inspections and interference in the captaincy by the governors-general; and it was largely due to the donatário's efforts that the appointment was made.[83] Henrique Correia da Silva also must have seen the handwriting on the wall. As the man designated to replace D. Luis de Sousa as governor-general, he immediately submitted his resignation, informing the Crown that if he could not go to Pernambuco, he would not go to Brazil.[84] Finally, the king's tacit support of Matias de Albuquerque in his struggles with the governors-general gives strength to the belief that Madrid saw the presence of Duarte's brother in Brazil as an ideal way to restrain overambitious royal officials.

To a great extent the Crown's action succeeded. Pernambuco's defenses were strengthened; the governors-general remained at their

80. ANTT, Chancelaria de Filipe II, Doações, liv. 42, fols. 206–206v.

81. For the relationship between rumors of a Dutch attack on Brazil and Matias de Albuquerque's appointment as capitão-mor of Pernambuco, see the petition of the Condessa de Alegrete, BNL/FG, 1555, fol. 314.

82. Regarding the fourth donatário's marriage to D. Joana de Castro, see ANTT, Chancelaria de Filipe II, Doações, liv. 31, fols. 277v–278. D. Diogo de Castro, the future Conde de Basto, was several times governor of Portugal.

83. Frei Vicente, História, p. 425.

84. Ibid., pp. 425–426.

posts in Bahia; there was more progress and efficiency in the conquest of the north of Brazil; and much of the widespread corruption was curtailed. As a bonus, those on the sidelines were treated to an exciting clash between centralized authority in Bahia and donatarial privilege in Pernambuco.

The tone of the dispute was set almost from the moment Matias de Albuquerque arrived in Pernambuco in May of 1620 to serve in his brother's place as capitão-mor of Pernambuco. Fresh from a successful three-year tour of duty in North Africa and the Mediterranean and angered by interference in what the Albuquerque Coelho family considered the sacrosanct fields of patronage in the Brazilian Northeast and the provisioning of Maranhão and Pará, Matias wasted no time in rectifying what he felt were two decades of abuses by the governors-general and their allies.[85] Within weeks of his arrival in Brazil, the new capitão-mor reported to the Crown that the breastworks and forts of the captaincy were in a sorry state.[86] In an exposé of irregularities in Pernambuco several months later, Matias insinuated that the administration of the captaincy was not much better than its defenses.[87] He contended that during the stay in Pernambuco by the governors-general, corruption and neglect had almost become a way of life. A new day of reform had dawned for the captaincy of the Albuquerque Coelho family.

On 25 September 1620, the governor and capitão-mor of Pernambuco wrote to the king: "It seems proper to me to advise Your Majesty of some matters which I found in this captaincy approved by custom, but not by law nor by the order of Your Majesty." Before he signed this damning indictment, the new capitão-mor had brought to light a string of abuses in Pernambuco. First, Albuquer-

85. For Matias de Albuquerque's activities in the Mediterranean, see BNL/ FG, 1555, fols. 312–314 and 326. These are summarized in ANTT, Chancelaria da Ordem de Cristo, liv. 63, fols. 64–65; and AGS, Sect. Prov., lib. 1468, fols. 124–130v.

86. Letter of Matias de Albuquerque, Olinda, 7 June 1620, in *Livro primeiro*, pp. 304–305.

87. Matias de Albuquerque to king, Olinda, 25 September 1620, AHU, Pernambuco, Papéis Avulsos, caixa 1. The discussion in the following paragraphs is based on this letter. In his correspondence with the king, Matias did not identify the almoxarife by name. However, Gaspar Pereira, a Pernambucan notary public, who drew up the affidavits dealing with the almoxarife's misconduct, disclosed that it was João de Albuquerque who was guilty. See the *certidão* of Gaspar Pereira, dated Olinda, 16 September 1620, AHU, Pernambuco, Papéis Avulsos, caixa 1.

que reported that treasury and customs officials, including the provedor and the clerks, were unlawfully imposing a tax of eight *vinténs*
per *peça* on all Negro slaves entering the port of Recife. This included both those disembarking as well as those staying aboard
slave ships using Pernambuco as a port of call on the Anglo-Spanish
Indies run. Most slavers did not have liquid assets, and they usually
had to sell about ten peças of slaves (often at a loss) to pay this tax,
Because a considerable number of well-laden slave ships came to
Pernambuco, treasury and customs officials had reaped a great profit
which they divided among themselves—the more important officials
receiving a greater share of the "take." Second, the irate governor
complained that the treasury clerk of Pernambuco illegally supplemented his regular earnings by forcing newly enlisted recruits assigned to the presidio of Pernambuco to pay him one cruzado on their
enlistment and another cruzado after each year of service.

In addition to the venality of these royal officials, there were other
improprieties. Matias de Albuquerque pointed a finger at the governor-general of Brazil and the keeper of the royal stores (*almoxarife*) of Pernambuco, accusing the former of interfering with his
authority in the family's captaincy and the latter of behavior "characterized by insolence and boldness." The capitão-mor's charges
related to an incident in which João de Albuquerque, the almoxarife,
had been ordered by D. Luis de Sousa to send more than two hundred and fifty pounds each of powder, lead, and fuses to Paraíba
for the fortress of Cabedelo. However, the munitions happened to
be those given to Matias de Albuquerque by the king for the defense
of Pernambuco (in anticipation of a Dutch attack), and entrusted
to the keeper of the royal stores. Angered, because similar supplies
were readily available from other sources and the danger of enemy
activity was acute, Matias de Albuquerque reprimanded the almoxarife, who, in turn, informed the capitão-mor that he obeyed
only the governor-general and the provedor-mor of Brazil. In reply
to this "insolence," Matias angrily informed the king that insubordination by Crown officials had to stop, emphasizing that if he,
as the capitão-mor, were to have the responsibility for fortifying and
defending Pernambuco, he had to have the authority that went
with it.

Less than a month later, after receiving a similar report from
his brother, Duarte de Albuquerque Coelho added his own cry of
indignation. Writing to the king from Lisbon on 9 December 1620,

the donatário lashed out against D. Luis de Sousa's leadership. His letter deserves to be quoted at length:

> I have understood that D. Luis de Sousa, governor-general of the State of Brazil, entrusts to various people tasks which in my captaincy touch on the service of Your Majesty; moreover, these persons do not measure up to the demands of the job. A case in point is the *provedor da fazenda* to whom was given recently the job of provisioning Maranhão—one that is incompatible with the position of *provedor*. Since it has always been customary to give the task of provisioning [the newly-opened areas] to the capitães-mores of that place [Pernambuco] because the persons who serve there are the most qualified, and since on my part I am concerned with the promptness with which Your Majesty's wishes should be carried out (since my brother governs in my place), it seems only proper that I bring these matters to Your Majesty's attention so that Your Majesty may be better served.[88]

These two letters received immediate attention from the Council of the Treasury (*Conselho da Fazenda*) whose decision of 15 December 1620 was a resounding victory for Matias and his brother.[89] The unauthorized practices of taxing slaves and new soldiers in Pernambuco were condemned and ordered stopped, and explanations were demanded from the accused of why they had been acting without orders from the king. The defiant keeper of the royal stores was severely reprimanded for his behavior toward Matias de Albuquerque, and a letter was soon sent to D. Luis de Sousa informing him that the next time he dealt with matters in Pernambuco, he should work through the capitão-mor and not at cross purposes with him.

The council's recommendation in reference to the provisioning of Maranhão, however, had the greatest effect on the Albuquerque Coelho family's morale. The council informed the Crown reports had been received that in the supplying of Maranhão "there were some matters very detrimental to the service of Your Majesty and the good of Your Treasury," including the sending of "worthless goods at excessive prices" along with materials of no use in Per-

88. Duarte's letter is annexed to his brother's of 25 September 1620 in AHU, Pernambuco, Papéis Avulsos, caixa 1.

89. Consulta of the Conselho da Fazenda, 15 December 1620, in AHU, cod. 32, fols. 176v–178. Another copy of this consulta with different marginal notes can be found in AGS, Sect. Prov., lib. 1473, fols. 521–522v.

nambuco which were being unloaded for a profit in Maranhão. To
get at the bottom of this corruption, the Council of the Treasury
recommended that Matias de Albuquerque be instructed to undertake a secret investigation. Following the suggestions of Duarte de
Albuquerque Coelho, the council further advocated that the provisioning of Maranhão be taken out of the hands of Pernambuco's
provedor da fazenda and that Matias de Albuquerque, as capitão-
mor, be placed in charge of provisioning that new conquest. This
report was addressed to D. Filipe II, but he died on 31 March 1621,
and it fell to his son, D. Filipe III, to put most of it into execution.
By September 1621 the suggestions of the Council of the Treasury
were being implemented in their entirety. In fact, D. Filipe III even
went further than the council's earlier recommendations and ordered the treasury officials in Pernambuco to open all their account
books for Matias' examination.[90]

This order, of course, was a serious blow to the governor-general's
influence in Pernambuco. In dismay, Luis de Sousa complained to
D. Filipe III that because Albuquerque was supervising the provisioning of Maranhão and was "independent of the governor-
general in many matters dealing with the treasury," the donatário's
brother was "much more than a capitão-mor." "So great is his
sovereignty," Sousa lamented, "that no one there [in Pernambuco]
dares to antagonize him."[91] By this time, Matias de Albuquerque
had assumed many of the trappings of a lord-proprietor, and he had
refused to subordinate himself to the governor-general as had previous capitães-mores. Though D. Luis de Sousa's complaints of
Matias' disobedience resulted in an investigation and a mild slap on
the wrist in the form of a carta régia, dated 26 November 1623, for-
bidding the donatário's brother from acting as if he were the lord-
proprietor, they did little to hamper Albuquerque's activity in Pernambuco.[92] The capitão-mor was also reprimanded for his attitude
toward the leadership in Bahia by Manuel Pinto da Rocha, the
ouvidor-geral (later, chancellor of the Relação) stationed in Brazil's

90. Though there is evidence that D. Filipe II had already started to implement the Council of the Treasury's recommendations (see the marginal notes
on the consulta cited in the preceding note), it was not until his son's reign that
full attention was given to them. See king to Matias de Albuquerque, AHU,
cod. 35B, fol. 32v.

91. *Livro primeiro*, pp. 335–336.

92. King to Sousa, Madrid, 10 February 1621, *AMP*, III:2, 115. For the carta
régia, see *CCLP*, III, 106.

capital, who sharply reminded him that in two earlier letters Matias had been using "language very different from that which had been used by his predecessors" and instructed him to pay more respect to the governor of Brazil. Albuquerque angrily scribbled on the back of Pinto da Rocha's note: "I observe more the laws of His Majesty than their corruption."[93]

These words probably made a still greater impression on the governor-general when the smouldering question of who should appoint Tomé Mendes' successor to the position of patrão da ribeira and juiz dos calafates in Pernambuco flared up again. Though the exact sequence of events is hazy, before the conflict was resolved three of Luis de Sousa's chief supporters in Pernambuco—João Pais Barreto, Vicente Campelo, and Manuel de Matos—had been imprisoned. This much is clear. Matias de Albuquerque supported Antônio Vicente Cochado, who, because of his services in the conquest of Maranhão, had been awarded the vacant post by the Crown on 7 June 1620.[94] At the same time, Manuel de Matos, Pernambuco's provedor, and a protégé of D. Luis de Sousa, backed Lourenço Vaz Cerveira, the governor-general's choice. During the last two-and-a-half weeks of November 1620, the two sides attempted to outmaneuver each other. Although Cochado followed the instructions of the capitão-mor, he was unable to get his appointment registered in the provedor's office. In fact, Manuel de Matos threatened Cochado with fines and sanctions if he tried to exercise his office. At this juncture, Matias de Albuquerque, who thought the entire matter (as he, perhaps with mock surprise, expressed it to the king) "seemed more the effect of inadvertence than passion" sent a clerk to bring to Matos' attention the fact that Antônio Vicente Cochado was serving under the authority of a royal writ. The provedor heatedly replied that Cochado's document was worthless and that it had been obtained surreptitiously. Manuel de Matos further asserted that only the appointee of the governor-

93. For Pinto da Rocha's letter, see *Livro primeiro*, pp. 291–292. A photographic reproduction of Matias de Albuquerque's comment is found opposite p. 290. For Pinto da Rocha's promotion to chancellor of the Relação, see ANTT, Chancelaria de Filipe III, Doações, liv. 1, fol. 130.

94. Consulta of the Conselho da Fazenda, 26 March 1621, AHU, cód. 33, fols. 46v–48. Antônio Vicente Cochado was being awarded the position "por ser o prim^ro piloto q̃ foj ao descobrim^to do maranhão E despois o obrigar V mag^de a ir seruir em nauios aquella Conquista quatro ou cinco uezes e ter seruido nas partes do Brasil muitos annos."

general would be recognized. D. Luis de Sousa, it was claimed, had been given authority by the Crown in his regimento to name men to various posts in Brazil.[95] This claim was all Matias de Albuquerque needed to hear, for it recalled memories of his encounter with the almoxarife of Pernambuco a few months earlier. In his report to the king, the capitão-mor made a special point of contrasting the strong feelings of loyalty which Manuel de Matos had towards his benefactor, the governor-general, with the provedor's disregard in following the monarch's own provisions and orders.

The reaction of the Council of the Treasury was swift and similar to that which Matias de Albuquerque's earlier letters had elicited: praise for the capitão-mor's alertness and condemnation for the provedor's audacity in failing to execute the king's orders.[96] But the council's recommendations for Manuel de Matos' punishment were much more severe than those which had been advocated for João de Albuquerque's misbehavior. The council suggested that the provedor da fazenda be immediately suspended from his post, imprisoned, and shipped back to Portugal for a hearing. At about the same time, the Albuquerque Coelhos felt the proper opportunity had arrived to settle old scores with João Pais Barreto and Vicente Campelo for their treatment of Cristóvão de Albuquerque. The aid of D. Diogo de Castro was enlisted, and soon the president of the *Desembargo do Paço* started an investigation into the circumstances of Cristóvão de Albuquerque's imprisonment and the controversy over the appointment of the new patrão da ribeira—matters which even D. Luis de Sousa admitted "had been marked by excesses on both sides."[97] Soon the former capitão-mor (Pais Barreto) and the captain of the fort of Recife (Vicente Campelo) were imprisoned "with great fanfare."[98] Finally, after many arguments by the principals engaged in the controversy and much pen-pushing by the tribunal of the Desembargo do Paço and by members of the Council of the Treasury, a halt was called to this long-drawn-out conflict. On 23 February 1624, D. Filipe III ordered that nothing more be

95. For D. Luis de Sousa's claim, see AHU, cód. 34, fols. 24–25. There is a similar provision in the regimento of Francisco Giraldes (1587), par. 45. See *RIHGB*, 67:1, 234.

96. AHU, cód. 33, fols. 46v–48. Also cf. king to Matias de Albuquerque, 6 May 1622, AHU, cod. 35B, fols. 30–30v. The capitão-mor was praised for reporting abuses in Pernambuco. See king to Albuquerque, 22 May 1621, AHU, cód. 35B, fol. 31.

97. *Livro primeiro*, p. 340.   98. *Ibid.*, pp. 335, 340.

said on the subject and that there be no more proceedings against any of the persons involved in the original dispute.[99] By that time it was clear that the Albuquerque Coelhos had been victorious. Never had the prestige of a capitão-mor been so high. Not only had the governor-general been prevented from making appointments in the donatário's captaincy, but the Crown had been prompted to reassess its earlier policy of allowing governors-general to name minor officials in the overseas possessions.[100]

One of the results of Matias de Albuquerque's probings into corruption in the conquest of Maranhão was the indictment (on a variety of charges) of the governor-general himself.[101] D. Luis was accused of sending goods to Maranhão at excessive prices, often close to twice their value. It was further claimed that many supplies for which Sousa received payment never arrived and that both the governor-general and his protégé, Francisco Barbosa, had a personal interest in the provisioning of Maranhão, since they themselves acted as suppliers. Finally, Sousa was charged with acting in collusion with several of the Crown's purveyors to defraud the royal treasury.[102] Later, at his residência, D. Luis brushed aside these accusations by emphasizing that in the provisioning of Maranhão only the established prices were charged. And, the governor added, if there were by chance any misappropriation of funds or profiteering, it must have occurred after he left Pernambuco for Bahia.[103] Since, for reasons explained later, no residência was taken in Pernambuco, the charges against the governor-general were never proved or disproved—though the Council of Portugal on another occasion slyly remarked that "he returned from Brazil very wealthy."[104]

The bad feelings existing between the governor-general and the Albuquerque Coelhos did not end when D. Luis de Sousa's term of office came to a close. On his way back to Portugal the governor-

99. CCLP, III, 114. The Desembargo do Paço had previously directed three consultas to the Crown, dated 10 May and November 1622 and 23 February 1623.

100. Consulta of the Conselho da Fazenda, 12 February 1622, AHU, cód. 34, fols. 24–25.

101. For D. Filipe III's authorization, see AHU, cód. 35B, fol. 32v. References to the investigation itself are found in Livro primeiro, p. 416, along with pp. 336 and 343.

102. Livro primeiro, p. 409.   103. Ibid., pp. 413–416.

104. AGS, Sect. Prov., lib. 1467, fol. 714.

general sailed to Pernambuco where he planned to rendezvous with
the fleet readying its departure from Recife.[105] To D. Luis de Sousa's
surprise, when he attempted to land there, he discovered that "he
had to remain aboard ship eight or nine days, because Matias de
Albuquerque would not allow him to visit the captaincy."[106] Furthermore, the capitão-mor of Pernambuco refused to talk to the
governor-general and, as Sousa complained, attempted to appoint
a man of his own choice as commander of the *frota*.[107] As an added
insult—in a week already filled with humiliations and abuse for
the governor-general—when Albuquerque sailed past the ship on
which Sousa was "quarantined," he gave D. Luis no sign of recognition and even failed to doff his hat.[108]

Sousa's reception by the donatário and his relatives when he
reached Lisbon in 1622 was even chillier.[109] The governor-general's
cousin, Duarte de Albuquerque Coelho, refused to visit or to con-
verse with him.[110] Soon D. Diogo de Castro, by now one of the
governors of Portugal, inaugurated a secret investigation into D.
Luis de Sousa's behavior as governor-general.[111] Placed in the hands
of *desembargador* Manuel Coutinho de Castelo Branco, the devassa
was held in Lisbon and lasted nine or ten months. Many Pernambucan settlers, treasury officials, merchants, and ship captains were
questioned. Meanwhile, in Pernambuco, Matias de Albuquerque was
investigating the governor's conduct in provisioning Maranhão.[112]

Sousa objected to these investigations, accusing D. Diogo de
Castro of acting without royal orders, and in a series of petitions

105. *Livro primeiro*, p. 343; Frei Vicente, *História*, p. 428.
106. *Livro primeiro*, p. 335.
107. *Ibid.*, p. 343; cf. Frei Vicente, *História*, p. 428.
108. *Livro primeiro*, p. 335.
109. Though the exact date of D. Luis' departure for Portugal is not certain,
it was no earlier than November of 1621. See Frei Vicente, *História*, p. 427,
who mentions that Sousa was in Bahia when his successor arrived on 12 October.
D. Luis seems to have stayed in the Brazilian capital for the celebrations mark-
ing the arrival of a new governor-general. He also spent eight or nine days
cooling his heels in Pernambuco. D. Luis de Sousa did not arrive at the court
in Madrid until the summer of 1622. See *Livro primeiro*, p. 333. For his frosty
reception by Duarte de Albuquerque Coelho, see *ibid.*, pp. 335, 343.
110. The governor-general and the donatário were cousins (within the second and third degree) and had been good friends before Sousa left Portugal for
his Brazilian assignment. *Livro primeiro*, p. 343.
111. *Ibid.*, pp. 333–334, 338, and 343.
112. *Ibid.*, p. 342.

requested that both D. Diogo and Manuel Coutinho de Castelo Branco be reprimanded and punished and that the devassas taken in Pernambuco and Lisbon be declared null and void.[113] At the same time, D. Luis tried to persuade the Crown not to go ahead with the two-fold residência in Bahia and Pernambuco, as planned, but to limit to Bahia alone the investigation of Sousa's activities as governor-general. As he explained to the king, no testimony damaging to himself should be accepted in Pernambuco "because almost all of that [captaincy] is composed of relatives, friends, followers, and dependents of Duarte de Albuquerque; justice officials are appointed by him; and by grants of land and by the quitrents they pay to him, they are all his subjects."[114]

On 25 October 1623, D. Filipe III seems to have restricted the residência in Pernambuco, for he ordered that neither the protégés of Matias de Albuquerque nor persons appointed to offices by Duarte de Albuquerque Coelho, nor followers of either be permitted to testify.[115] Despite these concessions to D. Luis de Sousa, however, it is clear that the king still planned to go ahead with a limited residência in Pernambuco, an assignment given to desembargador Pero Casqueiro da Rocha.[116] But Sousa's successor as governor-general, Diogo de Mendonça Furtado, thwarted such plans. He claimed that due to the death of the chancellor of the Relação, Manuel Pinto da Rocha, and the absence of João Sousa de Cárdenas who was conducting devassas in the south of Brazil, there would be a shortage of desembargadores in Bahia to take care of the great backlog of cases in the Brazilian capital if another desembargador went to Pernambuco. In the meantime, in Bahia, a residência which turned out to be favorable to D. Luis was begun on 9 January 1624 and ended about 16 March of the same year.[117] A short time later, on 10 May 1624, Bahia was seized by the Dutch. In the intervening year before Brazil's capital was recovered by the Portuguese, D. Luis de Sousa contributed three thousand and three hundred cruzados and thirty moios of wheat for biscuits for the campaign, and the king, in turn, seems to have forgotten about the residência planned

113. Ibid., pp. 333–334 and 342. Though D. Luis de Sousa made several petitions that no residência be held in Pernambuco, the best expression of his feelings is found in ibid., pp. 337–338.

114. Ibid., p. 335.   115. Ibid., p. 359.

116. AGS, Sect. Prov., lib. 1467, fol. 714 and Livro primeiro, p. 337.

117. Livro primeiro, pp. 359–416.

for Pernambuco.[118] Thus, as far as D. Filipe III was concerned, the
dispute between the Albuquerque Coelhos and D. Luis de Sousa
had come to a close.

Though the struggle between the governors-general in Bahia and
the capitães-mores and governors of Pernambuco reached its greatest intensity during the administration of D. Luis de Sousa, it did
not end with the arrival of his successor, Diogo de Mendonça
Furtado. Again controversy flared up, fueled by the questions of
the provisioning of Maranhão by Pernambuco and its dominant role
there, and the jurisdiction of the governor-general within Pernambuco itself.

The development of northeastern and northern Brazil was an
important and urgent problem for Matias de Albuquerque. As
Capistrano de Abreu remarked in his review of Oliveira Lima's
Pernambuco: seu desenvolvimento histórico: "If we want to assign
an epithet to each century of our history, it would be 'Pernambuco'
in the sixteenth century, 'Bahia' and 'São Paulo' in the seventeenth,
'Minas Gerais' in the eighteenth, and 'Rio de Janeiro' in the period
that will soon end."[119] It was over the Brazilian Northeast, in particular, that Pernambuco exercised this hegemony. Almost from the
start, the captaincy of the Albuquerque Coelho family, by providing
men, money, munitions, and supplies, had played an important role
in opening up Brazil's northern frontier. Although Pernambuco
lagged behind São Paulo as the nucleus *par excellence* of Brazilian
frontier activity, it was clearly the second most important center of
Brazilian expansion during the colonial period.

Even though, at times, Bahian ouvidores-gerais such as Dr. Fernão
da Silva or Martim Leitão might head the expeditions of "conquest,"
the bulk of their forces came from Pernambuco. Frei Vicente do
Salvador's comment regarding da Silva's campaign of the mid-
1570s—the ouvidor included among his followers "all the men on
foot and on horseback and Indian allies that he could round up in
Pernambuco and Itamaracá"—could easily be applied to the countless follow-up expeditions bent on the conquest of the Northeast.[120]

118. AGS, Sect. Prov., lib. 1467, fls. 714–715v. For D. Luis' contribution, see
Frei Vicente, *História*, p. 472. No residência was ever taken in Pernambuco.
119. Quoted by José Honorio Rodrigues, *História e historiadores do Brasil*
(São Paulo, 1965), p. 51. An English translation is found in *Perspectives on
Brazilian History*, ed. E. Bradford Burns (New York, 1967), p. 177.
120. Frei Vicente, *História*, p. 219.

Merchants in Olinda and Recife became wealthy supplying food, seed, livestock, utensils, and arms for the many boatloads and wagonloads of soldiers and settlers leaving Pernambuco for the new lands to the north. Many relatives of the donatários of Pernambuco saw in the Brazilian Northeast opportunities for duplicating Duarte Coelho's success. Thus, it is not surprising that the crucial half-century (1580–1630) of Portugal's early expansion into northern Brazil was dominated by such kinfolk of the Albuquerque Coelhos as the Albuquerque Maranhão clan, the Coelho de Carvalho family, the Cavalcantis and the Mouras. Even such non-relatives as Manuel Mascarenhas Homen, the capitão-mor of Pernambuco, caught the expansionist fever. For his efforts in Rio Grande do Norte in the years 1597–1602, Mascarenhas Homen was properly credited with being the "conqueror" of that region.[121]

The lengthy stays of the governors-general in Pernambuco during the first twenty years of the seventeenth century threatened the supremacy of many of the important interest groups in the captaincy vis-à-vis the Brazilian Northeast. Within months of Matias de Albuquerque's arrival in Pernambuco, moves were afoot to stop this threat. As noted earlier, Pernambuco's capitão-mor was amazingly successful in his efforts to thwart the governors-general's influence in northern Brazil. But before the Albuquerque Coelho family could consolidate their newly won gains, Diogo de Mendonça took advantage of a political vacuum in northern Brazil and appointed men to two important posts there—the interim governorship of Maranhão and the captainship of the garrison of Grão Pará.[122]

At the suggestion of Gaspar de Sousa, Diogo de Meneses, Alexandre de Moura, and others, D. Filipe II had decided to separate the government of Maranhão and Pará from that of the remainder of Brazil, as early as 20 June 1618, but all sorts of delays prevented the king's wishes from becoming a reality. Though both an ouvidor-geral and a governor were appointed in 1619, the new state did not come into being until 13 June 1621.[123] The Spanish-born governor-elect, D. Diogo de Carcamo, died early in 1623, before he could set

121. See the comments of the Jesuit, Padre Jácome Monteiro, in HCJB, VIII, 405.

122. Frei Vicente, História, p. 429.

123. Mathias C. Kiemen, O.F.M., The Indian Policy of Portugal in the Amazon Region, 1614–1693 (Washington, D.C., 1954), p. 26. Also AGS, Sect. Prov., lib. 1516, fols. 12–12v.

sail, and on 23 September 1623, Francisco Coelho de Carvalho, a relative of the donatário of Pernambuco, was named governor of Maranhão and Grão Pará.[124]

In the meantime, Jerônimo de Albuquerque, capitão-mor of Maranhão, and Jerônimo Fragoso de Albuquerque, capitão-mor of Pará, two influential figures in the opening up of the Brazilian Northeast to Portuguese settlement and both relatives of Pernambuco's donatário, had died. In the confusion caused by Carcamo's death, D. Filipe II's death, Lisbon's lack of activity in the affairs of northern Brazil, and Matias de Albuquerque's preoccupation with the struggle to restore donatarial authority in the captaincy of Pernambuco, Mendonça Furtado was able to use his prerogative of naming officials to vacant positions by appointing Antônio Monis Barreiros as interim captain of Maranhão, to replace Jerônimo de Albuquerque, and appointing Bento Maciel Parente as Jerônimo Fragoso's successor.[125] Though this must have rankled Matias de Albuquerque, the capitão-mor had the consolation that Monis Barreiros would have to stop in Pernambuco for supplies (which he did, departing 11 March 1622) and thus many of the details of the expedition would still be in the hands of Pernambucans.[126] By mid-1622, Matias de Albuquerque was, in fact as well as in theory, superintendent for the Northeast.

The capitão-mor of Pernambuco saw his responsibility toward the Brazilian North country as two-fold: first, to secure what had already been explored and settled by the Portuguese; second, to continue this work of exploration and settlement. Matias' concern for the security of the Northeast is evidenced by his role in the construction of Fort Conceição near the city of Filipeia in Paraíba and his quick response to the Dutch threat at the Bahia da Traição.[127]

124. Kiemen, *Indian Policy*, p. 27.

125. Frei Vicente, *História*, p. 429.

126. See consulta of the Conselho da Fazenda, 2 August 1623, in Studart, *Documentos para a história do Brasil*, I, 300–303.

127. See the petition of the Condessa da Alegrete, BNL/FG, 1555, fol. 315. Matias de Albuquerque also wanted to play a role in further explorations of northern Brazil. When the Crown, early in 1623, sent Captain Luis Aranha de Vasconcelos and a caravel from Lisbon to explore and fathom the Amazon River "because of rumors that it would be easier and cheaper to transport silver from Potosí that way" and gave orders that the capitães-mores of Pernambuco, Rio Grande do Norte, Maranhão and Pará give to Aranha de Vasconcelos all that was necessary, Matias with his accustomed alacrity contributed greatly to the expedition. In fulfilling these royal orders, Albuquerque not only supplied

Albuquerque kept the entire northeastern coast alerted to possible foreign attacks, and he continually sent arms and munitions to the various captains and forts in the area.[128] He was also interested in the material welfare of the new "conquests." Periodically, thousands of cruzados worth of supplies, ranging from foodstuffs to cattle and seed, were sent along with trained mechanics (especially to aid in the construction of sugar mills) and numerous ships.[129] As can be seen from two pieces of royal correspondence, dated 1621 and 1623, Pernambuco was expected to aid in provisioning the Northeast with a variety of goods, ranging from a chalice, monstrance, bell, and statue of St. Sebastian—for Martim Soares Moreno in Ceará—to cattle, oxen, and the necessary machinery for a sugar mill owned by Bento Maciel Parente in Grão Pará.[130] Perhaps Matias' prompt attention to the needs of the Northeast spoiled the captains stationed there. After he stepped down from his post late in 1626, there seems not to have been the same close cooperation between the north of Brazil and officials (especially royal ones) in Pernambuco and Bahia. In 1628 and 1629 Martim Soares Moreno was bitter in his complaints to the king that the governor-general (Diogo Luis de Oliveira) was disobeying royal orders by not sending needed arms and soldiers to Ceará and that Pernambuco's provedor da fazenda was not forwarding money for the salaries of the soldiers already there.[131]

---

seventeen men and a launch from Pernambuco but sent along his trusted friend, the capable pilot, Antônio Vicente Cochado. See Frei Vicente, *História*, p. 429; AGS, Sect. Prov., lib. 1467, fols. 688–691v. By sending on the voyage the man he had installed in the post of patrão da ribeira, Matias probably felt he could exert some influence (at least indirectly) on the results of any new discoveries and thus strengthen Pernambuco's hegemony over northern Brazil. Nor was the capitão-mor of Pernambuco the only one interested in the exploration of the Amazon. A similar tactic was tried by Bento Maciel Parente of Ceará, but it failed. Frei Vicente, *História*, p. 430.

128. See, for example, the consulta of the Conselho da Fazenda, 5 March 1623, AHU, cód. 35, fols. 234v–235v.

129. See Studart, *Documentos para a história do Brasil*, I, 300, for one of many examples of supplies being sent to Maranhão from Pernambuco. Also cf. king to Albuquerque, 28 January 1621, AHU, cód. 35B, fols. 28v–29. For skilled technicians, see king to Albuquerque, 13 September 1622, AHU, cód. 35B, fol. 35v.

130. Luis da Silva to Provedor da Fazenda of Pernambuco, 30 March 1621, AHU, cod. 35B, fol. 29; Consulta of the Conselho da Fazenda, 22 August 1620, AHU, cod. 32, fol. 107v; and king to Matias de Albuquerque, 4 September 1623, AHU, cod. 35B, fol. 45v.

131. Luis da Silva to Provedor da Fazenda of Pernambuco, 30 May 1628, in Studart, *Documentos para a história do Brasil*, II, 220–221; Martim Soares

The high point of this cooperation between Pernambuco and the Brazilian North should have been reached in mid–1624 with the arrival in Recife of Francisco Coelho de Carvalho, the governor of the new state of Maranhão and Grão Pará. Coelho de Carvalho was a relative of the donatário of Parnambuco as well as a trusted associate. With Matias de Albuquerque presiding over Pernambuco and the "vassal" captaincies of Itamaracá, Paraíba, and Rio Grande do Norte, and Francisco Coelho de Carvalho in charge of Maranhão and Grão Pará, the Albuquerque and Coelho clans could hope to effectively control half of Brazil. But the Dutch invasion of Brazil in 1624 dashed these hopes. When Coelho de Carvalho arrived in Pernambuco from Lisbon to pick up supplies and make preparations for completing his voyage, the Dutch threat was so great (Bahia had already been captured) that the new governor of Maranhão was asked to stay on in Pernambuco and was placed in charge of Recife, where he remained for almost two years.[132] Though Matias gave his cousin five ships and twenty thousand cruzados' worth of provisions for Maranhão, it was not until 13 July 1626 that Coelho de Carvalho could continue his expedition.[133] By the end of that year Matias had been replaced as capitão-mor of Pernambuco by André Dias da Franca, and the Albuquerque Coelho dream of a Pernambuco-Maranhão axis had been destroyed before it could become a reality.

Matias de Albuquerque's dispute over interference by the governors-general in the affairs of his brother's captaincy flared up again with the arrival of Diogo de Mendonça Furtado's ship off the coast of Pernambuco in late September or early October 1621. Although the new governor-general later had words of praise regarding Matias de Albuquerque's handling of the provisioning of Maranhão, he clashed initially with the capitão-mor by renewing the question that had previously poisoned relations between his predecessor and the Albuquerque Coelho family—the appointment of officials to positions in Pernambuco. Soon after he arrived, he named one of his protégés, Gregório da Silva, captain of Recife,

Moreno to king, 17 October 1628, *ibid.*, pp. 221–222; consulta of the Conselho da Fazenda, 10 March 1629, AHU, cód. 38, fols. 59–59v.

132. For the "vassal" captaincies, see the contemporary comments of Brandão, *Diálogos*, pp. 20–21. For Coelho de Carvalho, see Frei Vicente, *História*, pp. 455–456, and AGS, Sect. Prov., lib. 1536, fol. 182.

133. Frei Vicente, *História*, pp. 509–510; BNL/FG, 1555, fols. 316v–317; AGS, Sect. Prov., lib. 1536, fol. 182. The latter states that only four ships accompanied Coelho de Carvalho.

a post temporarily vacant because of Vicente Campelo's imprisonment. But Matias de Albuquerque would have none of this and immediately limited Silva's jurisdiction to the royal fort itself, giving charge of the settlement of Recife to one of his own supporters.[134]

Several months later, in February 1622, the same issue reoccurred. This time, the office of provedor da fazenda, around which much of the conflict between Matias de Albuquerque and D. Luis de Sousa had revolved, was the center of controversy. When the capitão-mor of Pernambuco imprisoned Manuel de Matos and shipped him off to Portugal in mid–1621 for disobeying the king's orders regarding the appointment of the captaincy's patrão da ribeira, Albuquerque received permission to name Matos' successor. His choice was licenciado Domingos da Silveira, a former official of the Olinda town council and procurador da fazenda.[135] Silveira's term of office was to be six months, though his alvará seems to have implied that if the Crown did not appoint his successor within that time, the licenciado would continue in office until someone else was named to fill the vacancy. On 30 July 1621, Silveira was installed in his post by Matias de Albuquerque. By the end of January of the following year no action had been taken by the king regarding the licenciado's replacement; thus Silveira made ready to continue in office for another six months. In the meantime, the governor-general decided to name one of his protégés, João Rebelo de Lima, to Silveira's post. But when Rebelo de Lima reached Pernambuco, Matias refused to permit him to assume office. While Rebelo de Lima appealed to the Relação in Bahia to sustain his appointment, Matias, furious at what he considered further evidence of interference by the Bahian authorities, angrily complained to the Crown. He accused Diogo de Mendonça Furtado of acting fradulently and outside his jurisdiction; he attacked the desembargadores of the High Court for their interference and called for their reprimand; and he compared this episode with the Cochado case which had also been marked by a governor-general's intervention.[136]

134. Frei Vicente História, pp. 425–426. For the governor-general's words of praise, see Livro primeiro, p. 313. Vicente Campelo's imprisment can be inferred from ibid., p. 335.

135. Details regarding the Domingos de Silveira episode are found in Matias de Albuquerque to king, Olinda, 1 June 1622, AHU, Pernambuco, Papéis Avulsos, caixa 1. For Domingos da Silveira's activity as a member of the Olinda town council, see Livro primeiro, p. 148.

136. King to Matias de Albuquerque, 20 September 1622, AHU, cod. 35B,

Three months later, the king thanked the capitão-mor "for having proceeded well in all these matters" and informed him that the mass of materials Matias had gathered was being carefully studied. The final outcome of the controversy is shrouded in mystery, though before the incident was concluded, João Rebelo de Lima had been added to the list of Matias de Albuquerque's prisoners.[137]

The year 1623 was not much more peaceful. Here again, the chief difficulty centered on the two-fold problem of jurisdiction over questions dealing with Pernambuco and the lack of communication and cooperation between the governor-general and the capitão-mor. In one case, Mendonça Furtado, at the king's order, had planned to send desembargador Pero de Casqueiro to Pernambuco to report on the collection of newly imposed taxes (the receipts from which were to bolster Pernambuco's defenses) and to view the progress being made on the captaincy's fortifications.[138] Though, according to the Crown's orders, Albuquerque and the desembargador were supposed to work closely together on this undertaking, the governor-general failed to notify the capitão-mor, thereby inviting further trouble.[139]

Later that same year there was another bothersome dispute in the Iberian peninsula over jurisdiction in Pernambuco—possibly the aftermath of Gregório da Silva's experience in which he was allowed authority only over the fort and not over the settlement of Recife. This time, Antônio Carneiro Falcato, the newly appointed captain of the fort of Recife, occupied the Crown's attention. Two questions were raised: Should the captain of the fort be subordinate to the capitão-mor of Pernambuco? Did the fact that the captain was installed by the capitão-mor give the latter authority over the former? The answers to these queries seem not to have been presented to the Crown, although D. Filipe III was curious to know "by what

---

fol. 37v. The Crown evidently went along, at least tacitly, with Silveira's continuance in office. See letter of Luis da Silva to Domingos da Silveira, Lisboa, 11 March 1622 in AHU, cód. 35B, fol. 34.

137. *Livro primeiro*, p. 335.

138. *CCLP*, III, 96. As it turned out, Pero de Casqueiro, who was also to take D. Luis de Sousa's residencia in Pernambuco, never arrived there. See *Livro primeiro*, p. 337 and AGS, Sect. Prov., lib. 1467, fol. 714. It seems that Matias de Albuquerque and the town council of Olinda were not too enthusiastic about sending part of the money being collected for the repair and upkeep of fortifications in Bahia. See *CCLP*, III, 124.

139. *Ibid.*, p. 106. Coincidentally, Diogo de Mendoça Furtado had been complaining of similar behavior on the part of the Crown. See *ibid.*, p. 96.

order in the writs of the captains of the said fort was the clause inserted that they should be under the control [of the capitão-mor] of Pernambuco" and "if the captain proprietor of Pernambuco or whoever is serving in his place has any writ in which it is ordered that the captain of Recife be under his command."[140]

For the next few years the issue of the governor-general of Brazil *vs.* the governor and capitão-mor of Pernambuco became academic, for on 10 May 1624, Diogo de Mendonça Furtado and a handful of his associates were captured by the Dutch after the rest of the inhabitants had fled the city. When the secret orders were opened to discover Mendonça Furtado's successor, Matias de Albuquerque headed the list. As thirteenth governor-general of Brazil as well as capitão-mor of Pernambuco, Matias easily solved any practical problems dealing with matters of jurisdiction in Pernambuco.[141] In fact, the two-and-a-half years Albuquerque served as governor-general were probably the high points in almost a century of donatarial rule in Pernambuco. By the eve of his departure for Portugal on 18 June 1627, Matias had returned the captaincy of the Albuquerque Coelhos to the type of strong rule that had been only a hazy memory since Duarte Coelho's last years in Brazil.

As a military man who would brook no insubordination in Pernambuco, and as brother of the lord-proprietor interested in restoring firm control over the captaincy to his family, the capitão-mor was somewhat of a reformer, exposing and cleaning up graft and corruption in Pernambuco. By adopting the role of "crime-fighter," Matias had much to gain. Not only could his actions be used to impress the Crown (which they did), but they could serve to discredit enemies of the Albuquerque Coelho family and to tighten the family's control over Pernambuco.

The abolition of the Relação stationed in Bahia provided the finishing touches to the Albuquerque Coelho family's triumph. Though the Brazilian Relação had been in the planning stages early in the reign of D. Filipe I, its first officials did not arrive in Bahia until

140. Consulta of the Conselho da Fazenda, 4 December 1623, AHU, cod. 35, fols. 232–232v. D. Filipe III's questions are annexed to the above consulta and dated 7 March 1624.

141. Though several Brazilian historians have not included Matias de Albuquerque on their list of Brazil's governors-general, recent study has shown that he was a bonafide governor. See especially, Hélio Vianna, "Acréscimos à Biografia de Matias de Albuquerque," *RIHGB*, 251 (1961), 45–46.

5 June 1609.[142] Almost from the beginning this new institution had been a thorn in the side of many Pernambucans—especially those belonging to the captaincy's establishment. Ambrósio Fernandes Brandão, one of the chief spokesmen for Pernambuco's (as well as the rest of the Northeast's) wealthy sugar planters, felt so strongly about the Brazilian High Court that in his *Diálogos das grandezas do Brasil* he devoted almost three-fourths of his survey of Bahia to the subject of the Relação.[143] In Brandão's opinion, Brazil could do very well without the court. Its operational expenses were considerable, and he felt that the money could be best used elsewhere. In addition, the author of the *Diálogos* argued that it was easier for the majority of Brazilians to get to Lisbon than to journey to Bahia. Since most of the settlers in Brazil had relatives in the capital of the Portuguese empire, all that they had to do was send a chest of sugar to Lisbon to cover expenses, and appeals and other legal matters could easily be resolved there. On the other hand, few Brazilians had relatives in Bahia, and the trip to the Brazilian capital from other parts of Portuguese America was difficult, expensive, and time-consuming.[144]

Brandão's solution must have pleased the donatário of Pernambuco and those in the captaincy who were tired of desembargadores meddling in their business and saw the Relação as another instrument of Bahian interference. The Brazilian High Court would be abolished and Brazil would be divided into three *comarcas* or districts with centers in Paraíba, Bahia, and Rio de Janeiro, each of which would be headed by a corregedor. Pernambuco and all of Brazil north of it would be under the jurisdiction of Paraíba, which would serve as a court of appeals for all the cases before the judges and ouvidores of Pernambuco, with further appeals and matters outside of Paraíban jurisdiction going to a proposed Relação in Lisbon.

142. Varnhagen, *História Geral*, II, 105. The Relação's regimento is found in *CCLP*, I, 258–265. The best treatment of this important institution is found in Stuart Schwartz, "The High Court of Bahia: A Study in Hapsburg Brazil," (Ph.D. Diss., Columbia University, 1968).

143. *Diálogos*, pp. 31–34. In Diálogo Primeiro, which surveys the different captaincies in Brazil, three of the four-and-a-half pages of printed text dealing with Bahia are devoted to the Relação.

144. Not everyone in Brazil agreed with Brandão's claims. See "Rezoens q̃ darão os m^dores da Bahya para se não estinguir a R^cão" in BNL/CP, cód. 647, fols. 69–72. The entire document is found in Schwartz, "The High Court of Bahia," appendix 1.

The author of the *Diálogos* cleverly suggested Paraíba and not Pernambuco for the seat of Brazil's northern judicial district "because it [Paraíba] is a royal city." In this way, Duarte de Albuquerque Coelho and those sympathetic to the lord-proprietor of Pernambuco would be free of royal interference in their captaincy. Though this point was not expressly made by Brandão, clearly it was uppermost in his mind, for he emphasized that his proposed corregedores would not be allowed to enter the captaincies of their comarcas except for the prescribed visitations. Furthermore, these judges could not spend more than thirty days in a captaincy. If they remained more than a month, no one was obliged to obey them.[145]

Though little of Duarte de Albuquerque's correspondence dealing with this period has been uncovered, clearly he was opposed to the Relação.[146] He saw it as an arm of centralization of royal authority. The fact that the Relação was located in Bahia only aggravated an already touchy situation. As indicated earlier, the fourth donatário had the Crown's permission to appoint ouvidores in Pernambuco, and, according to D. Luis de Sousa, the Albuquerque Coelho family had complete control of the judicial apparatus in their captaincy. Thus, Duarte was in no mood to see Bahian judges interfering in the affairs of Pernambuco.

There is no doubt about the attitude of Matias de Albuquerque towards the officials of the Relação: he had a thorough dislike for them. As mentioned previously, in 1620 Matias angrily replied to the chancellor of the High Court, Manuel Pinto da Rocha, that he observed the laws of His Majesty more than their corruption. In 1622 Albuquerque created a stir when a member of the court, desembargador Pero de Casqueiro, planned to visit Pernambuco. The same year, after the Relação took up the appeal of João Rebelo de Lima who claimed that Albuquerque was keeping him out of the post of provedor da fazenda of Pernambuco, the capitão-mor complained angrily to the king of the High Court's interference in his captaincy's affairs.

The Dutch seizure of Bahia in 1624 gave Albuquerque his long-awaited chance to even the score. The huge, thousand-man Bahian garrison was in desperate need of clothing, bedding and supplies. Albuquerque and others were able to use Bahia's critical defense

145. Brandão was also upset by the stays of the governors-general in Pernambuco. See *Diálogos*, p. 31.
146. BNL/CP, cód. 647, fol. 71.

needs and the mounting unpopularity of the Relação to persuade
the Crown to abolish the High Court and to use the money customarily appropriated for it for the garrison of Bahia.[147] On 5 April
1626, D. Filipe III did just that.[148]

Pernambuco had come full turn in the struggle between centralization and donatarial authority. From 1602 to 1619 while the
governors-general and, to a lesser extent, the Crown ran roughshod
over the lord-proprietor's prerogatives, strong donatarial rule in
Pernambuco seemed a relic of the past. The arrival of Matias de
Albuquerque dramatically reversed this trend, as D. Luis de Sousa
ruefully observed in the quotation that begins this essay. A new
day had dawned in Pernambuco's history as a proprietary colony.

In the years after control over Pernambuco was regained from
the Dutch (1654) and the deaths of Matias de Albuquerque (1647)
and Duarte de Albuquerque Coelho (1658), there were no more
strong donatários to preserve the gains Albuquerque had made. But
the Pernambucan governors themselves continued to free the captaincy from the power of centralized government in Bahia. André
Vidal de Negreiros, Jerônimo de Mendonça Furtado, and Fernão de
Sousa Coutinho stood up to the pretensions of the governors-
general despite their complaints and even shows of force.[149] D. Vasco
Mascarenhas (Conde de Óbidos), viceroy of Bahia from 1663 to
1667, blamed the erosion of his power and authority in Pernambuco
on the disorders caused by the Dutch wars.[150] Perhaps he would
have been closer to the truth if he had stressed the tradition of independence from Bahian interference firmly established by Matias
de Albuquerque during his six years as governor and capitão-mor
of Pernambuco.

147. King to governors of Portugal, Baluastro, 31 January 1626, AGS, Sect.
Prov., lib. 1520, fol. 6v.
148. CCLP, III, 158; see also AGS, Sect. Prov., lib. 1520, fols. 35v, 47v and 53.
149. Alden, Royal Government, pp. 35–39.
150. In a letter to Jerônimo de Mendonça Furtado, dated 26 April 1664, the
Conde de Óbidos remarked: "A ambição dos Governadores que houve nessa
Capitania [Pernambuco], depois de as guerras se acabarem, introduziu quererem
mais jurisdição que a que lhes tocava." DH, IX, 164. For a reference to Matias
de Albuquerque, see ibid., p. 135.

DAVID M. DAVIDSON:

How the Brazilian West Was Won: Freelance & State on the Mato Grosso Frontier, 1737-1752

It has long been a tenet of Brazilian historiography that the winning of the Brazilian West, unlike the gradual, largely state-supervised occupation of the northern and southern colonial frontiers, was primarily the achievement of the intrepid *bandeirantes* of São Paulo.[1] These volatile frontiersmen shattered the front line of Spain's missionary advance in the early seventeenth century, thus leaving an open land in the Brazilian Southwest that eventually fell to Portugal, and their sudden discoveries of gold at Cuiabá (1718–1722) and western Mato Grosso (1734–1736), on the fringes of the Spanish Jesuit territories of Moxos and Chiquitos, thrust upon the metropolis the hitherto unsettled far western lands. The subsequent decade and a half, when Portugal extended secure control to the Far West, is often treated perfunctorily as a brief, if necessary, epilogue to the heroic bandeirante movement. Historians of the *Paulistas* might applaud the diplomatic efforts of Alexandre de Gusmão (who was, after all, a Brazilian) to win Spain's recognition of Portuguese sovereignty in Mato Grosso in the Treaty of Madrid (1750). But in the light of nationalism the lengthened shadow of the bandeirante has obscured the crucial role of the state in shaping and securing the western frontier, and the contingent nature of the process by which this was achieved.[2]

1. For an introduction to the themes and historiography of the bandeirantes, see Richard M. Morse, ed., *The Bandeirantes: The Historical Role of the Brazilian Pathfinders* (New York, 1965); a welcome addition to the extensive literature on Brazilian territorial formation is the useful summary in Rollie E. Poppino, *Brazil: The Land and the People* (New York, 1968), pp. 68–112.

2. See, e.g., the traditional treatment in Basílio de Magalhães, *Expansão geográfica do Brasil colonial* (3rd ed.; Rio, 1944), pp. 267–289, 357–358, and Afonso d'Escragnolle Taunay, "Os primeiros anos de Cuiabá e Mato Grosso," *Anais*, IV Congresso de História Nacional (Rio, 1950), I, 143–505, and the revised summary in Taunay's *História das bandeiras paulistas*, (2nd ed.; São Paulo, 1961), II, 13–106. The role of the state is given greater weight by Jaime

MAP 2

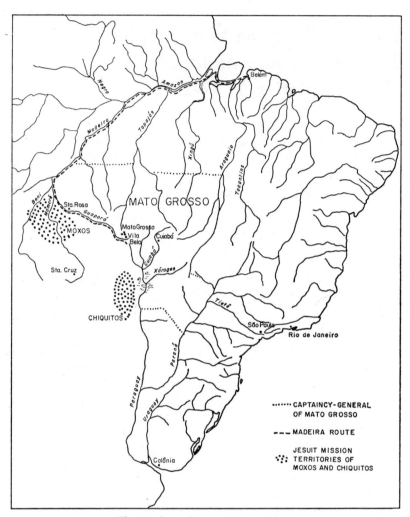

The Madeira-Guaporé River Route

If it appears, as is commonly assumed, that Paulista gold discoveries and the ensuing spontaneous rush bequeathed the territory
of Mato Grosso to Portugal, Brazilian historical writing has not
sufficiently stressed that these same events projected the western
lands into the arena of geopolitical contests between the two Iberian
powers for control of strategic or profitable lands in colonial South
America. Settlement alone did not guarantee that the West would

be Portuguese, though it did prompt imperial ministers to preserve territorial gains, and confirmed their conviction that the fact of occupation should be the legitimate basis for territorial possession in America. To overlook such decisions at critical historical moments, and especially at the juncture of intense geopolitical conflict of the mid-1730s, is to run the risk of accepting a kind of Brazilian manifest destiny as a suitable explanation for territorial expansion. There is much of value in arguments that certain cultural or geopolitical "imperatives" shaped and informed the territorial formation of Brazil, but such imperatives must be viewed as both the results of aspirations, strategies, and decisions, and their flexible guidelines. The role and nature of such imperatives will be clarified as this paper unfolds, but for the moment suffice it to suggest that possession of the West, disputed by Spain in the mid-1730s, remained in doubt until the eve of the Madrid agreement. Portuguese sovereignty was only then guaranteed after pre-emptive, defensive, and diplomatic efforts.

In light of such considerations, this paper submits that the critical stage in the winning of the Brazilian West spanned approximately the years from 1737 to 1752, after the initial gold strikes and settlement, and during a time of increased state participation. Within this brief span the Portuguese occupied Mato Grosso, sketched a western border along the Guaporé, Mamoré, and Madeira rivers, and, in opening navigation between Mato Grosso and Pará along these same rivers in 1752, created a bureaucratic, commercial, and logistic artery that, like its southern counterpart along the monsoon route, integrated the Far West into the empire.[2a] Focus on the hitherto neglected role of the state, however, need not imply underestimation of the instrumental contributions of its frontiersmen to the incorporation of Mato Grosso. Precisely the combined, interdependent efforts by state and and frontiersmen brought about Portuguese success. Furthermore, the international setting of the

---

Cortesão in numerous studies, especially his *Alexandre de Gusmão e o tratado de Madrid (1750)* (9 vols., Rio, 1950–1960), I:2, 135–178 and *passim*, (hereafter cited as *AGTM*), and in Arthur Cézar Ferreria Reis, *Épocas e visões regionais do Brasil* (Manaus, 1966), pp. 85–89, 301–320. Reis, p. 89, following Cortesão, explicitly raises the question of the contributions of private and public initiative to the territorial formation of Brazil and cautions: "Há, é certo, que examinar a matéria com rigor e sem exageros nacionalistas."

2a. For the monsoon route, see n. 40.

action requires consideration of their relationship to groups engaged in a similar interplay within the empire of rival Spain.

Thus, the process by which the Brazilian West was won can be clarified within a framework of intersecting national and international relations of four parties: the imperial states of Portugal and Spain, and their respective groups of freelances—the Paulistas, miners, and merchants of Mato Grosso, and the Jesuits of the Moxos and Chiquitos missions. Interplay occurred along international or horizontal lines between the imperial states, and between their freelances. Simultaneously, national or vertical interplays evolved between the metropolitan governments and their freelances. Both national and international relationships were characterized by conflict, accommodation, and other more ambiguous forms of mutual influence; and from the intersections of these relationships in Europe and America, policy and action on both sides of the frontier were shaped. Freelances, for example, shared certain goals of their governments, yet pursued private interests which often conflicted with state intentions, but which at times unintentionally fulfilled them. Freelances opposed each other when private or state interests clashed, then assisted each other when private interests met tangentially; in the process they fostered and hindered, executed and molded the imperial strategies of their governments. The governments, in turn, directed their freelances to execute state policies, yet could not fully harness freelance energies and interests, and in effect delegated to their "agents" a certain freedom of action which was used sometimes to violate, sometimes to fulfill state policies. Finally, the imperial states interacted with each other in the same pattern of conflict and cooperation that marked the relations of each with its freelances. Out of this process was ultimately fashioned a mutually acceptable accommodation in the West.

The above relationships are best illuminated by brief consideration of the geographical foundations of historical action in the West before the heightened international tensions of the mid-1730s. Of the many striking elements of continental geography that guided the formation of the Iberian empires, none had deeper historical implications than the nature and direction of the great Amazon and Paraguay-Paraná-Plate river systems whose major trunks ramify to the far reaches of the South American heartland, where their various sources arise within a few miles of one another in the Brazilian

West. These rivers offered routes of navigation or, when water-borne travel was impeded, as on stretches of the Paraguay-Paraná system, provided useful guidelines for overland movement.[3]

During the late seventeenth and early eighteenth centuries, four largely independent European advances along the fluvial basins converged on, and in so doing defined, the territory that became the Brazilian West. Two uncoordinated vectors of Portuguese penetration, one from São Paulo by freelance initiative, the other, largely state-directed, from Belém do Pará, closed pincers-like upon the Far West, while the expansion of Moxos from Upper Peru and of Chiquitos from Tucumán and Paraguay seemed to wedge between the two Portuguese movements. By approximately 1737, bandeirantes had traversed the Paraguay-Paraná basin to the vicinity of the Xarayes flood plain and upper Paraguay, settled the mining campus of Cuiabá and Mato Grosso in the watershed of the Paraguay and Amazon systems, and then entered the Guaporé of the Amazon system. Jesuits of Chiquitos had erected their missions along the western fringes of the Xarayes-Paraguay and made frequent entries northward between the Paraguay and Guaporé. The Moxos missions had expanded down the Mamoré and the southern affluents of the Guaporé, and the fathers periodically sent their wards onto the upper Madeira.[4] Finally, Portguese missionaries, soldiers, and merchants had inched up the Amazon, Madeira, and lower Mamoré, and made initial contact with the northernmost missions of Moxos. Francisco de Melo Palhêta's famous expedition of 1722–1723 had even carried Portuguese claims to the lower Guaporé, though disease, difficulties of navigation, and Indian resistance restricted settlement and effective penetration to the lower Madeira.[5]

With the aid of hindsight and accurate cartography the modern observer notes that such a convergence of moving frontiers prefigured the limits of the Brazilian West along the fluvial lines of the

3. On the historical implications of Brazil's river systems, see, e.g., Moacir M. F. Silva, *Geografia dos transportes no Brasil* (Rio, 1949), pp. 1–47; Jaime Cortesão (and Pedro Calmon), *Brasil* (Barcelona, 1956), pp. 31–40.

4. On Chiquitos, see Juan Patricio Fernández, *Relación historial de las misiones de indios chiquitos que en el Paraguay tienen los padres de la Compañía de Jesús* (2 vols., Madrid, 1895), and José Aguirre Achá, *La antigua provincia de Chiquitos* (La Paz, 1933). On Moxos, see Ruben Vargas Ugarte, *Historia de la Compañía de Jesús en el Perú* (Burgos, 1964), III, and José Chávez Suárez, *Historia de Moxos* (La Paz, 1944).

5. Alexandre Rodrigues Ferreira, "Relação circunstanciada do Rio da Ma-

Xarayes-Paraguay and Guaporé-Mamoré-Madeira rivers. Men on
the spot, however, lacked such a perspective and were only dimly
aware of the paths they had traced through the South American
heartland and of the existence and location of one another. They
nevertheless formed a pattern of riparian outposts slowly approach-
ing each other on the same complex river networks—a kind of
water-borne society in formation where most communication,
travel, and settlement was guided along rivers. It is not surprising,
then, that in the years of increased international rivalry after 1737,
when frontiersmen learned of their spatial relations to one another,
rivers served as arteries of communication and commerce, strategic
lines of defense, and channels of conflict.

Rivers also offered the metropolitan governments salient geographic features for locating and delineating their alleged possessions in distant, insufficiently charted lands. Cartography of the
period assumes an X-ray quality wherein a skeletal and rudimentary
aqueous structure articulates the nebulous land mass.[6] Territory
was defined in relation to fluvial structure, and the contest for the

deira, e seu territorio, desde a sua fóz, até a sua primeira Cachoeira chamada
de Santo Antonio," BNRJ, I–21–1–36; HCJB, III, 383–393, 400–401; IHGB/CU,
arq. 1–2–26, fols. 43v.–44, 53–54, 63v–64. In November 1722, Captain-General
of Pará João da Maia da Gama dispatched Sergeant-Major Francisco de Melo
Palhêta to lead a troop up the Madeira to Santa Cruz de la Sierra to assert
Portugal's claim to that river, block the expansion of Spanish missionaries
down the Madeira, and open commerce with Upper Peru to "tap the silver of
Potosí," (Maia da Gama's letter to the king of 15 August 1723 is summarized
at length in the royal order of 18 Feb. 1724, BNRJ, 7–2–21, n. 279). Palhêta's
troop reached Moxos the following August, where he informed the Jesuits and
the governor of Santa Cruz that Portugal possessed the Madeira from its mouth
to the meeting of the Mamoré and Guaporé (thus including the lower Mamoré);
he then returned down the Mamoré and sailed eastward along the Guaporé for
six days before returning downriver to Belém the same year. See the anonymous
diary of the journey "Narração da viagem e descobrimento que fez o sargento
mór Francisco de Mello Palheta no Rio da Madeira. . . ," in J. Capistrano de
Abreu, Caminhos antigos e povoamento do Brasil (2nd ed.; Rio, 1960), pp. 219–
248. Palhêta's meeting and correspondence with the Spaniards is related in
documents in Pablo Pastells (and F. Mateos), Historia de la Compañía de Jesús
en la provincia del Paraguay (8 vols., Madrid, 1912–1949), VI, 282–285, 317–318,
347–349, 352–353, 370–371, (hereafter cited as HCJPP).

6. On the cartography of colonial Brazil, see Isa Adonias, A cartografia da
região amazônica. Catálogo descritivo (1500–1961) (2 vols., Rio, 1963), whose
excellent work is broader in scope than the title suggests, and Jaime Cortesão,
"Apontamentos das aulas do curso de história da cartografia, geografia das
fronteiras do Brasil e mapoteconomia," Rio, 1945. (Mimeographed.)

Far West after 1737 became in large measure a struggle on, and for, strategic waterways of the South American hinterland.

The emergence of rivers as geopolitical instruments, both foci and vehicles of imperial rivalry, is explained in part by the type of expansion discussed above, and in part by the nature of Portuguese imperial policy toward the western lands before 1737. During the seventeenth and eighteenth centuries, state policy in varying degrees either directed or was fashioned by the course of the inland advance, but its seeds were planted during the first century and a half of Brazilian history. The Portuguese had inherited a vague concept of Brazil's western boundary in the Tordesillas line, traced in 1494 by the Iberian powers along a meridian 370 leagues west of the Cape Verde Islands. Yet the precise inland path of the demarcation remained a matter of speculation and controversy until the refinement of cartographic techniques in the early eighteenth century. In consequence, the line proved more effective as an instrument of policy than as a barrier to action. The line was manipulated with considerable freedom by both imperial governments in pursuit of their interests; its primary significance lay in Portuguese efforts to adjust it to changing geopolitical circumstances, or, when these efforts appeared unfeasible, to seek a more favorable alternative for delimiting an expanding sphere of sovereignty.

The first notion of rivers as possible alternatives to (or, euphemistically, definitions of) the Tordesillas line evolved together with Portuguese awareness of the nature of the *terrae incognitae* behind the narrow coastal strip. In fact, the interrelated concepts of *uti possidetis* and organic interior limits, both potentially antagonistic to the Tordesillas principle, were foreshadowed in two of the most impelling myths of the distant interior to originate in the sixteenth and early seventeenth centuries—the first, of a mysterious land harboring precious metals and gems, the second, of this same land as an island continent bounded in the interior by two great rivers, born of a central lake, that flowed to the Atlantic.[7] Both myths, amalgams of European preconceptions and assorted indigenous lore,

7. The following discussion of myths is based primarily on Sérgio Buarque de Holanda, *Visão do paráiso: Os motivos edênicos no descobrimento e colonização da Brasil* (Rio, 1959), pp. 78–123, and Jaime Cortesão, *Introdução à história das bandeiras* (2 vols., Lisbon, 1964) I, 91–132, 163–241, and *passim*; see also the brief summary in Morse, *The Bandeirantes*, pp. 16–19.

assumed shape in the crucible of Luso-Spanish rivalry for political
and economic advantage, and became for a time mutually reinforcing
impressions of the West. As matrices of aspirations and strategies,
the myths heralded pre-emptive claims to specific targets in the interior. The first myth implied the extension of Portugal's limited
sphere of sovereignty to wealth-bearing lands when circumstances
and resources would permit. The appetite for mineral wealth,
whetted by Indian tales, grew after Spain's discovery of silver at
Potosí in 1545, and for another one hundred and fifty years the
Portuguese intermittently gnawed on the bone of an "other Peru."
By a priori reasoning and the fact of occupation, the mines of the
interior would be Portuguese.

The second myth, as Jaime Cortesão suggests, revealed possible
legitimate limits of an expanded sphere of sovereignty along the
rivers of the Amazon and Paraguay systems. Indian rumors that the
headwaters of these rivers arose from a common source in the continental heartland coincided with a growing Portuguese conviction
that the Amazon delta and the Platine estuary formed the natural
northern and southern limits of the nascent colony, and the most
obvious points of access to the fabled riches of the interior. Suspecting that the two river mouths lay west of the Tordesillas line,
and hence in Spain's possession, the Portuguese claimed them in a
stratagem of state-directed cartography. During the first half of the
sixteenth century, royal cosmographers sketched the line intersecting the coast north of the Amazon and south of the Plate. After
mid-century, they gave the island myth cartographic expression in
quest of the same geopolitical goal. Official maps depicted a central
lake whence a southern river in the approximate position of the
Paraná-Paraguay flowed to the Plate, while a northern river corresponding to the Tocantins-Araguaia emptied into the Amazon
delta. By the mid-seventeenth century, the configuration had been
shifted westward, with the lake corresponding to the Xarayes, the
southern river to the Paraguay, and the northern river to the
Madeira-Mamoré. As Portuguese mapmakers extended the island
configuration westward, they assiduously traced the Tordesillas division along this fluvial inner frontier. From the pursuit of the
northern and southern limits of Brazil, a mythical western limit
emerged, part political creation—the projection inland of two strategic river systems—and part symbolic reflection of geographical
realities.

The early myths offer insights into the premises of state action
in the West in the late seventeenth and eighteenth centuries, but
they did not stimulate sustained official action during the first century of colonization when government priorities resided emphatic-
ally in the maintenance and defense of the settlements of the littoral.
Especially during the second half of the seventeenth century, the
Portuguese state actively sought components of the myths in response to changing domestic and international circumstances. The
government-prompted search for mines and the official attempts to
capture the Platine estuary and Amazon river systems grew out of
a policy of expanding the limits and wealth of the Brazilian colony,
which was then assuming central importance within the Portuguese
empire.[8] Whether the state sought possible boundaries, fluvial or
otherwise, in the distant interior is still a matter of speculation.[9] To
be sure, the concept of a clearly circumscribed western hinterland
did not become important to the metropolis until the mines of the
Far West were discovered and became a focus of international
competition. It is striking, however, that in the course of westward
expansion the myths were simultaneously realized and "exorcised,"
as Sérgio Buarque de Holanda noted,[10] as the Portuguese state and
its freelances alike gradually discovered the realities on which the
myths had been based. The Far West of the eighteenth century
became a near perfect analogue of the original myths—a gold-
bearing land bounded, with but one minor gap, by the Amazon and
Paraguay systems. Similarly, Portuguese policy at the time was informed by the same aspirations and strategies as those that under-
lay the mythical expressions.

The metropolitan response to the Paulista gold strikes at Cuiabá
crystallized, and in a sense actualized, a potential state policy toward
the lands of the Far West. During the latter part of the seventeenth
century, the state had encouraged explorations for precious metals
in the lands known as the *vacaria*, the "cow country" between the

8. See, e.g., Manoel Cardozo, "Dom Rodrigo de Castel-Branco and the Brazilian El Dorado, 1673–1682," *The Americas*, I (1944), 131–159; Mario Rod-
ríguez, "Dom Pedro of Braganza and Colônia do Sacramento, 1680–1705,"
HAHR, XXXVIII (1958), 179–208; C. R. Boxer, *Salvador de Sá and the Struggle
for Brazil and Angola, 1602–1686* (London, 1952), pp. 385–388.

9. See Cortesão's argument for a state-promoted search for interior limits in
his *Rapôso Tavares e a formação territorial do Brasil* (Rio, 1958). Cortesão's
logic is attractive, at times brilliant, but he fails to marshal convincing evidence
to support his thesis of geopolitical intent.

10. *Visão do paraíso*, p. 15.

Paraná and Paraguay rivers extending toward the abandoned Jesuit
mission fields of Itatín. The region had become an arena of bandeirante activity, and was apparently considered by Paulistas to be
the westernmost frontier of São Paulo. Lacking adequate maps and
forced to rely on impressionistic accounts by bandeirantes, metropolitan authorities were reluctant to claim or settle the region for
fear of conflict with Spain.[11] Nonetheless, that once gold was discovered the state would claim the potentially disputable territory is
evident from its vigorously positive reaction to the Cuiabá strikes
in a region even farther west of the vacaria, and thus even more
likely to cause conflict with Spain. Upon hearing that Paulistas had
found signs of gold near the Paraguay river, "so near to where
Spaniards reside," the Count of Assumar, captain-general of Minas
Gerais and São Paulo, hoped to avoid an international incident by
ordering the bandeirantes to leave the region in January 1719. Significantly, however, an agent was to reconnoiter the area to determine its location and the extent of neighboring Spanish settlement.
In no "populous town" were found nearby, the captain-general suggested that Portugal establish a colony to prevent Spain from ad-
vancing on "our lands." Three months later Assumar informed
Lisbon that there was no Spanish settlement in the immediate vicinity, just a Jesuit mission (Chiquitos) across the Paraguay and
that, in any case, the Paulistas had already made camp. In addition,
he recommended the creation of a new captaincy-general of São
Paulo, carved from Minas Gerais, which would allow its govenor
greater freedom to preserve Portugal's newly claimed frontier.[12] In
October, the Overseas Council approved the proposals, and a royal
resolution the following January created the new captaincy-general
and decreed the founding of a settlement in the Far West, "so that
once established it can impede the Spaniards from occupying that
district."[13] Although authorities lacked a clear understanding of the

11. Conflicting views of the state role in the vacaria are in Magalhães, *Expansão geográfica*, pp. 183–189; Taunay, *História das bandeiras paulistas*, I,
147–151; Mário Monteiro de Almeida, *Episódios históricos da formação geográfica do Brasil* (Rio, 1951), pp. 51–54. See also the anonymous report in João
Pandiá Calógeras, *A política exterior do império* (2 vols., Rio, 1927–1928), I,
173–175.
12. The captain-general's account is summarized in the *consulta* of the
Overseas Council, 31 Oct. 1719, IHGB/CU, arq. 1–1–25, fols. 156–159.
13. *Ibid.*; royal letter to captain-general of Rio de Janeiro 21 Feb. 1720, *DI*,

location of the new mines, they asserted a pre-emptive claim to the lands and extended administrative machinery to secure them. During the 1720s, fiscal and judicial authorities were dispatched to the West, the town of Cuiabá was incorporated, and the new captain-general of São Paulo himself visited the new municipality. The presence of gold and the right of occupation were sufficient justification for expanding the sphere of Portuguese sovereignty far to the west in lands that probably fell to Spain's side of Tordesillas division.

The overseas councillors suspected that the new mines, if not most of the Portuguese outposts in the Amazon and central interior, were to the west of a reasonable interpretation of the Tordesillas line, and immediately planned a comprehensive reconnaissance of the whole interior of Portuguese America aimed at a realistic appraisal of the extent of Portuguese occupation and of geographic features that might delimit these holdings more suitably than did the arbitrary and controversial line of demarcation. In April 1719, the Overseas Council ordered that an engineer be sent to the West to draft a map of the principal natural landmarks of the region, "indicating the river or mountains he deems most suitable to serve as division and separation in that area between the dominions of the two Crowns."[14] In August 1720, the council again emphasized the need for an adequate map of the West and a "natural" western border, and expanded considerably the scope of the survey. Two foreign Jesuit "mathematicians" (the *padres matemáticos*) would be commissioned to explore the backlands of São Paulo and the Amazon and to prepare detailed charts for a more informed and favorable version of the boundaries of the colony.[15]

The search for organic colonial borders, begun two centuries earlier at the northern and southern fringes of Brazil, was here catalyzed by the western discoveries and extended to the far hinterland. The quest became urgent after 1722 when the internationally respected French royal cartographer, Guillaume Delisle, through a more sophisticated calculation of longitude, placed the north bank of the Plate and the mouth of the Amazon (and hence the lands to

XLVII, 90; royal *provisão* to Assumar, 12 Aug. 1720, *DI*, XLIX, 275–278; *alvará*, 2 Dec. 1720, *DI*, XLVII, 94–96.

14. Consulta of Overseas Council, 29 Apr. 1719, IHGB/CU, arq. 1–1–25, fols. 146–148.

15. Consulta of Overseas Council, 23 Aug. 1720, IHGB/CU, arq. 1–1–25, fols. 276–278v.

the west) on Spain's side of the Tordesillas division.[16] During the
1720s, Portugal held an initial advantage over her rival since Spain
had not yet learned of the far western gold strikes. Yet Portuguese
imperial authorities themselves had little knowledge of the actual
location of the mines or their proximity to Spanish territory. Later,
however, both imperial governments became increasingly aware of
converging frontiers in the interior of the continent, and it is significant for the course of events in the West that this occurred in
the mid-1730s, precisely at a time of bitter hostilities between the
two powers over possession of Colônia do Sacramento on the Platine
estuary. The Platine war 1735–1737 had ended in a tense armistice,
an "armed truce" as Cortesão described it.[17] This tension was projected westward when the imperial governments entered the contest
for the western lands. By the time of the Convention of Paris (March
1737), when the Iberian powers agreed to resolve the problem of
Colônia,[18] secret preparations were underway in both courts which
would go beyond the issue of the Plate to include the great land mass
of the continent. Neither government could locate the occupied territories of the interior with assurance, both feared encroachments
into their lands, and both hoped to determine the extent of penetration of the other and to trace borders that would restrain aggression
and preserve strategic regions.

Ministers in Lisbon in the 1730s were acutely conscious of Portuguese westward expansion and the need to incorporate the new
territory into the empire. The commitment to possession and the
search for boundaries, begun a decade earlier, were energized by
the new royal secretary, Alexandre de Gusmão. Born in Brazil, educated at Bahia, Coimbra, and the Sorbonne, Gusmão entered the
royal service at the age of nineteen as secretary to the ambassador
to Paris, and later served for eight years as diplomatic agent in

16. Delisle, "Détermination géografique de la situation et de l'étendue des
différentes parties de la terre," *AGTM*, III:1, 206–221; see also the chart in
AGTM, I:1, following p. 276, which compares Delisle's map of 1722 with a
contemporary Portuguese map, both of which are superimposed on the actual
configuration of the Brazilian coast; for an excellent discussion of the impact
of Delisle's findings on the development of cartographic research in Portugal,
see Cortesão's treatment in *AGTM*, I:1, 273–321.

17. *AGTM*, I:2, 59–81.

18. Convention of Paris, 15 Mar. 1737, in Carlos Calvo, ed., *Colección
completa de los tratados, convenciones, capitulaciones, armisticios y otros actos
diplomaticos de todos los estados de la América latina* (11 vols., Paris, 1862–
1869), II, 210–224.

Rome, before his appointment in 1730 as secretary to João V. For the next two decades Gusmão was influential in shaping colonial policy and the boundaries of Brazil. An active participant in the negotiations with Spain over Colônia, Gusmão concluded that the resolution of colonial antagonisms depended on the clear definition of Portugal's territorial priorities, and on an uncontestable basis for the possession of disputed lands. He and the elder statesman, Luís da Cunha, considered the pasturelands of the South, the forest and agricultural products of the Amazon, and the mines of the Center and West more valuable to the metropolis than the scanty contraband trade conducted through Colônia. Although Portuguese ministers would not relinquish their claims to Colônia and the Platine estuary until Spain's resolute determination convinced them that such pretensions were hopeless, royal policy under Gusmão from the mid-1730s was directed toward the occupation and defense of Rio Grande, the West, and the Amazon. Like the councillors of the 1720s, Gusmão suspected that a substantial part of the Brazilian interior lay to the west of the Tordesillas line; and like his predecessors, he looked to occupation as a more effective basis for sovereignty than the traditional division, and to natural landmarks as the only adequate guidelines for territorial demarcation. Although Gusmão was the first Portuguese minister to state with clarity and sophistication the principles of uti possidetis and natural borders, he drew upon trends already expressed in Portuguese imperial thought.[19]

In the Brazilian West, however, Gusmão still faced the perennial problem of insufficient geographical knowledge. The cartographic survey entrusted to the padres matemáticos more than a decade earlier had not yielded information upon which Portugal could base her claims. The Jesuit cartographers, Domingos Capassi and Diogo Soares, did not arrive in Brazil until 1730, and although they finally produced useful sketches of the southern and central regions, neither of them fulfilled the original request of the Overseas Council to reconnoiter the Amazon and Far West.[20] Portugal's tasks remained

19. Two excellent studies of the public life and policies of Gusmão by Jaime Cortesão are his short summary, "Alexandre de Gusmão e o Tratado de Madrí," *Revista de História*, no. 4 (São Paulo, 1950), pp. 437–452, and the extended treatment in *AGTM*, I:1–2.

20. The original Italian Jesuits, João Baptista Carbone and Domingos Capassi, arrived in Lisbon in 1722. Carbone remained as advisor to João V and was replaced by the Portuguese Diogo Soares, who sailed with Capassi to Brazil

those of a decade earlier—to locate the mines, determine their proximity to the Spanish missions, and delineate a border for the far western settlements and the Portuguese outposts of the Amazon. To these ends Gusmão sought to accelerate and systematize the geographic survey of the interior, and called upon colonial officials to report on the distances between Portuguese and Spanish settlements. Aware of possible fluvial communications between the states of Maranhão-Pará and Brazil, and suspecting that such rivers or combinations thereof might serve as adequate guidelines for a boundary through the uncharted lands, he urged the exploration of rivers flowing from the mining communities.[21]

By 1736, although Portuguese authorities did not know of the Madeira's eventual connections via the Mamoré and Guaporé to the mines of Mato Grosso, the Portuguese were convinced that the Madeira formed a border with Spanish America. In that same year Gusmão's close associate and mentor, Luís da Cunha, sketched his concept of the ideal borders of Portuguese America. The coastal limits, he suggested, should be the Vicente Pinzón River north of the Amazon, and the Platine estuary in the South.

> And the inland boundaries could be the Paraguay river which empties into [the Plate], ascending it as far as the Xarayes lake, even though it [the Paraguay] seems to originate much farther away; from there drawing a line westward for a distance of 100 leagues, as seen on the map, until encountering the Madeira river whose waters merge with those of the Amazon.

Cunha urged that "we should use all means and all occasions which might present themselves to establish the aforesaid boundaries."[22]

This vision of Brazilian western limits accurately reflected the state of knowledge of freelances and authorities alike. Paulistas in Mato Grosso did not discover the Guaporé until 1737, and even then were unaware of its eventual course into the Mamoré-Madeira.

---

in 1730. Capassi died in 1736 in São Paulo; Soares continued his activities until his death in Goiás in 1748. On their labors, writings, and maps, see HCJB, VIII, 130–132; IX, 130–137; and Jaime Cortesão, "A missão dos padres matemáticos no Brasil," Studia, I (Lisbon, 1958), 123–150.

21. Cortesão suggests that Gusmão was seeking the link between the Madeira and upper Paraguay rivers in the mid-1730s, AGTM, I:2, 149–150.

22. Pedro de Azevedo & Antônio Baião, eds., Instruções inéditas de D. Luís da Cunha a Marco António de Azevedo Coutinho (Coimbra, 1929), p. 215.

The Portuguese in the Amazon had ventured to the lower Guaporé in 1723, but were similarly unaware that the Mamoré-Guaporé led to Portuguese-occupied lands. The line drawn from the Xarayes swamp to the Madeira symbolized the missing link—the Mamoré-Guaporé—between the far western mines and the Amazon outposts. The Portuguese, however, did not learn of the complete connections between them until Spanish activities helped to make it possible.

Spain's interest in the territory that would eventually become the Brazilian West was largely strategic. Silver deposits and an abundant labor supply restricted colonization, and the attention of the metropolis, to the plateaus and fringes of the Andes. To the northeast, the governorship of Santa Cruz and the missions of Moxos and Chiquitos formed a vast though sparsely settled buffer zone between the mines of Upper Peru and the advance posts of Portuguese America, located, as far as the Spaniards knew, somewhere in the distant interior. The arrival of Palhêta at Moxos in 1723 had given colonial authorities a better idea of the extent of Portugal's expansion upriver from the Amazon, and increased the strategic importance of Santa Cruz and the missions, particularly since Spaniards reached the ill-founded conclusion that Palhêta's expedition was the vanguard of a larger Portuguese force which would invade Potosí by way of the Madeira-Mamoré. The governor of Santa Cruz asserted Spain's rights to the Madeira, but preferred to bolster existing defenses along the Mamoré and into Moxos toward the Guaporé, rather than to advance downriver into the Amazon.[23]

Notwithstanding Madrid's theoretical claims to the greater part of the continent, no efforts were made to settle the inhospitable and still unknown lands beyond the Mamoré-Guaporé and Xarayes flood plain which became Mato Grosso. This territory was of little value to Spain as long as Portugal did not settle or, more important, use the region as a base from which to advance toward Upper Peru. From the time of the bandeirante attacks of the 1690s, the Jesuits of Chiquitos had been specifically charged with the surveillance of

23. Governor of Santa Cruz Francisco Antonio Argomosa Ceballos to Palhêta, S. Lorenzo, 7 July 1724; Argomosa Ceballos to Crown, S. Lorenzo, 6 Oct. 1724; Viceroy of Peru Castelfuerte to Crown, Lima, 13 Nov. 1724; royal cédula, 25 July 1725; HCJPP, VI, 317–318, 347–349, 370–371, 432–433, 519–522.

this frontier, as were the missionaries of Moxos after the scare induced by Palhêta's arrival. Yet despite their *entradas* toward Mato Grosso and Cuiabá, the fathers did not learn of the Portuguese mines until the early 1730s, more than a decade after the first discoveries of gold at Cuiabá, and only then from Paiaguá Indians who had attacked Portuguese canoes sailing the Paraguay toward São Paulo. Once informed, the fathers evidently did not consider the news of sufficient importance to notify the lay authorities. Not until 1734, after the viceroy of Peru had heard similar rumors and requested information from the governor of Santa Cruz, who in turn consulted the superior of Chiquitos, did the fathers inform state officials of their suspicion of Portuguese mines located somewhere near the Paraguay River.[24] But by the time this information reached Spain, the court at Madrid had already been shocked into recognizing Portugal's expansion to the west.

In the summer of 1735, a disaffected Portuguese fortune hunter and turncoat, Francisco Esteves de Cervera, approached officials in Spain with the first report that Portugal had discovered mines in lands which he claimed were obviously far to the west of the Tordesillas division.[25] The following year he presented to Spanish Prime Minister José Patiño a map which purported to show the location of the mines in Cuiabá, Goiás, Minas, and São Paulo, and requested permission to lead an invasion to regain the usurped lands in return, of course, for a considerable share of the booty.[26] Spanish authorities were quick to associate Portuguese expansion to the west with similar encroachments in the South and in the Amazon. In light of the bitter hostilities already in progress in the Plate, the court was disposed to take Cervera's proposals seriously. In August 1736, Francisco Esteves' documents were dispatched to

24. Argomosa Ceballos to Father Superior of Chiquitos Agustín Castañares, S. Lorenzo, 10 Oct. 1738; Castañares to Argomosa Ceballos, S. Javier, 12 Dec. 1738, *HCJPP*, VII, 327–329, 331–332; Father Superior of Chiquitos Esteban Palozzitto Governor of Paraguay Rafael de la Moneda, S. Rafael, 8 Jan. 1744, AGI, Charcas, leg. 384 (also *HCJPP*, VII, 548–549).

25. Carlos de los Ríos to José Patiño, Tuy, 28 Aug. 1735 and 13 Apr. 1736, AGI, BA, leg. 302.

26. See Cervera's various proposals, especially "Observaciones y modo para restaurar las tierras usurpadas por los Portugueses en los dominios de S. M. . . ," attached to royal order to Governor of Buenos Aires Miguel de Salcedo, 16 Aug. 1736, AGI, Audiencia de Buenos Aires (hereafter cited as BA) leg. 302 (also *HCJPP*, VII, 337–339).

Buenos Aires with instructions to Governor Miguel de Salcedo to begin preparations for the conquest of the mines.[27]

Already committed to evicting the Portuguese from Colônia, Santa Catarina, and Rio Grande, Salcedo relished the opportunity to extend this objective to the mines of the West. He was convinced that Cuiabá lay in Spanish territory, and that its presence menaced not only the Paraguay River system, but also Santa Cruz, Potosí, and possibly even Peru. Salcedo's convictions were confirmed by the reports of Captain Juan Antonio de la Colina of the Royal Spanish Navy, who had arrived in Buenos Aires in 1737 after a brief imprisonment in Rio de Janeiro. Colina had also heard that Cuiabá lay beyond the Tordesillas line, six months travel from São Paulo along the Tietê-Paraná-Paraguay river route. Throughout the latter half of 1737, Salcedo and Colina inundated Madrid with highly impressionistic intelligence reports in which they called for a massive offensive against all Portuguese-held territories along the Plate-Paraguay from Colônia to Cuiabá.[28]

By the time the reports reached Madrid, ministers at court were reconsidering the issue of colonial borderlands. A month after the signing of the Paris Convention, at roughly the same time that Alexandre de Gusmão was undertaking to resolve Brazil's boundaries, Spanish authorities began to collect cartographic materials upon which to plot the distribution of Iberian settlement in America.[29] Like Gusmão, the Spaniards realized the necessity of continued reconnaissance of the interior. But unlike the Portuguese, who cautioned against overt acts of aggression on the frontier, Madrid continued to look forward to the reconquest of the north bank of the Plate and the Portuguese mining communities of the West. Throughout 1737 and 1738, the question of the mines remained of intense concern in the policy debates at Madrid, and the ablest councillors and cosmographers were assigned to outline a plan of action. Yet the obstacles to the formation of a decisive policy were formidable. Spaniards now wondered if the occupation of Cuiabá were directly related to Portugal's conscious expansionism in the Plate,

27. Royal order to Salcedo, 16 Aug. 1736, AGI, BA, leg. 302.
28. Salcedo to ministers in Madrid, Buenos Aires, 23, 26 Aug., 17, 20 Nov., 4 Dec. 1737, AGI, BA, leg. 534; Charcas, leg. 161 (also HCJPP, VII, 289–293).
29. José de la Quintana to Marquis of Torrenueva, Madrid, 11 Apr. 1737, AGI, BA, leg. 534.

and thus, if the occupation formed the threat to Paraguay, Santa Cruz, or Potosí that Salcedo, Cervera, and Colina had suggested. Indeed, authorities in Spain put little stock in the reports of their impassioned informants, particularly in the latter's ill-founded geographic notions. For, after a year of study, no one at court could locate Cuiabá, or the other mines for that matter, on the map. Without this information it was impossible to determine who held sovereignty over the mines. The king's advisors considered it significant that Madrid had received no word from the governors of Santa Cruz or Paraguay, the two military commanders who should have been most aware of Portuguese penetration into their districts.[30] With circumspection, then, packets were dispatched in October 1738 to the viceroy of Peru and the governors of Paraguay and Santa Cruz bearing copies of the reports by Salcedo and Colina, with orders to conduct a complete reconnaissance of the Portuguese mines. If the military commanders deemed them to be in Spanish territory, the commanders were to work together, and with the governor of Buenos Aires, to dislodge the Portuguese from the lands of the Crown of Spain.[31]

Although the governor of Santa Cruz, Francisco Antonio Argomosa Ceballos, had not yet reported to Spain, he had already begun the search for Cuiabá with the aid of Spain's missionaries in Moxos and Chiquitos. In response to the governor's inquiry of 1734, the father superior of Chiquitos, Bartolomé Blende, had replied that the Portuguese mines were probably situated beyond the Paraguay, though he was unaware of the precise location.[32] In mid-1738, disquieting rumors reached Santa Cruz from Buenos Aires that Cuiabá was more populous than São Paulo and Bahia, and was well defended by two small forts bearing sixteen pieces of artillery; all of these rumors were greatly exaggerated.[33] With these notices in

30. Dispatches of Torrenueva, Sebastián de la Quadra, Quintana, Francisco Molinillo, and others, June–Oct. 1738, AGI, BA, leg. 302 (also *HCJPP*, VII, 322–324).

31. Royal cédulas, and dispatches of Torrenueva, 8 Oct. 1738, to Villagarcía, Moneda, and Argomosa Ceballos, AGI, Charcas, leg. 161; BA, leg. 302.

32. Argomosa Ceballos to Castañares, S. Lorenzo, 10 Oct. 1738, *HCJPP*, VII, 328.

33. "Copia de un capítulo de carta que persona de todo credito escribió al Gobernador de Santa Cruz. . . ," 20 July 1738, AGI, BA, leg. 534 (also *HCJPP*, VII, 316–317).

hand, Argomosa Ceballos heard that the Jesuits of Chiquitos had seen the Portuguese mines, and in October he requested information from the new father superior, Augustín Castañares.[34]

Castañares' report of two months later, based on a careful study of the maps at his disposal, the testimonies of Chiquitos Indians and others who had fled Cuiabá, and an excursion Castañares himself had made to the north in December 1737, conveyed data only slightly more reliable than the earlier rumors. The father could offer little concrete news of the precise location of the Portuguese, but he did note that north of the mission of San Rafael and beyond the Xarayes lay at least two mining communities—Cuiabá to the east of the Paraguay River, and another (Mato Grosso) to the west of the river and possibly near the missions of Moxos—with smaller sites between them. Castañares suggested that the Portuguese could mobilize some 40,000 men capable of bearing arms (a seven-fold exaggeration), and stressed the awesome offensive might of the Paulistas who could undoubtedly, he felt, defeat the Spaniards as they were then organized. Though he cautioned against violence, the father suggested that the projected invasion should proceed up the Paraguay River toward the smaller western sites, since Cuiabá was better able to defend itself. In the meantime, he promised Jesuit cooperation in the surveillance of the area.[35]

Such hazy geographic notions and the gross exaggeration of the population and military forces of the mining communities only increased Argomosa Ceballos' fears. In hurried letters of January 1739 to the Audiencia of La Plata (Charcas), the viceroy of Peru, and the Crown, he called for arms, munitions, and funds, alluded to Portugal's notorious expansionist tendencies, and stressed the ease with which the Portuguese could conquer the missions, Santa Cruz, and Potosí, if immediate measures were not taken. The governor urged the continued reconnaissance of the region by Jesuits and their Indians, and even considered, somewhat foolishly, sending Castañares to demand evacuation of the mines. In a more realistic vein, Argomosa Ceballos suggested that a Spanish expeditionary

34. Argomosa Ceballos to Castañares, S. Lorenzo, 10 Oct. 1738, HCJPP, VII, 327–329; Argomosa Ceballos to Crown, S. Lorenzo, 8 Jan. 1739, AGI, Charcas, leg. 218 (also HCJPP, VII, 340).

35. Castañares to Argomosa Ceballos, S. Javier, 12 Dec. 1739, HCJPP, VII, 331–337.

force sent up the Paraguay could certainly weaken the mines by severing their vital communications with coastal Brazil along the Paraná-Paraguay rivers.

The governor's vision of the strategic and logistic problem had widened considerably, though, for Castañares had provided the first news of the existence of the Mato Grosso mines near the Guaporé and the possible movement of Portuguese toward Moxos. With Palhêta's expedition clearly in mind, Argomosa Ceballos suspected that the Portuguese hoped to reach the Guaporé-Marmoré, and to open fluvial communications into the Amazon basin by which they could receive necessary support from Pará. He ordered the superior of Moxos to establish sentinels along the Guaporé to search for Portuguese on the river.[36] The governor's wish to prevent navigation between Mato Grosso and Pará was in fact a short step ahead of Portuguese knowledge and intentions. But in focusing attention on the river route, still unknown in its entirety to the Portuguese, his measures would ultimately be self-defeating.

By mid-1740, Argomosa Ceballos' warnings about Portuguese expansion in the West, taken in conjunction with the continued occupation and fortification of Colônia, Santa Catarina, and Rio Grande, erased any remaining doubts in Madrid of her rival's true intentions. The royal instructions to the new governor of Buenos Aires, who was to continue Salcedo's cooperation in the offensive against the mines, were not merely rhetorical in declaiming that "the intention and design of the Portuguese has been, not only in time of hostilities, but equally in that of Peace, to further and extend their boundaries into my territories and Dominions by all the means and outrages to which cleverness and malice have prompted them."[37] But the governor of Paraguay had not yet reported to Spain, and the Council of the Indies considered the information from Santa Cruz an insufficient basis for planning an effective invasion of the mines. The councillors shelved Argomosa Ceballos' request for an immediate offensive until more specific data could be gathered. They called for more precise information

36. Argomosa Ceballos to Crown, S. Lorenzo, 8 and 11 Jan. 1739; acts and *provisiones* of the Audiencia of La Plata, 10 and 17 Feb., 21 Mar. 1739; act of Audiencia of Lima, 26 Nov. 1739; AGI, Charcas, leg. 207 (also *HCJPP*, VII, 283–284, 340–341, 343–345, 365–366).

37. Royal instructions to Domingo Ortiz de Rosas, 12 July 1740, AGI, BA, leg. 42; see also dispatches of Quintana and Torrenueva to Rosas, Madrid, 12 July 1740, AGI, BA, legs. 42, 302 (also *HCJPP*, VII, 377–378).

about the location, population, military forces, and fortifications of the mines; their communications with coastal Brazil and Pará; the distances to Santa Cruz and Asunción; and which routes through Moxos and Chiquitos to the mines could carry heavy materials, supplies, and troops. Upon the council's recommendation, in March 1741 the king once again ordered the governors of Santa Cruz and Paraguay, with the cooperation of authorities in Buenos Aires and Peru and the Jesuits of Moxos and Chiquitos, to collect the information necessary to dislodge the Portuguese.[38]

After five years of laborious machinations, hampered by an ignorance of continental geography and an ineffectual frontier intelligence system, the Spaniards had scarcely improved on the knowledge they had had in 1736. They had acquired a somewhat better idea of the location of the mines, but they had seriously misjudged the intentions of the Portuguese in the West and the actual state of the mining settlements. In fact, a well-executed invasion would probably have succeeded, for the communities of Cuiabá and Mato Grosso, distant from the principal centers of Portuguese power, were neither as populous, wealthy, and well-defended, nor as aggressive as Spanish reports suggested.

The settlers of Portugal's far western outposts were still struggling to stabilize their precarious existence. The total population of the region, including whites, slaves, freedmen, and domesticated Indians, probably did not exceed 6,000 by 1740. Of these, perhaps half lived in or around Cuiabá, still the major demographic center once the rush of 1736 to the new gold strikes at Mato Grosso had subsided. The rest of the population remained in the Mato Grosso washings or settled in sites along the Guaporé and on the Cuiabá-Mato Grosso road. In the absence of regular military units, the defense needs of the communities were served by a haphazard militia organization or by the traditional *bandeiras*, formed on an ad hoc basis to meet the sporadic attacks of nearby Indians. There were no fortifications and there was little, if any, artillery. Gold extraction in the Cuiabá district, notwithstanding a few minor strikes in the 1730s, remained at the minimal level reached a decade earlier. Primitive mining techniques and the shortage of water prevented

38. Comments of councillors, 21 Aug., 9 Nov. 1740, attached to Argomosa Ceballos to Crown, S. Lorenzo, 8 Jan. 1739, AGI, Charcas, leg. 218; final decision of council, 2 Dec. 1740, AGI, Charcas leg. 161; royal cédulas 8 Mar, 1741, AGI, BA, leg. 534; also *HCJPP*, VII, 341–343, 405–407, 419–422.

penetration of deeper lodes and hampered the substained exploitation of surface deposits and stream beds. The readily available gold washings of Mato Grosso, less abundant than the original strikes at Cuiabá, were nearly exhausted by 1740. The slow growth of agriculture beyond the bare subsistence level brought relief from the famines of the 1720s to Cuiabá, but the settlers of Mato Grosso, some 300 miles to the west, were forced to subsist largely on hunting and fishing, irregular plantings of maize, manioc, and beans, and the collection of fruits and wild rice. Nearly everything else necessary to life in the West—livestock, salt and similar processed foodstuffs, clothing, tools, arms, munitions, and all other manufactures, slaves and luxuries—still had to be imported from the coast at exorbitant prices that most settlers could ill afford.[39]

Until the late 1730s, the community was dependent for its imports on commerce along the Tietê-Paraná-Paraguay route from São Paulo, the only legally sanctioned line of communication to the western settlements over one thousand miles from the coast.[40] Yet repeated harassment of the merchant convoys by Paiaguá Indians seriously

39. On the early history of Cuiabá and western Mato Grosso see the following eighteenth-century chroniclers who owe as much to each other as to the sources they consulted: José Barbosa de Sá, "Relaçaó das provoaçoens do Cuyabá e Mato groso de seos principios thé os prezentes tempos," ABNRJ, XXIII (1901–1904), 5–58; Joaquim da Costa Siqueira, "Chronicas do Cuyabá," Revista do Instituto Histórico e Geográfico de São Paulo, IV (1898–1899), 4–217; Filippe José Nogueira Coelho, "Memorias chronologicas da capitania de Mato-Grosso principalmente da Provedoria da Fazenda Real e intendencia do ouro," RIHGB, XIII:2 (1850), 137–199; "Anal de Vila Bela desde o primeiro descobrimento dêste sertão do Mato Grosso, no ano de 1734," Congresso do mundo português (19 vols., Lisbon, 1940), X, 303–320; useful modern studies are Taunay, "Os primeiros anos de Cuiabá e Mato Grosso"; Sérgio Buarque de Holanda, Monções (Rio de Janeiro, 1945), esp. pp. 66–93; a brief summary in English is in C. R. Boxer, The Golden Age of Brazil, 1695–1750 (Berkeley, 1962), pp. 254–267. On conditions in the mid-1730s, see João Gonçalves Pereira (ouvidor of Cuiabá) to Crown, Cuiabá, 20 Sept. 1740, AHU, Papeis Avulsos, Mato Grosso (hereafter cited as MT), maço 2; various proposals from settlers of Cuiabá describing the state of mining and calling for corrective measures in AHU, MT, maços 1–5; Domingos Gomes Beliogo to Martinho de Mendonça de Pina e Proença, 2 Mar. 1734, IHGB/CU, arq. 1–3–3, fols. 278–279v.; correspondence of Captain-General of São Paulo Sarzedas in DI, XL, XLI, passim.

40. The monsoon route, as it became normalized after 1723–1725, usually began at Araritaguaba (Pôrto Feliz), coursed down the Tietê and Paraná, up the Pardo, then briefly overland to the Coxim and Taquari, onto the Paraguay, and finally up the Cuiabá; see the fine studies of this route in Holanda, Monções; Taunay, História das bandeiras paulistas, II, 109–184; and, Leonardo Arroyo, Relação do rio Tietê (São Paulo, 1965).

endangered the survival of the monsoon route. Initiated in 1725, Paiaguá attacks increased in intensity and destructiveness into the following decade, prompting a series of defensive measures from the Cuiabanos and the captain-general of São Paulo. But neither the official declaration of war against the marauders, nor the dispatch of various bandeiras and attempts at surveillance could insure fully the safety of this lifeline of empire.[41] Though the monsoon route continued to function in later years, the settlers of the mines sought new trade routes and alternative sources of supply to maintain their beleaguered community.

The search for markets led the westerners to blaze the overland trail to Goiás in 1736–1737,[42] to dispatch an ill-fated trade embassy to the Guaicurú, horse-riding nomadic pastoralists to the southeast,[43] and, finally, to consider commercial relations with the Jesuits of Chiquitos. This final step was quite natural: the missions had an adequate supply of cattle, cotton cloth, and foodstuffs in demand in the mines, while Portuguese gold would have benefited the fathers' trade with Santa Cruz. Yet the imperial governments of Spain and Portugal had adamantly prohibited trade between their freelances on the frontier. Portuguese authorities were especially wary of international contacts in the West. In 1723 the captain-general of São Paulo expressly forbade communication with the neighboring Spaniards or forays into Spanish territory, for fear of revealing the existence and location of the new mines.[44] From all

41. On the Paiaguá attacks, see Sá, "Relaçaó," pp. 15–18, 24, 26, 30–36, and Costa Siqueira, "Chronicas do Cuyabá," pp. 31–32, 59, 61, 65–66; see the lively first-hand account of the Paiaguá by the old Indian fighter Antônio Pires de Campos, "Breve noticia que dá o capitão . . . do gentio barbaro que ha na derrota da viagem das minas do Cuyabá e seu reconcavo," RIHGB, XXV (1862), 439–440; scattered historical references also appear in Alfred Métraux, "Ethnography of the Chaco," Handbook of South American Indians, I, 197–370, esp. pp. 203, 214, 217, 224–225, 308.

42. Pereira to Crown, Cuiabá, 7 Oct. 1736, AHU, MT, maço 1; Antônio de Pinho e Azevedo to Pina e Proença, Trahiras, 7 Jan. 1737, BNL/CP, cod. 618, fols. 24–25v; Sá, "Relaçaó," pp. 36–37.

43. Pereira to Crown, Cuiabá, 7 Oct. 1736, AHU, MT, maço 1; Manoel Roiz Torres to Crown, Cuiabá, 30 June 1738, AHU, MT, maço 2; Sá, "Relaçaó," pp. 39, 41. On the Guaicurú see Pires de Campos, "Breve noticia," pp. 439–441; Holanda, Monções, pp. 162–168; Métraux, "Ethnography of the Chaco," pp. 200, 201–203, 210, 214–217.

44. "Reg.º do Regim.to q́ Levou p.ª as novas minas do Cuyabá o M.e de Campo Regente João Leme da Sylva," 26 June 1723, DI, XII, 106; see also Rodrigo Cézar de Menezes to viceroy of Brazil, São Paulo, 2 May 1722, DI, XX, 26.

accounts Cuiabanos had obeyed the injunction, but by the late 1730s they felt they had compelling reasons to justify a commercial embassy to the missions.

There was at the time a general suspicion in Cuiabá that Spaniards were planning action against the mines. This fear derived not from direct knowledge of the actual plans, but from a set of circumstances which, well-founded or not, led to the same conclusion. It was the firm conviction of most settlers that Paiaguá harassment of Portuguese canoes on the Paraguay was condoned, if not openly encouraged, by Spaniards, especially after the brutal assault in 1730 from which the Indians carried their gold booty to trade with the colonists of Paraguay province.[45] Spaniards did, in fact, barter tools, arms, and other goods in return for gold they knew to be Portuguese. But they were as intimidated by the Paiaguá as were the Portuguese, and had suffered Paiaguá attacks to the very fringes of Asunción periodically throughout the past century.[46] Scourge to both parties, the Paiaguá were both the means by which Spaniards first learned of the existence of Portuguese mines, and the source of information which first caused the Portuguese to suspect hostile plots by the Spaniards.

The fears of the Cuiabanos increased in 1736 and 1737 when Field Master Manoel Dias da Silva arrived in the West with news that Spaniards were considering moving on Cuiabá.[47] At roughly the same time, various individuals reported that Spanish Jesuits had penetrated Portuguese territory as far north as the headwaters of the Paraguay River in an attempt, so the miners claimed, to remove the Indians from Portuguese control. One of these Jesuit entradas was probably that conducted by Father Castañares in late 1737, sometime before he became consultant for Spanish invasion plans.

45. The Paiaguá attack of *ca.* June 1730 on a monsoon heading down the Paraguay for São Paulo, in which crown magistrate Antônio Alves Lanhas Peixoto was killed, was the first recorded instance in which Indians stole gold; see Sá, "Relaçaó," pp. 26–28; Costa Siqueira, "Chronicas do Cuyabá," pp. 65–66. Captain-general of Rio Luís Vahia Monteiro was also quick to assume that the attack was in some way fostered by Spaniards: see his dispatches of Nov.–Dec. 1730, Jan. 1731, ANRJ, cod. 80, vol. 4, fol. 53, cod. 84, vol. 3, fols. 37v–38, 52v–53v, 89v–90.

46. See Boxer, *Salvador de Sá*, pp. 90–93, on Paiaguá attacks in Paraguay in the seventeenth century.

47. Costa Siqueira, "Chronicas," pp. 105–106, n. 1; Taunay, *História das bandeiras paulistas*, II, 79–80.

On the basis of this tenuous evidence, the crown magistrate (*ouvidor*) of Cuiabá, João Gonçalves Pereira, held a series of inquiries in mid-1739 to determine the proximity of the missions, and to "ascertain whether or not the Spaniards and the Indians of their missions could invade the settlements of this district." In August and September, Pereira and the municipal council of Cuiabá informed the king and the captain-general of São Paulo of Spanish encroachments on Portuguese soil, and of the dangers of an invasion. They called for the fortification and strategic settlement of the region, and the use of missionaries to bring the Indians of the frontier securely under Portuguese rule.[48] In February of the following year, the magistrate and the council voted to send an expedition to reconnoiter Chiquitos. The expedition would determine the distance between the mines and the first mission, ask the Jesuits to discourage Spanish cooperation with the Paiaguá, and, most important, begin secret trade relations with the missions.[49] In his reports to the authorities after the bandeira departed, Pereira made no reference to the commercial purpose of the expedition, nor did he state that the expedition was to visit the missions. The magistrate had earlier requested permission to trade with the Spaniards, but he carefully divorced such designs from the "exploring bandeira" which, as he stated, was only for reconnaissance purposes.[50] Probably, even if he did not believe in the reality of an invasion or Spanish hostility, Pereira exaggerated such fears to justify the expedition. Indeed, the intendant of the treasury in Cuiabá claimed that the ouvidor and his merchant cronies had manufactured the invasion scare as a pretext to open trade—and thus find a secret outlet by which to avoid the fifth on gold—and that the decision was taken over the intendant's determined opposition.[51] The expedition was, in fact, financed pri-

48. Pereira to Crown, Cuiabá, 6 Sept. 1739, AHU, MT, maço 3; Cuiabá council to Crown, 30 Aug. 1739, AHU, MT, maço 5; captain-general of São Paulo Luís Mascarenhas to Pereira, Goiás, 20 Apr. 1740, *DI*, LXVI, 32–34; Sá, "Relaçaó," p. 39.
49. Torres to Mascarenhas, Cuiabá, 28 Feb. 1740, AHU, MT, maço 2; Sá, "Relação," pp. 39–41.
50. Pereira to Crown, 6 and 20 Sept. 1739, 4 Dec. 1740, AHU, MT, maço 3.
51. Torres to Mascarenhas, Cuiabá, 28 Feb. 1740, Torres to Crown, Cuiabá, 20 Aug. 1740, AHU, MT, maço 2. Torres' testimony is somewhat suspect, however, since he had been placed under arrest by Pereira for alleged malfeasance, and consequently bore a grudge against Pereira and many of the leading settlers of Cuiabá who opposed his vigorous attempts to enforce royal fiscal regulations in the West. Pereira's testimony is even more suspect.

marily by the merchants of Cuiabá, and it bore a letter of introduction from Luís Rodrigues Vilares, a leading businessman of the town who had commercial connections on the coast.[52] Freelance economic interests clearly violated state policy, though the ultimate result would be beneficial to both.

In July 1740, Antônio Pinheiro de Faria led a small group of Portuguese and Indians southward to Chiquitos, where he encountered Spanish Indians reconnoitering in search of the Portuguese. In the heart of the continent, the two freelance espionage enterprises converged. The Indians dutifully led Faria to the mission of San Rafael, the nerve center of the Jesuit surveillance network, where they arrived in the last week of August. After a brief exchange of formalities and the presentation of gifts, the Portuguese informed the Jesuits quite unabashedly of the economic hardships of the mines and their ardent wish for a mutually beneficial commercial interchange. The fathers firmly refused the offer. They noted the long-standing prohibition of trade across the frontier, informed the visitors that the mines were in Spanish territory, and declared that they would rather expel them from the area than trade with them. Faced with such obstinancy, the Portuguese embassy returned to Cuiabá in October, without having accomplished its mission. Later the same year, another expedition, dispatched from the mines of Mato Grosso, also visited San Rafael to open commerce, but it received an even colder reception. The fathers had been given strict orders to avoid all contacts with the Portuguese. Trade, of course, was out of the question.[53]

52. Sá, "Relaçaó," p. 39, noted that the expedition was financed by the town council, Pereira, and the principal citizens of Cuiabá, who were "mais interesados em que se estabelese negocio com os Castelhanos que era o projeto da impresa do que impedir desem favor a Payagoazes." Pereira admitted that the expedition was financed mainly by merchants (Pereira to Crown, Cuiabá, 20 Sept. 1740, AHU, MT, maço 3). Torres claimed that Vilares was the prime mover behind the expedition, which was probably true (Torres to Mascarenhas, Cuiabá, 28 Feb. 1740, AHU, MT, maço 2). A Spanish translation of Vilares' letter to the Chiquitos fathers dated Cuiabá, 22 June 1740, is in AGI, Charcas, leg. 207 (also HCJPP, VII, 376–377).

53. Father Superior of Chiquitos Bartolomé Mora to Argomosa Ceballos, S. Rafael, 12 Sept. 1740; Mora to Audiencia of La Plata, S. Rafael, 15 Sept, 1740; Argomosa Ceballos to José Casimiro Gómez García, Santa Cruz, 17 Sept. 1740, AGI, Charcas, leg. 207 (also HCJPP, VII, 386–391); Esteban Palozzi to Mora, S. Rafael, 28 Dec. 1740, HCJPP, VII, 412–416; Palozzi to Moneda, S. Rafael, 8 Jan. 1744, AGI, Charcas, leg. 384 (also HCJPP, VII, 550–551); Sá, "Relaçaó," pp. 40–41, agrees essentially with the Jesuit accounts, though he adds other

The brief meeting of freelances energized the imperial strategies of both governments in a manner quite disproportionate to its meager results on the frontier. Pereira's reports of 1739 and 1740, sent during and after the expedition to Chiquitos, provoked varying reactions from Portuguese colonial authorities. In November 1740, Luís Mascarenhas, captain-general of São Paulo, provisionally denied the ouvidor's original request to trade with the Spaniards until a decision arrived from Lisbon.[54] Three months later, upon hearing of the completed Faria expedition, though unaware of its commercial intentions, the captain-general sent a stinging complaint to the king in which he questioned Pereira's competence and sanity, and hinted of duplicity in the ouvidor's actions. Mascarenhas doubted that Spain was plotting against the mines, but was quick to suggest that the magistrate's alarmist views might well become self-fulfilling prophecies if he continued such patently illegal measures. He wrote immediately to Pereira to put an end to his activities.[55] By 1742, Mascarenhas had heard of the secret commercial purpose of the original expedition and of Pereira's plan to send another bandeira. The captain-general considered this news "totally incredible, unless the said magistrate is demented, or blind with ambition."[56] He reminded the ouvidor forcefully of his earlier admonition, and ordered him "not to provoke, or allow to be provoked, the least communication, and even less, commerce, between the Dominions of Portugal and Castile, for in the present circumstances this matter is much more delicate than your grace imagined."[57]

Matters were indeed delicate, for ministers in Lisbon feared that Pereira's actions would cause a break with Spain.[58] The reports from Cuiabá alerted the court to the possibility, so belabored by Pereira and the Cuiabá town council, that Spain was in fact plotting against the mines. Thus, though councillors in Lisbon had no direct knowledge of Spanish plans already underway, they were led circuitously to believe in the possibility of such machinations by the unsub-

sidelights and incorrectly gives the date of the expedition as April; the dates provided in the Jesuit letters are corroborated in Pereira's letters to the Crown of 20 Sept. and 4 Dec. 1740, AHU, MT, maço 3.

54. Mascarenhas to Pereira, Goiás, 7 Nov. 1740, DI, LXVI, 52–53.
55. Mascarenhas to Crown, Trahiras, 13 Feb. 1741, AHU, MT, maço 3.
56. Mascarenhas to Viceroy Galveas, 14 Oct. 1742, DI, LXVI, 64–65.
57. Mascarenhas to Pereira, 14 Oct. 1742, DI, LXVI, 63.
58. Mascarenhas to Galveas, 14 Oct. 1742, and to Gomes Freire de Andrada, n.d., prob. Nov.–Dec. 1742, DI, LXVI, 65–66, 74–75.

stantiated, self-interested, yet nonetheless essentially accurate, information from their volatile frontiersmen in the West.

In 1740–1743, the Overseas Council, convinced of the necessity for defensive moves, suggested various measures designed to secure the far western mines which they now saw as the "bulwark" of Portugal's far-flung possessions in the interior of the continent. As an indispensable precautionary step, the council clearly restated its desires to sever all Portuguese entries into Spanish territory for fear of provoking Spain. The council, on the recommendation of the Cuiabanos, also authorized the conversion of Indians by missionaries to be sent to the strategic area. It rejected on tactical and financial grounds, however, Pereira's suggestions for the fortification of the Cuiabá River. Instead, the council elaborated upon the ouvidor's recommendation for the strategic settlement of the West, and called for the erection of a new town with privileges and exemptions sufficient to entice colonists to the frontier. A prime strategy of Portugal already employed in the South and Amazon basin, Crown-promoted colonization would guarantee Portuguese occupation, contribute to the formation of a standing defensive force, and spare the royal treasury undue expense.[59]

The expeditions of the Portuguese prompted their metropolis to take action; they were equally important catalysts for Spanish plans. The same intricate relay and interpretation of information occurred on both sides of the frontier. Just as Pereira and the Cuiabá council sent notices to São Paulo and Lisbon, so did the fathers of Chiquitos inform the governor of Santa Cruz and the Audiencia of La Plata, who in turn informed each other, the viceroy of Peru, and the king. The Jesuit fathers related their encounters, with no speculation on the ulterior motives of the Portuguese. Argomosa Ceballos, however, now even more adamantly convinced of the need for an invasion, was appalled at the ease with which the Portuguese entered Spanish territory at will and the dangers this held for the security of the frontier. He saw in the miners' desire for trade nothing less than the ultimate ruin of the Spanish settlements, and repeated most of the suggestions he had made the year before.[60] The

59. Consultas of Overseas Council, 10 Nov. 1740, 4 Mar. and 5 Apr. 1742, royal letter to Mascarenhas, 2 Mar. 1741, AHU, MT, maço 5; consultas of Overseas Council, 30 Jan. 1741, 25 Feb. 1743, IHGB/CU, arq. 1–2–2, fols. 215–219v, 252–253.

60. Argomosa Ceballos to Audiencia of La Plata, S. Lorenzo, 6 Oct., 4 Dec.

Audiencia of La Plata also felt the threat of trade, and prohibited communication with the Portuguese, rejecting, however, the governor's call to arms until more information, and aid and advice from Paraguay and Peru, could be obtained. Moreover, the Audiencia could not finance the troops, arms, and supplies that Argomosa Ceballos requested, and could barely scrape together two hundred pounds of dry refined powder.[61] The viceroy of Peru considered these reports interesting, approved of what had been done, and asked for more information.[62] The chain of correspondence dragged on through the overlapping jurisdictions of the Spanish bureaucracy until April 1742, when, at about the time the Portuguese Overseas Council was reviewing Pereira's reports on the expeditions, the news finally reached the Council of the Indies in Madrid.[63]

Aided by the geographic notices unwittingly provided by the free-lance expeditions to Chiquitos, Spanish councillors at last considered they had sufficient information to begin serious preparations for the invasion. The reports from Chiquitos and Argomosa Ceballos, which supplemented Castañares' earlier dispatches, and cartographic research conducted in Madrid gave an adequate notion of the location of the Portuguese settlements and routes of access between the mines and the missions. The *fiscal's* report of August 1742, approved by the Council of the Indies eleven months later, outlined Spanish strategy. A military force would ascend the Paraguay River with the intent either to invade the mines, or if this proved difficult, to sever possible supply routes to the west along the rivers communicating with São Paulo and Pará. The resolution of problems

1740; Argomosa Ceballos to Crown, La Plata, 18 July 1741, AGI, Charcas, leg. 207 (also *HCJPP*, VII, 393–396); Argomosa Ceballos to Quintana, Santa Cruz, 6 Oct. 1740, AGI, Quito, leg. 158; Argomosa Ceballos to Gómez García, Santa Cruz, 16 Nov. 1740, *HCJPP*, VII, 401–402.

61. Acts and decisions of the Audiencia of La Plata, 17–19 Oct. 1740, 17 Feb., 11 Apr., and 7 Oct. 1741, AGI, Charcas, leg. 207 (also *HCJPP*, VII, 388–389, 409–410).

62. Villagarcía to Audiencia of La Plata, Lima, 30 Dec. 1740 and 2 June 1741, and attached act of the Audiencia of Lima, AGI, Charcas, leg. 207 (also *HCJPP*, VII, 416); Governor of Paraguay Moneda also conducted an investigation of Portuguese expansion, the results of the inquiry being dispatched to Madrid in the "Diligencia esecutada por el Señor Coronel Don Rafael de la Moneda Governador y Capitan General en esta Provincia del Paraguay por orden de S.M. sobre si con efecto los Portuguese ocupen varias minas en los territorios del Paraguay," 4–18 Sept. 1741, AGI, Charcas, leg. 207 (also *AGTM*, III:2, 35–51).

63. José del Campillo to Villanueva, Aránjuez, 21 Apr. 1742, AGI, Quito, leg. 158 (also *HCJPP*, VII, 450–451).

of supply and transport along the unpopulated stretch of the Paraguay above Asunción would be entrusted to the Jesuits of Chiquitos who, under the pretext of missionary activity, would establish provisioning stations on the Paraguay and its affluents up to the Xarayes. The cooperation of the Jesuits, their surveillance work, and the use of their neophytes as troops and labor were indispensable to the success of Spanish plans.[64] In July and August 1747, the minister José de la Quintana conferred with the Jesuit procurators of Paraguay, Peru, and the Indies, and brought them fully into the enterprise.

Within these meetings state geopolitical strategy merged with the traditional goal of the Jesuits for a united, well-defended chain of missions through the interior of the continent. Father Juan José Rico, procurator of Paraguay Province, agreed to found the desired sites along the Paraguay, which would not only assist the invasion, but would also fulfill the Jesuits' century-old hope of opening fluvial communications between the Guaraní missions of Paraguay and the reductions of Chiquitos.[65] Earlier the council had granted Rico's request to strengthen Chiquitos, the weakest of the mission territories, by instituting the payment of tribute by the Indians. Theoretically, the Indians of Chiquitos were not vassals of the Crown until such tribute was paid, and if this seemed a fine distinction, it assumed importance once news of the Faria expedition arrived in Madrid. The requirement of tribute would provide necessary funds for missionary labors, afford the Jesuits a more secure foothold in the region, and officially consolidate under the Crown the frontier directly facing the Portuguese mines.[66]

64. Report of the fiscal, 3 Aug. 1742, and decision of the council, 10 June 1743, AGI, Quito, leg. 158 (also HCJPP, VII, 451–454); Villanueva to Quintana, Madrid, 28 June 1743, AGI, Quito, leg. 158.

65. Rico to Quintana (?), Madrid, 3 July 1743, and to council, Madrid, 16 July 1743, AGI, Quito, leg. 158 (also HCJPP, VII, 507–508). On earlier attempts to open the Chiquitos-Paraguay fluvial route, see Guillermo Furlong, "De la Asunción a los Chiquitos por el Río Paraguay. Tentativa frustrada en 1703," Archivum Historicum Societatis Iesu VII (1938), 54–79, and Eulália Maria Lahmeyer Lobo, "Caminho de Chiquitos às missões guaranis de 1690 a 1718 (ensaio interpretativo)," Revista de História no. 39 (1959), 67–79; no. 40 (1960), 353–384; no. 41 (1960), 85–90; no. 42 (1960), 413–433.

66. On the consolidation of Chiquitos, see Rico's "Memorial" of 14 Jan. 1743, attached documents of the council, 14–31 Jan. 1743, and royal orders of 17 Dec. 1743, HCJPP, VII, 475–479, 534–539; see also the account in Pierre Xavier de Charlevoix, Historia del Paraguay (6 vols., Madrid, 1910–1916), VI, 116–129.

The Jesuits also agreed to foster the expansion of Moxos eastward toward Xarayes for communications with Chiquitos, to cut off possible Portuguese navigation into Moxos or the Amazon basin, and to provide alternative points of departure for the invasion of the mines. Quintana considered the stretch between Xarayes and the Madeira along the Guaporé-Mamoré of such importance that he suggested placing armed flotillas along these rivers. He also urged the advance of Moxos down the Madeira to the Amazon to close this route to the Portuguese, and, as the Jesuits had hoped a century earlier, to connect with the missions of Mainas (from Quito). The fathers of Mainas once again were to move eastward down the Amazon to the Madeira, and, if possible, to gain control of the Negro river.[67]

The convergence of Jesuit and state interests, though centering on the problem of the mines, went beyond these considerations to produce a coherent Spanish imperial vision of the continental interior strikingly similar to that of the Portuguese. Both governments had responded to the activities on the frontier with a heightened awareness of, and concern for, the western lands. Portugal hoped to consolidate the western mines, while Spain called for similar measures in Chiquitos. Both sought to occupy strategic regions, and to unite these territories along the rivers that could integrate their possessions in America. Spain now realized the importance of the fluvial line along the Paraguay-Xarayes and the Guaporé-Mamoré-Madeira, precisely the line that Luís da Cunha (though unaware of the Mamoré-Guaporé) cited in 1736 as Brazil's ideal western limit. Yet just when Spain began to assert control over these rivers, Portugal's willful freelances sailed from Mato Grosso to Moxos and Pará to project the Guaporé-Mamoré-Madeira finally, and fully, into Portugal's view.

Hard times and faltering mine production spurred slave hunters, prospectors, and fishermen of Mato Grosso down the Guaporé. In April 1742, the Paulista Francisco Leme do Prado and the Portuguese Manoel Felix de Lima organized a troop of impoverished miners and adventurers, with the intention of gaining quick profits from reported gold deposits on the Guaporé, and of trading with the missions of Moxos, whose easternmost reductions were re-

67. Report of Quintana, Madrid, 7 Aug. 1743; procurator-general of the Indies Ignacio de Altamirano to Quintana, Madrid, 3 July 1743, AGI, Quito, leg. 158.

putedly less than a month's travel downstream. Departing from
Mato Grosso in June, the group soon encountered Spanish Indians
who directed them to the missions. In each reduction the Portuguese
requested permission to trade for cattle and horses, and in each
they were received warmly, entertained graciously, but denied commerce. The Jesuits were wary of their visitors, but notwithstanding
earlier orders to prevent Portuguese entry into Moxos, they apparently feared to act, until a stern reprimand arrived from the
governor of Santa Cruz ordering the priests to expel the Portuguese
immediately. By that time the group had divided and, failing to meet
Felix de Lima's party as planned, Leme do Prodo's troop sailed
up the Guaporé to Mato Grosso in January 1743.[68]

Reports of this trip soon reached Justice Pereira, who immediately
had the *juiz ordinário* of Mato Grosso interrogate the party. Rather
than punish the freelances for violations that Pereira himself had
committed three years earlier, the magistrate ordered Leme do Prado
and the chronicler José Barbosa da Sá to return to Moxos, ostensibly
in the service of the state. Under the pretext of seeking trade, they
were to report on the location, forces, arms, and general state of
Moxos and Santa Cruz; the possibility of a Spanish invasion of the
mines; and, significantly, on the course of the Guaporé and the possible fluvial communications between the missions and Portuguese
settlements of the Amazon.[69] On their return downriver in March

68. The basic sources for the expedition, prepared by participants, are published in *AGTM*, III:2, 52–80; Robert Southey, *History of Brazil* (3 vols., London, 1810–1819), III, 310–332, bases his accurate account on the above sources,
and on an MS. drafted by Lima, which is now apparently lost (see *ibid.*, p.
311, n. 5, pp. 342–343); see also the hitherto unknown dispatch of Captain-
general of Pará João de Abreu Castelbranco to Crown, Pará, 24 Feb. 1743, and
the attached "Auto de preguntas," and "Lista das pessoas," AHU, Pará, caixa
11; see also the brief accounts in Sá, "Relaçaó," p. 42, and "Anal de Vila Bela,"
p. 309.

69. The documents prepared by Pereira in *AGTM*, III:2, 52–80, do not state
that the second expedition was sent to gather information, but rather that Leme
do Prado returned to Moxos voluntarily and without instigation; Sá, "Relaçaó,"
p. 43, states that he and Leme were sent expressly for reconnaissance purposes;
see the list of items in *AGTM*, III:2, 64–80, in which it is not clear whether they
were formulated as questions to guide a reconnaissance mission, or drawn up
after the troop returned. Cortesão, *AGTM*, I:2, 155–161, argues that this trip
was part of a "vasto serviço de informação geográfica por meio de espionagem
lançada em quase todo o territorio circundante do Brasil," which was begun ca.
1739–1740 under the direction of Gusmão. He can not muster any evidence,
however, to indicate that Pereira or the members of the expedition were acting
on specific orders from Gusmão.

1743, the Portuguese encountered the new mission of Santa Rosa, the first Spanish reduction established on the eastern bank of the Guaporé. The padre of Santa Rosa informed them that the governor of Santa Cruz had ordered the Guaporé fortified and settled to prevent Portuguese navigation downstream and was planning an invasion of the mines with the assistance of the Jesuits. Leme do Prado and Barbosa de Sá received no cooperation from the now alert Jesuits in other missions and returned to Mato Grosso two months later. There the Portuguese answered a detailed questionnaire prepared by Pereira, and Leme do Prado dicated a narrative of the trip. Pereira appended a summary of the events and sent the documents to Lisbon sometime in September 1743. They described the missions of Moxos with some accuracy and stressed Spain's hostile attitude and desire to control the rivers, though they did note that the missions were ill prepared for a successful invasion of the mines. The miners also provided the first account of the course of the Guaporé from Mato Grosso to the Mamoré. Basing their testimony on discussions with the fathers themselves, the Portuguese noted that the Guaporé-Mamoré flowed into the Amazon basin, again the first concrete evidence of river connections between the mines and the Amazon. Indeed, they suggested that their missing companions might have sailed that route to Pará.[70]

Lima and his three comrades had done precisely that. They had waited in Moxos for some three weeks, then decided to continue downriver. Lima stated that the Jesuits informed him of the course of the Mamoré-Madeira into the Amazon, though it seems odd that the fathers would reveal such strategic information, given the intention of the governor and Jesuit authorities to block the Portuguese. Nevertheless, their contact with the Moxos priests enabled Portuguese freelances to learn of the Mamoré-Madeira route and to travel it. Sometime in or before February 1743, after an arduous four-month trip of constant hardships, Lima's group, the first Portuguese to sail the full course of the river route between Mato Grosso and Pará, arrived in Belém. Surprised at the audacious undertaking, the captain-general of Pará nevertheless apprehended them for

70. *AGTM*, III:2, 62–63, 64–80; Sá, "Relaçaó," p. 43, exaggerates the range of travels of the expedition; Pereira also sent a sketch map of the Guaporé-Mamoré and the missions of Moxos, the "[Carta da rede e bacia hidrográfica do rio Guaporé e outros rios e ribeirões em Mato Grosso,]" AHU, Mapas e Plantas, MT.

violation of the law of 1733 which prohibited the opening of new routes to the mines, and after a brief interrogation, sent Lima and a companion to Lisbon for further questioning.[71]

The feats of men on the spot in Brazil led directly into the formulation of imperial policy in Lisbon. The news from Mato Grosso and Pará not only confirmed Portugal's view of the importance of the West, especially in light of its newly discovered proximity to Moxos and the repeated suggestions of Spanish hostility, but also fulfilled hopes for a western border that would link the distant mines to the Amazon basin.[72] This information was of particular importance, for the death in 1746 of the Spanish king, Felipe V, long a determined opponent of rapprochement with Portugal, opened the doors to negotiations by which the courts of Lisbon and Madrid could finally resolve the issue of colonial boundaries. Discussions commenced in 1747 and continued until the signing of the Treaty of Madrid in January of 1750, the first negotiated settlement between the Iberian powers to delineate their colonial possessions in South America in their entirety.

Portugal's intention, as stated principally by Alexandre de Gusmão, the royal secretary, was to win Spanish recognition of Portugal's sovereignty over her occupied territories in Rio Grande, the central and far western mining districts, and the greater part of the Amazon valley. In return for this recognition, and for a tract along the Uruguay River embracing the Spanish mission territory known as the Seven Peoples, Portugal would cede Colônia and full control of the Platine estuary to Spain. In the West, Gusmão hoped to establish the Guaporé-Mamoré down to the Madeira as a border between the Portuguese mines and Spanish missions; recognition of this border would require the removal of the Moxos fathers from the east bank of the Guaporé. He expected to guarantee navigation rights to the Madeira, thus assuring possible water-borne communications between the West and the Amazon. The Portuguese minister called for a permanent treaty that would annul the Tordesillas pact, for although Portugal had admittedly usurped lands in America,

71. Castelbranco to Crown, Pará, 24 Feb. 1743, and attached documents, AHU, Pará, caixa 11; Southey, *History of Brazil*, III, 332–341, describes the trip from the Lima MS.; Crown to Castelbranco, 17 June 1744, BAPP, cod. 848, no fol. (also *AGTM*, III:2, 81–82).

72. See Cortesão's discussion in *AGTM*, I:2, 171–172, 260.

Spain was guilty of similar violations in the East. He urged the acceptance of the principle of *uti possidetis* by which "each of the parties retains that which it has occupied," except for the exchanges mentioned, and that borders follow clearly discernible landmarks to avoid misunderstandings.[73]

Spanish negotiators sought control of the Platine estuary and a definite halt to Portugal's westward expansion. Thus, they were willing to relinquish claims to the mines, most of the Amazon, and the southern plains in return for Colônia and assurance of a stable inland border.[74] The invasion plans so patiently elaborated were apparently shelved when negotiations began,[75] and although Spain did assert nominal sovereignty over the mines during the proceedings, the claim was doubtless a ploy to achieve other objectives, just as Gusmão used Portugal's hold on Colônia as a lever to pry desired territories from Spain. The Spaniards also looked to the Guaporé-Mamoré as a border, but were still definitely opposed to Portuguese navigation on the rivers for fear of Portuguese entry to Moxos and Santa Cruz, and of Portuguese communications between the mines and Amazon basin. Between 1744 and 1746, the Moxos fathers founded two more reductions—San Miguel and San Simón—on the east bank of the Guaporé, probably to limit Portuguese use of the river.[76]

Despite their desires to settle imperial problems, neither government trusted the other's good will. Both parties continued defensive measures on the frontier which they hoped would guarantee the success of their objectives. Spain dispatched additional missionaries

73. Portugal's objectives are outlined in documents in *AGTM*, IV:1, 99–113, 168–184, 224–241, and summarized in Cortesão's narrative of the negotiations and goals of both powers in *AGTM*, I:2, 231–316.

74. See n. 73 and *AGTM*, IV:1, 96–97, 147–152, 154–161, 207–208, 209–218.

75. No mention of the invasion plans appears in Spanish documents consulted dated after 1743; investigations on the frontier did continue throughout the 1740s: see AGI, Charcas, legs. 207, 217, 246, 384, and *HCJPP*, VII, 506, 548–551, 583–585. The governors of Paraguay and Buenos Aires considered the mines too distant to pose a threat to Paraguay Province: Rosas to Campillo, Buenos Aires, 3 Dec. 1743, and Moneda to Crown (?), Asunción, 24 Apr. 1744, AGI, Charcas, leg. 246; authorities in Santa Cruz and La Plata still felt threatened by the presence of Mato Grosso: Gómez García to Crown, La Plata, 2 Feb. 1745, AGI, Charcas, leg. 207 (also *HCJPP*, VII, 575–576).

76. The Jesuit catalogue of 1748 lists the Indian population of the three missions on the Guaporé: S. Miguel—3444, S. Simón—493, Sta. Rosa—388, *HCJPP*, VII, 748.

to Moxos and Chiquitos, and retained the reductions on the Guaporé, and the Portuguese sought to strengthen their hold on the West and assure control of the Guaporé-Mamoré-Madeira.

Even before negotiations got underway in Madrid, the Portuguese had adopted precautionary measures to defend the mines. Because the earlier decisions of the Overseas Council had not been implemented, in 1745 the council again authorized the dispatch of missionaries to the West in hopes of counteracting the progress of Spanish Jesuits in the conversion of the Indians, and thus the possession of the frontier zone.[77] The Portuguese also obtained papal approval of the creation of the bishoprics of São Paulo and Mariana (Minas Gerais) and the prelacies of Goiás and Cuiabá. The councillors were sincerely concerned with the spiritual well-being of their settlers; but they were also aware of the legitimacy the papal sanction gave to the occupation of the West.[78] A year later the council again prohibited trade and communications with the missions in direct response to Pereira's reports of 1743. Yet the ministers were clearly upset by the presence of Spanish Jesuits on the Guaporé and Spain's intention to prevent Portuguese navigation on that river. Though they wanted no action taken yet against Santa Rosa, the councillors again recommended the founding of a new town on the frontier to foster settlement that could stop the Spanish advance.[79]

Finally, in January-May 1748, the council called for the creation of a new captaincy-general of Mato Grosso, separated from that

77. Consulta of Overseas Council, 1745, IHGB/CU, arq. 1-2-2, fols. 298–301v; the Cuiabá town council repeated its request for missionaries to the Crown on 3 Oct. 1744, AHU, MT, maço 5; the Overseas Council discussed the question again in 1746, and the following year ordered Captain-general of Rio Gomes Freire de Andrada to confer with the Jesuit Provincial: provisão to Andrada, 13 July 1747, ANRJ, cod. 952, vol. 34, fol. 5. The first Jesuits did not reach the West for another four years.

78. See esp. parecer of Overseas Council, 10–22 Apr. 1745 and attached royal resolution, 22 Apr. 1745, and the papal bull "Candor Lucias Aeternae" of Benedict XIV, 8 Dec. 1745, AGTM, III:2, 156–187, 191–200; see also Cortesão's discussion in AGTM, I:2, 173–175.

79. Parecer of Overseas Council, 26 Apr. 1746, and attached royal resolution, 27 June 1746, AHU, MT, maço 5 (also AGTM, III:2, 83–86); Mascarenhas to crown magistrate of Cuiabá Manoel Antunes Nogueira, Santos, 5 Oct. 1747, DI, LXVI, 202, sends news of the new vila to be established in the West; Mascarenhas' bando, Santos, 9 Oct. 1747, DI, XXII, 199–202, posts the privileges to be conceded to settlers of the new town as stated in the provisão of 5 Aug. 1746; see also provisão to Andrada, 21 Aug. 1747, ANRJ, cod. 952, vol. 34, fol. 53.

of São Paulo. The name was significant, for though the captaincy would include the town of Cuiabá—the most populous settlement in the West—the camps of Mato Grosso were some thirty miles from the Guaporé and the sites closest to the missions of Moxos. The captain-general would reside for the greater part of the year in the new town to be established in Mato Grosso to "make the colony of Mato Grosso so powerful that it be held in respect by its neighbors, and that it serve as bulwark of all the interior of Brazil." Not only would the presence of a superior military officer and royal troops contribute to defense, but the new captaincy-general would symbolize the permanent occupation of the Far West under the Crown, giving a firm basis to the operation of *uti possidetis*.[80]

With measures underway to hold the western mines, Portugal simultaneously sought to assure navigation rights on the Guaporé-Mamoré-Madeira rivers. In 1744, after Lima's journey, Gusmão had firmly reiterated the ban on river travel between Maranhão-Pará and the mines of Brazil to avoid the flow of contraband gold, in effect closing the newly discovered Madeira route to traffic.[81] As negotiations proceeded in Europe, he maintained the prohibition, and doubtless assumed that such measures would relieve tension along the Guaporé-Mamoré as well as testify to Portugal's good faith at the conference table. But while Gusmão diligently pursued his goals through diplomatic channels, Portugal's incorrigible frontiersmen in Mato Grosso sailed the rivers of the West with impunity.

The persistent need for sources of supply continued to entice miners and merchants down the Guaporé toward Moxos. Despite the efforts of the new royal magistrate of Cuiabá to prevent trade with the Spaniards,[82] by 1747 the Portuguese had established commercial relations with the fathers of Moxos. The Jesuits were ill prepared to thwart Portuguese navigation; moreover they were often willing to trade so far as their superiors did not specifically and repeatedly prohibit it. From all accounts, the men of the frontier, despite imperial considerations, maintained a mutually beneficial co-

80. Parecer of Overseas Council, 29 Jan. 1748 and attached royal resolution, 7 May 1748, AHU, MT, maço 3 (also *AGTM*, III:2, 127–131); royal letter, 9 May 1748, which decrees the new captaincy-general is in Estevão de Mendonça, *Datas mato-grossenses* (2 vols., Niteroi, 1919), I, 243–244.

81. Provisões to Castelbranco, 16 and 17 June 1744, BAPP, cod. 878, no fol.

82. Sá, "Relaçaó," pp. 44, 46; Costa Siqueira, "Chronicas do Cuyabá," p. 100; "Anal de Vila Bela," p. 310.

existence, interruped at intervals when authorities intervened.[83]

Other freelances, in emulation of Lima, sailed the Guaporé-Mamoré-Madeira to Pará. At least one trip was undertaken between 1744 and 1746, but its consequences are not known.[84] Another expedition, under the direction of José Leme do Prado and Francisco Xavier de Abreu, made the voyage sometime between 1747 and late 1748 in the impressively short span of fifty-two days.[85] The most spectacular voyage, the first upriver journey from Pará to Mato Grosso, was achieved by the notorious merchant-adventurer of the backlands, João de Sousa Azevedo. A skilled *sertanista* and audacious enterepreneur, Azevedo had sailed the full course of the Tapajós from Mato Grosso to Pará in 1746–1747, then set out from

83. José Gonçalves da Fonseca related that in 1747 a Mato Grosso surgeon, Francisco Rodrigues da Costa, maintained a flourishing traffic in salt, dry goods, wax, and cotton cloth with the fathers of Exaltación (Moxos), "com interesse da qual estabeleceu huma quazi sociedade," but the Jesuits halted the trade a year later on orders from the superior: "Navegação feita da cidade do Gram Pará até á bocca do rio da Madeira. . . ," *Collecção de noticias para a historia e geografia das nações ultramarinas, que vivem nos dominios portuguezes, ou lhes são visinhas* (7 vols., Lisbon, 1812–1867), IV, 131–132. Fonseca also noted a similar pattern between Mato Grosso and Chiquitos: "Noticia da situação de Mato-Grosso e Cuyabá: estado de umas e outras minas e novos descobrimentos de ouro e diamantes," *RIHGB* XXIX:1 (1866), 382–383. A striking example of coexistence, apart from commerce, occurred between the Portuguese outlaw society on the Ilha Comprida (on the Guaporé) and the Jesuits of the nearby Guaporé missions. The freebooters alternated between slave hunting, fishing, aiding the fathers to reduce Indians—which bolstered Spain's position on the river—and harassing the missions: see the "Anal de Vila Bela," pp. 310–311, and the especially vivid description of the outlaw society by Fonseca, who spent a harrowing visit on the island in March 1750. Though he found the Portuguese outcasts vulgar and terrifying, Fonseca nonetheless considered them an effective buffer against possible Spanish expansion. "Navegação," pp. 119–123.

84. "Anal de Vila Bela," p. 310, relates that in *ca.* 1743, Miguel da Silva, Mathias Corrêa's brother, and a Dutchman, Gaspar Barbosa, following Lima's example, set said for Pará, and that Corrêa was killed by Indians and Barbosa lost in the rapids; the chronicle does not reveal the ultimate fate of the expedition. Henrique de Beaurepaire Rohan, "Annaes de Matto Grosso," *RIHGSP*, XV (1910), 67, dates the expedition in 1744. Costa Siqueira, "Chronicas do Cuyabá," p. 100, states that a group left Mato Grosso in 1745 to trade with Pará, a few died at the rapids, but others completed the voyage and returned the following year with merchandise. It is not clear if these sources refer to the same expedition.

85. Captain-general of Pará Francisco Pedro de Mendonça Gorjão to Crown, Pará, 22 Apr. 1749, AHU, Pará, caixa 3; "Anal de Vila Bela," p. 311, states that they left Mato Grosso in 1747; Fonseca, "Navegação," pp. 370–372, wrote that they were nearing Pará on the lower Amazon in late 1748; evidence does not permit a more precise dating.

Belém in late 1748 and shortly encountered Leme do Prado and Abreu, who informed him of the Madeira route. João de Sousa took their advice; some nine months later he reached the far western outpost, sold his goods, and returned down the Madeira on the last leg of the first commercial round trip between the West and Pará.[86] At about the same time, another group departed the mines for Belém.[87]

Despite Gusmão's guarded policy, the Madeira route was already in operation. Pressing commercial necessity had led freelances again to Moxos, then to Pará along the Guaporé-Mamoré-Madeira, in violation of state policy. Shortly, however, freelance commercial interests merged with state geopolitical and logistical considerations in common agreement on the usefulness of the Madeira route.

86. On Azevedo's Arinos-Tapajós voyage, see the nineteenth-century copy of an eighteenth-century narrative by Ricardo Franco de Almeida Serra, evidently based on Azevedo's own account, "Noticia da viagem de João de Sousa de Azevedo," attached to Almeida Serra's "Memoria geographica do Rio Tapajós," BNRJ, I—31-17-3; the "Noticia" was later published in João Severiano da Fonseca, *Viagem ao redor do Brasil, 1875–1878* (2 vols., Rio, 1880–1881), I, 68–72; Mendonça Gorjão to Crown, Pará, 26 Sept. 1747, AHU, Pará, caixa 12, reports and notes that Azevedo presented him with an "Informação" of 26 Aug. 1747, which probably refers to the "Breve informação que dá João de Sousa de Azevedo ao General do Estado do Maranhão, do descobrimento das Minas de Santa Isabel no Rio Orinoz," listed in Joaquim Heliodoro da Cunha Rivara, *Catálogo dos manuscriptos da bibliotheca publica eborense* (4 vols., Lisbon, 1850), I, 30; Mendonça Gorjão to Cardeal da Mota, Pará, 3 Nov. 1747, AHI, lata 288, maço 8, pasta 8; royal letter to Mendonça Gorjão, 9 July 1748, BAPP, cod. 880, doc. 42 (also *AGTM*, III:2, 131–132); Azevedo described the voyage in his petition of 1749–1750, AHU, MT, maço 5; see also Fonseca, "Noticia," pp. 369–371, and João de São José e Queirós, "Viagem e visita do sertão em o bispado do Gram-Pará em 1762 e 1763," *RIHGB*, IX (1847), 92–95. On the Madeira voyage see Mendonça Gorjão to Crown, Pará, 22 Apr. 1749, AHU, Pará, caixa 3; Azevedo's petition of 1749–1750, AHU, MT, maço 5; Mendonça Gorjão to Pedro de Mota e Silva, Pará, 10 Sept. 1750, AHU, Pará, caixa 13; "Anal de Vila Bela," pp. 311–312; Fonseca, "Noticia," pp. 370–372. See the general studies of Azevedo by Virgílio Corrêa Filho, "João de Sousa Azevedo," *Revista do Instituto Historico de Mato Grosso,* XXIII–XXIV:xlv–xlviii (1941–1942), 39–60; Arthur Cézar Ferreira Reis, "Paulistas na Amazônia e outros ensaios," *RIHGB* CLXXV (1941), 233–248, 315–329; Afonso de E. Taunay, *História geral das bandeiras paulistas* (11 vols., São Paulo, 1924–1950), VIII, 245–258.

87. Mendonça Gorjão to Crown, Pará, 25 Oct. 1749, AHU, MT, maço 7; Mendonça Gorjão to Mota e Silva, Pará, 15 Sept. 1750, AHU, Pará, caixa 13, notes that a group of seven miners from Mato Grosso arrived in Pará in 1749; "Anal de Vila Bela," p. 314, records the expedition, but dates it, probably incorrectly, in 1750; two petitions of *ca.* 1749 by an intinerant preacher who accompanied the troop are in AHU, MT, maço 7.

Although unaware of these travels on the Madeira, by 1748 ministers in Lisbon had decided to take steps to open the Madeira route. They feared that Spain's forces in Moxos and Chiquitos would take control of the rivers, and possibly of the mines themselves, if measures were not adopted for the defense of the river route. The supposed ease by which Mato Grosso could receive supplies and troops from Pará along the Madeira in time of need was a primary consideration in the decision to create the new captaincy-general in May 1748.[88] The following September, just four days after Secretary of State Marco Antônio de Azevedo Coutinho sent to Madrid Gusmão's first request for a western border along the Guaporé-Mamoré-Madeira and for the removal of the Jesuits from the Guaporé,[89] Azevedo Coutinho informed the captains-general of Rio de Janeiro and Pará that the route might be opened to navigation. To Gomes Freire de Andrada in Rio, Azevedo Coutinho cited

the importance of securing navigation on the aforesaid river, which the Spaniards are attempting to usurp from us, and by means of [that navigation], and of communications with Pará, increase our forces in the backlands of Mato Grosso, so that rather than fear the superiority which the Spaniards now enjoy because of the number of people they have in the villages of Moxos and Chiquitos, let them fear ours.[90]

But before a decision could be reached, the Portuguese Court needed a more precise account of the rivers, the state of Mato Grosso, and the forces of the Spaniards. The secretary ordered Francisco Pedro de Mendonça Gorjão, captain-general of Pará, to dispatch immediately a secret expedition from Belém to reconnoiter the entire length of the route and to report promptly on its findings.[91] In January 1749, Antônio Rolim de Moura, newly appointed captain-general of Mato Grosso, was instructed to bolster Portuguese defenses in the West, neutralize the effects of Santa Rosa by fostering

88. Parecer of Overseas Council, 29 Jan. 1748, AHU, MT, maço 3 (also *AGTM*, III:2, 129).

89. Azevedo Coutinho, to Tomás de Silva Teles, Lisbon, 11 Sept. 1748, and attached "Réplica de Alexandre de Gusmão," *AGTM*, IV:1, 168–184; Azevedo Coutinho to Silva Teles, Lisbon, 22 Nov. 1748, and attached "Primeiro plano da Côrte de Portugal," *AGTM*, IV:1, 224–241.

90. Azevedo Coutinho to Andrada, Lisbon, 15 Sept. 1748, *AGTM*, III:2, 133–134.

91. Azevedo Coutinho to Mendonça Gorjão, Lisbon, 15 Sept. 1748, *AGTM*, III:2, 135–138.

settlement in adjacent regions, and establish his residence in the new town to be founded on or near the Guaporé. He was to promote fishing and navigation on the Guaporé "so that negligence on our part shall not encourage the Spaniards in their pretensions to master them." The opening of the Madeira route to navigation, he was informed, "will be the most efficacious means of destroying that pretension and of fortifying the lands of your jurisdiction."[92] Portuguese fears increased considerably some three months later when the ambassador to Madrid reported that Spain was still definitely opposed to granting navigation rights on the rivers.[93] Azevedo Coutinho replied that "as to the navigation of the Guaporé or Madeira river, by no means must we desist from it, because upon it depends the stability and strength of Mato Grosso. . . . This point of our free navigation on the said river is of such consequence that we must sustain it at all costs."[94] A month later, however, under pressure to complete the negotiations, the Spaniards agreed to Portugal's terms, and in January 1750, the Treaty of Madrid was signed.

The terms of the treaty fulfilled Portugal's hopes of preserving the West and its river connections to Pará. Article III granted to Portugal all the land she occupied in the Amazon basin and Mato Grosso. Articles VII and VIII stipulated that Brazil's western border be drawn in a straight line from the mouth of the Jaurú River (an affluent of the Paraguay) to the southern bank of the Guaporé where it meets the Sararé, then proceed down the Guaporé, Mamoré, and Madeira to a point mid-way between the mouths of the Mamoré

92. Royal instructions to Rolim de Moura, 19 Jan. 1749, Marcos Carneiro de Mendonça, ed., *A Amazônia na era pombalina* (3 vols., São Paulo, 1963), I, 15–24, esp. pp. 18–19 (hereafter cited as *AEP*).

93. Silva Teles to Azevedo Coutinho, Madrid, 2 Apr. 1749, *AGTM*, IV:1, 281.

94. Azevedo Coutinho to Silva Teles, Lisbon, 28 Apr. 1749, *AGTM*, IV:1, 292–293; Gomes Freire de Andrada supported this view in a dispatch to Azevedo Coutinho from Rio de Janeiro, 10 Mar. 1749, BNRJ, I–13–4–10, no. 5. The timing of the publication of the first edition of Bernardo Pereira de Berredo's *Annaes historicos do Maranhão* (Lisbon, 1749) suggests a state-directed effort to claim possession of the rivers of the Amazon. Berredo, former captain-general of Maranhão (1718–1722), managed to include in his history numerous proofs of Portugal's right to the Amazon basin and its rivers; a prefatory note by the procurator-general of the Jesuits in Maranhão, Bento da Fonseca, includes a brief historical account, though he confuses the dates, of some of the Portuguese expeditions on the Madeira after 1718 (when Berredo's history ends). Fonseca concludes, "Com estes noticias fico certo ser a demarcação do interior da nossa America cortando pelo rio Madeira ao Mato Grosso."

and Madeira, whence another straight line would extend westward
to the Javarí River. In Article XIV Spain ceded to Portugal the
missions on the eastern bank of the Guaporé, offering the Indians
the option of remaining in Portuguese hands or repairing with the
Jesuits to the west bank. Finally, Article XIX declared navigation on
rivers serving as borders to be open to both powers. Thus, the treaty
guaranteed Portuguese navigation on the Guaporé, lower Mamoré
and upper Madeira, and placed the lower Madeira within Portuguese
territory to complete the fluvial chain.[95]

The treaty sanctioned Portugal's hold on the West, but the Portuguese had few illusions about the need to maintain that hold. Dis-
trustful of Spain's legal commitment, they moved cautiously to
assure the defense of Mato Grosso and its secure incorporation into
the empire. To state and freelance alike, the maintenance, perhaps
the very survival, of the far western outpost depended in large measure on the use of the Madeira for commercial, logistic, and bureaucratic communications with Pará. Throughout 1750 and 1751,
though metropolitan ministers hoped to open navigation, they de-
ferred action pending departure of the binational border commis-
sions charged with surveying the boundaries sketched provisionally
in the Treaty of Madrid.[96] In April 1751, the newly appointed captain-general of the state of Grão-Pará and Maranhão and chief
Portuguese commissioner for the northern demarcations, Francisco
Xavier de Mendonça Furtado, was instructed to investigate the possible benefits of opening the Pará-Mato Grosso connection in light
of Portugal's increased interest in the development of the Amazon.[97]
By mid–1752, metropolitan authorities considered the time propitious to act, and they had received abundant encouragement from
freelances and bureaucrats in Brazil, who enthusiastically recommended navigation on the Madeira route for the defense and well-
being of both Pará and Mato Grosso.

From Mato Grosso came the dispatches of Captain-General Rolim
de Moura, who had finally arrived at Cuiabá in January 1751, then
proceeded to the Guaporé where he founded the new capital of

95. Portuguese text in *AGTM*, IV:1, 460–490.
96. Azevedo Coutinho to Silva Teles, Lisbon, 21 March 1750, and Silva Teles
to Azevedo Coutinho, Madrid, 27 March 1750, *AGTM*, IV:2, 214–219; consulta
of Overseas Council, 15 Apr. 1751, AHU, Pará, caixa 16.
97. Royal instructions to Mendonça Furtado, 31 May 1751, *AEP*, I, 26–38,
esp. p. 37.

Mato Grosso, Vila Bela da Santíssima Trindade, in March 1752.[98]
From Pará arrived the reports of outgoing Captain-General Mendonça Gorjão and Bishop Miguel de Bulhões, both of whom based
their recommendations largely on the findings of the reconnaissance
expedition dispatched in pursuance of Azevedo Coutinho's orders.[99] In July 1749, Sergeant-Major Luís Fagundes Machado and
the secretary of the Pará government, José Gonçalves da Fonseca,
led the troop from Belém up the Madeira, arriving in Mato Grosso
after nine month's travel; they returned downriver in September
1750, to arrive in Belém three months later. The reports of this first
officially sponsored round trip of the Madeira route afforded a wealth
of pertinent data on the state of Mato Grosso and the neighboring
Spanish missions, and the first abundantly detailed description of
the full course of the river route.[100] By January 1752, the incoming
captain-general of Pará, Mendonça Furtado, was also able to report
on his investigations, basing his opinions on various interviews with
skilled backlanders in Pará, including Fonseca, and above all João
de Sousa Azevedo. Having completed another illegal roundtrip in
1749–1750, Azevedo was fully prepared to report on the rivers
of the West. Moreover, the following year he had been forced into
the royal service by Mendonça Gorjão and sent back to the Madeira
to construct canoes and huts for use of the border commission that
would ascend to Mato Grosso. João de Sousa informed the two
captains-general of Pará of his findings, and prepared a set of papers
which, for all their disorganization and rusticity, yielded insights
of value to Portugal.[101]

98. Rolim de Moura to Diogo de Mendonça Côrte Real, Cuiabá, 27 June and
8 Aug. 1751, IHGB/CU, arq. 1–2–4, fols. 1–4, 11; same to [same?], Vila Bela, 28
May 1752, *RIHGB*, CCLXIII (1964), 194–196. Two brief, impressionistic accounts
of the founding of Vila Bela are Henrique de Campos Ferreira Lima, "Vila Bela
da Santíssima Trindade de Mato Grosso—o seu fundador e a sua fundação,"
Congresso do mundo português, X, 291–301, and Virgílio Correia Filho, "Fundação de Vila Bela primeira capital de Mato Grosso," *Anais*, IV Congresso de
História Nacional (Rio, 1952), X, 31–52.

99. Mendonça Gorjão to Côrte Real, Pará, 1 and 3 Dec. 1751, and Bishop
Bulhões to Côrte Real, Pará, 12 Jan. 1752, IHGB/CU, arq. 1–2–9, fols. 74–92,
503–547. The letters are published in Arthur Cezar Ferreira Reis, *Limites e
demarcações na Amazônia brasileira* (2 vols., Rio, 1947–1948), II, 138–158.

100. Drafted sometime between Dec. 1750 and Jan. 1752, the reports of the
expedition are preserved in MS. copies in IHGB/CU, arq. 1–2–9, fols. 102–468,
and inventoried in *RIHGB*, LXVII:1 (1906), 92–93. The major writings are
Fonseca's "Navegação," and "Noticia," cited in note 83 above.

101. Mendonça Furtado to Côrte Real, Pará, 20 Jan. 1752, *AEP*, I, 181–190.

All the informants agreed that the Madeira-Mamoré-Guaporé rivers offered the most convenient line of communication to the Far West, for trade, travel, mails, or transport of heavy equipment. Although navigation on the route suffered from some eighteen to twenty rapids and hostile Indians, the informants still contrasted it favorably with that of the shorter though more difficult supply runs from São Paulo along the monsoon route, with its ferocious Paiaguá and over one hundred rapids, and the tedious overland march to Bahia and Rio de Janeiro through Goiás. High transport costs on the southern routes forced prices beyond the settlers' reach, prevented a steady flow of abundant, cheap imports, and reduced the purchase of slaves and accumulation of capital; and thus contributed to the decline of gold production. But if Pará supplied Mato Grosso, they claimed, the West would receive a higher volume of less expensive slaves, manufactures, and foodstuffs, mine production would revive, Belém would swell with the gold of the West, the royal treasury of Pará would finally cover its perennial deficit, and the Amazon North might emerge from its century of poverty. Missionaries could sail the rivers to bring the heathen into Christ's— and Portugal's—fold, and settlers would flow westward to populate the frontier and safeguard the mines from the everpresent threat of Spanish encroachments.

To be sure, the most convincing reason for the opening of the Madeira route was the security of the West. Heavy Portuguese traffic and the establishment of settlements or forts would assure control of the rivers, just as the transport of troops and supplies from Pará would guarantee the safety of the mines. Strategically placed settlements would also provide supply and rest stops for merchants and travelers, guard against Indian attacks, and serve as fiscal checkpoints for the registry of gold exports. The Madeira route, the informants believed, promised to be the outer wall of Brazilian defense, the major lifeline to the West, and the first channel of integration between the States of Brazil and Grão-Pará leading toward a greater Portuguese America.

On Azevedo's forced entrance into the royal service, see Mendonça Gorjão to Mota e Silva, Pará, 10 Sept. 1750, AHU, Pará, caixa 13, and petitions of Azevedo in BAPP, cod. 666, fols. 19–20, AHU, MT, maço 5, and BAPP, cod. 665, fol. 31. Azevedo expressed his opinions in his "Parecer" of 16 Jan. 1752, RIHGB, CLXXIX (1943), 185–203, a more complete version of which can be found in IHGB/CU, arq. 1–2–9, fols, 561–604, and in another "Parecer" of 26 Jan. 1752 in IHGB/CU, arq. 1–2–9, fols. 492–502.

With such fervent recommendations in hand, the king opened trade and navigation along the Madeira route in October 1752. To facilitate commerce, he exempted slave imports to Mato Grosso from the imposts (*entradas*) customarily levied on chattels entering mining districts and authorized the creation of a monopoly in Pará to export moderately priced salt to Mato Grosso.[102] Four years later, the newly founded Pará Company opened commercial relations with western merchants, and the colonial secretary ordered periodic material assistance dispatched from the royal treasury of Pará for the support of Crown operations in the West.[103] For the remainder of the century the Madeira route was indispensible to the maintenance and defense of the Brazilian West.[104]

The interests of state and freelances here coincided in measures which brought to fruition nearly two decades of imperial planning and frontier activity. Portuguese success in defending, defining, and integrating the West was clearly the result of the combined efforts, albeit haphazard and unplanned, of authorities and frontiersmen, and of the forceful posture each assumed relative to its international counterpart. Gusmão "bandeirized' state diplomacy, striking with iron purpose and logic toward well-defined objectives. The Spanish government's position was essentially defensive and sedentary, similar to that of its own freelances. Spain did initially challenge Portugal's claim to the West; and the projected invasion, though it never materialized, seemed to pose a threat to the mines. The threat itself, whatever its seriousness, prodded Portugal to take defensive measures. In this sense, Spanish policy, and the failure of authorities and Jesuits to implement it, both encouraged and enabled the Portuguese to secure the West and confirmed the outcome at the conference table. Portuguese freelances, clearly the most dynamic of the interacting groups, pursued commercial interests which, deflected and guided by the Jesuits, threw into focus rivers by which the West was circumscribed and incorporated into the empire. In

102. Royal resolution, 23 Oct. 1752, attached to consulta of Overseas Council, 7 Aug. 1752, *AGTM*, II:2, 341; two royal provisões, 14 Nov. 1752 to Mendonça Furtado, BAPP, cod. 884, docs. 17, 19; two provisões, 14 Nov. 1752 to Rolim de Moura, AHU, MT, maço 8.

103. Tomé Joaquim da Costa Côrte Real to Rolim de Moura, 7 July 1757, 22 Aug. 1758, *O Archivo* (Cuiabá, 1904–1905) I:1, 24; I:2, 52–53; Côrte Real to Bulhões, 8 July 1758, BAPP, cod. 668, fol. 103.

104. See my "Rivers & Empire: the Madeira Route and the Incorporation of the Brazilian Far West, 1737–1808" (Ph.D. diss., Yale University, 1970), Chapters 2–4.

the West the traditional nomadic-sedentary antagonism, which had marked the bandeirante-Jesuit encounters a century earlier in Guairá and Itatín, still worked to the Portuguese advantage. The fathers had performed admirable frontier services for Spain, but their inbred fear of Paulistas, and a well-developed sense of self-preservation, seemingly operated at critical times to undermine Spanish strategy. Nonetheless, whereas both Portuguese freelances and Jesuits often preferred to further their own interests when these interests seemed threatened or contained by imperial considerations, such Portuguese action fortuitously aided the state. Although the frontiersmen of Mato Grosso seemed to keep one step ahead of the metropolitan government, they followed the path of imperial interest, just as they violated state strategy only to fulfill state aspirations. Portuguese freelances were necessary to the winning of the West, but the state proved to be the sufficient agent. Freelances settled isolated nuclei and revealed strategic rivers; the state defined such rivers as boundaries and in so doing gained an area far more extensive than that actually held or traveled by freelances.

The state won space in the West—*espaço* in its temporal and spatial connotations—a vast, sparsely populated territory whose value to Portugal was, and indeed to Brazil still is, largely extrinsic and potential. Within the evolving geopolitical strategies of metropolitan ministers from Pombal to Linhares, Mato Grosso was viewed as the indispensable rearguard of Portugal's more valuable possessions, and accepted as a financial liability in return for its frontier services. For the duration of the colonial era, the sprawling captaincy-general remained an archipelago of impoverished, scattered outposts and settlements whose boom days lay in the past, and whose true value is only now being realized.

KENNETH R. MAXWELL:

The Generation of the 1790s and the Idea of Luso-Brazilian Empire

Between 1786 and 1808, critical changes occurred in the attitudes of Brazilians and Portuguese which were to have profound repercussions on the later development of Portuguese America. Internal and external influences combined and interacted to suggest a peculiarly Luso-Brazilian solution to the problems of nationalism and colonialism, republicanism and monarchy. This paper attempts to delineate some of these changes, to seek causes, and to explain results.

During October 1786, Thomas Jefferson, the envoy of the United States in France, received a letter from the ancient University of Montpellier signed only with the pseudonym *Vendek*. The writer indicated that he had a matter of great consequence to communicate, but as he was a foreigner he wished Jefferson to recommend a safe channel for correspondence. Jefferson did so at once. In a second letter *Vendek* declared himself a Brazilian. The slavery in which his country lay was "rendered each day more insupportable since the epoch of your glorious independence," he wrote. Brazilians had decided to follow the example of the North Americans, he continued, to break the chains that bound them to Portugal and "relive their liberty." To solicit the aid of the United States was the purpose of his visit to France. "Nature made us inhabitants of the same continent," *Vendek* told Jefferson, "and in consequence in some degree compatriots."[1]

Vendek, José Joaquim Maia e Barbalho, who arranged a secret rendezvous and met Thomas Jefferson near Nîmes, was a native of Rio de Janeiro.[2] He had entered the faculty of medicine at Montpellier in 1786, having previously matriculated at the University of Coimbra in Portugal where he studied mathematics.[3] Maia may have

1. *Vendek* to Jefferson, Montpellier, 9 October 1786; *Vendek* to Jefferson, Montpellier, 21 November 1786; Jefferson to *Vendek*, Paris, 26 December 1786; *Vendek* to Jefferson, Montpellier, 5 January 1787, *Anuário do Museu da Inconfidência* (hereafter cited as *AMI*) II (Ouro Preto, 1953) 11–13.
2. Thomas Jefferson to Mr. Jay, Marseille, 4 May 1787, *ibid.*, 13–19.
3. "Estudantes Brasileiros em Coimbra 1772–1872," *ABNRJ*, LXII (1940) 174;

been commissioned by merchants in Rio de Janeiro to enter into contact with the American envoy.[4] Probably he was one of a group of students who during the early 1780s had joined hands at Coimbra and vowed to work for the independence of their homeland.[5] An accurate account of Jefferson's encouraging but non-committal response to *Vendek* reached Brazil via Domingos Vidal Barbosa, another Brazilian student at Montpellier.[6]

Maia and Vidal Barbosa were not alone in their educational accomplishments or their political enthusiasms. Between the Marquis of Pombal's reform of the University of Coimbra in 1772 and 1785, three hundred Brazilian-born students had matriculated there.[7] Others continued their studies or went directly to the faculty of medicine at Montpellier, where fifteen Brazilian-born students matriculated between 1767 and 1793.[8] Vidal Barbosa, a landowner from the captaincy of Minas Gerais, was an enthusiastic propagandist for the writings of the Abbé Raynal, passages of which he was in the habit of reciting by heart.[9] Raynal was a dominating influence in the thinking of many educated Brazilians during the 1780s. His *Histoire philosophique et politique des établissements et du commerce des Européens dans les deux Indes* was invariably part of the greatest private libraries in the colony, and a much quoted textbook for many of those inspired by the example of the United States.[10]

Manoel Xavier de Vasconcelos Pedrosa, "Estudantes Brasileiros na Faculdade de Medicina de Montpellier no fim do século XVIII," *RIHGB*, CCXLIII (April–June, 1959) 35–71.

4. Such was the view expressed in *Autos de devassa da inconfidência mineira* (hereafter cited as *ADIM*), (7 vols., Rio de Janeiro, 1936–1938) II, 81–95. It is difficult to identify with any certainty the merchants in Rio de Janeiro who might have been implicated in this enterprise. Possibly the idea had something to do with Francisco de Araujo Pereira, for he is cited at a later date as being openly critical of the colonial administration (*ADIM*, I, 280), and he was, according to Viceroy Lavradio, the only merchant in the city worthy of the name; the rest Lavradio dismissed as being simple commissaries (Lavradio, *Relatório*, *RIHGB*, IV [2nd edition, 1863] 453.)

5. Visconde de Barbacena to Martinho de Melo e Castro, Vila Rica, 11 July 1789, *AMI*, II, 68.

6. Jefferson made a detailed report on his conversation with *Vendek* and his response to the request for aid, Jefferson to Mr. Jay, Marseille, 4 May 1787, *ibid.*, 17.

7. "Estudantes Brasileiros em Coimbra," 141–181.

8. "Estudantes Brasileiros . . . Montpellier," *RIHGB*, CCXLIII, 40.

9. *Ibid.*, 41, 48–50; for comments on Vidal Barbosa's habit of citing Raynal, *ADIM*, II, 59.

10. For the influence of Raynal on the thinking of Luís Vieira da Silva and

Raynal's *Histoire* contained an extensive account of Brazil, presented a contemptuous picture of Portugal, condemned British political and economic influence, and recommended that the ports of Brazil be opened to the trade of all nations.[11] During 1785, José Bonifácio de Andrada e Silva, a *Paulista*, who matriculated at Coimbra in the same year as Maia, was writing poems, heavy with a bewildering profusion of heroes, including Rousseau, Locke, Voltaire, Pope, Virgil, and Camões, which attacked "the horrid monster of despotism."[12] José Alvares Maciel, son of a wealthy merchant, landowner, and tax farmer in Vila Rica (today Ouro Preto), and a contemporary of Maia at Coimbra, traveled to England.[13] Maciel spent a year in Britain studying manufacturing techniques and whenever possible obtaining accounts of the American Revolution. He discussed the possibility of Brazilian independence with sympathetic English merchants.[14] Even on the far off frontiers of Portuguese America ideas and opinions subversive to the colonial system were aired. During 1786, Antônio Pires da Silva Ponte was denounced to Martinho de Melo e Castro, secretary of state for the overseas dominions, for his rebellious discourses in Mato Grosso. Ponte had claimed that his homeland, Minas Gerais, would become "the head of a great kingdom."[15]

---

the members of the Literary Society of Rio, see *ADIM*, I, 445–465, II, 95, IV, 207, and *ABNRJ*, LXI, 384, 409–412, 435. Also "Relação completa dos livros pelos autores," Rio de Janeiro, 10 April 1791, [the books of Dr. Antonio Teixeira da Costa] cited by Herculano Gomes Mathias, *A coleção da casa dos contos de Ouro Preto* (Rio de Janeiro, 1966) 145; and "Sequestro feito em 1794 nos bens que forão achados do bacharel Mariano José Pereira da Fonseca extrahido do respectivo processo," *RIHGB*, LXIII (1901) 14–18.

11. *Histoire philosophique et politique des établissements et du commerce des Européens dans les deux Indes.* (Amsterdam, 1770), 4 vols. in 8. For wider ranging discussions of intellectual currents in late colonial Brazil, see Alexander Marchant, "Aspects of the Enlightenment in Brazil," in A. P. Whitaker, ed., *Latin America and the Enlightenment* (2nd edition, Ithaca, N.Y., 1961) 95–118; E. Bradford Burns, "The Enlightenment in Two Colonial Libraries." *Journal of the History of Ideas*, XXV (1964) 430–438; E. Bradford Burns, *Nationalism in Brazil: A Historical Survey* (New York, 1968) especially 23–26. And for a fascinating and broadly based discussion of Portuguese intellectual development see "The 'Kaffirs of Europe,' the Renaissance, and the Enlightenment," in C. R. Boxer, *The Portuguese Seaborne Empire, 1415–1825* (London, 1969), 340–366.

12. Octávio Tarquínio de Sousa, *História dos fundadores do império do Brasil: I, José Bonifácio* (Rio de Janeiro, 1960) 63.

13. Maciel matriculated in 1782 and graduated in 1785. Maia matriculated in 1783, "Estudantes Brasileiros em Coimbra," 172, 174.

14. *ADIM*, II, 40, 251; IV, 400.

15. José de Lacerda e Almeida to Martinho de Melo e Castro, 24 September,

The designation of Minas Gerais as the potential leader of an emancipated colony was not surprising. The captaincy had become the cultural center of late colonial Brazil.[16] Among the native-born whites, there existed a highly literate élite. For forty years rich *mineiros* had been sending their sons to the University of Coimbra. In 1786, twelve of the twenty-seven Brazilians matriculated at Coimbra were from Minas, and in 1787, ten of nineteen.[17] Doyen of the older generation of Brazilian-born graduates was the gracious poet Cláudio Manuel da Costa, a wealthy Vila Rica lawyer, who had entered Coimbra in 1749. In 1759 he had been elected a member of the *Academia Brasilica dos Renascidos* of Bahia, a short-lived literary and historical association, one of the few enterprises which had genuinely sought to embrace the whole of Portuguese America as its parish. Accumulating landed estates and slaves, the successful young Brazilian had been appointed secretary to the government of Minas, a post he held between 1762 and 1765 and again from 1769 to 1773. In 1771 he was appointed attorney to the Third Order of Saint Francis of Vila Rica, one of the most prestigious sodalities in Minas' capital.[18]

The poet's elegant town house was a gathering place for the intellectuals of the captaincy. Among his regular visitors during the 1780s was the superior crown magistrate (*ouvidor*) of Vila Rica, Tomás Antônio Gonzaga, an ambitious and fastidious legalist, son of one of Pombal's confidants. Gonzaga's father was a Brazilian-born magistrate who had served as ouvidor of Pernambuco, as a judge of the Bahian High Court, intendant-general of gold, first minister of the Inspection House of Bahia, and as a judge of the High Court of Oporto. He had personally presented his son's dissertation on the natural law to Pombal. The treatise was dedicated to the marquis, described in the preface as "that hero and lover of

1786, Mato Grosso, maço 12. I am grateful to David Davidson of Cornell University for drawing this important letter to my attention.

16. See comments by C. R. Boxer, "Some Literary Sources for the History of Brazil in the Eighteenth Century" (Oxford, 1967).

17. "Estudantes Brasileiros em Coimbra," 181–187.

18. Alberto Lamego, *Mentiras históricas* (Rio de Janeiro, 1947) 113–120; "Sequestro," Cláudio Manuel da Costa, *ADIM*, I, 356–364; "Traslado dos sequestros," *ADIM*, V, 263–276; M. Rodrigues Lapa, *As "Cartas Chilenas": Um problema histórico e filológico, com prefácio de Afonso Pena Júnior* (Rio de Janeiro, 1958) 28, 37; Lúcio José dos Santos, *A Inconfidência Mineira: papel de Tiradentes* (São Paulo, 1927) 234–239.

true science." Tomás Antônio Gonzaga was born in Oporto but brought up almost entirely in Brazil. He had attended the Jesuit college at Bahia, witnessing the expulsion of the Black Robes in 1759. He was nominated ouvidor of Vila Rica in 1782. Long an admirer of the works of Cláudio Manuel da Costa, he himself was a poet of merit and originality. The two men formed the center of a group which embraced Ignácio José de Alvarenga Peixoto, ouvidor of São João d'El Rei, and Luís Vieira da Silva, canon of the cathedral of Mariana, the episcopal seat of Minas Gerais.[19]

Ignácio José de Alvarenga Peixoto, a Brazilian graduate of Coimbra, had composed some fulsome verses in honor of the Marquis of Pombal and his family. His appointment as ouvidor of the *comarca* of Rio das Mortes in Minas Gerais was a consequence of these poetic endeavors. He himself selected the post because of his vast landed estates, slave holdings, and mining interests in the area, though the Portuguese government did not ordinarily sanction such initiative.[20] Luís Vieira was a well known and persuasive preacher, much in demand on solemn and festive occasions, of which there were many in the ecclesiastical calendar of Minas Gerais. An erudite and thoughtful cleric in his early fifties, he had studied at the Jesuit college in São Paulo during the 1750s, and was appointed to the chair of Philosophy in the seminary at Mariana in 1757. He was elected commissary of the Third Order of Saint Francis of Vila Rica in 1770. Luís Vieira was outspoken in his enthusiasm for the events in North America. He held that the European powers had no right to dominion in America. The Portuguese monarchy had spent nothing on the conquest of Brazil, and the Brazilians themselves had restored Bahia to the Crown from the Dutch, and ransomed Rio de Janeiro from the French. Luís Vieira, a man who had never left Brazil, was close in opinion to those conspiratorial students who had attempted to negotiate with Thomas Jefferson in France.[21]

19. *Obras completas de Tomás Antônio Gonzaga: I, Poesias, cartas chilenas*, ed., M. Rodrigues Lapa (Rio de Janeiro, 1957) ix–xv; "Auto de inquirição summario de testemunhas," Vila Rica, 26 May 1798, ADIM, II, 441–452; "Direito Natural accommodado ao estado civil catolico, offerecido ao Ill° e Ex° Sn^r Sebastião José de Carvalho e Mello, Marquês de Pombal, por Thomás Antônio Gonzaga," BNLCP, códice 29.

20. M. Rodrigues Lapa, *Vida e obra de Alvarenga Peixoto* (Rio de Janeiro, 1960) x, xxvii, xxviii.

21. Conego Raimundo Trinidade, *São Francisco de Assis de Ouro Preto*

The Vila Rica circle was not the only group of like-minded and intelligent men who met informally to discuss poetry, philosophy, and the events in Europe and America. Similar groups of lawyers and writers met in São João d'El Rei and elsewhere in the captaincy for conversation and cards.[22] The members of the Vila Rica circle, however, by the quality of their writing, and by their position, influence, and wealth, stood at the apex of Minas society. Books and information often reached them more rapidly than official dispatches which had to pass through the cumbersome bureaucracy from Lisbon to the secretariat of the captaincy. The canon Vieira's cosmopolitan collection of books, some 600 volumes all told, contained Robertson's *Histoire de l'Amerique*, and the *Encyclopédie*, as well as the works of Bielfeld, Voltaire, and Condillac.[23] Cláudio Manuel da Costa was reputed to have translated Adam Smith's *Wealth of Nations*.[24]

Literate and open-minded, the intellectual élite of Minas Gerais proved creative and original.[25] The history of the captaincy became

(Rio de Janeiro, 1951) 197–200, 222–228; "Avaliação dos livros sequestrados, conego Luís Vieira da Silva," *ADIM*, I, 445–465; "Auto de perguntas," Rio de Janeiro, 20 November 1789, *ADIM*, IV, 292–293; "Auto de continuação de perguntas" Rio de Janeiro, 21 July 1790 (*sic*; this must be 1791, for the interrogating judge in this instance, Chancellor Vasconcellos Coutinho, did not arrive in Rio de Janeiro until late December 1790) *ibid.*, 304; Vicente Vieira da Mota, Witness, Vila Rica, 23 June 1789, *ADIM*, I, 110–111; Vicente Vieira da Mota, Witness, Vila Rica, 3 August 1789, *ADIM*, III, 336; "Auto de perguntas," Rio de Janeiro, 19 July 1791, *ADIM*, V, 19–20; *AMI*, II, 68.

22. Rodrigues Lapa, *Alvarenga Peixoto*, xxxii.

23. "Avaliação dos livros sequestrados," *ADIM*, I, 458; Also see José Ferreira Carrato, *Igreja, Iluminismo, e Escolas Mineiras Colonias: Notas sôbre a cultura da decadencia mineira setecentista* (São Paulo, 1968) 113–114; and Eduardo Frieiro, *O Diabo na Livraria do Cônego* (Belo Horizonte, 1957).

24. According to Santos, *Inconfidência mineira*, 237, "esse manuscripto foi sequestrado e perdeu-se. . . ." This information probably came from Joaquim Noberto de Sousa Silva, "Commemoração do centenário de Cláudio Manuel da Costa," *RIHGB*, LIII: I (1890) 150, who cited Cônego Januário da Cunha Barbosa's *Parnaso Brazileiro*.

25. There is a very large bibliography on the cultural flowering of Minas Gerais during the late eighteenth century; especially useful studies are, Augusto de Lima Junior, *A capitania de Minas Gerais, origens e formação* (3rd edition, Belo Horizonte, 1965) 123, 191–193; José Ferreira Carrato, *As Minas Gerais e os Primórdios do Caraça* (São Paulo, 1963) 57–62; Fritz Teixeira de Salles, *Associações religiosas no ciclo do ouro* (Belo Horizonte, 1963) 27, 36, 65, 71; Sílvio de Carvalho Vasconcellos, "Architectura colonial Mineira," *Iº Seminário de estudos mineiros, Universidade de Minas Gerais* (Belo Horizonte, 1956) 67; Curt Lange, "Música Religiosa de Minas Gerais," *MEC* (Ministério da Educação e Cultura, Rio de Janeiro, May–June, 1958) 19–25; Francisco Antônio Lopes,

the theme of Cláudio Manuel da Costa's epic poem *Vila Rica*, and the subject of a lengthy prose dissertation by him replete with statistical tables.[26] During 1781 Alvarenga Peixoto reflected this powerful self-awareness in his *canto genetlíaco*, an enthusiastic apology for the riches, men, and promise of the Brazilian land. He compared the deeds of the *Mineiros* to those of Hercules, Ulysses, and Alexander. And he did not fail to include "strong and valiant" slaves in his panegyric. In a portentous phrase which could well have applied to the rest of his countrymen, the poet asserted: "They are worthy of attention."[27]

Gonzaga, Cláudio Manuel da Costa, and the canon Luís Vieira were men "who have ascendancy over the spirits of the people," the commandant of the Minas Dragoons told Alvarenga Peixoto in 1789.[28] All three were involved in the plot to foment an armed uprising against the Portuguese Crown during late 1788 and early 1789.[29] Much later an inquiry into the implication of one of the conspirators described the intention of the Minas movement as

---

História da construção da igreja do Carmo de Ouro Preto (Rio de Janeiro, 1951); for the extensive bibliography on the Minas Baroque, an excellent introduction is provided by Germain Bazin, *L'Architecture Religieuse Baroque au Brésil*, (2 vols.; Paris and São Paulo, 1956) I, 173–213; and by Robert C. Smith Jr., "The Arts in Brazil: Baroque Architecture," in Harold Livermore, ed., *Portugal and Brazil*, (Oxford, 1963) 349; and his "Colonial Architecture of Minas Gerais," *The Art Bulletin*, XXI (1939) 110–142.

26. "Noticia da capitania de Minas Gerais por Cláudio Manuel da Costa," IHGP, *lata* 22, doc., 13.

27. Rodrigues Lapa, *Alvarenga Peixoto*, xli, 33–38.

28. "Continuação de perguntas feitas ao . . . Alvarenga Peixoto," Rio de Janeiro, 14 January 1790, *ADIM*, IV, 138.

29. For a summary of the evidence against the conspirators, see Desembargador José Pedro Machado Coelho Torres to Luís de Vasconcellos e Sousa, Rio de Janeiro, 11 December 1789, with "a lista das pessoas . . . dando hum idea das prezumsoens, out prova que rezulta contra cada hum deles," AHU, Minas Gerais, caixa 92, folder no. 47. Some discussion in English of the Minas conspiracy can be found in Manoel Cardoso, "Another document on the Inconfidência Mineira," *HAHR*, XXXII (1952) 540–551; and Alexander Marchant, "Tiradentes and the Conspiracy of Minas," *HAHR*, XXI (1941) 239–257; the standard account in Portuguese remains Lúcio José dos Santos, *A Inconfidência Mineira*, supplemented recently by two articles by Herculano Gomes Mathias, "O Tiradentes e a cidade do Rio de Janeiro," *Anais do Museu Histórico Nacional*, XVI (1966) 102, and "Inconfidência e Inconfidentes," *Anais do congresso comemorativo do bicentenário da transferência da sede do governo do Brasil da cidade do Salvador para o Rio de Janeiro* (3 vols.; Rio de Janeiro, 1967) III, 250; and by Célia Nunes Galvão Quirino dos Santos, *A Inconfidência Mineira* (Separata do Tomo XX dos *Anais do Museu Paulista*, São Paulo, 1966).

being "to change the government of Minas from monarchical to democratic."[30] At the time, however, as far as the evidence shows, the word democratic was never used. The American Revolution was thought especially pertinent because the Minas conspirators saw the course of events in North America as remarkably similar to their own situation. "Nothing caused the break [between Britain and her colonies] but the great duties that were imposed," one of the conspirators claimed.[31] The demands of the Portuguese government that the colossal arrears due on the royal fifth of the gold production of the captaincy be made up by the imposition of a per capita tax (derrama) on the Minas population, seemed all too reminiscent of the duties levied on the American colonists. The conspirators concluded that "the Abbé Raynal had been a writer of great vision, because he had prognosticated the uprising in North America, and the captaincy of Minas Gerais because of the imposition of the derrama was now in the same circumstances."[32] Their intention was to establish a republican and constitutional state in Minas Gerais. Parliaments were to be set up in each town.[33] These would be subordinate to a supreme parliament (um parlamento principal). A university was to be founded in Vila Rica.[34] The plotters contemplated the total abrogation of past laws and statutes.[35]

How far the institutions to be established imitated those in North America is not clear. There is some evidence of opposition to a slavish imitation of the North American example—at least as far as the arms of the state were concerned, and perhaps on more fundamental matters.[36] However, circulating among the conspirators was the Recueil de Loix Constitutives des États—Unis de l'Amérique, published in Philadelphia in 1778, which contained the Articles of

30. The reference came concerning a petition by Padre Oliveira Rolim, one of the priests implicated in the plot, August, 1822, RAPM, IX (1904) 624.

31. "Continuação de perguntas feitas a Francisco de Paula Freire de Andrade," Rio de Janeiro, 29 July 1791, ADIM, IV, 230.

32. "Auto de perguntas feitas ao Freire de Andrade," Rio de Janeiro, 16 November 1789, ADIM, IV, 207.

33. "Continuação de perguntas feitas ao vigário . . . Carlos Corrêa," Rio de Janeiro, 27 November 1789, ADIM, IV, 171.

34. Sentença de Alçada (1792), Santos, Inconfidência Mineira, 591.

35. "Joaquim Silverio dos Reis and Carlos Corrêa, auto de acareação," Rio de Janeiro, 13 July 1791, ADIM, IV, 193.

36. "Continuação de perguntas feitas ao . . . Alvarenga Peixoto," Rio de Janeiro, 14 January 1790, ADIM, IV, 147.

Confederation, and the constitutions of Pennsylvania, New Jersey, Delaware, Maryland, the Carolinas, and Massachusetts.[37] The conspirators also possessed constitutional commentaries by Raynal and Mably.[38] Gonzaga, despite his disparagement of democracy in his treatise on the natural law, was even at that time a firm supporter of the contractual nature of government. The king, the young Gonzaga had written, was a mandatory of the people, a minister of God, the end of whose rule was the utility of the people. Gonzaga's acrimonious dispute with the government Luís da Cunha Menezes of Minas, immortalized in his *Cartas Chilenas*, had centered on the dangers of arbitrary rule. His memorials to court during the 1780s strongly emphasized the legal and moral restraints on the actions and power of the executive.[39]

The minas plot was betrayed. With others, Gonzaga, Cláudio Manuel da Costa, Alvarenga Peixoto, and the canon Luís Vieira, were arrested. The ideology of the Minas conspiracy, however, influenced by the success of the American Revolution and the impact in Brazil of the ideas of Raynal and others had projected the movement into a much greater context. There had been uprisings far more damaging in lives and property before. The Vila Rica uprising of 1720, for example, was more dramatic in action and more bloody than the non-events of 1788–1789. But no previous plot had possessed motivations so fundamentally anti-colonial and so consciously nationalistic. Members of an important segment of that group in society on whom the metropolitan government most relied for the

37. "Translado e Appensos, No. 26; neste lugar e debaixo do No. 26 vai apo aos Autos originais o livro em Frances intitulado, Recueil des Loix Constitutives des Etats Unis de l'Amerique," AHU, Minas Gerais, caixa 92. This book was lost, stolen or strayed from the archives, but I have been able to locate a copy of *Recueil des Loix Constitutives des Colonies Angloises confédérées sous la dénomination d'États-Unis de l'Amérique-Septentrionale* (Philadelphia, 1778) in the rare book collection of The Newberry Library, Chicago. This is certainly an edition of the work in the hands of the Minas conspirators, the short title page corresponding exactly to the listing in the confiscations.

38. "Item, le droit public de l'Europe de Mably, tres volumes em oitavo," avaliação dos livros, *ADIM*, I, 461; and for other books by Mably, "Termo de encerramento, Marianna," *ADIM*, I, 466.

39. There is a vast bibliography on the *Cartas Chilenas*, their attribution, identification of the characters, and so on. Hardly a literary scholar or historian in Portugal or Brazil has not at some time discussed the work. I have relied heavily on M. Rodrigues Lapa's masterly, *As "Cartas Chilenas"*, though it is unlikely that even this profound and careful study will prove to be the definitive work.

exercise of power at the local level, in one of Brazil's most important, most populous, and most strategically placed captaincies, had dared to think that they might live without Portugal. Inspired by the example of North America and by current political theory, they had questioned what had been unquestioned. The new mental climate was not something that could be concretely defined, but it was obvious to all, and most especially to the agents of the metropolitan government in Brazil.[40] Men in Minas had thought they could be free, independent, and republican.

The conspiracy in Minas Gerais had occurred at a special moment in time. The plot was concerted before the French Revolution. But the arrests, the trial, and the sentencing of those involved, coincided with growing revolutionary turmoil in Europe. Rumors of possible French invasion had been bandied around among the conspirators, but they meant the France of the Old Regime. The chronological relationship of the Minas conspiracy to the French Revolution is important. The Minas oligarchs had believed they could control and manipulate the popular will. They had taken as their example and American Revolution, where political readjustments had taken place without social upheaval. But the example of the American patriots had not prepared them for the events of the French Revolution, particularly not for the spectacular repercussions of the French Revolution in the Americas. The revolt of the slaves in the French sugar island of Saint Domingue during 1792 brought an awful awakening to those slaveowners who had talked naively of republics and revolt while ignoring the social and racial consequences of their words. The British scientist, traveler, and writer, John Barrow, who was in Rio de Janeiro during 1792, noted the change "black power" had brought. "The secret spell that caused the Negro to tremble in the presence of the white man is in a great degree dissolved," he wrote. "The supposed superiority by which a hundred of the former were kept in awe and submission by one of the latter is no longer acknowledged."[41] Martinho de Melo e Castro recognized at once the threat the Saint Domingue revolt posed for

40. See, for example, the comments by Desembargador Torres, *ADIM*, VI, 932–403, and by Chancellor Vasconcellos Coutinho to Martinho de Melo e Castro, Rio de Janeiro, 30 July 1791, AHU, Minas Gerais, caixa 94.

41. John Barrow, *A Voyage to Cochinchina in the Years 1792 and 1793* (London, 1806) 117–118.

Brazil. He warned the governors against "the pernicious and perverse intent of the [Jacobin] clubs established in France to propagate the abominable and destructive principles of liberty, in order to effect by these means the fatal revolution." And he warned that it was these abominable principles that caused "the fire of revolt and insurrection that made the slaves rise against their masters . . . in Santo Domingo."[42]

The innocuous Literary Society of Rio de Janeiro, with its dedication to Raynal and Mably, and its alleged sympathy for the Minas conspirators, was an obvious target for the nervous colonial administration. In 1794, its members were arrested and subjected to prolonged interrogations. The society, founded in 1785 by Luís de Vasconcellos e Sousa, the former viceroy, had attempted to form a secret inner conclave where "good faith and secrecy might be maintained among the members." Democratically constituted, it was to discuss "philosophy in all its aspects." Among the papers confiscated from Jacinto José da Silva, a graduate in medicine from Montpellier, were two remarkable letters from a colleague, Manuel José de Novais de Almeida, which dramatically underlined the impact of the revolt in Saint Domingue on his contemporaries. In February 1791, Dr. Novais de Almeida had written enthusiastically of the "equality of men." But by May 25, 1792, his comments had a different tone. "I am very worried with respect to the Americas," he told da Silva. "What happened in French [America] demonstrates what might one day happen in ours, which god permitting I shall never see, for I am a friend of humanity. . . . Sell the slaves that you possess, have the generosity to grant them their freedom, you will have fewer enemies."[43]

42. Martinho de Melo e Castro to Bernardo José de Lorena, Lisbon, 21 February, 1792, *DI*, XLV (1924) 449–452.

43. "Autto do exame que fizerao o Dez[embargador] Ouv[idor] G[eneral] do Crime Francisco Alvarez de Andrade, e o Dr. Intendente General do Ouro, Caetano Pinto de Vasconcellos MonteNegro, em todos os Papeis do Dr. Jacinto José da Silva," Rio de Janeiro, 8 January, 1795, which together with the rest of the documents concerning the Literary Society is published in *ABNRJ*, LXI (1939) 241–523, especially 364–370. The nervousness of the Rio administration had been very obvious the year before (1794), when the Brazilian Juiz de Fora of Rio turned over an anonymous letter he had received recommending an uprising and the methods by which it should be carried out, "Autos de Exame e Averiguação sobre o a autor de uma carta anonima escrita ao juiz de fora do Rio de Janeiro, Dr. Balrazar da Silva Lisboa (1793)," *ABNRJ*, LX, 261–313.

The example of the Antillean revolt was especially pertinent for white Brazilians. In Minas Gerais the population in 1776, excluding Indians, was over 300,000, or 20 percent of the total population of Portuguese America. Over 50 percent of the population of Minas was black, and the remainder equally divided between *pardos* and whites. In 1786, the number of freemen to slaves was placed at 188,712 to 174,135.[44] In Bahia, the capital city of Salvador had a population of 40,000 during the 1790s, and the total for the captaincy was near 280,000, or 18 percent of the total population of Portuguese America. Half the population was slave. José da Silva Lisboa, a Brazilian graduate of Coimbra and Professor of Philosophy in Bahia, estimated that a mere quarter of the population was white.[45]

The only racial overtones during the Minas conspiracy had come in the form of vague comments attributed to Manoel da Costa Capanema, and the evidence which linked him to the conspirators was so slight that he was absolved by the court of inquiry (*Alçada*).[46] José Alvares Maciel had regarded the presence of so large a percentage of blacks in the population as a possible threat to the new republic, should the promise of their liberation by the Portuguese induce them to oppose the native whites. Alvarenga Peixoto recommended that the slaves be granted freedom, which would make them the passionate defenders of the new state, committed to its survival. Maciel, however, pointed out that such a solution might be self-defeating, for proprietors would be left with no one to work the mines. The conspirators appear to have reached a compromise solution whereby only the native-born black and mulatto

44. "Taboa das habitantes da capitania de Minas Gerais, 1776, noticia da capitania de Minas Gerais," IHGB, lata 22, doc., 13; Dauril Alden, "The Population of Brazil in the late Eighteenth Century: A Preliminary Survey," *HAHR*, XLIII (1963) 173–205; "População da provincia de Minas Gerais, 1776–1823," *RAPM*, IV (1899) 249–276.

45. "Mappa da enumeração da gente e povo desta capitania da Bahia, December, 1780," *ABNRJ*, XXXII (1910) 480; Thales de Azevedo, *Povoamento da cidade do Salvador* (São Paulo, 1955) 201; José da Silva Lisboa to Domingos Vandelli, Bahia, 18 October, 1781, *ABNRJ*, XXXII (1910) 505; Vilhena put the proportion of whites at nearer a third, Luiz dos Santos Vilhena, *Recopilação de noticias soteropolitanas e Brasilicas, contidas em XX cartas (1802)* ed. by Braz do Amaral (3 vols.; Bahia, 1922, 1935) I, 49.

46. The statement attributed to him was: "Estes branquinhos do Reino que nos quirem tomar a terra cedo os havemos de deitar fora," Sentença da Alçada, Santos, *Inconfidência Mineira*, 607–617.

slaves would be freed in the interests of the defense of the state.[47] The proposition was itself a startling one for 1789, but the conspirators seem to have totally underestimated the consequences of their actions. They assumed the situation could be controlled with ease, just as they assumed the uprising could be instigated, manipulated, and controlled in their own interests.

In the climate of opinion that followed the Saint Domingue revolt, the discovery of plans for an armed uprising by the mulatto artisans of Bahia during 1798 had a very special impact; the plans demonstrated what thinking whites had already begun to realize: ideas of social equality propagated within a society where a mere third of the population was white would inevitably be interpreted in racial terms. The Bahian affair revealed the politicization of levels of society barely concerned with the Minas conspiracy. The middle-aged lawyers, magistrates, and clerics in Minas Gerais (most of them opulent, members of racially exclusive sodalities, and slave-owners) contrasted markedly with the young mulatto artisans, soldiers, sharecroppers, and salaried school teachers implicated in the Bahian plot. Embittered and anticlerical, the Bahian mulattoes were as opposed to rich Brazilians as to Portuguese dominion. They welcomed social turmoil, proposed the overthrow of existing structures, and sought an egalitarian and democratic society where differences of race would be no impediment to employment and social mobility. The pardo tailor, João de Deos, who at the time of his arrest possessed no more than 80 reis and eight children, proclaimed that "All [Brazilians] would become Frenchmen, in order to live in equality and abundance. . . . They would destroy the public officials, attack the monasteries, open the port . . . and reduce all to an entire revolution, so that all might be rich and taken out of poverty, and that the differences between white, black and brown would be extinguished, and that all without discrimination would be admitted to positions and occupations."[48]

It was not the North American patriots that provided the example for João de Deos and his colleagues. It was the sans-culottes. It was

47. "Perguntas feitas a José Alvares Maciel," Rio de Janeiro, 26 November, 1789, *ADIM*, IV, 398.
48. "Denuncia publica, jurada . . . que da Joaquim José da Veiga, homen pardo forro . . . ," 27 August 1798, *ADIB*, I, 8; Cel. Ignácio Accioli de Cerqueira e Silva, *Memorias históricas e políticas da Bahia* (hereafter cited as *MHPB*), ed. Braz do Amaral (6 vols.; Bahia, 1940) III, 93.

not the constitutional niceties of the United States that inspired
them. It was the slogans of the Paris mob. Handwritten manifestoes
appeared throughout the city on August 12 of 1798.[49] Addressed to
the "Republican Bahian people" in the name of the "supreme
tribunal of Bahian democracy," the manifestoes called for the ex-
termination of the "detestable metropolitan yoke of Portugal."[50]
Clergy who preached against popular liberty were threatened. "All
citizens, especially mulattoes and blacks," were told that "all are
equal, there will be no differences, there will be freedom, equality
and fraternity."[51] There was no equivocation over slavery: "All
black and brown slaves are to be free so that there will be no slavery
whatsoever."[52] The government would be "Democratic, free and
independent."[53] "The happy time of our liberty is about to arrive,
the time when all will be brothers, the time when all will be equal."[54]

Long before they had concerted even the most rudimentary plan,
the Bahian artisans were caught red-handed.[55] The causes of the
plot had been an amalgam of social resentments, high food prices,
and the impact of the revolutionary slogans of France. The appoint-

49. F. Borges de Barros, "Copia de varios papeis sediciosos que em alguns
lugares públicos deste cidade se fixarão na manha do dia 12 de agosto de 1798,"
Anais do Arquivo Público da Bahia, II (1917) 143–146; Carlos Guilherme Mota,
"Ideia de revolução no Brasil no final do século XVIII" (mestrado, cadeira de
história de civilização moderna e contemporânea, Universidade de São Paulo,
1967). I am most grateful to Professor Mota for the opportunity of using his
valuable unpublished work. For a brief account in English of the Bahian plot see
R. R. Palmer, *The Age of Democratic Revolution*, II, 513, Two documentary collections are available. *A Inconfidência da Bahia, Devassas e Sequestros* (hereafter cited as *ADIB*) (2 vols.; Rio de Janeiro, 1931); "Autos de devassas do levantamento e sedição intentados na Bahia em 1798," *Anais do Arquivo Público
da Bahia*, XXXV, XXXVI (1959–1961). The most important recent study is a detailed quantitive article by Katia M. de Queiros Mattoso, "Conjoncture et
Société au Brésil à la fin du XVIIIe Siècle: Prix et Salaires à la veille de la
révolution des Alfaiates, Bahia 1798," *Cahiers des Amériques Latines*, V (Jan.–
June, 1970) 33–53.
  50. "Aviso ao clero e ao povo Bahinense indouto," *MHPB*, III, 110.
  51. "Prelo," *MHPB*, III, 109.
  52. "Denuncia pública . . . que da o capitão do regimento auxiliar dos homens
pretos Joaquim José de Santa Anna," *ADIB*, I, 13.
  53. "Auto . . . para proceder a devassa pela rebelião e levantamento pro-
jectada nesta cidade, para se estabelecer no continente do Brasil, hum governo
democratico . . . ," 28 August 1798, *ADIB*, I, 7.
  54. "Aviso," *MHPB*, III, 106.
  55. "Os conspiradores que foram presos," *MHPB*, III, 99–102; also see
account by Braz do Amaral, *ibid.*, 96–97, and Afonso Ruy, *A primeira revolução
social brasileira (1798)* (São Paulo, 1942).

ment of a white *sargento-mor* as commandant of the auxiliary regiment of free pardos crossed racial lines, and placed the mulatto regiment in an unfavorable relationship with the regiment of free blacks, the famous *Henriques*, with its black commandant colonel.[56] The price of manioc flour, the basic subsistence food, had risen during the previous four years from 640 reis per *alqueire* to between 1280 and 1600 reis.[57] "The most vile meat imaginable was selling for prices twice what it was worth," according to the Professor of Greek in Salvador, Luís dos Santos Vilhena.[58] The mulatto artisans and soldiers, many of them literate, had been receptive to revolutionary ideology.

But the appearance of the manifestoes in Bahia, the demand for "liberty, equality and fraternity," and the racial composition of the conspiratorial conclave, provoked a reaction out of all proportion to the incidents themselves. Since 1792, slaveowners throughout the Americas had barely hidden their concern that the revolution in the Caribbean might prove contagious. For slaveowners in Brazil at least, the actions of Bahian mulattoes made the contagion a concrete reality. After 1798 all white men in Portuguese America faced the question posed by Admiral Campbell, commandant of the Brazilian squadron of the Portuguese Navy during the early nineteenth century: was it indeed true that "the transactions at St. Domingo had plainly evinced that there was no stability in the sovereignty of whites in a country necessarily worked by blacks?"[59]

The government in Lisbon suspected that more important and influential men might be behind the Bahian conspiracy, a concern understandable in the light of events in Minas Gerais. In addition there had been rumors in Portugal "that the principal people [of Bahia] were infested . . . with the abominable French principles . . . with great affection for the absurd and intended French constitution. . . ." If French troops landed, it was said, the city would unite with them. Specifically, the wealthy priest and entrepreneur Francisco Agostinho Gomes was denounced to the authorities in Lisbon.

56. "Denuncia . . . que da . . . Santa Anna," *ADIB*, I, 12.

57. Vilhena, *Cartas*, I, 159; Carlos Guilherme Mota, "Mentalidade Ilustrada na colonização Portuguesa: Luís dos Santos Vilhena," *Revista de História*, No. 72 (1967) 405–416.

58. Vilhena, *Cartas*, I, 128–129.

59. Donald Campbell, London, 14 August 1804, Chatham Papers, Public Record Office, London (hereafter cited as PRO) 30/8/345 part 2, f. 223.

The governor of Bahia, D. Fernando José de Portugal, was instructed to investigate these charges.[60]

Gomes was an erudite and enlightened man with as fine a private library as that which canon Luís Vieira had built up in Minas Gerais. Thomas Lindley, who met him at the turn of the century, was singularly impressed. "In the French I noticed Alembert's Encyclopedia, Buffon, and Lavoisier, among our own authors he had chiefly selected natural history, political economy, travels and philosophical works. . . . Robertson's America he particularly commended and Smith's Wealth of Nations. . . ." Lindley also noted how Father Gomes praised the works of Thomas Paine.[61] D. Fernando, however, found nothing to incriminate Gomes. The ideas and organization of the Bahian conspiracy were such, he wrote, "that no persons of consideration, or understanding, or who had knowledge or enlightenment had entered. . . ."[62] With respect to the priest, he pointed out to Lisbon that "the reading of English papers did not make a man a Jacobin." Moreover, he found it highly improbable that any of the principal people of the captaincy were implicated in the Bahian conspiracy. He had no indication of this implication among either the business men and the men in public office, or the people of property, all of whom reacted strongly when the seditious papers appeared. Those involved in the plot were all of the lower class (classe ordinária). "That which is always most dreaded in colonies are the slaves, on account of their condition and because they comprise the greater number of the inhabitants," he told Lisbon. "It is therefore not natural for men employed and established in goods and property to join a conspiracy which would result in awful consequences to themselves, being exposed to assassination by their own slaves." He did not seek "to apologize for the inhabitants of Bahia," he wished "only to express his sentiments."[63]

60. D. Rodrigo de Sousa Coutinho to D. Fernando José de Portugal, Queluz, 4 October 1798, MHPB, III, 95. The suspicion that more important members of society were implicated has been put forward by both Ruy, A primeira revolução, and Antônio de Araujo de Aragão Bulcão Sobrinho, "O patriarcha da liberdade Bahiana, Joaquim Inácio de Sequeira Bulcão," RIHGB, 217 (1952) 167–185, though neither has presented any evidence.

61. Thomas Lindley, Authentic Narrative of a Voyage from the Cape of Good Hope to the Brazils . . . in 1802 and 1803. . . (London, 1817) 66–68.

62. D. Fernando José de Portugal to D. Rodrigo de Sousa Coutinho, Bahia, 20 October, 1798, MHPB, III, 123.

63. D. Fernando José de Portugal to D. Rodrigo de Sousa Coutinho, Bahia, 13 February, 1799, MHPB, III, 132–134.

D. Fernando had made a vital distinction, and his comments stressed the change which had occurred since 1792. The sugar planters and their apologists desired "liberty," to be sure, and the more literate of them were avid disciples of European thinkers; but the theories that appealed to them articulated and provided justification for their own self-interest, and this self-interest, D. Fernando discerned, was not in conflict with the colonial relationship. The liberty the planters most desired was the freedom Bishop Azeredo Coutinho proposed in his memorial on the price of sugar, presented to the Lisbon Academy of Sciences in 1792. It was the liberty "for each to make the greatest profit from his work."[64] Freedom for capitalist enterprise was not the freedom João de Deos had in mind. As D. Fernando saw, the firmest opponents of the demands of the Bahian mulattoes would be the Bahian planters, for it was they, not Lisbon, who had most to lose if those demands were met.

Paradoxically the slave revolt in the West Indies had added acuteness to the sugar planters' demands for freedom from government interference and control, just as the events in Saint Domingue had stimulated apprehensions about the racial balance of the population, and produced the socio-economic situation out of which the Bahian conspiracy emerged. Collapse of French sugar production in the West Indies during the 1790s gave Bahia the opportunity for economic renaissance.[65] So profitable had sugar become and so high the prices fetched on European markets that, according to Luís dos Santos Vilhena, "there is no one who does not wish to be a sugar planter."[66] Azeredo Coutinho, who before becoming an ecclesiastic had

64. "Memória sobre o preço do açúcar (1791)," *Obras econômicas de J. J. da Cunha de Azeredo Coutinho (1794–1804)*, apresentação de Sérgio Buarque de Holanda (São Paulo, 1966) 175–185. The Academy of Sciences had been founded in 1779. Some indication of its importance to the intellectual life of the period can be obtained from Antonio Baião, *A Infância da Academia 1788–1794* (Lisbon, 1934); Antonio Ferrão, "O segundo duque de Lafões, e o marquês de Pombal (subsídios para a biografia do fundador da Academia das Ciências)," *Boletim da Segunda Classe, Academia das Ciências de Lisboa*, XIX (1924–1925) 407–588. For listing of the Academy's publications, see Moses Bensabat Amzalak, *Do estudo e da evolução das doutrinas econômicas em Portugal* (Lisbon, 1928). For Azeredo Coutinho, Manoel Cardozo, "Azeredo Coutinho and the intellectual ferment of his times," Henry H. Keith and S. F. Edwards, eds., *Conflict and Continuity in Brazilian Society* (Columbia, S.C., 1969) 72–103, and E. Bradford Burns, "The role of Azeredo Coutinho in the Enlightenment of Brazil," *HAHR*, XLIV (May, 1964) 145–160.

65. Caio Prado Junior, *A formação do Brasil contemporâneo, colónia* (7th edition, São Paulo, 1963) 126, 159.

66. Vilhena, *Cartas*, I, 158; "Exportação da Bahia para Portugal (1798),"

administered a sugar mill in Brazil, urged that full advantage be taken of the favorable market conditions provided by the "providential revolution of the French colonies." As the price of sugar rises, he wrote, "the greater becomes our production and our commerce."[67]

The sugar boom was partly responsible for the favorable balance of trade with the metropolis enjoyed by Bahia during the 1790s, as a result of which it became necessary to send bullion from Portugal to Brazil.[68] It was a spectacular reversal of circumstances. A mere forty years before, Brazilian gold had provided the mainstay of colonial exports to Lisbon. Azeredo Coutinho's essay on the commerce of Portugal and her dominions attempted to rationalize the new situation. "The mother country and the colonies taken together ought to be regarded as the farm of a single farmer," he wrote. "The owner of many estates does not care whether such and such a one procures him more revenue, but he only rates the collective revenues of the whole. If the mother country could not consume all the produce of the colonies or provide sufficient manufactures so that instead money had to be sent, what prejudice could arise to the mother country? The more colonial products it possesses, the more it has to dispose to foreigners. Though the mother country be in this case made the debtor to the colonies, yet it becomes, at the same time, a creditor doubly considerable in its claims upon the foreigner."[69]

The high price of sugar led planters to exploit all available land.

---

ibid., I, 53; Comment on the high price of South American products was made by Robert Walpole to Lord Grenville, Lisbon, 12 October, 1791, PRO, Foreign Office, 63/14. For price of Brazilian sugar on the Amsterdam market see N.W. Posthumus, *Inquiry into the History of Prices in Holland* (2 vols.; Leiden, 1946, 1964) I, 122, 124.

67. "Memória sôbre o preço do açúcar," *Obras econômicas*, 175–185.

68. In 1796 the value of goods exported to Portugal from Bahia was assessed at 3,702,181,721 reis, and the value of goods sent from Portugal to Bahia at 2,069,637,404 reis, "Tableau général de la valeur des marchandises importées dans le royaume de Portugal." Adrien Balbi, *Essai statistique sur le royaume de Portugal et d'Algarve* (2 vols.; Paris, 1822) I, 431.

69. "Ensaio econômico sôbre o comércio de Portugal e suas colônias . . . D. José Joaquim da Cunha de Azeredo Coutinho, Bispo em outro tempo de Pernambuco . . . e actualmente Bispo d'Elvas . . . ," *Obras econômicas* (Lisboa, MDCCCXVI) 59–172. There is an English translation published in 1807, *An Essay on the Commerce and Products of the Portuguese Colonies in South America, especially the Brazils* . . . (London, 1807). The quotations are taken from this edition, 154–155.

They strongly resented the obligation imposed by law to plant subsistence crops. Professor Luís dos Santos Vilhena condemned the great sugar producers for their failure to plant sufficient manioc and warned that such an unthinking pursuit of their self-interest threatened famine. He firmly believed that plantation owners should be obliged to plant manioc, for there was no other source of supply available. Vilhena held that "European ideas" which had led to the removal of price controls on meat and manioc were responsible for the shortage of subsistence food and for high prices. Such ideas should only be applied in a place like Brazil after the most careful attention had been paid to local factors. In Europe, one nation in time of dearth might have recourse to its neighbors for added supplies, but mutual dependence was impossible in South America, where food supplies were inelastic. Vilhena saw a direct relationship between the removal of price controls and "the ineffectual uprising and cruel massacre" projected by the Bahian mulattoes in 1798.[70]

The "European ideas" Vilhena especially condemned were those of Adam Smith and J. B. Say. Both economists were used by João Rodrigues de Brito and Manuel Ferreira da Câmara to document and justify their rejection of state interference to regulate production or control the prices of commodities. Rodrigues de Brito and Ferreira da Câmara had been consulted over the state of agriculture in Bahia, and their responses were a clear defense of the interests of the great sugar planters. Manuel Ferreira da Câmara, speaking as proprietor of the great sugar mill of Ponte, categorically rejected all laws and regulations that restricted the liberty of the proprietors. He was violently opposed to the Inspection House which regulated the prices of sugar and tobacco, and also to the public granary established by Governor D. Rodrigo José de Menezes in the city of Salvador during 1785 in an attempt to provide regular food supplies at reasonable prices to the population. These institutions, Câmara claimed, "had been set up out of the fantasy of those in government as obstacles to the freedom of commerce." He attributed the granary "to a zeal more religious than practical. . . ." He could conceive of nothing worse than that commodities "should be sold for less than they cost to produce or transport." He boasted that he had not "planted a single foot of manioc in order not to fall into the absurdity of renouncing the best cultivation of the country for the worst." Each

70. Vilhena, Cartas, I, 128–129; I, 159; II, 445–448.

"must be master to do what most benefits him, and what benefits him is that which most benefits the state."[71]

For Rodrigues de Brito, admissible direction in agricultural matters by the government could be reduced to three points: "the granting of liberties, facilities, and instruction." The proprietor should not be forced to plant manioc. De Brito opposed "restrictions that prevented our farmers from taking their goods to the places where they could obtain most value." He argued in favor of the removal of the prohibitions against the *comissários volantes*, the itinerant free traders outlawed by the Marquis of Pombal during the 1750s. He was strongly opposed to price fixing. Freedom should be allowed capitalist enterprise, and in order to encourage the capitalist to participate in agricultural improvement, the institutional and judicial obstacles to investment should be removed. "Intolerable inconveniences placed on the capitalist in the matters of debt collection and foreclosure should be abolished," he contended, and in particular "foreign investment should be welcomed."[72]

The apologists for the sugar planters were making a frontal attack on the whole concept of state regulation and government interference in economic matters. Yet the planters' demands were so closely related to their own self-interest that they were also limited by them. Planters desiring emancipation from government interference did not necessarily desire emancipation from the colonial relationship with Portugal. To Ferreira da Câmara, Rodrigues de Brito, and Azeredo Coutinho, *laissez faire* was not synonymous with free international commercial exchange. It was this basic distinction that another disciple of Adam Smith, D. Fernando José de Portugal, whose elimination of price controls in Bahia provoked Vilhena's criticism, had evidently perceived in 1798. The sugar interests did not lead the demand for free international commerce for one simple reason. Brazilian sugar was sold in the continental European market, for which Lisbon was a logical and necessary entrepôt. Britain, the most likely candidate for any free trade relationship outside the Luso-Brazilian commercial system, placed prohibitive duties on the importation of Brazilian sugar, in the interests of its own sugar colonies in the West Indies.

71. Carta II, M[anuel] F[erreira] da C[âmara], *Cartas econômico-políticas sobre a agricultura e commercio da Bahia . . . pelo Desembargador João Rodrigues de Brito e outros* (Lisbon, 1821) 80–85.
72. Carta, I, João Rodrigues de Brito, *ibid.*

The marriage in the writing of Azeredo Coutinho between his attack on state interference and his restatement of the basic tenets of mercantilist colonial policy was a perfect rationalization of the situation. He held up the English Navigation Acts as "a pattern of imitation to all seafaring nations." It was "in the true interests of both [metropolis and colony] that the colony be permitted to carry on a direct trade with the mother country only, and that they [the colonists] should not have fabrics and manufactories of their own especially of cotton, linen, wool and silk." In fact, the interests of Brazil, defined as the interests of the great sugar planters, were compatible with those of Portugal.[73]

The point of view of the planters of the littoral, so accurately stated by Azeredo Coutinho, gained added weight during the 1790s as a result of the sugar boom, and of the temporary removal of any political influence from Minas Gerais, a region not dominated by an export-oriented plantation economy. The strongly regionalist emphasis of the Minas conspirators had verged at times on economic nationalism. The *alferes* Silva Xavier claimed that once free and a republic like English America, Brazil might become even greater than English America, owing to better resources. With the establishment of manufactories, he said, there would be no need to import commodities from abroad.[74] Proposals for trade and commercial arrangements were noticeably absent from the discussions of the Minas plotters, and many believed that there was no necessity whatsoever to invite the support of foreign powers, for they would rush to establish relations with the new state on account of its natural riches.[75] But the influence of such views was suppressed in the aftermath of the failure of the uprising.

There were Brazilians, however, less closely linked to the interests of the sugar planters, who came to the same conclusion as Dr. Novais de Almeida in his letter to Jacinto José da Silva. The basic issue, as they perceived it, was slavery itself. D. Fernando had

73. *An essay on the commerce*, 155–157.
74. Witness, Vicente Vieira da Mota, Vila Rica, 22 June 1789, *ADIM*, I, 108; Witness, Vicente Vieira da Mota, Vila Rica, 3 August 1789, *ADIM*, III, 334; Witness, José Aires Gomes, Vila Rica, 28 July 1789, *ADIM*, I, 207; Witness, José Aires Gomes, Vila Rica 30 July 1789, *ADIM*, III, 319–320; "Continuação de perguntas feitas ao coronel Alvarenga," Rio de Janeiro, 14 January 1790, *ADIM*, IV, 141.
75. "Continuação de perguntas feitas ao Padre José da Silva de Oliveira Rolim, Vila Rica, 13 November 1789, *ADIM*, II, 288.

found it necessary to expell a Capuchin friar from Bahia during 1794 for his anti-slavery statements.[76] Professor Luís dos Santos Vilhena observed soberly that he was "not persuaded that the commerce in slaves is so useful as it seems." He believed that "Negroes were prejudicial to Brazil."[77] A similar attitude had been expressed some years before by his colleague, Professor José da Silva Lisboa, secretary of the Bahian Inspection House. Although he recognized the importance of slavery and sugar to the Bahian economy, Silva Lisboa did not believe that the number of slaves imported brought a commensurate increase in population or agricultural production. And, like Vilhena, he believed slavery was responsible for many of the ills of Brazilian society.[78]

The suggestion of slave emancipation was anathema to the planters. Azeredo Coutinho thought abolitionist sentiment sufficiently threatening to warrant a blistering attack on "the insidious principles of the philosophic sect." What would happen to the agriculture of Brazil and in consequence the commerce and prosperity of Portugal if slavery was abolished? he asked. To Azeredo Coutinho "necessity has no law, because she is the origin of all law," and necessity clearly demanded the continuance of the slave trade. "To those that accuse me of occupying myself with a study more proper to a farmer or business man than to a Bishop, it is necessary to remember that before I was a Bishop I was, as I continue to be, a citizen linked to the interest of the state." He attacked those who "in the depths of their studies presume to give laws to the world without having dealt at first hand with the people of whom they speak." The bishop's concern at the growth of emancipationist sentiment was evidently justified, for his defense of the slave trade was refused by the Lisbon Academy of Sciences, and he was forced to publish a French edition in London. When he sought again in 1806 to have his polemic published in Portugal, the Royal Board of Censorship denied permission, on the ground that although slavery might be tolerated in present circumstances, nothing should be said to make its elimination even more difficult.[79]

76. Dom Fernando José de Portugal to Martinho de Melo e Castro, Bahia, 18 June 1794, *RIHGB*, LX (1897) 155–157.
77. Vilhena, *Cartas*, I, 136, 139–140.
78. José da Silva Lisboa to Domingos Vandelli, Bahia, 18 October, 1781, *ABNRJ*, XXXII (1910) 502, 505.
79. "Análise sôbre a justiça do comércio do resgate dos escravos da costa

No one was advocating immediate abolition, but a small group of men was beginning to regard slavery as the source of social ills in Brazil, and was starting to think in terms of an alternative model for Brazilian development, in which European immigration and free laborers would replace slavery. Vilhena's objections to slavery were not so much the result of "humanitarian" sentiment, as they were a practical response to the problem of a society where the racial balance appeared to be dangerously unstable. In fact, despite Azeredo Cutinho's calumny, those few who urged eventual emancipation of the slave did so not because of the humanity of blacks, but because they wished to see blacks eliminated. Saint Domingue was especially important in transforming José da Silva Lisboa's vague prejudices into concrete opinions. During 1818 he expressed publically a point of view which had been developing for over thirty years. The progress of São Paulo, he said, was due "to the extraordinary preponderance [there] of the white race." Rio Grande do Sul, the granary of Brazil, likewise had been colonized by "the Portuguese race, and not the Ethiopian population." Taking the example of Madeira, he asserted that "experience had shown that once the supply of Africans has been cut off the race does not decrease and decline but becomes better and whiter. . . ." He wished to see the cancer of slavery eliminated from the Rio de la Plata to the Amazon. "Was the best area in America to be populated by the offspring of Africa or of Europe?" he asked. To avoid "the horrid spectacle of the catastrophe that reduced the Queen of the Antilles to a Madagascar," Brazil should be prevented from becoming a "Negroland."[80]

The question of slavery raised fundamental questions about the most desirable course for Brazilian development. And during the 1790s that question was beginning to divide enlightened men. Dis-

d'Africa (1798)" Obras econômicas; Sonia Aparecida Siqueira, "A escravidão negra no pensamento do bispo Azeredo Coutinho, contribuição ao estudo da mentalidade do último inquisidor geral," I, Revista de história, XXVII (1963) 349–365, II Revista de história, XXVIII (1964) 141–198. D. Fernando José de Portugal significantly also supported the views of the sugar planters with respect to slavery, see D. Fernando to Martinho de Melo e Castro, Bahia, 18 June 1794, RIHGB, LX (1897) 155–157.

80. José da Silva Lisboa, Memória dos benefícios políticos do governo de el-rei nosso senhor dom João VI (1818) (2nd edition, Rio de Janeiro, 1940) 160, 169–175.

cussion about development resulted in a striking paradox. Those
who were the strongest supporters of laissez faire when it meant
removal of the regulatory functions of the state were also most
committed to the slave trade and slavery. Those who supported
government interference, particularly in the control of prices and in
the guarantee of sufficient supplies of subsistence food to the population, were also most opposed to the slave trade and slavery.
Novais de Almeida and Vilhena saw the slave population as enemies within, and José da Silva Lisboa believed Brazil would not
develop without the creation of a free labor force and the Euro-
peanization or whitening of the population. Bishop Azeredo Coutinho saw slavery as essential to Brazilian prosperity. Those who
attacked laissez faire where it demanded the removal of what
they considered judicious government controls would be most in
favor of free international commerce, because free trade promised
to stimulate European immigration, and offered the possibility of
an alliance with Great Britain against the slave trade. Yet at the
same time, because the solution to Brazil's problems by opponents
of laissez faire was based on fear of the racial composition of the
Brazilian population, they would be the least likely to take any
initiative that might provoke the disaster they foresaw and sought
to avoid. The division was profound. Vilhena attacked those "European ideas" he held responsible for creating the conditions that led
to the Bahian plot. Azeredo Coutinho attacked the "humanitarians"
and "philosophers" whose utopian concepts threatened, in his
opinion, to destroy Brazilian prosperity.

Republicanism had been discredited by its abortive uprising in
Minas Gerais and later association with social and racial turmoil,
and Brazilians were in very basic disagreement over fundamental
issues; thus there was room for metropolitan initiatives. And for
the white minority in Portuguese America, the failure of the oli-
garchic movement in Minas Gerais during 1789, and the threat from
below revealed by the Bahian artisans in 1798, provided two powerful incentives for compromise with the metropolis. Psychologically,
the situation was propitious for accommodation. The recognition
of this fact by influential members of the Portuguese government
during the 1790s had profound impact on the future development
of Brazil.

During 1788 Luís Pinto de Sousa Coutinho became Portugal's

foreign minister.[81] He was a man with firsthand knowledge of Brazilian conditions, having distinguished himself as governor of Mato Grosso (1769–1772) before succeeding Martinho de Melo e Castro as minister plenipotentiary to the Court of St. James.[82] In Britain he had provided William Robertson with information on South America for Robertson's famous history, a service he had also provided for the Abbé Raynal some years earlier.[83] Once back in Lisbon, Luís Pinto made contact with Brazilian intellectuals, many of them students of Domingos Vandelli, an Italian scholar brought to Portugal by Pombal as part of his program of educational reform. On May 31, 1790, Luís Pinto sent two young Brazilians and a Portuguese colleague on a grand European tour of instruction at the expense of the Portuguese government. The Brazilians were Manuel Ferreira da Câmara and José Bonifácio de Andrada e Silva. The group was instructed to proceed to Paris and take courses there in physics and mineralogy. Two years at Freiburg would be spent gaining "all practical knowledge." Afterwards the scholars were to visit the mines of Saxony, Bohemia, and Hungary, and to return to Portugal by way of Scandinavia and Great Britain.[84]

Manuel Ferreira da Câmara, the leader of the expedition, had close links with those caught up in the events of Minas Gerais. His elder brother, José de Sá Betencourt, who graduated from Coimbra in 1787, was implicated on several occasions during the judicial inquiry into the conspiracy, and had fled from Minas by way of the backlands to Bahia. His uncle had been a member of the Bahian High Court, and his wealthy relatives were proprietors of the sugar mill of Ponte. (Manuel Ferreira administered this estate from 1801

81. Caetano Beirão, D. Maria I, 1777–1792 (3rd edition, Lisbon, 1944) 88, 341–342; Simão José da Luz Soriano, História da Guerra Civil (Lisbon, 1866) I, 349–350.

82. Ibid., 355–356.

83. Robertson, History of America, I, xiv; J.-M. Quérard, La France littéraire, ou dictionnaire bibliographique des savants . . . (10 vols.; Paris, 1827–1839) VII (1835) 473. I am grateful to Holden Hall of The Newberry Library for bringing to my attention this connection between Luís Pinto and Raynal.

84. Instrução, Ajuda, 31 May 1790, in Marcos Carneiro de Mendonça, O Intendente Câmara, Manuel Ferreira da Câmara Bethencourt e Sá, Intendente Geral das Minas e Diamantes 1764–1835 (São Paulo, 1958) 26–27. Among the Brazilians' distinguished colleagues at Freiburg were Alexandre de Humboldt and Andrés Manuel del Río; see Charles Minguet, Alexandre de Humboldt, Historien et Géographe de l'Amérique Expagnole (1799–1804) (Paris, 1969), 44–45.

to 1807; from it he wrote his observations about the agriculture of Bahia.)[85] At the time that Manuel Ferreira received his instructions for the study tour of Europe, the Portuguese government had known for three months of his brother's suspected implication in the projected uprising in Minas Gerais.[86]

Luís Pinto's extension of the powerful protection of his office during the critical year 1790 to these young Brazilian scholars, and his remarkable act of faith in sponsoring the visit of Manuel Ferreira and José Bonifácio to the center of European social and political upheaval, coincided with a series of public criticisms of the attitudes and assumptions which had dominated policy-making since the fall of Pombal in 1777. In 1790 D. Rodrigo de Sousa Coutinho, Luís Pinto's successor, published under the auspices of the Lisbon Academy of Sciences his "discourse on the true influence of mines of precious metals on the industry of the nations that possess them, and especially the Portuguese." D. Rodrigo was Pombal's godson. He was related by marriage to Mathias Barbosa, one of the famous Minas pioneers, and as a result possessed extensive properties in the captaincy. In his discourse, D. Rodrigo took issue with the view that mines were responsible for Portugal's decadence, as the *Encyclopédie* had stated. He attributed the stagnation of Portugal to the effects of the Methuen treaty of 1703.[87] D. Rodrigo was preparing the way for Manuel Ferreira da Câmara's paper on "physical and economic observations about the extraction of gold in Brazil," in which the young Brazilian made an eloquent plea for improved methods and techniques. Manuel Ferreira recom-

85. Carneiro de Mendonça, *Intendente Câmara* 9–10.

86. Martinho de Melo e Castro acknowledged receipt of the first notice of the conspiracy in a letter to the Minas governor, the visconde de Barbacena, dated 9 March 1790. A much corrected minute of this dispatch in Melo e Castro's own hand survives at the AHU, Minas Gerais, caixa 92. Ignácio Ferreira da Câmara, a cousin of Manuel Ferreira and José de Sá, had been a student at Montpellier, *MHPB*, VI (1940) 283.

87. D. Rodrigo de Sousa Coutinho, "Memória sôbre a verdadeira influência das Minas dos metaes preciosos na indústria das nações que as posuem e especialmente da portuguesa," *Memórias econômicas da Academia*, I (1789), cited by Amzalak, *Evolução das doutrinas econômicas*, 106–107, and Carneiro de Mendonça, *Intendente Câmara*, 18–20; Marqués do Funchal, "Certidão do baptismo de Dom Rodrigo de Sousa Coutinho," *O Conde de Linhares, Dom Domingos António de Sousa Coutinho* (Lisbon, 1908) 186. For information on D. Rodrigo's Minas connections, see Miguel Costa Filho, *A cana de açúcar em Minas Gerais* (Rio de Janeiro, 1963) 92, 97, and John Mawe, *Travels in the Interior of Brazil* (London, 1812) 181–182.

mended that mining companies be promoted and encouraged by royal privileges. These companies should not be monopolies, but organizations which could mobilize capital for rational exploitation. He suggested that mining colleges be set up in Brazil to provide skilled mining engineers.[88] The papers of both D. Rodrigo and Manuel Ferreira implied that the imposition of fiscal demands on Minas Gerais had been wrong, and that what Minas Gerais needed was not increased tax burdens but rational reform and modern technology.

When Melo e Castro died in March 1795, Luís Pinto took over as interim secretary of state for the overseas dominions.[89] On May 27, 1795, he forwarded to the Brazilian governors a circular which contained a startling admission of past mistakes. "Defects in policy and fiscal restrictions had until now held back the progress of Brazil," he wrote. "Her Majesty, desiring to calm her subjects as much as possible," had made important decisions. First, the salt-gabelle would be abolished in Brazil. Second, the mining and manufacture of iron would be encouraged, especially in Minas and São Paulo.[90] Both measures promised to ameliorate two principal irritants to the white minority in Brazil. And one of the few areas of agreement between Luís dos Santos Vilhena and Bishop Azeredo Coutinho was opposition to the salt monopoly, due to its restrictive effect on the development of salt meat production.

To formulate programs and implement the reforms, Luís Pinto relinquished his temporary portfolio to D. Rodrigo de Sousa Coutinho in 1796.[91] D. Rodrigo had impressive credentials. He had been a student at the College of Nobles, established by Pombal to create a "virtuous" nobility in Portugal.[92] In 1779 he had visited

88. Carneiro de Mendonça, "Memória de observações físico-econômicas acêrca da extração do ouro do Brasil, por Manuel Ferreira da Câmara," *Intendente Câmara,* 499–523.

89. Luís Pinto's first dispatch as secretary of state for the overseas dominions was dated 26 March, 1795, AHU, códice 610, f. 194v–195; the death of Melo e Castro was announced to the governors in Brazil on 30 March 1795.

90. Luís Pinto de Sousa Coutinho to Bernardo José de Lorena, Queluz, 27 May, 1795, Arquivo do estado de São Paulo, *caixa* 63, N. orden 421, *livro* 171, f. 159–161. For the complete transcription see Carneiro de Mendonça, *Intendente Câmara,* 174–175, and *DI,* XLV (1924) 466–468.

91. Luís Pinto announced the appointment of D. Rodrigo, 9 September, 1796, *DI,* XLV (1924) 486.

92. Rómulo de Carvalho, *História da fundação do colégio real dos nobres de Lisboa, 1761–1772* (Coimbra, 1959), 182–186.

France and observed what he described as its "parasitic and useless court" and its "chaotic financial situation."[93] In Paris he met Abbé Raynal. He told Raynal that the "population and resources of France would have made her insupportable to the rest of Europe were it not for the disorder of her financial administration." Raynal replied that "Providence had given France the forces but refused her good sense. France would indeed be terrible if her natural power was matched by a just and wise administration." Writing to his sister, D. Rodrigo later wondered: "What would be better for Europe, to be a factory of the English or a slave of France? The only thing that can console us is the almost total impossibility of France reforming her system of government."

D. Rodrigo was right in his analysis but wrong in his prediction. Reform in France had come through revolution, and as he had seen, the geopolitical consequences for Portugal threatened to be an intolerable choice between the Great Powers. Moreover, he attributed the collapse of the French monarchy to its fiscal situation. His opposition to monopolies and the contracting of revenues, and his fervent support of an efficient and solvent financial administration, grew from his belief that intelligent reform was essential if Portugal were to avoid a similar collapse. The financial problem was especially relevant because one of the prime issues in Minas Gerais was the tax farms. The "good administration of the royal exchequer would contribute most to the opulence and conservation of the vast overseas dominions," the new secretary of state observed.[94] To achieve sound fiscal policies, D. Rodrigo planned "wise and enlightened reforms, executed by intelligent men, capable of forming well-organized systems, the utility of which would be recognized by all."[95] His optimism epitomized that of the Enlightenment itself.

The immediate problem was the status of mining in Minas Gerais. Theoretical debate and practical suggestion centered on this. D. Rodrigo would base his measures "on the most liberal principles, if it is legitimate to adopt to our language the sense which the English attribute to that word."[96] Domingos Vandelli, in a memorial

93. D. Rodrigo to Dona Marianna de Sousa Coutinho, Fontainebleau, 4 August, 1779, Funchal, *Linhares*, 191–194.

94. "Plano sôbre o meio de restabelecer o crédito público e segurar recursos para as grandes despesas, 29 October 1799," *ibid.*, 172–179; "Plano de fazenda," 14 March 1799, *ibid.*, 155–168.

95. "Discurso, IV," *ibid.*, 135.

96. "Discurso, II, *ibid.*, 120.

on the gold of Brazil, complained that policy had previously been "left only in the hands of people ignorant of mineralogy to the grave prejudice of the state." Decision about whether gold mines were advantageous or prejudicial to Portugal he left to "those who know how to calculate the true interest of nations." He recommended that practical experience be taken into account, especially that of scholars who might have been to Germany.[97] D. Rodrigo consulted Antônio Pires de Silva Ponte, who embodied his thoughts in an essay on the mines. He emphasized the necessity for more training in the mathematical and physical sciences and metallurgy because "of the present great difficulties in extracting gold." He criticized the fact that in Minas Gerais the value of gold was kept artificially below its value outside the captaincy. He went so far as to suggest that the royal fifth be abolished and replaced by a tax on luxury goods proportional to their price. He noted that Minas abounded in agricultural and pastoral riches whose development should be encouraged. "The royal revenues do not depend so much on the fifth of the gold . . . as in the number of consumers (consumidores) and inhabitants in the region."[98] José Eloi Ottoni, in a memorial on the state of the captaincy, agreed that the extraction of gold was now beyond the capacities of the miners. He pointed to the absurd expense of the importation of iron and steel into Brazil. It was important to promote agriculture and commerce with the interior by removing import taxes. Communications should be opened, especially along the Rio Doce and the Rio Sao Francisco. He did not mean to suggest that all manufactures be permitted in Brazil, but he did think it wise to allow those which provided substitutes for items which "from negligence we buy from foreigners, iron, steel, saltpetre."[99] Azeredo Coutinho, like Ottoni, pointed to the absurd price of iron in Minas Gerais. A quintal of iron which in Portugal cost about 3,800 reis, he said, would in Minas Gerais be worth 19,000 reis, and in Goias and Mato Grosso 28,000 reis. It was "absolutely necessary that schools of mining be immediately

97. "Memória . . . sôbre as Minas de Ouro do Brasil por Domingos Vandelli," *ABNRJ*, XX (1898) 266–278.
98. "Memória sôbre a utilidade pública em se estrahir o ouro das minas e os motivos dos poucos interêsses que fazem os particulares que minerão actualmente no Brasil, por António Pires da Silva Pontes Leme [sic]," with a letter to D. Rodrigo, *RAPM*, I (1896) 417–426.
99. "Memória sobre o estado actual da capitania de Minas Gerais por José Eloi Ottoni, estando em Lisboa no anno de 1798," *ABNRJ*, XXX (1908) 303–318.

established in São Paulo, Minas Gerais, Goias, Cuiabá and Mato Grosso."[100]

D. Rodrigo mobilized a task force of erudite Brazilians in America to provide practical information. José Vieira Couto and José Teixeira da Fonseca Vasconcelos were instructed to collect information on salt deposits, especially in the São Francisco river valley.[101] João Manso Pereira, subsidized by local tax money, was to conduct mineralogical and metallurgical investigations and experiments in São Paulo, Minas Gerais, and Rio de Janeiro.[102] Joaquim Veloso Miranda, a student of Vandelli, whose information had been used by the Italian scholar in his memorial, was appointed secretary to the new governor of Minas, José de Lorena, a close personal friend of D. Rodrigo and a disciple of the Abbé Raynal.[103] Veloso Miranda was instructed to continue his studies of the natural resources of the region and most especially of the deposits of saltpetre. José de Sá Betencourt received a commission to investigate the copper and saltpetre deposits at Jacobina.[104] The secretary of state outlined explicitly the objective of these various investigations. He told Veloso Miranda "that orders might perhaps be issued to the governor to establish the manufacture of gunpowder on the account of the royal exchequer . . . as soon as sufficient saltpetre was

100. "Discurso sôbre o estado actual das minas do Brasil," Obras econômicas, 190–229.

101. Rodrigo de Sousa Coutinho to Bernardo José de Lorena, Queluz, 18 March 1797, AHU, códice 610, f. 202v. Also "Memória sôbre as Minas da capitania de Minas Gerais, suas descripções, ensaios, e domicílio próprio, a maneira de itinerário com hum appêndice sôbre a nova lorena diamantina, sua descripção e utilidades, que d'êste país possa resultar ao estado, por ordem de sua alteza real, 1801, por José Vieira Couto," IHGB, lata 18, doc., 17.

102. D. Rodrigo de Sousa Coutinho to Bernardo José de Lorena, Queluz, 18 March 1797, AHU, códice 610, f. 202.

103. D. Rodrigo de Sousa Coutinho to Bernardo José de Lorena, Queluz, 21 February 1797, AHU, códice 610, f. 201v, and D. Rodrigo to Joaquim Veloso de Miranda, Queluz, 18 March 1797, AHU, códice 610, f. 202v; Carvalho, Fundação do colégio dos nobres, 182–186; D. Rodrigo to Lorena, Queluz, 11 October 1798, AHU, códice 610, f. 215v–216; Lorena's comments on Raynal in DI, XLV 10–11.

104. D. Rodrigo de Sousa Coutinho to D. Fernando José de Portugal, 2 March 1798 and letter from José de Sá, Bahia, 7 October 1797, MHPB, VI 278. Some observations on cotton by José de Sá had been favorably received in Lisbon and published as Memória sôbre a plantação dos algodões e sua exportação; sôbre a decadência da lavoura de mandiocas no têrmo da villa de Camamu, comarca dos Ilheos, governo da Bahia . . . por José de Sá Bitencourt (Lisbon, 1798).

found."[105] Governor Lorena was informed that the proposed iron works would be set up on the account of the exchequer and iron sold at "a price discrete and wise, equally beneficial to the royal exchequer and the inhabitants. . . ."[106] When Manuel Ferreira returned to Portugal during 1798, D. Rodrigo at once called for his views on the proposed legislation.[107]

After three years of study and planning, the outlines of a general policy for the empire as well as specific legislative drafts had been composed.[108] During 1798, D. Rodrigo formally presented his ideas to the council of state of Portugal.[109] He intended, he told the councillors, to "touch rapidly on the political system that it is most convenient for the crown to embrace in order to conserve its vast dominions, particularly those of America, that are properly the base of the greatness of the throne. . . ." D. Rodrigo asserted that "the dominions in Europe do not form any longer the capital and center of the Portuguese Empire. Portugal reduced to herself would within a very brief period be a province of Spain." He advised that the empire be regarded as being composed "of provinces of the monarchy, all possessing the same honors and privileges, all reunited with the same administration and all contributing to the mutual and reciprocal defense of the monarchy." Brazil should be divided into two centers of power, Rio de Janeiro in the south and Pará in the north. It was essential, he said, to "occupy our true natural limits," and in particular the northern bank of the Rio de la Plata. The choice of governors was important for the maintenance of justice and the efficient administration of the royal exchequer; with higher salaries, he believed, governors would have less incentive to become embroiled in business. Associations should be formed to exploit the

105. D. Rodrigo de Sousa Coutinho to Joaquim Veloso de Miranda, Queluz, 17 September 1799, AHU, códice 611, f. 7.

106. D. Rodrigo de Sousa Coutinho to Bernardo José de Lorena, Queluz, 20 September 1798, AHU, códice 610, f. 212v–213v.

107. Carneiro de Mendonça, Intendente Câmara, 33–66.

108. Numerous drafts for the future legislation were made: for some of these see AHU, Minas Gerais, caixa 57, document 221. (This is mistakenly dated 1780 on the folder. These projects were written between 1798–1800, the first drafts in the name of Queen Maria I, and the later ones in that of Dom João, the prince regent. Dom João formally became prince regent of Portugal in 1799 though he had been exercising the function of head of state since 1792.)

109. Discurso de D. Rodrigo de Sousa Coutinho, document no. 4 (I) Carneiro de Mendonça, Intendente Câmara, 277–299. This is from the Coleção Linhares, BNRJ I, 29–13–16.

mines more efficiently. The number of high courts in Brazil should
be increased, and the need for appeal to Lisbon abolished. He proposed that taxation be reformed so that it would "be productive but
not fall heavily on the contributors." The tax contract system would
be abolished because it fell unequally and because most of the money
remained in the hands of the tax farmers. Duties on slaves, iron,
steel, copper, lead, gunpowder, and metropolitan manufactures
sent to the interior of Brazil would be removed. The royal fifth
would be reduced to a tenth, and the value of gold in Minas Gerais
revalued to its market price.

The ideas of his Luso-Brazilian braintrust were very evident in
the plan for empire proposed by the secretary of state. And the
urgency of implementation of the plan was increased by the Bahian
episode. D. Rodrigo sensed more acutely than most the opportunities the situation presented, and he distinguished more clearly than
most between the necessity of enlightened reforms and the dangers
posed by the revolutionary slogans of the French Revolution. The
severity with which he treated the Bahian mulattoes and the favors
he continued to bestow on the Brazilian graduates of the University
of Coimbra were indicative of his point of view.[110] His fear of
revolution made it essential that "the federative system, the most
analogous to Portugal's position in the world, be conserved with the
greatest firmness and pure good faith."[111] He attacked "the banal
declamations" of those who claimed "that in the . . . difficult
circumstances of the moment great reforms should not be attempted and only palliatives employed; experience had shown the
opposite."[112]

D. Rodrigo had employed many erudite Brazilians in the process
of decision making. He had encouraged others to undertake state-
sponsored scientific expeditions in Brazil. He had been especially
responsive to those who were connected with the Minas conspiracy.

110. Three of the leaders of the Bahian plot were hanged, beheaded, and
quartered in the center of the city of Salvador. The rest of the plotters were
taken to Africa and abandoned along the African coast. C. R. Boxer has attributed the clemency displayed by the Crown toward the Minas conspirators,
of whom only the alferes Silva Xavier (Tiradentes) was hanged, in comparison
with the severity of the repression of a similar movement in Goa during 1787,
to "colour prejudice." The same could be argued in the Bahian episode. Boxer,
Portuguese Seaborne Empire, 199–200.
111. "Discurso I," 22 December 1798, Funchal, Linhares, 108–109.
112. "Plano de Fazenda," 14 March 1799, ibid., 168.

The exiled José Alvares Maciel, for example, forwarded a memorial on the iron mines in Angola. It was favorably received and Maciel was given an official mission to investigate the situation more closely.[113] The members of the Literary Society of Rio de Janeiro, languishing in jail since 1794, were released.[114]

In 1800 D. Rodrigo was appointed president of the Royal Treasury.[115] The position had been created by Pombal as the linchpin of the government, and its occupant was principal minister of the Crown. At the treasury, Pombal's godson had the opportunity to implement the reforms he had long regarded as most important, for which draft legislation was prepared. The royal decree of April 24, 1801, "in favor of the inhabitants of Brazil," promulgated the reforms outlined by Luís Pinto in 1795. The salt monopoly was abolished and the mining and manufacture of iron permitted.[116] Manuel Ferreira da Câmara was nominated General Intendant of Mines and the Sêrro do Frio [the Diamond District].[117] Antônio Pires da Silva Ponte was appointed governor of the captaincy of Espírito Santo.[118] José Bonifácio de Andrada e Silva became Intendant of Mines and Metals in Portugal.[119] There was precedent for the appointment of Brazilians to such high positions in the metropolitan and colonial administrations. But the nomination to a new and important post second only to the governor of Minas of a man whose brother had been seriously implicated in the proposed uprising of 1789, and the appointment as a governor in Brazil of a Brazilian whose loyalty had been gravely questioned in 1786 were little short of revolutionary.

113. José Alvares Maciel to D. Rodrigo de Sousa Coutinho, 7 November 1799, AHU, Minas Gerais, caixa 94.

114. Devassa of Literary Society, introductory notes, ABNRJ, LXI (1939) 241–245.

115. Soriano, História da guerra civil, II, 296–297.

116. José da Silva Lisboa, Synopse da legislação principal do Senhor Dom João VI (Rio de Janeiro, 1818) 28.

117. Carta régia, 7 November 1800, and instrução, in Carneiro de Mendonça, Intendente Câmara, 86–91.

118. RAPM, I (1896) 417 note; also ABNRJ, LXII (1940) 145.

119. "Carta de merce, concedendo a José Bonifácio de Andrade e Silva o cargo de intendente geral das minas e metais do Reino, 25, VIII, 1801," Obras científicas, políticas, e sociais de José Bonifácio de Andrade e Silva (3 vols.; Santos, 1964) III, 29. For a detailed discussion of the activities and publications of many Brazilian scholars encouraged by D. Rodrigo during the late eighteenth century see Maria Odila da Silva Dias, "Aspectos da Ilustração no Brasil," RIHGB, 278 (January–March, 1968) 105–170.

In the meanwhile, however, the war in Europe had forced Portugal to face the choice D. Rodrigo had foreseen while in France during 1779. His views on the importance of Brazil made it logical that, when he was consulted in 1803 on the European situation, he should recommend that the prince regent of Portugal, D. João, establish the seat of the monarchy in America. The idea was not original.[120] The proposal that the monarch leave for Brazil was a recurrent suggestion in times of difficulties. But to D. Rodrigo the factors in favor of the move were not merely those imposed by the deteriorating international situation. D. Rodrigo told the prince regent that "Portugal is not the best and most essential part of the monarchy." In his opinion a mighty empire might be established in South America. There the offensive might be taken against the Spaniards, and natural frontiers be established at the Rio de la Plata. As he saw the situation, the prince regent would have little choice, in the event of a showdown between the Great Powers over Portugal. If the French took Lisbon, then the British would take Brazil. It was better to anticipate both moves by taking the initiative.

The plan to transfer the court to Brazil, espoused by D. Rodrigo in 1803, was eminently acceptable to white Brazilians. Canon Luís Vieira da Silva had considered the establishment of Rio de Janeiro as the seat of the Portuguese monarchy the best possible solution to Brazil's problems in 1789.[121] Alvarenga Peixoto, in an ode to the Queen in 1792, pleaded for her to visit her American subjects.[122] One of the few points to emerge from the investigation arising out of the seemingly trumped-up charges against Captain Francisco de Paula Cavalcante and others in Pernambuco during 1801, was the evident concern in Brazil about what would happen if the prince regent did not establish himself in America in the event of the loss of Portugal.[123]

In 1789, important members of the Minas oligarchy had been prepared to move in armed rebellion against the Portuguese Crown and to establish an independent and republican government. After

---

120. "Quadro da situação política da Europa, apresentado ao Principe por D. Rodrigo de Sousa Coutinho," 16 August 1803, Angelo Pereira, D. João VI, Príncipe e Rei I, 127–136 (Lisbon, 1953).

121. Witness, Vicente Vieira da Mota, Vila Rica, 22 June, 1789, ADIM, I, 111.

122. Rodrigues Lapa, Alvarenga Peixoto, lii–liii.

123. "Devassa de 1801 em Pernambuco," edited by J. H. Rodrigues, DH, CX, 151. For some comments on this so-called conspiracy see Cardozo, "Azeredo Coutinho," in Keith and Edwards, eds., Conflict and Continuity, 84.

1792 "men established in goods and property," to use the words
of D. Fernando José de Portugal, were wary of republicanism. The
slave revolt in the Caribbean frightened slaveowners throughout
the Americas. The sugar boom in Brazil, in part a result of the
collapse of production in Saint Domingue, brought with it social
and economic problems which in turn were partly responsible for
the proposed uprising of the mulatto artisans of Bahia. The Bahian
manifestoes of 1798 confirmed that the slogans of the French Revolution propagated within a society like that of Portuguese America
brought with them the risks of racial upheaval, risks that the
American Revolution, the inspiration of the Minas conspirators,
had not brought. After 1792 both the great slaveowners of the
coastal plantations and the chastened Mineiros were prepared for
an accommodation with the metropolis. Even more than the reforms
and reorganization proposed by D. Rodrigo, the establishment of
the monarchy in Brazil was a welcome and hopeful compromise
which offered political change without social disintegration.

The Brazil plan was anathema to many in Portugal. Admiral
Campbell attributed the opposition to "the French, but also the
Spanish influence, and finally to a greater part of the nobility, who
dread the idea of seeking their fortunes in a new country while they
can grasp at the shadow in their own."[124] The plan was unthinkable
to Portuguese merchants and industrialists who, unlike D. Rodrigo
with his extensive properties in Minas Gerais, had much to lose
and nothing to gain by such a move. Nor was D. Rodrigo's distinction between reform and revolution appreciated by those who
saw subversion in all Enlightenment philosophy. Combating nationalism overseas he had underestimated nationalism at home. His
regulations of Portugal to a secondary status in his federative scheme
provoked ferocious opposition.[125] The limitations of D. Rodrigo's
influence were made apparent by his failure to protect his protégé,
Hypolito da Costa, from arrest and imprisonment for masonic
activities on his return from the United States, a visit D. Rodrigo
himself had sponsored.[126] José Joaquim Vieira Couto, brother of

124. Donald Campbell, London, 14 August 1804, Chatham Papers, PRO,
30/8/345 (2) f. 224.
125. For an account of the violence of the merchants' opinions see Robert
Walpole to Lord Grenville Lisbon, 9 September 1795, Foreign Office 63/21.
126. Mecenas Dourado, *Hypólito da Costa, e o Correio Brasiliense* (2 vols.;
Rio de Janeiro, 1957), I, 47–67; Carlos Rizzini, *Hypólito da Costa e o Correio
Brasiliense* (São Paulo, 1957) 9, 13.

the scientist José Vieira Couto, who came to Lisbon on behalf of the residents of the Diamond District, was also arrested and imprisoned on the orders of the intendant of police, Pina Manique.[127] Manuel Ferreira da Câmara remained intendant of mines in name only, and was forced to remain at his estate in Bahia waiting in vain for instructions to proceed to Minas Gerais.[128] When, in late 1803, the prince regent submitted the new mining legislation to ministers in the government regarded by D. Rodrigo as incompetent to judge the issue and opposed to his objectives, he found his position no longer tenable, and resigned.[129]

The setback was temporary. D. Rodrigo had accurately foreseen the course of events. In November 1807, the showdown between Britain and France over Portugal took place. With a British fleet off Lisbon and a French army marching across the frontier, the move to Brazil became essential if the monarchy was to survive at all.[130] But when the Portuguese fleet sailed from the Tagus with the court of Portugal aboard, plans were ready for the new situation. A vindicated D. Rodrigo was reappointed to the government to implement the blueprint he and his associates had drawn up during the 1790s.

The fact that Dom João arrived in Brazil so well prepared was important to the success of the establishment of monarchy in Portuguese America. And the warm reception accorded the European court in Brazil was also important. Part of the reason for both the preparation and the cordial reception lay in the course of events between 1789 and 1808. The timing of the Minas conspiracy and the

127. Ibid., 12–13; Also, "carta de Diogo Ignacio de Pina Manique em que trata sucintamente dos serviços prestados a tranquilidade publica combatendo os Jacobinos e maçons," 4 Sept. 1798, IHGB, lata 177, doc., 8.

128. D. Rodrigo told Manuel Ferreira, "I hope that you have that quality of obstinacy necessary to overcome the obstacles of ignorance and those who oppose the public wellbeing." Carneiro de Mendonça, Intendente Câmara, 103.

129. Ibid., 113–118, 491.

130. The painful process by which the council of state during 1807 came to the conclusion which D. Rodrigo had consistently upheld has only recently become clear, thanks to the discovery of the papers of the council of state by Alan K. Manchester in the Arquivo Nacional, Rio de Janeiro. See his article "The Transfer of the Portuguese Court to Rio de Janeiro," in Keith and Edwards, eds., Conflict and Continuity, 148–183, translated as "A transferência da corte portuguesa para o Rio de Janeiro," RIHGB, CCLXXVII (October-December, 1967) 3–44. Some of these documents have been published by Eneas Martins Filho, O conselho do estado português e a transmigracão da família real em 1807 (Rio de Janeiro, 1968).

Bahian plot, and the relationship between the chronology of events in Brazil, the French Revolution, and the slave revolt in Saint Domingue, caused a shift among white Brazilians from a flirtation with republicanism to an optimistic acceptance of monarchy. Sympathetic ministers in the Portuguese government, especially during the period of D. Rodrigo de Sousa Coutinho's control of the Department of Overseas Dominions between 1796 and 1800, encouraged many Brazilians who might have been nationalists—indeed many who had been sympathetic with the republican movement in Minas Gerais—to join in the highest levels of policy making. This collaboration between Brazilian intellectuals and enlightened ministers produced an imperial idea, Luso-Brazilian in inspiration, which moved beyond nationalism to a broader imperial solution, and sought to defuse metropolitan-colonial tensions.

The idea of Luso-Brazilian empire possessed weaknesses. The circumstances which compelled influential Brazilians to seek an accommodation during the 1790s were not permanent phenomena. Basic differences of opinion existed on vital matters such as slavery. In addition, the opposition in Portugal to the Luso-Brazilian concept was seriously underestimated, and had been neutralized only by the French invasion. In 1808, moreover, the viability and acceptability of the blueprints had yet to be tested. How fundamental these weaknesses might be only the future would reveal. But whatever the impact of the imperial idea itself, the Luso-Brazilian generation of the 1790s, which gave it shape, was to be extremely influential. D. Rodrigo became the principal minister of the first new world monarchy. José da Silva Lisboa was the ideologue of free trade. Manuel Ferreira da Câmara became intendant of mines and his family was instrumental in securing Minas Gerais and Bahia for Dom Pedro I. José Bonifácio de Andrada e Silva became the patriarch of Brazilian independence. And it is also noteworthy that following 1789, in the Lisbon Academy of Sciences and in the writing of private individuals, debates were opened on topics such as laissez faire, slavery, and the slave trade, which were to dominate discussion of Brazilian development for much of the nineteenth century.

Pierre Chaunu entitled a discussion of the transition of Portuguese America from colony to independent nation, *Heureux Brésil*.[131] If Brazil was indeed fortunate in its monarchical solution, in being spared the agonies of nineteenth-century Spanish America,

131. Pierre Chaunu, *L'Amérique et les Amériques* (Paris, 1964) 216.

part of the cause must be sought not in the Brazilians' lack of imagination, instruction, and enlightenment, or even in vague attributes of their national character, but in the perspicacity of the generation of the 1790s, who brought reason to the analysis of colonial problems, and with optimistic faith projected a grandiose concept of Luso-Brazilian empire.

SOCIOECONOMIC ASPECTS

STUART B. SCHWARTZ:

Free Labor in a Slave Economy:The Lavradores de Cana of Colonial Bahia

For more than one hundred years sugar ruled Brazil. From the end of the sixteenth to the beginning of the eighteenth century the cultivation of sugar provided Brazil with its *raison d'être* and shaped the society that grew around it. Even after its decline in the colony's total economic production, sugar continued to mold the land of the coastal Northeast and the lives of the people upon it. Social scientists, historians, and novelists have probably written more about the plantation life of the Brazilian Northeast than about any other region or aspect of the Brazilian past. Many of these authors, writing from the vantage point of the late nineteenth century, have traced the outline of the colonial Northeast in a sharp contrast of black and white, slave and master, and paid little or no attention to social elements that do not readily fit the authors' model of a semi-feudal, almost manorial agrarian society based on slavery.[1] Slavery and *latifundia* undoubtedly cast a long shadow over the colonial past, but our histories, peopled with governors, planters, slaves, and a few missionaries, have left little space for the artisan, small farmer, wage laborer, poor white, and freed slave. The stories

1. The classic, of course, is Gilberto Freyre, *The Masters and the Slaves,* Samuel Putnam trans. (2nd ed. in English; New York, 1956). The literature on sugar is enormous. Deserving of special mention are Manuel Diegues Júnior, *O Banguê nas Alagoas* (Rio de Janeiro, 1949) and José Wanderley Pinho, *História de um engenho do Recôncavo* (Rio de Janeiro, 1946). In the 1940s, José Honório Rodrigues published a series of articles in the pages of *Brasil Açucareiro* which in their totality constitute an extremely important contribution to the study of the colonial sugar economy. As guides to sources, the reader is directed to Rodrigues' "Notas á literatura brasileira sôbre açúcar no século xvii," *Brasil Açúcareiro,* XXV (1945), no. 5, 420–424; "A literatura brasileira sôbre açúcar no século xviii," *Brasil Açúcareiro,* XX (1942) no. 1, 6–25: "A literature brasileira sôbre açúcar no século xix," *Brasil Açúcareiro,* XIX (1942), no. 5, 16–38. The best short descriptions of the colonial sugar economy are Alice P. Canabrava's "A grande propriedade rural," in Sérgio Buarque de Holanda, ed., *História geral da civilização brasileira,* 5 vols. to date (São Paulo, 1959—), I:2, 192–217; and Frédéric Mauro, *Le Portugal et l'Atlantique au xviie siècle* (Paris, 1960), chaps. III, IV.

of the latter group constitute a relatively unwritten series of chapters in Brazilian social and economic history. This paper, therefore, is intended as a preliminary probe into the history of one sector of the free population of colonial Brazil, the *lavradores de cana* (cane growers) of Bahia.[2]

A number of conceptual and methodological problems must be stated here as a preface. Since secondary literature on the lavradores de cana is virtually non-existent, much of the following discussion must be limited to matters of definition and description as a necessary step toward more interpretive treatment. This limitation, however, raises a second problem, for the primary materials that serve as the basis for our discussion often fail to resolve the questions the historian finds most interesting. In many ways writing the history of the cane growers is similar to writing the history of the plantation slaves, for both histories can only be written through the records of others or from the impersonal ledgers and account books of contracts long forgotten and harvests long past. For these reasons the papers of the plantation of Sergipe do Conde in Bahia present a unique source of information. These account books, letters, contracts, and legal transcripts, some of which are published but most of which remain in manuscript, offer a window to the past and a unique source on the history of the lavradores de cana.[3]

2. I have used the term cane growers as the best translation of lavradores de cana because the more frequently used "tenants," "copyholders," or "share-croppers" refer to forms to tenure that were not necessarily common to all.

3. The major collection of the papers of Engenho Sergipe do Conde is located in ANTT, Cartório dos Jesuitas. In the series *Documentos Históricos* published by the Biblioteca Nacional do Rio de Janeiro, the following volumes relating to Sergipe do Conde have appeared: LXIII (1944) "Tombo das Terras pertencentes a' Igreja de Santo Antão da Companhia de I.H.S. Bahia, Livro V," and a continuation in LXIII (1944), and LXIV (1944). The Instituto do Açúcar e do Álcool of Rio de Janeiro has published in its series *Documentos para a história do açúcar* (hereafter cited as *DHA*), Engenho Sergipe do Conde: Livro das Contas (1622–1653); and Engenho Sergipe do Conde: Espólio de Mem de Sá (1569–1579). The following manuscript ledgers of Engenho Sergipe have been used in conjunction with the published account books: 1611 (maço 14, no. 4); 1612–1613 (maço 17, no. 19); 1654–1656 (maço 17, no. 22); 1669–1670 (maço 17, no. 24); 1680–1681 (maço 17, no. 25); 1699–1700 (maço 17, no. 27); 1704–1706 (maço 17, no. 28); 1705–1716 (maço 17, no. 28); 1722–1723 (maço 17, no. 30); 1725–1726 (maço 17, no. 31). A preliminary evaluation of the Engenho Sergipe ledgers for the years 1622–1635 is presented in Frédéric Mauro, *Nova História e novo mundo* (São Paulo, 1969), 135–148. A statistical analysis of Engenho Sergipe for the years 1622–1652 appears in Mircea Buescu, *História econômica*

Sergipe do Conde was one of the largest and certainly the most famous of the sugar plantations in colonial Brazil. Founded by Governor Mem de Sá in the 1560s, it passed to his daughter in 1572 and became part of her dowry when she married Dom Fernando de Noronha, count of Linhares, in that year. Upon her death in 1612, the plantation became embroiled in a three-way lawsuit involving the Jesuit College of Santo Antão of Lisbon, the Jesuit College in Bahia, and the Charitable Brotherhood (Misericórdia) of Bahia. This dispute dragged through the courts until a final decision in 1659.[4] Absentee ownership, the many legal disputes, and eventual Jesuit control should caution us against generalizing too readily from the records of Sergipe do Conde. Whenever possible, corroborating evidence has been used in conjunction with these records, and if the method is tenuous it at least has distinguished precedent. The still unsurpassed description of the Brazilian sugar economy written by Antonil (the Jesuit Father Andreoni) relied heavily on its author's short stay at Sergipe do Conde in 1689.[5]

Engenho Sergipe do Conde lay in the midst of the Bahian Recôncavo, those lands that encircled the Bay of All Saints (Maps 3 and 4).[6] This region, along with its counterpart in Pernambuco, formed the heart of the colonial sugar economy. In the 1530s sugar cultivation began in earnest and by the 1570s it had become a major economic activity on the northeastern coast. Royal land grants (*sesmarias*) had stimulated early colonization, and the process in-

---

do Brasil (Rio de Janeiro, 1970). Unfortunately, this volume came to the author's attention after this paper was submitted for publication.

4. The best short descriptions of this complex legal tangle are found in *HCJB*, V, 243–251; and A.J.R. Russell-Wood, *Fidalgos and Philanthropists: The Santa Casa da Misericórdia of Bahia 1550–1755* (Berkeley, 1968), 91–92.

5. For this paper two editions of Antonil were used. João António Andreoni, *Cultura e opulência do Brasil*, Alice P. Canabrava, ed. (São Paulo, 1967) has a fine introduction, but the recent edition by Mlle, Andrée Mansuy, André João Antonil, *Cultura e opulência do Brasil por suas drogas e minas*, Travaux & Mémoires de l'Institut des Hautes Etudes de l'Amérique Latine, no. 21 (Paris, 1968), is especially useful since the extensive notes and introduction are based on the papers of Engenho Sergipe. I have followed Mlle. Mansuy's argument that Antonil visited Sergipe do Conde in 1689, although his work was first published in 1711.

6. Engenho Sergipe do Conde was located in the area near the present towns of Santo Amaro and São Francisco do Conde. São Francisco do Conde was the subject of Harry W. Hutchinson's community study, *Village and Plantation Life in Northeastern Brazil* (Seattle, 1957). On Santo Amaro there is Herundino da Costa Leal, *História de Santo Amaro* (Salvador, 1964).

MAP 3

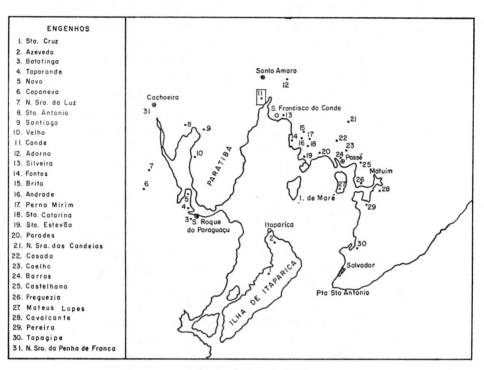

ENGENHOS

1. Sta. Cruz
2. Azevedo
3. Batatinga
4. Taparande
5. Novo
6. Copaneva
7. N. Sra. da Luz
8. Sto. Antonio
9. Santiago
10. Velho
11. Conde
12. Adorno
13. Silveira
14. Fontes
15. Brito
16. Andrade
17. Perna Mirim
18. Sta. Catarina
19. Sto. Estevão
20. Parades
21. N. Sra. das Candeias
22. Casada
23. Coelho
24. Barros
25. Castelhano
26. Freguezia
27. Mateus Lopes
28. Cavalcante
29. Pereira
30. Tapagipe
31. N. Sra. da Penha de Franca

The Recôncavo in 1630

tensified after the arrival of Tomé de Sousa, first governor-general, in 1549. Tomé de Sousa granted a large number of sesmarias in the Recôncavo and his example was followed by royal officials in Bahia and elsewhere. Although by the mid-seventeenth century some of these grants encompassed miles of inland territory exceeding at times "whole provinces in Portugal," the majority of these coastal sesmarias were smaller in scale, usually one or two leagues square.[7]

7. One league equals between 5,555 and 6,600 meters. Sebastião Cardoso de Sampaio wrote to the Crown in the 1670s "que houve pessoa q. pedio e impetrou sesmaria q. comprehende mais terra q. hua provincia inteira de Portugal." This document is reprinted in José Pinheiro da Silva, "A capitania de Baía," *Revista portuguesa de história*, pt. iv, XI (1964), 93. An interesting quantitative analysis of sesmarias was presented by Célia Freire A. Fonseca, "Colonização e doações de terras no Brasil colonial," (mimeo), a paper presented to the VI International Colloquium of Luso-Brazilian Studies (1966). Her analysis of 1.141 Paraíban sesmarias showed 87.5 percent smaller than four leagues square. Two good

MAP 4

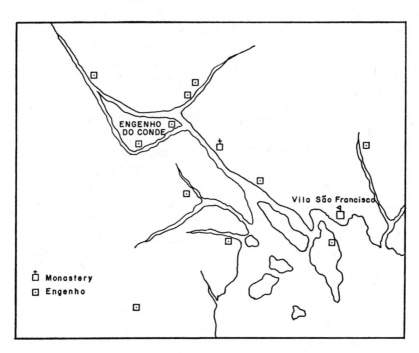

Sergipe do Conde and its Environs

The grants of the sesmarias had the desired effect of fixing colonists on the land. Holders of these grants erected sugar mills
(*engenhos*) and planted the land in cane. Often the mill owners
(*senhores de engenho*) subdivided their lands by renting or selling
portions to those men who lacked the capital or credit to set up
their own mills and who were willing to grow cane for others. In
fact, the instructions Tomé de Sousa received from the Crown not
only advocated the granting of sesmarias, but also recognized the
need to provide for cane growers. This recognition can be taken as
royal acknowledgment of an existing situation in which senhores
de engenho had already come to depend on cane growers to supply

studies of the sesmaria in microcosm are provided by José Antônio Gonsalves
de Mello in "Sesmaria de Santo André de Muribeca, Origem do Engenho dos
'Guararapes'," *Revista do Arquivo Público* (Recife), VI (1949), 217–248; and
"O Engenho Guarapes e a Igreja dos Prazeres," *ibid.*, XIII–XIV (1958), 5–13.
The best general study is Costa Porto, *Estudo sôbre o sistema sesmarial* (Recife,
1965).

the mills.[8] In the early days of the Brazilian sugar industry, planters viewed renting or sharecropping as an effective way of sharing costs and risks without losing control of the land.

The cane growers, however, were only one element of free labor that the plantations of the Recôncavo drew upon. Skilled and unskilled laborers provided a wide range of skills, services, and goods on a wage basis. Artisans had arrived in considerable numbers in the company of Tomé de Sousa's expedition, and both town and plantation found good use for their services.[9] A large plantation like Sergipe do Conde maintained a permanent staff of ten to twenty salaried employees who served as artisans and technicians. These men might earn simple salary (*soldada seca*), but more often they also received room and board. Although one estate manager claimed that a large engenho might have twenty whites performing these tasks and eating at the estate's expense, other evidence indicates that slaves and occasionally freedmen also filled these positions.[10]

The account books of Engenho Sergipe do Conde clearly indicate that skilled and unskilled laborers provided a wide spectrum of services on a less permanent basis. Smiths, carpenters, barber-surgeons, and priests often came to the plantations from Salvador to perform necessary tasks. The engenho paid them on a piecework or a daily basis. No *safra* (harvest) passed without payments to these hired workers, and salaries at Engenho Sergipe amounted to 19 percent of the total expenditures.[11] Moreover, every year the plantations expected to employ an extra boatman, woodcutter, or

8. "Regimento de 17 de Dezembro de 1548 do Governador Geral do Brasil," *Documentos para a história do açúcar*, I (*Legislação*) (Rio de Janeiro, 1954), 45–62. See also Wanderley Pinho, *História*, 310. For comparative purposes see W. K. Marshall, "Metayage in the Sugar Industry of the British Windward Islands, 1838–1865," *Jamaican Historical Review*, V, (May, 1965), 28–55; and Roger Ransom and Richard Sutch, "The Rise of Sharecropping in the American South (1865–1900): A Preliminary Report," Southern Economic History Project, Working Paper, No. 1 (Berkeley 1969).

9. *DH*, XIV, "Mandados, provisões, doações;" XXXVIII, "Mandados, 1549–1552."

10. Father Andreoni (Antonil) noted that slaves provided some skilled labor. By the early eighteenth century, slaves filled even the most important position of sugar master. Governor Luís Cezar de Meneses wrote to the Crown in 1706 that, "os mestres de assucar que hoje se achão nos engenhos que ha no Recôncavo desta cidade da Bahia são muy poucos por cuja causa sevalem muitos senhores de engenho, de seus escravos para este menister." APB, Ordens régias 7, no. 440, 441 (Bahia, 6 Nov. 1706).

11. Mauro, "Contabilidade teórica," 143.

cowboy, or to pay an Indian for carrying a message or to reward a slave hunter for returning a runaway. Such un- or semiskilled laborers constituted a third category in the free labor force.

In the sugar country, therefore, the lavrador was one type of free laborer among others, but even here we must establish a more precise definition. The term lavrador essentially means tiller or farmer, but during the colonial period it had a variety of other meanings. In the late eighteenth century, for example, the term lavrador was commonly used to describe anyone engaged in agriculture, even a great senhor de engenho.[12] Generally, however, a distinction did exist between the senhor de engenho (mill owner) and the lavrador de cana (cane grower). Not all lavradores were cane growers, for the term also applied to subsistence farmers (lavradores de roça) and tobacco farmers (lavradores de fumo).

The above distinctions are not presented to satisfy the author's desire for neat categories, but are essential for an understanding of the economic and political activities of the groups mentioned. The free laborers in colonial Brazil did not constitute a third segment of the population somewhere between masters and slaves, but, rather, constituted a series of four to six social groups partially differentiated by class, race, and political goals. The lavradores de cana took considerable pride in their title and usually set themselves apart from the other farmers. Despite the antagonisms and conflict born in their relationship to the mill owners, the lavradores de cana identified their interests with those of the owners and the sugar sector in general. Petitions to Crown or town council usually bore the signatures of both growers and owners.[13] If sugar was king and the mill owners his barons, the lavradores hoped to be his squires.

Land: Tenure, Size, and Pattern

Land stood at the core of the cane grower's existence. It determined his relationship to the engenho and his position in society. The types of tenure that tied the lavrador de cana to the engenho

12. João Rodrigues de Brito, Cartas economico-politicas sôbre a agricultura e commercio da Bahia (Lisbon, 1821), 1–24, uses "lavrador" in this sense which appears to be based on common usage.

13. For example, see the petition of 1639 from the senhores de engenho and lavradores de cana to the Count of Torre; Biblioteca do Itamaraty, Cartas do Conde de Torre, I, 102.

had firm roots in Portugal's agrarian traditions, for the forms of
purchase, rent, and sharecropping used in northeastern Brazil followed medieval precedents in form if not always in proportion and
frequency of use.[14] By far the most advantaged were those men
who possessed full and clear title to lands acquired by purchase or
grant. Such independent ownership gave them considerable leeway
in bargaining with mill owners over the grinding of the cane. Although the division of the sugar produced of this "free cane"
appears to have been a standard 50 percent to the engenho and
50 percent to the cane grower, the lavrador de cana could negotiate
other advantages like the loan of slaves and oxen or preferential
treatment in the assignment of the grinding schedule at the mill.

Planters probably preferred to rent at a fixed rate so that all risk
would fall on the lavrador, but far more common was the so-called
partido de cana in which the lavrador de cana leased land from the
mill with certain restrictions on its use and the disposal of the
produce. These contracts varied from place to place over time.
Engenho owners favored the *partido de terço* (third) or *partido de
quarto* (fourth) in which the lavrador de cana agreed to pay the
engenho one-third or one-fourth of his half of the sugar produced
from cane.[15] In the instructions issued to Christóvão Barroso in
1607, the countess of Linhares specifically ordered that he try to
rent lands at the "third."[16] This contract placed a heavy burden on
the lavrador de cana since in each safra he would receive only one-
third of the sugar his cane produced. A particularly bad harvest

14. Armando Castro, *A evolução económica de Portugal dos séculos xii a xv*,
7 vols. (Lisbon, 1966), V, 75–122; Henrique da Gama Barros, *História da admin-
istração pública em Portugal*, 11 vols. (2nd ed., Lisbon, 1945–54), VII, VIII, IX.
A fine summary of modern agricultural practices in Brazil is presented in T.
Lynn Smith *Brazil: People and Institutions*, 2nd ed. (Baton Rouge, 1963), chaps.
11–14.

15. For a general description see Mansuy, *Cultura*, 260. Adriaen van der
Dussen, *Relatório sôbre as capitanias conquistadas no Brasil pelos holandeses
(1639)*, José Antônio Gonsalves de Mello, trans. and ed. (Rio de Janeiro, 1947),
93–95. In the *Diálogos das grandezas do Brasil* (1618), José Antônio Gonsalves
de Mello, ed., (2nd ed.; Recife, 1966), 87–88, its author, Ambrósio Fernandes
Brandão, noted that a 50 percent division was sometimes made on "captive
cane" but only on rare occasions.

16. "Apontamentos que levão Christóvão Barroso que agora mando por
feitor da fazenda . . . ," (Lisbon, 23 March 1601), ANTT, Cartório dos Jesuítas,
maço 13, no. 14. These instructions on how to conduct the mill's business
should be compared with a similar document published by José Antônio Gonsalves de Mello as "Um Regimento de feitor-mor de engenho de 1663," *Boletim
do Instituto Joaquim Nabuco*, II (1953), 80–87.

could quickly spell complete failure for growers who farmed on this basis. On the other hand, the engenho owners usually rented their best lands in rather large parcels at the "third" rate. In Sergipe do Conde those lands along the bay or well-situated on rivers where the soil was good and transport easy rented at the "third," whereas lands without access to water transport were leased at the "fourth."[17] In Pernambuco similar criteria of fertility and access to cheap transport determined the contractual relationship of the planter and the cane grower.[18]

Because of the heavy rent obligations, only farmers of some substance accepted a large partido de terço. The mill owners encouraged this situation, because they wished to place their prime lands in the hands of those who could best cultivate them. In fact, the records of Sergipe do Conde indicate a definite reluctance to conclude a "third" contract with poor cane growers. In 1617 the Engenho Sergipe began to renegotiate contracts with its cane growers, and the estate manager, Manoel do Couto, refused to lease good lands at the "third" to poorer lavradores de cana despite their willingness. He claimed that their offers were "only words since they have not the capital, ability, or slaves necessary for those who must supply cane on the third."[19] Thus, the best cane lands went to those who already possessed some wealth and who could afford to meet the rigors of the one-third contract. Their substance did not preclude hard work and great effort. The industry of the lavrador de terço was proverbial. Bernardo Ribeiro, estate manager at Sergipe in 1612, observed that one poor farmer was "felling trees, hoeing, and planting the land at great cost to his pocket as if he would have to provide the terço."[20] Still, the large capital resources of many lavradores de terço should make clear that the cane growers were not poor white tenants.

In the boom days of the sixteenth and early seventeenth centuries engenho owners did not find it difficult to lease lands at the

17. Estevão Pereira "Dase rezão da fazenda que o Collegio de Santo Antão tem no Brazil, e de seus Rendimentos," ANTT, Cartório dos Jesuítas, maço 13, no. 20. This document has been published in *AMP*, IV (1931), 773–794; and as an appendix to Mansuy, *Cultura*, pp. 513–527.

18. Van der Dussen, *Relatório*, 93.

19. Manoel do Couto to countess of Linhares (Bahia, 20 Aug. 1617), ANTT, Cartório dos Jesuítas, maço 13, no. 7.

20. Bernardo Ribeiro to countess of Linhares (Bahia, 17 March 1612), ANTT, Cartório dos Jesuítas, maço 8, no. 190.

one-third or one-fourth rate. At Engenho Sergipe often one-third of the growers held land at the "third" in this period. By the late seventeenth century conditions had changed significantly. The falling price of sugar and the rush to the gold mines of Minas Gerais caused a dearth of available cane growers. By the 1690s the contract in Pernambuco was at one-fifth and in Bahia one-fifteenth or one-twentieth.[21] These conditions indicate the inability of the planters to find and hold lavradores de cana against the centrifugal forces of the gold of Minas Gerais and the prestige of mill ownership to which most lavradores de cana aspired.

The lease of a partido (arrendamento) varied as to provisions for length of tenure and reciprocal obligations, however, the contract concluded between lavrador de cana Custódio Lobo and the Engenho Sergipe indicates the general format.[22] Although Antonil reported that contracts in the 1680s were normally nine or eighteen years, in the 1640s the Engenho Sergipe preferred a six-year contract.[23] Custódio Lobo, however, agreed to accept a partido de terço for fifty years. He agreed to plant new cane fields and after the first three cuttings to bring his cane to the engenho where it would be divided two-thirds to the mill and one-third to the grower. If the mill manager felt that the grower's cane was not needed for a particular safra, Lobo was free to mill it at another engenho, but the engenho of Sergipe still received one-third of the sugar produced. Custódio Lobo could not sublease the partido or

21. Mansuy, *Cultura*, 260.
22. "Arrendamento de Custódio Lobo" (8 Aug. 1617), ANTT, Cartório dos Jesuítas, maço 12, n. 7.
23. Mansuy, *Cultura*, p. 94. On the preference for the six year contract see, "Treslado dos arrendamentos q. fes o P. Sebastião Vaz e o P. Simão de Soutomayor de varias terras do Engenho de Sergipe," ANTT, Cartório dos Jesuítas, maço 13, no. 32; and "Apontamentos . . . Christóvão Barroso," f. 2v. Professor José Antônio Gonsalves de Mello has discovered two contracts between lavradores de cana and the Engenho Suassuna in seventeenth-century Pernambuco. In the contract of 1638 concluded between Lavrador Jorge Saraiva and the Engenho Suasunna, the lavrador agreed to supply forty tarefas of cane for a nine year period. The sugar would be divided two-fifths to the lavrador and three-fifths to the engenho. The lavrador was allowed to plant foodstuffs on his property and to pasture his animals on the engenho's land. After nine years and two months the contract was terminated, and the lavrador was required to move, leaving behind all improvements made on the property. These somewhat favorable conditions for the lavrador may be related to the special conditions created by Dutch occupation of Pernambuco in this period. These documents are part of the Arquivo do Engenho Suassuna now housed in the Arquivo da Diretoria de Obras, Fiscalização e Serviços Públicos (Recife).

any part of it without the consent of the Engenho Sergipe, and then only under the same conditions and obligations stated in the original contract. Unlike many lavradores, Custodio Lobo was not obliged to provide the engenho with firewood.

Most striking in the Custódio Lobo contract is the clause which required Lobo or his heirs to surrender the partido and any improvements (bemfeitorias) to the owners of the Engenho Sergipe after fifty years. Such clauses served to keep the best sugar lands in large parcels under control of the senhores de engenho rather than subdivided among the lavradores de cana. Land hunger gripped the cane growers. Their inability to acquire ownership of the lands they worked hampered the growth of the lavradores de cana as a class, for the impermanence of their tenure made it difficult for a family to establish a secure economic base. The plaint of the cane growers sometimes reaches us through the dusty legal documents. Thus Pero Bras Rey, cane grower for twenty-five years, pleaded with the count of Linhares to sell him the tiny piece of land he had worked so long, so that he might leave it to his sons.[24]

A cane grower could labor fifty years on a parcel, so it is not surprising that many developed strong attachments to the land. The letter of Pero Bras Rey indicates this feeling, and other examples can be cited. Manoel do Couto, who on orders from the count of Linhares tried to dispossess a number of cane growers, found this a difficult task. Long occupancy made the cane growers "act like masters of their lands."[25] The conflict over ownership and use of land between mill owners and cane growers runs through the history of the Recôncavo like a steady hum, and if the records of Sergipe do Conde are a fair index the pitch sometimes rose to a deafening roar.

Engenho owners tried to hold their lands for a variety of reasons. Land, of course, had a social function in colonial society. Its possession carried with it status and recognition of its owner as a man of substance, but beyond this there existed persuasive economic reasons against outright sale. Chief among these was fear of com-

24. Pero Bras Rey to count of Linhares (Sergipe do Conde, 20 April 1609), ANTT, Cartório dos Jesuítas, maço 8, no. 188.
25. "Lembrança para a Senhore Condessa de Linhares sobre as suas fazendas de Sergipe," (Bahia, 20 Aug. 1617), ANTT, Cartório dos Jesuítas, maço 13, no. 7. The same document noted that lavrador de cana Francisco de Aguilar refused to vacate the land he had worked for forty years.

petition. Once land passed permanently into the hands of another, the senhor de engenho lost control over it. An enterprising lavrador could and did often establish his own mill. The proliferation of engenhos increased competition for available cane, firewood, and lavradores de cana, and consequently was opposed by the established mill owners. In 1615 the count of Linhares sought a restraining order to prevent some of his lavradores de cana from establishing mills on lands they had purchased. His lawyer, Jorge Lopes da Costa, informed him that since the land had been sold to them outright, nothing could be done.[26] Even poor cane growers tried to set up mills, often of the small *trapiche* variety.[27]

To meet this situation mill owners reverted to *emphyteusis*, lease in perpetuity but with restrictions, as a compromise solution. The owners found that some lands because of poor quality of location could not be leased on the fraction basis of the partido.[28] Sometimes lavradores de cana could lease these lands for prices below their real value, with the perpetual obligation to provide cane to the engenho.[29] To symbolize the continuing attachment of the land to the engenho, the senhor collected a symbolic rent (*fôro*), usually two chickens or a few *alqueires* of flour.[30] In this way the grower acquired virtual ownership but the cane remained a perpetual "captive" of the mill. The following examples illustrate the crucial difference between "free" and "captive" cane. In a sale made to Simão Borges in 1602, the vendor renounced "all rights, actions, pretensions, control, and usufruct and all present and future power that he or his heirs might have on the said land . . . and

26. Licenciado Jorge Lopes da Costa to count of Linhares (Bahia, 20 March 1615), ANTT, Cartório dos Jesuítas, maço 9, no. 230. Lopes da Costa wrote that attempts to eliminate *trapiches* had failed because the land had been sold outright to the current owners.

27. In 1682 a provision prohibited the erection of engenhos closer to each other than half a league. See IHGB, Lata 37, doc. 15 (28 Nov. 1682).

28. "Figua [a terra] mais de duas leguas do engenho . . . por estar tão longe não se pode dar de terço porque he imposivel virá as canas por terra por q. passão por 20 ou mais fazendas de outros lavradores . . . ," ANTT, Cartório dos Jesuítas, maço 9, no. 241 (Bahia, 3 May 1617). In the "Apontamentos . . . Christóvão Barroso," Barroso was instructed that, "if the lands that become vacant are so played out that none will accept them at the third, you will give them to whoever can make the best *partido*."

29. Mansuy, *Cultura*, 146.

30. Failure to pay the *fôro* for three consecutive years could lead to a forfeit of all rights to the land. See *Ordenações e leys do reyno de Portugal confirmadas e estabelecidas pelo senhor rey d. João IV* (Lisbon, 1747), IV, tit xxxix.

it is totally given, ceded, and transferred to the buyer and his heirs to hold, dispose of, and use as their own property as it now becomes by means of this instrument."[31] Compare this contract with that made between lavrador de cana Diogo de Leão and the Engenho Sergipe in 1670, in which the clause was repeated but with the additional "condition and obligation that all cane planted on the said land is perpetually obligated to be milled at the Sergipe do Conde as is already the case with the buyer's [other] farms."[32]

Lavradores did occasionally buy freedom from their cane by paying a sum to the engenho, but illegal disposal of cane seems to have been common. Engenho owners viewed the alienation of "captive" cane as a serious offense, and they used both force and the courts to impede it.[33] Antonil indicites that cases of illegal disposal rose sharply when a poor safra threatened some lavradores with ruin, and relatives then tried to help them meet their contractual obligations.[34]

The lavradores de cana, therefore, can be subdivided into a number of categories according to the nature of their relationship to the land they worked. Those who owned lands outright, free of obligations, constituted a privileged group. Lavradores de cana with "captive" cane can then be subdivided into sharecroppers (lavradores de partido), tenants, or owners with obligations. These categories played an important role in determining the relationship of the lavradores de cana to other groups in society.

From the days of the earliest sesmarias, the Recôncavo became a patchwork of grants and purchases, large and small. The sesmarias were often defined in loose terms—so many leagues along the coast by so many leagues "toward the sertão," and under such definitions exact measurements were impossible. Moreover, as in Portugal, Brazilian property definition and measurement gave great attention to surface features, so that the shift of a river's course could considerably alter the boundaries of a piece of land.

31. "Escritura de venda que fez Francisco de Negreiros . . . de uma sorte de terra acima do Engenho Sergipe a Simão Borges, DH, LXII (1943), 234.
32. "Escritura de venda que fazem os Colegios de Santo Antão de Lisboa e o desta cidade [Salvador] a Diogo de Leão . . . ," DH, LXII (1943), 240.
33. "Apelado do Colegio de Santo Antão de Lisboa contra Luís Correia Ribeiro sobre a obrigação de canas da Ilha Caíaba;" "Sentença de força do Colégio de Santo Antão contra Manuel de Araújo de Amorim sobre a obrigação de cana," DH, LXIII (1944), 39–134, 134–135.
34. Mansuy, Cultura, 96.

MAP 5

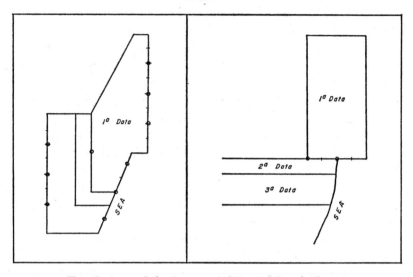

1ᵃ Data

1ᵃ Data

2ᵃ Data

3ᵃ Data

S E A

S E A

Two Surveys of the Sesmaria of Fernão Castelo Branco

In the colonial period, surface features were often used in conjunction with already defined neighboring properties as a means of establishing the perimeters of a parcel.[35] By the mid-seventeenth century the use of stone markers improved this situation, but indeterminate boundaries remained a constant source of conflict. Under Portuguese law, authentic survey measurements could only be performed by a royal magistrate.[36] These officials usually resided in Salvador or other towns, and they found trips to the agricultural regions an onerous and time-consuming task despite the extra fees they were entitled to charge.[37] Their lack of training for this task and the poorly marked boundaries contributed to the confusion. Map 5 indicates how two men, using the same definitions of a property's boundaries, arrived at very different interpretations of the property's configuration.[38]

35. Smith, *Brazil*, 259–260. Smith notes that many Brazilian land titles still contain the term *mais ou menos* (more or less).

36. See the discussion in Stuart B. Schwartz, "The High Court of Bahia: A Study in Hapsburg Brazil, 1580–1630," (Ph.D. diss., Columbia University, 1968), Chap. IV.

37. João Rodrigues Colaço to count of Linhares (Salvador, 15 Aug. 1597), ANTT, Cartório dos Jesuítas, maço 8, no. 92. Colaço noted that the judges appointed to perform the survey of the lands of the countess had not wanted to do so because of their other affairs.

38. Map 5 shows how various interpretations could be made of the written

Lands often went for years without adequate survey. Given this situation and the somewhat haphazard definition of some grants and sales, lavradores de cana often planted adjacent lands even though these did not fall within their existing contracts or purchases. These extra parcels, or *sobejos*, created great difficulties when attempts at accurate survey took place. Although individually the sobejos might be small plots, their aggregate importance can be seen in the estimate of Father Estevão Pereira who calculated the value of the sobejos of Engenho Sergipe in 1636 at 400,000 reis, an amount equal to the value of a medium-sized partido.[39] It should be noted, however, that cane growers were not the only offenders in this matter. Engenho owners also grabbed off unclaimed or unoccupied lands and then had to fight royal officers who wished to reclaim these lands for the Crown. Engenho Sergipe became embroiled in such a dispute in 1617.[40]

The holdings of the cane growers varied considerably in size and value. Although we lack information that would make it possible to compute the size of an average cane farm, there are clues that provide some idea of how much land a lavrador de cana put to use. Antonil informs us that one *tarefa* (the amount of cane that could be milled in one day) could be produced on a piece thirty *braças* per side).[41] If we use this figure as a base and multiply it by the number of tarefas, the size of the parcel under cultivation can be determined. A Jewish observer, Joseph Israel da Costa, stated in his memorial of the 1640s that a lavrador de cana usually owned twice as much land as he cultivated each year.[42] Hence a multiple of 2X can be used to indicate optimum holdings. These figures

definitions of a grant. In this case, the sesmaria granted to Fernão Castelo Branco composed of three parcels (*dadas*) was later included in the lands of Engenho Sergipe. The reader can see the differing measurements of these lands. The description that accompanied these figures is a lengthy and informative account of colonial surveying techniques. See "Rascunho das medições das terras de Sergipe," ANTT, Cartório dos Jesuítas, maço 14, no. 40.

39. Estevão Pereira, "Dase rezao da fazenda." See note 17.

40. In 1617 Desembargador Antão de Mesquita de Oliveira claimed that the countess of Linhares had taken far more land than was proper and that the lands of Sergipe do Conde had never been adequately surveyed. AHU, Bahia, papeis avulsos, caixa 1 (20 Aug. 1617).

41. 1 *braça*=2.2 meters.

42. Joseph Israel da Costa to the prince of Orange, (n.d.), The Hague, Algemein Rijksarchief, Loketkas 6, Staten Generaal West Indische Compagnie. The author wishes to thank Professor José Antônio Gonsalves de Mello for access to a photocopy of this document.

unfortunately do not take into account fluctuations in the number
of tarefas caused by changes in the quality of the cane, nor can
they indicate the considerable yearly fluctuations in the number
of tarefas a lavrador could produce. Nevertheless, the range seems
to coincide with records of land sales and evidence from Pernambuco provided in Adriaen van der Dussen's account of 1639.

Table 1 indicates the number of tarefas produced by each lavrador of the Engenho Sergipe in the safra of 1626/27. The number

TABLE 1

Size of Lands:

Lavradores de Cana of Engenho Sergipe

(Safra of 1626)

Lavrador	Tarefas	Minimum Hectares[a]	Maximum Hectares
António Jorge	27	11.88	23.76
Domingos Pereira	24	10.56	21.12
António Barroso	21	9.24	18.48
Beatris Delgada	19	8.30	16.60
Manuel Maciel Aranha	15	6.60	13.20
Fernão Cardoso	10	4.40	8.80
Gregório Francisco	9	3.96	7.92
António Rodrigues Pedreiro	8	3.52	7.04
Custódio Lobo	5	2.20	4.40
António Rodrigues Petinga	5	2.20	4.40
Manoel Esteves	4	1.76	3.52
Balthesar Gonsalves	3	1.32	2.64
António Paes	3	1.32	2.64
Amador Alvares	3	1.32	2.64
Francisco Gomes	3	1.32	2.64
António de Oliveira	2	.88	1.76
Bento de Araújo	2	.88	1.76
Gonçalo Luís	2	.88	1.76
Pedro João	2	.88	1.76
Viuva de Gaspar Alvares	2	.88	1.76
Francisco Ribeiro	2	.88	1.76
Gaspar de Araújo	1	.44	.88
Simão do Valle	1	.44	.88
Luís Mirandes	1	.44	.88
Francisco de Aguilar	1	.44	.88

SOURCE: DHA, II, Safra of 1626/27.

[a] Size in hectares has been computed by multiplying the number of tarefas by
the modern Bahian tarefa of .44 hectares.

of tarefas can also be used to calculate size of farm by using the
modern "Bahian tarefa" (a measure equal to .44 hectares) as a
measure. The results of these calculations indicate that the average
Bahian cane farm in the mid-seventeenth century included 3.07
hectares or, if we double the figures according to the information
supplied by Joseph Israel da Costa, 6.14 hectares. These figures
are, however, somewhat misleading for of the twenty-five lavradores represented in table 1, seventeen (68 percent) held lands under three hectares in size. Moreover, the four lavradores whose lands
exceeded eight hectares controlled 52 percent of the total land held.

TABLE 2

Size and Distribution of Lavrador Holdings
Engenho Sergipe, 1626–1627[a]

Holdings by size in Hectares	Number of Lavradores	Percent of Total Holdings	Percent of Land Held
0 – 3	17	68	24
3 – 8	4	16	24
8 plus	4	16	52

[a] Based on Table 1 Minimum Hectares.

By modern standards the size of these holdings seems small indeed. Certainly, the amount of cane an engenho could mill was limited by the technology of the period and the number of days in the
safra. Thus, there was no need of extensive holdings and lavrador agriculture was probably highly intensive. The small size of the
holdings indicated in table 1 may be misleading since the parcels
sold to lavradores de cana listed in table 3 are larger than seems
warranted by the tarefa calculation. The discrepancy can be explained by the inclusion of large tracts of non-arable land in a
cane grower's holdings, by a system of fallowing, or by the existence of contracts with more than one engenho. These possibilities
remain to be established.

Land values depended on the quality and location of the parcel,
and naturally varied over time. Table 3 lists a number of land sales
made in 1603 and 1604 in the vicinity of Sergipe do Conde and
suggests land values in the boom days of the sugar economy.[43]

43. In the early eighteenth century one tarefa (30 square braças) sold for
40,000 reis; "Escritura de uma sorte de terra que vendeu o capitão Luiz de
Sousa de Crasto ao donátario Manuel Garcia Pimentel (11 Aug. 1712)," DH,
LXIII (1944), 201–207.

The higher price per hectare of lands situated along the seacoast compared with those at some distance from the littoral probably reflects the former's lower operating costs because of the availability of water transport. The differences in value between the lands of Gonçalo Moreira and those of António Gonsalves Vieira demonstrates how location could influence the price of land. When the Engenho Sergipe sold lands to lavradores de cana for the cultivation of sugar cane, it maintained a semblance of legal domain (*senhorio*) over such parcels by requiring a yearly tribute of two hens. The size of the parcels and the dimensions of those indicated in table 1 are considerably greater than the plots of 50 to 60 braças described as average holdings in the subsistence district of Camamú.[44] Such disparities are indicative of the difference between the economic status of the lavrador de roça and the lavrador de cana.

The patterns of settlement and land use that emerged in the Recôncavo reflected the spontaneous growth of the sugar industry and the constant changes in ownership and development. New engenhos, land transfers, and shifting water courses created a crazy quilt of property. The ideal of each mill surrounded by its dependent cane growers on lands attached directly to the mill, like most ideals, was rarely achieved. Instead, a system of overlapping and intersecting boundaries developed, in which the lands of the engenhos and, most likely, the fields of the lavradores, were not contiguous.[45] In 1742, for example, the Engenho Sergipe bought out the competing Engenho de Pitinga because their lands were so intertwined that water transit rights could not be established. Map 6 shows this.[46]

A second aspect of the development of the Recôncavo also deserves mention here. The engenho in colonial Brazil had been a frontier institution, a factor of settlement that concentrated population in a region by providing protection as well as a locus of economic utility—a fact the planters never tired of pointing out when

44. Gonçalo Soares de França, "Dissertação da historia eclesiastica do Brasil" (1724), MS., Sociedade de Geografia de Lisboa (Reservados, 1–C–147).

45. Estevão Pereira wrote in 1635, "esta terra não está junta, mais dividida em 10 ou 12 partes ou quinhões metendosse entre huns e outros muitas propriedades alheias." See Mansuy, *Cultura*, 514.

46. Esquema do Engenho de Pitinga, ANTT, Cartório dos Jesuítas, maço 12, no. 44.

MAP 6

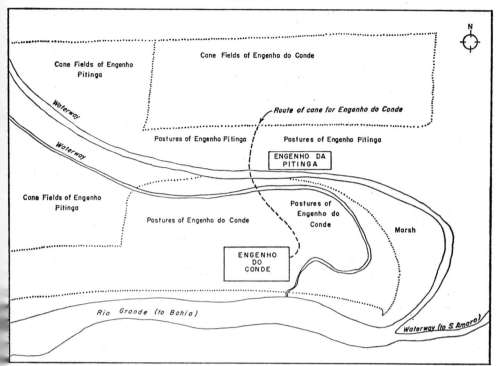

Location of the Canefields and Pastures of the Engenho Sergipe do Conde and the Engenho Pitinga (1742).

seeking some privilege.[47] But concentration around the engenho meant no concentration at all, for the engenhos assumed the functions of towns without providing many of the traditional urban services, or did so on a reduced and haphazard scale. As a result, secondary towns in the Recôncavo did not develop until the late seventeenth century, almost 200 years after the original settlement of the area.[48] The engenhos, so dependent on the primary port cities

47. For example, the sugar planters wrote in their petition of 8 January 1662, ". . . donde se fazem engenhos novos logo se povoa com vizinhança, lavradores de cabedais e operários de todos os oficios mecanicos e os mais deles com suas igrejas." Maria Izabel de Albuquerque, "Liberdade e limitação dos engenhos d'açúcar," *Anais do primeiro congresso de historia da Bahia* (Salvador, 1950), II, 491–499.

48. "Lourenço de Brito Correa pede licença para poder hua villa a sua custa, nas terras do Recôncavo do Brazil (23 Feb. 1663)," printed in José Pinheiro da Silva, "A Capitania da Baía," *Revista portuguesa de história*, XI (1964), 56–58.

TABLE 3
Sample Land Sales 1602–1063

Buyer	Area (in braças)	Total Price[a] (in milreis)	Hectares	Price[b] Per Hectare	Description
Diogo de Noronha	600 X 800	1,100	232.32	5	in the massapé
Amador Alvares Fereiro	150 X 400	400	29.04	14	on Rio Sergipe
Jácome Bravo	400 X 400	710	77.44	9	
Manuel Vandalle	350 X ?	880			sold with bemfeitorias on Pioca Island
António Fernandes	400 X 400	1,000	77.44	13	on seacoast in Patatiba
Francisco Ribeiro	500 X ?	1,100			in Patatiba
Balthesar Dias	700 X ?	960			on a point of land in Patatiba
Gonçalo Moreira	250 X 400	900	48.40	19	along the sea
Domingos Ribeiro	375 X ?	800			in Patatiba
António Gonsalves Vieira	250 X 400	700	48.40	14	
Manuel Alvares	100 X 600	380	29.04	13	on seacoast
João Ramos	400 X 400	1,150	77.44	15	
Belchior da Costa	700 X 700	940	237.16	4	contains a lake
Belchior Chaves	200 X 400	720	38.72	19	on seacoast
Simão Borges	250 X 400	510	48.40	11	along the salt marsh
João da Fonseca	250 X 250	480	30.25	16	
Padre Gaspar Dias	400 X 400	400	77.44	5	
Francisco Gil	600 X ?	1,400			on Rio Peroaçu; already surveyed
Bastião de Brito	500 X 500	600	121.00	5	on Rio Peguipe
Bernardo Ramos	200 X 400	250	48.40	5	
Luís Rodrigues		1,200			the island of Caraíba

SOURCE: ANTT, Cartório dos Jesuítas, maço 13, no. 6.

[a] All these sales included a yearly symbolic tribute of two hens to indicate their continuing attachment to Engenho Sergipe.

[b] To the nearest milreis.

of the coast, prevented the growth of secondary towns in the interior and served as poor substitutes for them.

The cane growers, artisans, and subsistence farmers, therefore, lived in the orbit of the engenhos without establishing the traditional nuclear agricultural settlements of Mediterranean Europe. Instead, a dispersed pattern, derived from the property arrangements between cane grower and mill owner, created an unconcentrated, free agricultural population. Each lavrador lived with family and slaves on his partido, separated from his neighbors and subject, not to community pressures, but to those of the senhor de engenho.[49]

Needs and Problems

There is no reason to give a description of the colonial sugar-making process, but several aspects of sugar agriculture which created special problems for the cane growers should be mentioned. Governors came and went and have served to measure time in our histories, but in the Recôncavo time moved in circles—from planting to harvesting and back again. Toward the end of February, growers began to plant the cane, and they continued to do so until late July or August. Three or four times a year the fields had to be weeded and cleaned and failure to do so resulted in weak cane and poor sugar. The cane growers turned their eyes skyward in October hoping for the seasonal rains, since rain from October to December followed by good sun thereafter produced the best growing conditions. Variations in this climatic pattern spelled disaster.

The uncertainty of weather, however, was only one danger.[50] Rats, insects, roadside theft, and foraging animals also constituted major threats to the cane crop. Unfenced cattle caused great damage, and frustrated cane growers sometimes killed stray animals.

More important were moves made in the 1690s that resulted in the foundation of the Recôncavo towns of Jaguaripe, Cachoeira, and São Francisco do Conde. See the listing in Nestor Goulart Filho, Evolução urbana do Brasil (1500–1720) (São Paulo, 1968), 86–88. The success of these towns stimulated the foundation of others like Jacobina; king to Marqués de Angeja (Lisbon, 17 Aug. 1717), APB, Ordens régias 11, no. 77.

49. Smith, Brazil, 260, presents a suggestive discussion of this pattern of settlement.

50. Mansuy, Cultura, 158.

Such killings resulted in accusations, recriminations, and vengeance.[51] Finally, in 1700, the lavradores of the Recôncavo obtained a legal decision that allowed them to kill cattle found within their cane fields without fear of legal penalty.[52] The reissue of this provision in 1709 and 1740 and a legal suit of 1785 indicate that the problem of unfenced cattle continued to plague the region.[53] To some extent, the problem was inherent in the nature of sugar agriculture.[54]

Oxen were indispensable to the cane growers. Transportation of the cane to the mill remained the grower's responsibility—thus the need for carts and oxen. The number of oxen needed by the grower varied according to the location of the land, but van der Dussen estimated that a lavrador de cana with forty tarefas of cane needed four to eight carts and six oxen for every two carts.[55] Roads were poor, bridges few, and if it rained during the safra the roads became a quagmire. Antonil noted that oxen often died drawing the heavy loads through the wet *massapé*.[56] In 1644 two lavradores de cana of the Engenho Sergipe secured release from their obligation because their land lay "far from the port and

51. Mansuy, *Cultura*, 158. The regimento of the feitor-mor of 1663 stated, "os canavais he lavouras da fazenda e fará que os lavradores façam o mesmo [cercar-os] porque nam he justo que os comao as lavouras quando elas custao tanto trabalho a prantar." In Pernambuco, the incidence of roadside theft moved the senhores de engenho and lavradores de cana to seek a law prohibiting the sale of loose cane; Flávio Guerra, *Alguns documentos de arquivos portugueses de interêsse para a história de Pernambuco* (Recife, 1969), 11.

52. Assento em q. se resolveo que fosse livre aos lavradores poderem matar os gados que acharem nos seus fructos sem por isso lhe poder ser formado crime (27 March 1700), IHGB, Lata 37, doc. 4, p. 9.

53. Reissue of the provision in 1709 is recorded in BGUC, Cod. 711, f. 123. The reissue followed an attempt in 1708 to legislate cattle-raising out of the manioc producing areas. See Governor João de Lencastre to ? (Bahia, n.d.), APB, Cartas do Governo 150. The law of 1740 was noted by Cristóvao Marques de Azevedo who complained about unfenced cattle in 1770 (BNRJ, II–34, 4, 36). In 1785 lavrador Manuel Fernandes Guimarães brought suit against João de Sousa da Camara for the damage caused by his cattle; Oficio do Juiz Ordinario da Villa de Maragogipe, BNRJ, 33, 21, 87. Similar complaints were voiced in Pernambuco; Guerra, *Alguns documentos*, 145.

54. Note in Map 4 the proximity of the *pastos* (pastures) of one engenho and the *canaviais* (cane fields) of the other.

55. Van der Dussen, *Relatório*, 94.

56. In 1716 the Crown ordered the superior magistrate of Bahia to build a bridge in the area of São Francisco do Conde since transport to the engenhos was impossible due to swampy conditions; AHU, Conselho Ultramarino, Codice 247, f. 73v. Mansuy, *Cultura*, 166.

when it rains they can not cart the cane."[57] Such conditions ruined
or imperiled a number of harvests in the 1720s and similar circumstances damaged the harvest of 1751. The royal officials who
reported the bad news usually noted the difficulties of transport.[58]
The working life of an ox has been calculated at three years, so
that the original investment and replacement costs for cattle figured
high among the cane grower's expenses.[59]

The German historian Hermann Wätjen claimed that lavradores
de cana received food from the mill owners, but there is no proof
to support this assertion.[60] Instead, it appears that lavradores
either grew some manioc and vegetables or bought these items
from the "miserable" manioc farmers who formed the lowest element of the free agricultural population. Cane growers tried to
plant as much as possible of their fields in profitable sugar cane.
As a result, the engenhos and the lavradores de cana bought much
of their foodstuffs from Indian villages, from poor farmers in the
Recôncavo, or from southern Bahia. Farmers in the Recôncavo
displayed a marked reluctance to cultivate manioc and preferred

57. "Treslado do arrendamento . . . ," ANTT, Cartório dos Jesuítas, maço
13, no. 32, f. 2v.

58. Beginning in the 1720s, the Viceroy in Bahia kept the Crown informed
on local harvest conditions. These letters can now be seen in the books of
gubernatorial correspondence of the Arquivo Público do Estado da Bahia. The
following exerpt indicates their content: "foy tão irregular o verão passado que
ficou ventagens ao Inverno e ouve huma chea tão formidavel que nao só passou
os limites do possivel mas ainda os mais antigos senão lembrão de outra semel-
hante e esta innudação produzio huns taes effeytos que empedio totalmente as
moagens arruinou as fabricas morrendo escravos, boys, e cavallos e ultimamente
empede as conduções e transportes." Viceroy Vasco Cezar de Meneses to king
(Bahia, 19 March 1727), APB, Ordens régias, no. 21. In 1751 Governor Diogo
de Mendonça Corte Real wrote to the king that engenhos far from the coast
were waiting for the sun to dry the effects of heavy rains so that the carts could
pass (esperar pelo bom tempo que enchuque os atoleiros para andarem os
carros). IHGB, Correspondencia do Governador da Bahia, Arquivo, 1, 1, 19.

59. Celso Furtado, *The Economic Growth of Brazil* (Berkeley, 1963), 47. Hermann Kellenbenz gives the price of an ox as 12,000 reis in 1618 and 20,000 in
1660. Engenho Sergipe, however, bought oxen at 2,000 to 4,000 reis per head
in the seventeenth century. Cf. Livro de Contas, 139; Hermann Kellenbenz,
"Einige Aspeckte der frühen Wirtschafts-und Sozialgeschichte des Nordesten
von Brasilien," *Jahrbüch für Geschichte von Staat, Wirtschaft und Gesselschaft
Latein-Amerikas* (1964), 56. I owe this reference to David Denslow's unpublished paper, "The First Brazilian Sugar Cycle," which he kindly put at my
disposal.

60. Hermann Wätjen, "The Dutch Colonial Empire in Brazil" (Peter Guild-
brandsen, trans.), typescript in the Bancroft Library, University of California,
Berkeley, 446.

instead to raise sugar cane or tobacco. Royal officials took steps to insure the availability of subsistence crops by limiting agriculture in Cairú and Camamú to food production.[61] As we shall see, the sugar producers' reluctance to plant manioc often caused food shortages that were most sharply felt by the slave population.

Another item essential to the sugar agroindustry of colonial Brazil and of concern to the cane growers was wood. Large amounts of firewood were necessary for boiling the cane syrup in the sugar making process and the mills of the Recôncavo and the Várzea displayed a voracious appetite for wood. The use of bagasse, so common in the seventeenth-century Caribbean, did not become widespread in Brazil until the next century.[62] The results of this technological failure could be seen in the depleted forest resources of the coast and the somewhat migratory nature of sugar agriculture in the eighteenth century. It took between fifteen and twenty tarefas of wood to produce ten tarefas of sugar, and as early as the first decade of the seventeenth century, deforestation had become a problem. Wood and cane became the two pillars of the sugar economy, items indispensable for success.[63]

61. The area of southern Bahia, the towns of Cairú, Camamú, São Jorge de Ilheús, and Boipeba traditionally produced manioc for the Recôncavo. Tobacco competed with manioc in certain areas of the Recôncavo. In 1639 the count of Torre prohibited the cultivation of tobacco in the southern towns in order to assure the supply of manioc flour. (Letters of the count of Torre, 5 and 12 Feb. 1639, Biblioteca do Itamaraty, Cartas do Conde da Torre, I, 95; II, 3.) In the eighteenth century similar restrictions, intended to secure the manioc supply, were imposed on Jaguaripe, Cachoeira, and Maragogipe. See king to Luís Cezar de Meneses (3 Aug. 1706) and Meneses to king (Bahia, 25 May 1708), APB, Ordens régias 7, no. 511, 511A. Manioc and tobacco still compete in the Recôncavo as is shown in E. Haskins, "An Agricultural Geography of the Bahian Recôncavo," (Ph.D. diss., University of Minnesota, 1956), 155–157.

62. Gilberto Freyre, Nordeste, 2nd ed. (Rio de Janeiro, 1951), Chap. III, "A Terra e a Matta." Wanderley Pinho, História, 141–161 collates a number of pertinent sources. On the failure to use bagasse (the stalks of the cane left after pressing) see the excellent article of Alice P. Canabrava, "A lavoura canavieira nas Antilhas e no Brasil," Anais do Prieiro Congresso da História da Bahia, IV (1950), 337–350.

63. The regimento of the Relação (High Court) of Bahia noted the problem of deforestation and instructed the judges to guard against it. The regimento is printed in José Justiano de Andrade e Silva, Colleção chronologica da legislação portugueza, 12 vols. (Lisbon, 1854), I, 258–265. See also APB, Ordens régias 3, no. 17 on the same problem in the 1690s. The competition for available firewood was fierce. In 1690 a group of men from the engenho of António da Rocha invaded the lands of the Jesuit-owned Engenho Pitanga. When two

The documents of the Engenho Sergipe do not provide a clear picture of the cane growers' role in the supply of firewood. Cristóvão Barroso described the grower's obligation to supply the wood necessary for processing his cane as "the custom of the land," but other documents of the period claimed he was not obligated.[64] It would appear that in the early seventeenth century the lavradores de cana supplied the necessary firewood, but that by mid-century the engenho bought firewood, often from the growers. A contract of 1648 noted that if the grower produced "firewood, boards, crates, or foodstuffs he will sell them, things being equal, to this engenho."[65] By the mid-seventeenth century the purchase of firewood from the cane growers became a regular item of the plantation's accounts and in fact amounted to 21 percent of operating costs.[66] The sale of firewood probably supplied the growers with extra funds, and some cane farmers also made crates which provided still another source of income.[67]

"The workings of the farms of Brazil depend on blacks and more blacks."[68] This observation held as true for the cane growers as it did for the mill owners. Slavery provided the labor needed for the planting, harvesting, and carting of the sugar. One account from the seventeenth century estimated that twenty slaves were

Jesuits tried to stop the intrusion and the theft of firewood, the interlopers insulted the fathers and beat one with a club (dando em hu delles com hu pao muyta pancada cuio excesso fora muyto escandallozo, e sentido dos moradores desse estado). King to António Luís Gonsalves da Câmara Coutinho (Lisbon, 7 Dec. 1690), APB, Ordens régias 1, no. 92.

64. Cristóvão Barroso to count of Linhares (1612), ANTT, Cartório dos Jesuítas, maço 13, no. 15. Bernardo Ribeiro wrote in the same year that "all the settlers who raise sugarcane on the plantation of Your Grace provide wood for processing." (Letter to count of Linhares, ANTT, Cartório dos Jesuítas, maço 9, no. 210.) But, a response to Barroso's statement noted that the lavradores de cana did not always provide wood (ANTT, Cartório dos Jesuítas, maço 13, no. 15).

65. Contract with the brothers Matheus and Pedro de Oliveira (1648), ANTT, Cartório dos Jesuítas, maço 13, no. 32.

66. DHA, Livro das Contas, 41, 84, 163, 247, 352. The tarefa of firewood consisted of eight cart-loads, each cart being seven spans high and eight long. It sold for 2,000 to 2,500 reis. On operating costs of Engenho Sergipe see Mauro, "Contabilidade teórica," 137–145.

67. "[T]em lavradores em Cergipe que lhas [caixas] fazem." Bernardo Ribeiro to count of Linhares (Bahia, 20 Sept. 1612), ANTT, Cartório dos Jesuítas, maço 9, no. 210.

68. Bernardo Ribeiro to count of Linhares (Bahia, n.d.), ANTT, Cartório dos Jesuítas, maço 8, no. 164.

required to produce forty tarefas of cane.[69] Unfortunately, the records of Engenho Sergipe reveal very little about the number and treatment of growers' slaves. Nevertheless, a few remarks from supporting materials shed some light on this topic.

The slaves of the lavradores de cana were used almost exclusively as field hands. To them fell the removal of trees, the planting, weeding, and cutting of the cane. During the safra each male slave was assigned a quota of cane to be cut. The slave was expected to cut seven "hands of cane" or 350 faggots a day. The women worked in the fields binding the cane into faggots. Children performed minor tasks and were often assigned to drive the cane-laden carts to the mill or to tend the animals in the pasture.[70] Field labor called for great exertion, but beyond this, other factors influenced the treatment of the growers' slaves.

Unlike the slaves of the mill owners, those of the growers did not labor at night amidst those Bosch-like scenes of whirring cogs and boiling couldrons that reminded more than one observer of hell.[71] Conversely, the demands of the partido de terço and the financial pressures on the lavrador forced him to demand optimum toil from his captive labor force. A man who owned ten or twenty slaves could ill afford the luxury, no matter what its social advantage, of employing his laborers in non-productive ways. The privileged house slaves and the liveried porters we have come to associate with the great plantations of the nineteenth-century found no place on the farms of the cane growers. Aside from the arduous labor, the numerical superiority of black slaves elicited a compensatory harshness from their masters. Planned terror was the means by which a cane grower or his driver worked the fields alone with twenty or thirty slaves.[72] Moreover, when ends did not meet, the lavrador de

69. Van der Dussen, *Relatório*, 93–94.

70. Mansuy, *Cultura*, pp. 162–165.

71. The Roman Catholic priests, Andreoni (Antonil) and Antônio Vieira, and the Jew, Joseph Israel da Costa, all used the image of hell as a fitting comparison with the engenho. It should be noted that a few references exist in the records of Engenho Sergipe to the rental of grower's slaves by the engenho for various tasks. See *DHA*, Livro das Contas, 221.

72. ". . . os castigão regurrosamente para que acudão a seu trabalho e como andão nus os magoão demasiadamente e dizem hé necessario assi porque outro modo não segeria a obra nem elles teriam o temor do Branco que se requere pois em hum engenho destes quando haja 8:10 Brancos he o mais e muitas vezes em hua fazenda de canaveis hu soo branco e 30, 40, 50 escravos que lhe obedesca . . . ," Joseph Israel da Costa to prince of Orange (1630s).

cana cut his costs of slave maintenance first. Although slaves undoubtedly constituted a major item of expense in the cane grower's
budget, a great deal of evidence exists showing that care and kind-
ness often gave way to the margin of profit. Time after time the
Crown intervened to force mill owners and cane growers to provide
adequate food for their slaves or at least to allow them free time to
cultivate their own crops.[73] The Crown intervened as early as
1606, but almost every man who wrote of conditions on the Bahian
plantations, from Antonil in 1689 to Rodrigues de Brito in 1807,
noted the same lack of proper care.[74]

As table 4 shows, the sugar growing parishes of the Recôncavo
often had a two-to-one ratio of slave to free inhabitants. It is impossible, however, to determine the precise number of slaves owned
by the senhores de engenho compared with the number owned by
the lavradores de cana. Some cane growers owned as many as thirty
slaves, but the average was probably between ten and twenty. One
method of estimating the number of slaves held by a lavrador is to
establish the ratio of slaves to acres of cane cultivated. If the general Caribbean calculation of one slave per acre is applied to Brazil,
a ratio of 2.5 slaves per hectare is indicated. Applied to the figures
of table 1, this ratio would produce an average of seven to fifteen
slaves per grower on Engenho Sergipe. The only check on these
figures is an early nineteenth-century comment by the French
traveler Tollenare, who stated that lavradores de cana on the Per-

73. The best summary of the problem of manioc production and supply in
the Recôncavo is presented in Gileno De Carli, "Geografia econômica e social
da cana de açúcar no Brasil," *Brasil Açucareiro*, X (1937), no. 2, 200–226. He
pointed out dire shortages in 1719 and 1724, while in Dutch Brazil (1640) and
the Recôncavo (1767) laws required lavradores to plant a certain amount of
manioc for each slave. José Antônio Gonsalves de Mello, *Tempo dos Flamengos*
(Rio de Janeiro, 1947), 175, 180–181, contains the best discussion of the resistance of the sugar sector to the planting of manioc in Dutch Brazil.

74. Philip III (II of Portugal) to India Council (30 April 1606), Biblioteca da
Ajuda, 51–V–48, f. 88, noted that plantation slaves in Brazil constantly stole
because of the inadequate provisions given them. In 1701, Governor Dom João
de Lencastre ordered plantation owners to set aside one day a week for the
slaves to grow their own food. See also Mansuy, *Cultura*, I, 126; C. R.
Boxer, *Race Relations in the Portuguese Colonial Empire* (Oxford, 1963), 111;
Luiz dos Santos Vilhena, *Recopilação de notícias soterpolitanas e brasilicas
contidas em XX cartas*, Braz do Amaral, ed., 3 vols. (Salvador, 1922–1935);
Rodrigues de Brito, *Cartas*, 3–4. Joseph Israel da Costa observed that the slaves
received dry manioc flour, once in a while a sardine or a mouthful of codfish,
and only water to drink. In their few free hours they would steal into the woods
to find land crabs or vegetables.

TABLE 4
The Bahian Population of 1724
(Selected Parishes)

Parishes	Number of Engenhos	Freemen				Slaves		Total
		Men	Women	Criados	Percent Free	Number	Percent	
Recôncavo								
N. S. da Purificação (Sergipe do Conde)	39	950	850	72	31	4152	69	6024
N. S. da Encarnação de Passé	8	713	648	122	36	2677	64	4160
N. S. do Socorro	12	289	315		30	1442	70	2046
São Miguel de Cotegipe	5	190	282	20	34	898	66	1390
Non-Sugar Areas								
Espírito Santo de Boipeba		323	327	25	56	552	44	1227
N. S. do Rosario de Cairú		525	406		44	1190	56	2121
N. S. da Assumpção de Camamú		448	750		54	1032	46	2230

SOURCE: Padre Gonçalo Soares de França, "Dissertações da historia eclesiastica do Brasil" (1724), ms. of Sociedade de Geografia de Lisboa (Reservados, 1–C–147).

nambucan plantations had between six and ten slaves each. The slave-to-acreage ratio indicates, however, that there were lavradores with as few as one slave and some with as many as thirty.[75]

Labor in the fields shared by poorer cane growers and slaves may have fostered close ties, but the social aspirations and the economic needs of the lavradores probably offset the growth of such feelings. At present, there is no proof of either alternative.

Slaves constituted the largest portion of the cane grower's original capital investment. Although the figure for slave purchases was high in the mid-seventeenth century, by the early eighteenth century the price of slaves and other basic commodities had risen sharply in response to the demand for those items in the booming mining areas to the south. Table 5 presents a rough estimate of a cane grower's original capital outlay in both periods. These figures are based on the needs of a lavrador de cana who produced forty tarefas each year.[76]

SOCIAL ASPECTS

Who then were the lavradores de cana? Obviously a wide gulf existed between a cane grower who produced one tarefa a year and a man whose fields yielded forty or fity tarefas. Counted among the lavradores de cana of Bahia were Catholic priests, New Christian (alleged crypto-Jewish) merchants, wealthy widows, and threadbare gentlemen. At Engenho Sergipe a number of lavradores de cana bore the honorific title of captain (of militia), more an indication of social position than military prowess.[77] A man like lavrador de cana Cosmé de Sá Peixoto, who served on the câmara of Salvador

75. Lista das informações e descripções das diversas frequezias do Arcebispado da Bahia (1755)," in *ABNRJ*, XXXI (1931), 203. The general figures on the Caribbean are presented in Ward Barrett, "Caribbean Sugar Production Standards in the Seventeenth and Eighteenth Centuries," in John Parker, ed., *Merchants and Scholars: Essays in the History of Exploration and Trade* (Minneapolis, 1965), 145–170. On Tollenare's comment see J. H. Galloway, "The Sugar Industry of Pernambuco during the Nineteenth Century," *Annals of the Association of American Geographers*, LVIII (June, 1968), 285–303.

76. These figures are based on entries in the Livros de Safra and on the account of Father Andreoni (Antonil). The cost for tools is simply a rough guess. Similar computations for a senhor de engenho can be seen in Mauro, *Le Portugal*, 215–216.

77. For example, Safra 1650/51: Jacome Antonio Merelo, Paulo Coelho, Manuel Fernandes de Ouro; Safra 1680/81: Francisco de Abreu; Safra 1704/05: Domingos Ferraz; Safra 1709/10: Estevão Machado. All from Livros de Safra, Engenho Sergipe.

TABLE 5
Original Capital Outlay of
a Lavrador de Cana[a]

	1620s		1720s	
Item	in Thousands of reis per unit	Total Outlay (in reis)	in Thousands of reis per unit	Total Outlay (in reis)
20 Slaves	45	900,000	140	2,800,000
36 Oxen	4	144,000	8	288,000
8 Carts	10	80,000	16	128,000
Tools		(est.) 20,000		(est.) 40,000
		1,144,000		3,256,000

[a] The cost of land has been omitted because not all lavradores de cana owned land.

and whose name figured prominently on many petitions from the sugar sector, had little in common with Pedro de Lima who in the safra of 1654/55 produced twenty arrôbas of sugar. Yet both men grew cane and most likely perceived a community of interest with each other and the sugar sector in general.

A petition of mill owners and cane growers sent to the Crown in 1662 and signed by more than one hundred individuals reveals cane growers like Dom Pedro Daça de Melo, "knight of the Order of Christ"; Luís Gomes de Bulhões, "lieutenant general of artillery and knight of the Order of São Bento de Aviz"; Luís Alvares Montarrôio, "Provedor da Fazenda e Alfândega"; Pero Borges Pacheco, "former attorney of the City of Bahia"; and Francisco Negreiros Sueiro, "Knight of Aviz, civil judge, many times municipal selectman, and cane grower for over forty-five years." Such men surely figured among the *gente principal,* the privileged few of the Bahian Recôncavo, and formed a select stratum among the ranks of the cane growers.[78] On the other hand, a 1702 attempt in Rio de Janeiro to limit cane growing to men who owned six slaves or more failed because too many cane farmers in that region had fewer than the required number.[79] Table 2 clearly shows that wide divergence between the many growers at Engenho Sergipe who produced a few tarefas and those few whose holdings constituted over 50 percent of the cane fields. In Brazil the economic spectrum of the lavradores

78. Albuquerque, "Liberdade e limitação," 491–499.
79. De Carli, "A Geografia econômica," 204.

de cana was broad, but socially they must as a group be considered an adjunct to the wealthy planter class, men of more or less the same social origins, but lacking the economic foundations capable of fully supporting their desires.

As might be expected, the records of Sergipe do Conde are sprinkled with references to family connections between lavradores de cana. The web of kinship often included individuals in the same occupation, and we find references to brothers and brothers-in-law mutually engaged in cane production.[80] Conversely, almost no information exists on the manner in which these lavradores disposed of their estates, so that it is impossible to know if land served as a cohesive force in maintaining the family unit. If it did not, ritual kinship (compadrio) may have served as a compensatory device to counteract the inability of land to maintain the cohesion of the family.

Compradio relations, extended families (parentelas), and mutual dependency surely existed, but the temptation to apply to them interpretations deriving from modern studies of such phenomena should be resisted. Only a close study of Recôncavo parish records can demonstrate whether the nature of compradio relationships varied over time and reflected changes in the economic and institutional character of the region. The familiar pattern of ritual kinship used to reinforce the master-client relations should not be superimposed on the colonial past, for it may have developed in response to the historical process.[81]

Two curious social categories appear among the lavradores de cana. The Engenho Sergipe counted among those who ground cane at the mill a number of religious institutions and individual clerics. As early as 1611 the Benedictine Fathers of Salvador were grinding cane in Sergipe do Conde, and in 1670 they acquired more cane fields

80. For example, in the safra of 1629/30 the brothers Duarte Alvares and Francisco Rodrigues both labored as cane growers for the Engenho Sergipe. *DHA*, Livro das Contas, 149. "Escritura de venda que fez Bernardo Ribeiro ao licenciado Francisco Lopes Brandao de uma sorte de terras sita na Patatiba," *DH*, LXIII (1944), 226, notes two cane growers related by marriage.

81. A good discussion of the extended family can be found in Charles Wagley, *The Latin American Tradition* (New York, 1968), Chap. IV. Emilio Willems has written extensively on this subject. See his "The Structure of the Brazilian Family," *Social Forces*, XXXI (1953), no. 4, 339–346; "A Familia portuguesa contemporânea," *Sociologia*, XVII (1955), no. 1, 6–55; "On Portuguese Family Structure," *International Journal of Comparative Sociology*, III (1962), no. 1, 65–79.

under obligation to the Engenho Sergipe. The Carmelites and the Franciscans also figure among the lavradores de cana of Sergipe do Conde, and the Jesuit College of Bahia appears in the safras of 1669/70, 1710/11, and 1711/12. The few clerics on the rolls of Engenho Sergipe seem to have been small lavradores, most likely only marginally involved in sugar agriculture. Harvests like that of Father Matheus de Mendonça, who produced thirty arrôbas in the harvest of 1650/51, and Father Gregório Mendes, with seventy-four arrôbas in 1680/81, are indicative of the level of clerical production.[82] Engenho Sergipe was typical, if the report of Adriaen van der Dussen is a fair gauge. The Dutchman's account lists a number of clerics involved in sugar agriculture and one who produced sixty tarefas of cane.[83] Moreover, a 1779 report noted clergymen in Bahia who served as plantation managers and some Capuchins who were mill owners.[84]

Even more surprising than the clerics are the many women listed among the lavradores de cana in Sergipe do Conde and in van der Dussen's account. The description of Pernambuco and Alagoas made in 1639 listed 144 individuals as lavradores de cana, of whom twenty-four were women (17 percent).[85] In fact, in van der Dussen's report all three lavradores de cana of the Engenho Alimbero were women. In Sergipe do Conde, hardly a harvest passed without one or two women appearing on the rolls of the lavradores de cana. Of the thirty-five harvests for which ledgers exist, only three list no women among the contributing growers. Often widows took over the property and responsibilities of their husbands. At times they figured among the most prosperous of the cane growers. Beatris Delgada, for example, produced large quantities of sugar at Sergipe do Conde in the 1620s. As might be expected, these wealthy and ethnically preferred women do not usually appear for long sequences in the account books, an indication either of their lack of difficulty in remarrying or of their inability to farm.

82. All citations for this paragraph are from the Livros de Safra for the years mentioned.

83. Van der Dussen, *Relatório*, 73. His account also lists the Benedictines and the Carmelites among the producers of sugarcane in Dutch Brazil. On the Benedictines see also, *Livro Velho do Tombo do Mosteiro de São Bento* (Salvador, 1945).

84. Report on the Captaincy of Bahia (1779); IHGB, 1, 1, 19.

85. Van der Dussen, *Relatório*, 21–22, 31–71.

These lady growers and their spiritual sisters who, like Dona Leonora Soares, became *senhoras de engenho* give the lie to traditional stereotypes of Portuguese protection of women.[86] Emilio Willems and others have pointed out that the strict double standard and the selection of women is an ideal behavioral norm that differs considerably from the real or even the expected patterns, especially in lower economic groups. The active women who contributed to the sugar industry of colonial Brazil added an interesting social dimension to the history of that agriculture.[87]

Beginning in the mid-sixteenth century, the Portuguese Crown took steps to stimulate the emigration of farmers from Portugal, the Azores, and Madeira.[88] Beyond this fact and the knowledge that crypto-Jews were occasionally engaged in sugar agriculture, we know little about the social background or ethnic composition of the cane growers.[89] One aspect, however, deserves special discussion. The large numbers of mulattoes, mestiços, and freedmen resulting from miscegenation and manumission comprised a pool of manpower in which the European element was small. Large numbers of freedmen and mulattoes served as free wage laborers in Brazil, often dominating certain skills and types of employment, but it would be wrong to believe that they entered into all occupations at the same rate. The records of Engenho Sergipe do Conde lack any direct reference to mulatto or Negro lavradores de cana. Such an omission cannot be interpreted as an accountancy color blindness,

86. Gabriel Soares de Sousa, *Notícia do Brasil*, Pirajá da Silva, ed. (São Paulo, 1940), 284.

87. Willems, "The Structure," gives examples of female economic activity, especially among low-income groups. Women lavradores were also connected to the sugar industry of Madeira in the fifteenth century. See the list printed in Virginia Rau and Jorge de Macedo, *O Açúcar da Madeira nos fins do século xv* (Lisbon, 1962), 37–43.

88. Carta régia of 11 September 1550, *DHA*, Legislação, 97–99.

89. Eduardo de Oliveira França's "Engenhos, colonização, e Cristãos-Novos na Bahia Colonial," *Anais do IV simpósio nacional dos professores universitários de história* (São Paulo, 1969), 181–241, notes a number of crypto-Jewish lavradores de cana who had been merchants and some who continued to engage in both activities. Arnold Wiznitzer, "The Jews in The Sugar Industry of Colonial Brazil," *Jewish Social Studies*, XVIII (1956), 189–198. Unfortunately, the best monographs on the Bahian population reveal very little about the composition of the rural areas. Cf. Thales de Azevedo, *Povoamento da cidade do Salvador*, (2nd ed.; São Paulo, 1955); Carlos Ott, *Formação e evolução étnica da cidade do Salvador*, 2 vols. (Salvador, 1955–57).

for often the records will specifically define an individual as *preto* (black) or mulatto. The only hints that exist to suggest the presence of cane growers of Afro-Brazilian origin are a few lavradores de cana listed without family name. "José Francisco" or a similar name may indicate slave origins, since bondsmen were often called by a Christian name, by a Christian name and the place of origin, or by a distinguishing physical characteristic (e.g., Manoel Congo, Bastião Grande). Or, "José Francisco" may simply indicate a certain familiarity with the accountant and hence the absence of a family name in the record.

In general, freedmen, Indians, and mulattoes served most often as un- or semiskilled manual laborers.[90] Some became skilled permanent employees of the engenho, performing important tasks as sugar masters, drivers, and craters. Those who did enter agriculture generally became subsistence farmers, where their lack of the credit and capital necessary for cane cultivation did not exclude them. Others labored on the cattle ranches which developed in marginal areas. Like much of the racial situation in Brazil, the exclusion of blacks from the ranks of the cane growers was not legislated but resulted from a number of social, historical, and economic factors. Undoubtedly, the exclusion was never absolute; but, as a group, the lavradores de cana probably had the smallest admixture of indigenous and African elements of any sector of the free laboring population.

It is difficult to establish the ethnic composition of the lavradores de cana; it is no easier to calculate the total number of cane growers at any one time. Van der Dussen demonstrated that the Pernambucan engenhos had between one and twelve lavradores de cana, with the highest frequency in the three to eight range. His listing, however, apparently included growers with "fazendas obrigadas."[91] Governor Gaspar de Sousa reported that in 1613 Paraíba had 220 men employed in growing sugar. At that time there were twelve

90. The account books of Engenho Sergipe are studded with references such as: "dinheiro que dei por hum mez a hu indio carapina q. trabalhou no engenho," (1628/29); "Ao mulato Barbosa por 100 dias que trabalhou nas barcas e dezoito sangrias que fes aos negros," (1628/29); "Aos negros de carregarem duas frasqueiras e mais fato," (1650/51).

91. Van der Dussen, *Relatório.* On occasion van der Dussen lists "partidos livres," thereby giving the impression that all other listings are of "captive cane."

engenhos in that captaincy, so that if we subtract twelve senhores de engenho, an average of seventeen growers per mill is indicated.[92] Sergipe do Conde, as one of the largest engenhos, perhaps indicates the maximum number of lavradores de cana that a mill possessed. As Graph 1 indicates, Engenho Sergipe at no time had over thirty growers. If we posit this as a maximum figure, the eighty Bahian engenhos of 1629 would have relied on at most 2,400 suppliers of sugar cane.[93] One-half or one-third that number is probably closer to the true figure. The number of growers per mill changed over time and reflected the prosperity of the industry. The graph below demonstrates that in the eighteenth century the Engenho Sergipe relied on fewer cane growers, a fact that supports the many complaints about the depopulation of agricultural regions as a result

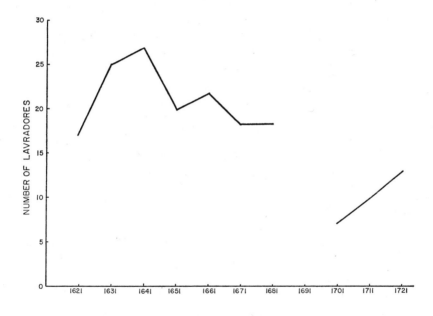

Graph 1.   Lavadores de Cana of the Engenho Sergipe, 1611–1721
(Based on ten-year averages)

92. King to Governor Gaspar de Sousa (Lisbon, 30 Aug. 1613), Biblioteca do Itamaraty, Correspondencia dos Senhores Álvaro e Gaspar de Sousa, ff. 259–260. The number of engenhos is established in (Diogo de Campos Moreno), Livro que dá razão do Estado do Brasil (1612), Hélio Viana, ed. (Recife, 1955).

93. Mauro, Le Portugal, 193, provides a listing of the number of engenhos at various dates.

of the Minas Gerais gold strikes. In short, the lavradores de cana appear as a predominantly white sector of the population, never large in numbers, but including men and women of social and economic importance. The cultivation of sugar cane was without question a respected and "honorable" occupation.

Conflicts, Mobility, and Change

"The senhores de engenho and lavradores de cana are the nerves of the body politick" wrote Wenceslao Pereira da Silva in 1738.[94] Recognition of the common bond between owners and growers, however, should not obscure their sometimes less than cordial relations. The senhores de engenho viewed themselves as a colonial nobility entitled to the prerogatives of and respect due to feudal lords. Their arrogance often knew no bounds. Mill owners looked upon their lavradores de cana as retainers who owed not only sugar cane but allegiance. The wives of the planters followed suit and treated the wives of the growers like servants. Through pressure or payment, senhores de engenho prevailed on growers to give false witness or carry out other illegal acts.[95]

Father Andreoni (Antonil) admonished the senhores de engenho to treat their lavradores well since the production of the mill depended on the success of the cane growers. Honest and helpful planters were, in fact, sought out by the lavradores.[96] The least powerful owners often proved the fairest. Luís dos Santos Vilhena, a Bahian professor, pointed out that the poorer senhores de engenho aided their lavradores de cana by loaning slaves and oxen and occasionally giving them some of the poorer grades of sugar (*panela*) which by right belonged entirely to the mill.[97] Santos Vilhena suggested that the more powerful and wealthy the senhor, the more tyrannical his treatment of the growers.

Although personality and the wealth of the senhor de engenho undoubtedly influenced owner-grower relations, a more important variable was the grower's formal contractual status. Mill owners

94. *Parecer* of Wenceslao Pereira da Silva, *ABNRJ*, XXXI (1913), doc. 347, 564.

95. Mansuy, *Cultura*, I, 96.

96. *Ibid.*

97. Santos Vilhena, *Recopilação*, I, 182. On the ideas of Santos Vilhena who was a professor of Greek in Bahia, see Carlos Guilherme Mota, "Mentalidade ilustrada na colonização portuguesa: Luís dos Santos Vilhena," *Revista de Historia*, 72 (1967), 405–416.

courted those lavradores de cana with "free cane," especially at
the time of the safra. These freeholders, unrestricted by contractual
obligations, could bargain with the senhores de engenho on an equal
footing. Sharecroppers and tenants, however, "were absolutely
dependent on the senhor de engenho who according to his caprice
keeps them beneath a servile oppression."[98] Throughout the colonial period and into the nineteenth century observers noted the
same abuses of the owner's power over the lavradores de cana.[99]
The master might fail to divide the sugar evenly or he might keep
the best for himself and give the grower sugar of inferior quality.
Another common abuse found the owner mixing the sugar of two
lavradores to even out the quality, but depriving one man of his
fair price.

The most damaging of all abuses by the mill owner could completely ruin a difficult or independent grower. Sugar cane had to be
cut at precisely the right moment to obtain the optimum yield of
syrup. If the cane was not pressed immediately after being cut, the
syrup would dry and sour, and the sugar produced would be poor.
Theoretically, before each safra the sugar master of the mill would
survey the cane fields and assign each grower a time for cutting
and pressing. Delay in the cutting was harmful, but failure by the
senhor de engenho to process the cut cane within three or four days
was disastrous. "The poor lavrador," said Santos Vilhena, "can see
in less than a week the loss of a year's labor."[100]

The lavradores de cana could ill afford to bring these matters to
court, but some did so. One such instance occurred in 1677, when a
grower argued that in return for furnishing his cane to the mill, the
engenho was obliged "to grind the cane at a fixed time, so many
tarefas per week with the condition that the party who fails in his
obligation must pay the other for all loss and damage."[101] The
constant repetition of these abuses indicates, however, that the
courts could do little to temper the relations between senhor de
engenho and lavrador de cana.

The cane growers, however, had a number of methods by which
they could apply pressure on the mill owners. One effective weapon

98. José de Silva Lisboa to Domingos Vandelli (1781), *ABNRJ*, XXXII (1914),
500–501.
99. Wanderley Pinho, *História*, 313.
100. Santos Vilhena, *Recopilação*, I, 183.
101. Cited in Wanderley Pinho, *História*, 312n.

was refusal to supply the mill with cane or firewood. A seventeenth-century observer noted that the cane growers' unreliability as suppliers was the greatest headache of the mill owners, who lived "dependent on the will of the cane growers."[102] Such remarks, however, do not balance the many references to the tyranny of the mill owner over the lavradores de cana.

Despite rivalry and mistreatment, association and cooperation with the mill owners offered definite benefits to the cane growers. From its inception the sugar industry had enjoyed a privileged and protected position in Brazil. Statements such as "who says Brazil says sugar" were common coin and fully accepted in governing circles. The prosperity of the colony depended on the sugar industry, and the Crown, after some hesitation, gave free rein to individual input and effort in developing Brazilian sugar. As early as 1551, those who built or renovated engenhos or planted cane were exempt from payment of the tithe for ten years, and similar privileges were extended throughout the sixteenth century and were renewed during the following century.[103] Although the Crown supported the efforts of tax farmers to collect the tithe during the seventeenth century,[104] the sugar interests continued to avoid payment of the tithe and other fiscal burdens by pleading that the unimpeded progress of the sugar industry constituted the soundest basis of the colony's prosperity. For example, in 1639, despite the Dutch menace and the need for small craft for the colony's defense, Governor Dom Fernando Mascarenhas ordered that the boats used by the sugar plantations be exempted from sequester, an action fully supported by the Crown.[105] The hope of the metropolis that it would reap benefits from the sugar industry's health and vigor gave the planters leverage with the Crown. The close association of the senhores de

102. Document of 1660 printed in Frédéric Mauro, Le Brésil au xviie siècle (Coimbra, 1961), 293.

103. DHA, Legislação, contains many of the sixteenth-century privileges.

104. The privilege of freedom from all taxes granted to new or renovated engenhos was often abused. Senhores de engenho who enjoyed the privilege bought sugar from those who did not and then shipped it to Europe tax-free. In 1608–1609, the matter was discussed by the Council of Portugal, and in 1612–1614 during the investigation of André Farto da Costa new restrictions were enforced. Cf. AGS, Secretarias Provinciales 1499, f. 54; 1500, ff. 26–27v; Regimento of André Farto da Costa, AHU, Bahia, papeis avulsos, caixa 1 (1612).

105. Bando (21 Feb. 1639), Biblioteca do Itamaraty, Correspondencia do Conde da Torre, II, no. 9; and king to D. Juan de Veiga Bazán (18 Aug. 1639), III, f. 155.

engenho with the lavradores de cana brought the latter too under this umbrella of privilege and exemption.

Of all the privileges sought, none was more ardently desired than freedom from the debts incurred with the mercantile sector. If we can believe the constant complaints of the sugar barons and their retainers, indebtedness to merchants and institutions that provided credit was a constant problem throughout the colonial epoch. Cane growers and mill owners purchased slaves on credit, offering their future harvest as collateral. Little is known about the actual mechanisms of credit, the fluctuations in sugar futures, or the rates of interest. Portuguese law prohibited usury, but techniques existed for extracting high interest rates.[106] The Misericórdia of Bahia lent money to the sugar sector at 6¼ percent, but rates sometimes went up to 20 to 24 percent.[107] Moreover, whatever the laws, means existed for securing even higher rates. For example, a common practice of the merchants consisted in accepting payment in sugar, but at a price fixed in the loan contract. By the time of the harvest or the fleet's departure, this price no longer expressed market realities, and the lavrador de cana or mill owner did not receive full value for his produce.[108] The chronic lack of specie in Brazil, which forced the use of sugar as a means of exchange, naturally aggravated this situation.[109] Defaulting on mortgage or loan brought foreclosure

106. Wanderley Pinho, História, 307–313, presents the best summary of this topic.

107. Russell-Wood, Fidalgos and Philanthropists, 70, 107, 197–198. There is, of course, the possibility that the senhores de engenho extended loans to the cane growers but I have been unable to find any reference to this practice.

108. Wanderley Pinho, História, 310. Examples of this abuse are mentioned in gubernatorial correspondence; APB, Ordens régias 2, no. 105; 7, no. 666. In 1690 the Crown established a commission to settle on a fair price for sugar two weeks before the departure of the fleet in an attempt to avoid the practice of unfair price-fixing. The merchants argued that the owners and growers falsified the weight and quality marked on the crates of sugar. Governor Francisco Barreto (1657–1663) ordered that each crate be stamped with the mark of the senhor de engenho or lavrador de cana and that these marks be registered with the municipal council of Salvador. (Arquivo da Câmara de Salvador, Livro das Portarias, 159, f. 239.) The Crown followed with an alvará in 1687 to enforce this system, but the merchants were still complaining in 1709. Cf. BNRJ II–33, 28. 27; APB, Ordens régias 7, no. 703, 704.

109. The problem of currency was chronic but intensified in certain periods. The separation from Spain (1640) and, therefore, from access to Peruvian specie caused a monetary crisis in Brazil. The late 1680s and 1690s saw another such period because of Portuguese payments to Great Britain. In 1693 Governor António Luís Gonçalves de Câmara Coutinho wrote to the Crown that "the colonists are so in need of money that they can buy nothing. They are in this

and either forced sale or acquisition of the mill by the merchant.

Complaints of the sugar sector against the merchants could be cited for almost any decade of the seventeenth or eighteenth century. A petition of 1632 will suffice. In that year the senhores de engenho and the lavradores de cana pleaded that the precipitous rise in the prices of the items necessary for sugar production had forced them to accept loans which they were now unable to pay. The creditors had attached their estates, and the petition listed sixteen planters who had recently lost their properties as a consequence. Said the planters, "when the mills close down then the cane growers, subsistence farmers and wood cutters will have no work and it will be necessary to depopulate the region as has already happened in Ilhéus and Porto Seguro."[110]

The sugar sector sought a law that would allow attachment only of their produce and not of their property and capital goods. Petitions designed to achieve this goal, written in more or less the same terms, continued until after the Luso-Dutch war (which, by the way, was led by disgruntled planters because of similar conditions of indebtedness to the Dutch West India Company).[111] Finally, in a law of 1663, the Crown acceded to the pleas of the planters, probably as a means of sweetening the special tax (donativo) imposed in Brazil to pay for the dowry of Catherine of Bragança.[112] The plant-

---

miserable state because there is none among them who does not live burdened with debts and unable to pay." (cited in Wanderley Pinho, História, 309). In 1736 Governor André de Mello e Castro, count of Galveas, wrote to the Crown of the lack of money, "because the metropolitan currency remains in the hands of the merchants and others who send it back to Portugal in the fleets and the local currency both of gold and silver circulates throughout the state, but the major part of it has passed to Piauí and Maranhão in exchange for cattle to supply this city." See APB, Ordens régias 32, no. 82; also C.R. Boxer, "Brazilian Gold and British Traders in the First Half of the Eighteenth Century," HAHR, XLIX (1969), no. 3, 454–472.

110. "Petição dos Senhores de Engenho e lavradores de cana," Arquivo da câmara do Salvador, Livros de Provisoes 155, f. 88ff.

111. This theme has been well-developed in Gonsalves de Mello's Tempo dos Flamengos. The close correlation between indebtedness and participation in the revolt against the Dutch was first noted by Father Antônio Vieira in his famous Papel Forte (BNRJ, 12, 2, 1, f. 74v.).

112. The pertinent documents on the law of 1663 and the petitions that brought it into being have been published in Mauro, Le Brésil, 270–307, José Pinheiro da Silva, "A Capitania da Baía," 63–77, Albuquerque, "Liberdade e Limitação," 491–499. This law was reinforced by others of 1673, 1674, 1681, 1683. See Francisco Adolfo de Varnhagen, História geral do Brasil, 5 vols. (7th ed.; São Paulo, 1962), III, 232.

ers' complaints, however, did not cease, as the memorial of João Peixoto Viegas (1687) and correspondence of the 1690s show.[113]

Although local officials sometimes failed to enforce the law of 1663, a more crucial turn of events was a decision of the High Court handed down in 1721.[114] The judges opened the whole matter again by questioning whether the law of 1663 applied to the fields of the cane growers as well as to the mills of the planters.[115] The cane growers apparently remained protected by the law, but their complaints of indebtedness and extortion continued. Phrases like "all are sorely indebted," "charged with debts and mortgages," "the calamitous and deplorable situation in which the planters and growers find themselves," remained the constant refrain of the sugar sector.[116] By the eighteenth century the battle had moved to a new level, and the planters began to petition for a debt moratorium, something they never achieved.[117] Planters and growers, therefore, shared a common bond in their need of, and in their antagonism toward, the merchants of Salvador.

We must ask, then, if the channels of mobility open to the lavradores de cana allowed for the attainment of their goals. Chief

113. João Peixoto Viegas, "Parecer e tratado feito sobre os excessivos impostos que cahirao sobre as lavouras do Brazil . . .," which appeared in *ABNRJ*, XX (1898), 212–223; king to António Luiz Gonçalves da Câmara Coutinho (Lisbon, 18 Dec. 1692), APB, Ordens régias 2, no. 105.

114. Bahian-born Desembargador João de Goes e Araújo reported to the Crown that local officials in Rio de Janeiro failed to enforce the law of 1663 and allowed attachment of sugar properties. ANTT, Chancelaria de Afonso VI, Livro 20, ff. 250–251.

115. The applicability of the law of 1663 to lavradores de cana had not been questioned until 1720, when, in a case brought to court by Dona Ana Cavalcanti against lavrador de cana Luís de Sousa de Castro, the Relação decided against him and apparently allowed the attachment of his fields by his creditor. The Câmara then appealed the case to the Crown, and the king, after soliciting the governor's opinion, issued an order that the law of 1663 be applied to cane growers who did not have mills. Cf. king to Vasco Fernandes Cezar de Meneses (Lisbon, 20 Nov. 1721), APB, Ordens régias 15, no. 52; BGUC, Livro dos assentos da Relação 706, ff. 42–43v. In Pernambuco similar privileges were finally obtained by the sugar sector in 1723. See BGUC, Livro dos assentos da Relação 707, ff. 152–154; and Guerra, *Alguns documentos*, 89–90. In Pernambuco the sugar sector had sought this privilege since the 1680s.

116. Wanderley Pinho, *História*, 204–207, includes a number of such references. See also the documents cited in José Honório Rodrigues, "Agricultura e economia açucareira no século xvii," *Brasil Açucareiro*, XXVI (1945), no. 1, 112–119; no. 2, 210–216; no. 3, 312–318; no. 4, 427–433; no. 5, 420–424; XXVI (1945), no. 1, 116–119; no. 2, 214–216.

117. Wanderley Pinho, *História*, 205–208.

among these goals was to establish a mill and become a senhor de engenho. The Italian Jesuit Andreoni (Antonil) put it succinctly: "senhor de engenho is a title to which many aspire for it means to be served, obeyed, and respected by many."[118] The social gratification and apparent economic benefits associated with this title drew many cane growers and others toward it, and scattered evidence of lavradores and even artisans who became plantation owners can be cited as indications of mobility. In the 1590s, Gaspar Nunez Barreto, a blacksmith's son, became a senhor de engenho. Cosme de Sá Peixoto, a lavrador de cana in the 1640s, could report in the 1660s that he lived on his engenho in Patatiba.[119] Such examples, however, should not obscure the fact that two other processes operated in the creation of new mill owners. First, there was a tendency toward multiple ownership, with some senhores de engenho holding up to four or five mills. Second, as already noted, merchants often acquired mills through foreclosure and sometimes held them, thereby joining the ranks of the planter class. The most prosperous mills probably belonged to persons in these two categories, men of substantial capital resources with access to credit facilities.[120]

Nevertheless, the lavradores de cana continued to aspire to mill ownership. A number of technological improvements in the late seventeenth century may have eased their progress, but evidence exists suggesting that the social benefits may have been greatly outweighed by economic loss, and that the scramble to set up new mills was very likely harmful to the sugar economy as a whole.[121]

118. Mansuy, *Cultura*, 84.

119. João Capistrano de Abreu, ed., *Primeira visitação do Santo Officio ás partes do Brasil: Confissões da Bahia 1591–92, 99*; Cosme de Sá Peixoto to Overseas Council (17 Jan. 1662), AHU, Bahia, papeis avulsos, caixa 8, 1st series non-catalogued.

120. Diogo Lopes Ulhoa owned three engenhos in Bahia in the late seventeenth century. Similar multiple holdings are noted in Pernambuco by Gonsalves de Mello in *Tempo dos Flamengos*, where he cites João Fernandes Vieira as the owner of five engenhos in the 1640s.

121. The Brazilian sugar agroindustry remained technologically conservative throughout the colonial period. Changes and improvements were few and often did not fulfill the claims of their inventors. Perhaps the most important innovation came after 1608, when either a Spanish priest or a Portuguese colonist named Gaspar Lopes Coelho introduced the three roller mills into Brazil. Cf. Frei Vicente do Salvador, *História do Brasil* (São Paulo, 1967), 2; AGS, Secretarias Provinciales 1473, ff. 38–39v. in which Gaspar Lopes Coelho claimed to be "first inventor and engineer of the engenhos de tres paos." (Lisbon, 19 July 1620). In the 1650s a Spaniard, Juan Lopes Sierra, introduced a new technique of

An extraordinary letter from the Juiz do Pôvo and artisan representatives of Bahia to the Overseas Council in Lisbon can be analyzed in this context.[122] Faced with the proliferation of engenhos and a decrease in sugar production, the Juiz do Pôvo sought a royal injunction against the creation of new mills. He observed that men "gave up being rich cane growers to become poor mill owners as is almost always the case." A lavrador de cana who could produce one hundred tarefas of cane found, upon establishing his own mill, that land for fifty tarefas had to be turned over to pasturage and other activities, so that, beside his capital outlay his cane production was cut in half. The Juiz do Pôvo could also have noted that skilled slaves who might cost 30 percent more than field hands also became a necessity when a grower established his own mill. Thus, while the number of mills increased, total production of sugar did not keep pace. Moreover, the new engenhos, located on marginal lands, produced less sugar per tarefas of cane. These charges by the Juiz do Pôvo seem to have some statistical validity, for whereas in 1650 three hundred engenhos in Brazil produced two million arrôbas of sugar, in 1670 five hundred engenhos produced the same amount.[123]

The proliferation of engenhos caused shortages in cane and firewood and "owners went begging at the doors of the lavradores" in search of cane. One might expect that such conditions would induce cane growers to remain as such and reap the benefits of the shortage by demanding more favorable terms; but instead they continued to seek the title of senhor de engenho out of either vanity or greed ("vaidade do nome ou o enganho da cobiça").[124] With the exception of one or two lavradores with great capital resources, the general result of this process was a large number of formerly successful lavradores de cana indebted up to their eye-teeth as mill owners.[125]

This grim picture was refuted by the lavradores de cana and the

---

wood use which cut down on firewood consumption. In 1663 Claudio Urrey invented a small mill which called for lower capital costs. These improvements did not revolutionize the industry, and others like that of Diogo Soares Alemão (1698) or Manuel de Almeida (1732) had even less impact. See APB, Ordens régias 5, no. 70; 29, no. 14, A, B; 2, no. 136.

122. Albuquerque, "Liberdade e limitação." This document and some others pertinent to the question are also published in Frédéric Mauro, Le Brésil, 270–307.

123. Mauro, Le Portugal, appendix, 516.

124. Mauro, Le Brésil, 279–307.   125. Ibid.

senhores de engenho, who, for their part, claimed that if some had gone under after setting up a mill, others had made a fortune. The sugar barons wanted no limitation placed on the number of engenhos developed, and chief among their arguments was that "it is unjust to deprive that lavrador or other person who has the capital for it from seeking his best interest in the establishment of a new mill for it is the greater glory of the state to have many rich subjects."[126] In effect, this argument underscored the importance of access to mobility as a means of inducing men to work as lavradores de cana. Only this importance can explain why engenho owners would support a proposal allowing the unlimited increase of competition. Eventual ownership may have been an ephemeral goal, but its possibility provided the requisite inducement for the lavradores de cana, and the mill owners seemed to realize this fact.

Certainly, the senhores de engenho also opposed limitations on expansion of the industry because of their own hopes of expansion or multiple ownership. Yet it is strange to find men with a monopoly control of an industry willing to allow the free access of competition. If opportunities did indeed exist for eventual lavrador ownership of an engenho, the colonial sugar industry contained the seeds of its own destruction. For a time would come when, faced with an inelastic market, profits would be increasingly divided among the continuously expanding number of mills. If such a process occurred at the same time that foreign competition began to cut into Brazil's percentage of the world sugar market, the effects would even more harmful.

If the Juiz do Pôvo was correct in his analysis that rich growers always became poor mill owners, the economic misjudgment of the lavradores de cana can only be explained by the compensating social values associated with plantation ownership. The model that suggests itself indicates that the prestige of mill ownership, the historical success of the senhores de engenho, and the hope of profit, outweighed current economic difficulties in the minds of the cane growers. The implications of such economically nonrational be-

126. The sugar sector claimed that the Juiz do Pôvo was an illiterate who had gotten the others to sign his memorial without their knowledge of the contents. António de Pinho later testified that, "sendo eu mister deste povo com un companheiro me mandaram na Camara assinar um papel que em contrario deste se fez a sua Magestade o qual me não leram nem eu soube o que era mais que disseram-me que o assinasse que era bem comum do povo." Albuquerque, "Liberdade e limitação," 498.

havior in the political sphere are broad indeed. First, the desire of lavradores de cana to become senhores de engenho led them to perceive a congruence of interests between themselves and the mill owners. As a group the cane growers never appear to have pursued interests of their own, independently of those of the senhores de engenho. Second, the marked inclination of the cane growers to join the ranks of the planters probably resulted in a continual depletion of the ranks of the very men whose economic resources and social origins best suited them to roles of leadership among the lavradores de cana and other free labor elements. The men best qualified to oppose the senhores de engenho most likely became the first to join them. Social goals operated to offset possible conflicts and antagonism, and real or apparent mobility was fostered by the planter class in order to maintain the existing patterns.

The lavradores de cana figured among the "important people" (gente principal) of the colony and were, therefore, elgible for election to municipal office—a privilege they did not share with artisans and subsistence farmers.[127] Such opportunities, the ability to own slaves, amass capital, and eventually set up a mill, gave the cane grower a sense of participation that seemed to promise him the social and economic benefits of the colonial system.[128] The achievement of his dreams depended on the vigor and stability of the sugar economy and the society that had grown around it. The closing decades of the seventeenth century brought a crisis in the sugar economy, and it is fair to ask in conclusion how the traditional social patterns adjusted to that crisis and how the cane growers reacted to these changes.

By any measure the 1680s initiated a time of crisis. External events, foreign competition, a fall in sugar prices, and a series of bad harvests placed the sugar economy of Brazil in jeopardy.[129] These difficulties lay beneath a number of social changes that also characterized the end of the century, for in the sugar areas of the coast there was a replacement of elites, an increase in central authority, and modifications in the pulse if not the form of social intercourse. The power of the sugar sector contracted in this period, but the

127. Vivaldo Coaracy, O Rio de Janeiro no século dezasete, 2nd ed., (Rio de Janeiro, 1965).

128. A.P. Canabrava, "A lavoura canavieira," 351–367.

129. The famous memorial of João Peixoto Viegas (1687) describes the difficulties of the sugar economy in that period. See ABNRJ, XX (1898), 213–223.

retreat was not a rout. In Pernambuco, the planter class fought to retain its power against the growing strength of mercantile groups but their battle (War of the Mascates) must be considered a rear-guard action.[130] In Bahia, planters simply pulled back to their redoubts—the engenhos. Such a withdrawal, however, had to affect the traditional patterns of both the Recôncavo and the city.

It has become somewhat commonplace to regard Brazilian colonial society as a static system in which great extended families maintained their sway generation after generation. Such a view, fostered by genealogical histories, diverts our attention from other themes in the colonial sugar economy, namely flux and mobility. The constant complaints of the sugar sector against foreclosure and insolvency may have been exaggerated, but they probably reflected the actual situation. Some senhores de engenho acquired two and three mills and founded dynasties, while many others lost everything in a generation. One need only glance at the maps of João Teixeira Albernaz, which at various times in the seventeenth century portrayed the Recôncavo, to see the constant changes in ownership that characterized the great century of sugar.[131] In a period of rapid expansion, overextension often resulted in rapid changes of mill ownership. Most likely this very factor of flux attracted men to the ranks of the cane growers, for although the structure of society remained somewhat static, opportunities for mobility were not closed. The lavradores de cana, so close to the social apex, had a vested interest in the maintenance of the structure as long as they continued to find opportunities for the attainment of their goals.

The second half of the seventeenth century brought a number of modifications of traditional sociopolitical patterns. First, the plant-

130. The War of the Mascates has been seen as a protonationalist movement, but it undoubtedly had economic origins reflecting the animosity between the Portuguese merchants of Recife and the Brazilian-born planters of Olinda. See C. R. Boxer, *The Golden Age of Brazil* (Berkeley, 1962), Chap. V, for a good summary. Bahia also had urban disturbances in this period. The 1703 "Maneta" tax-riot underlines this unrest.

131. The various atlases and maps drawn by João Teixeira Albernaz have been printed in Armando Cortesão and Avelino Teixeira da Mota, *Portugaliae Monumenta Cartographica*, 6 vols. (Lisbon, 1960) IV, plates 444, 449, 456. It was common for each series of maps of the Brazilian coast to have a separate leaf depicting the Bay of All Saints and the engenhos of the Recôncavo. Oliveira França, "Engenhos," 206, cites the Engenho de Paripe in Matium which was founded by Afonso Torres and passed through the hands of Jorge Gomes de Lamego, Baltazar Pereira, António Vaz and Gaspar Pereira Coelho all before 1618.

ers began to withdraw from urban life. Municipal institutions that had once been the bailiwicks of the sugar sector began in the 1680s to go begging for members.[132] Although the planters never fully surrendered their role in the Misericórdia and the Câmara, they no longer fought to control important positions in these bodies. By the 1690s, men like António Gomes, owner of two engenhos, pleaded poor health and financial loss in order to be excused from service in the municipal council, and one man went so far as to claim that his enemies had elected him to that body to do him a disservice.[133] Slowly, the merchants of Salvador moved to fill the vacuum created by the planters' withdrawal. Bahian society was in limbo at the turn of the century.[134]

On the engenhos a new conservatism could be seen. Expansion and overextension slowed, as the price of slaves rose and the planters began to turn from the economic goals of the seventeenth-century market orientation toward a more self-centered pattern in which social gratification became an over-riding concern.[135] Evidence from the Engenho Sergipe indicates that instead of using more lavradores de cana and thereby sharing the risks during the crisis of the 1690s, the engenho decreased its production, the contraction was accompanied by a reduction in the number of growers. The use of cane growers, which in the period of expansion had been a method for

132. Russell-Wood, *Fidalgos and Philanthropists*, 111, 120, shows how the planters withdrew from the controlling offices of the Misericórdia. A question can be raised, however, asking whether the câmaras of the newly formed Recôncavo towns replaced Salvador as the loci of planter power.

133. There are instances of this process as early as the 1620s, and in 1649 the Viceroy had to order men on the plantations to take up their duties in the municipal council. See C. R. Boxer, *Portuguese Society in the Tropics: The Municipal Councils of Goa, Macao, Bahia and Luanda* (Madison, 1965), 99–100. Petition of António Gomes was reported in a letter from the king to Governor António Luís Gonçalves da Câmara Coutinho (Lisbon, 23 Feb. 1690), APB, Ordens régias 1, no. 62, 62A. It was Manuel Marques who accused his enemies of electing him. AHU, Códice 51, f. 121v. (n.d.). Other petitions of a similar nature can be cited, such as those of Cosme de Sá Peixoto, AHU, Bahia, caixa 8 1st series noncatalogued; and that of Dom Jeronimo da Silveira e Albuquerque (Lisbon, 27 May 1737), APB, Ordens régias 34, no. 7. Silveira e Albuquerque claimed that his slaves would not labor during his absence in the city.

134. Russell-Wood, *Fidalgos and Philanthropists*, 120.

135. A tendency toward conspicuous waste had always existed on the plantations but it may have intensified in the eighteenth century, as Wenceslao Pereira da Silva pointed out in 1738. His *parecer* is printed in Eduardo de Castro e Almeida, "Inventario dos documentos relativos ao Brasil, Bahia 1613–1752," *ABNRJ*, XXXI (1913), 28–29.

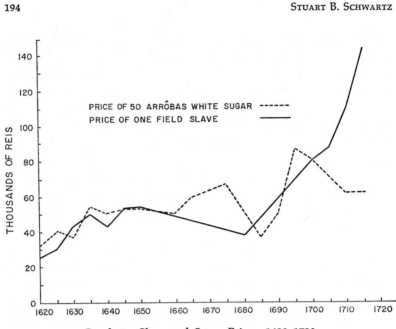

Graph 2. Slave and Sugar Prices, 1620–1720.

reducing capital costs and perhaps for providing intensive supervision of engenho property, now became unnecessary. Moreover,
the falling price of sugar reduced the margin of profit, out of which
the contractual obligations of the lavradores de cana were met.
Thus, their incentive to remain in the industry no longer existed.
(See graph above.)[136]

Increasing vertical integration of the growing and milling aspects
of the sugar-making process can be seen in the records of Engenho
Sergipe. Whereas in the mid-seventeenth century Engenho Sergipe
depended entirely on the cane of lavradores de cana, in the harvest
of 1669/70 plantation lands produced 38 percent of the sugar. By
the harvest of 1680/81, the engenho had reclaimed or bought back
other lands, including Pioca Island, and was producing over 50
percent of the sugar it milled. By 1700, this figure had risen to 84
percent. Table 6 represents the relative production of the plantation
and the lavradores at Engenho Sergipe.[137] Even after 1705, when

136. Slave and sugar prices in Graph 2 have been gathered from Mansuy,
Cultura; Mauro, *Portugal*; Wanderley Pinho, *Um engenho*; and the Livros de
Safra.
137. These figures are based on the Livros de Safra for the years cited.

production began to recover, the structure of the plantation's economy continued to reflect the much reduced role of the lavradores de cana. At Engenho Sergipe this movement had begun well before the Minas Gerais gold strikes and cannot be seen simply as a response to the conditions created by the rush. Instead, the process had begun as the planter class retreated from the cities, and it intensified after the discovery of gold in the interior.

TABLE 6

Sugar Production of Engenho Sergipe[a]

Selected Safras	Engenho-Controlled Land		Lavrador Lands		Total Arrôbas
	Arrôbas	Percent of Total	Arrôbas	Percent of Total	
1655/56	0	0	5138	100	5138
1669/70	2691	38	4404	62	7095
1680/81	3131	52	2842	48	5973
1690/1700	2062	84	380	16	2442
1704/05	4013	73	472	27	4485
1705/06	4707	83	998	17	5705
1707/08	2724	85	475	15	3199
1711/12	3732	61	2336	39	6068

[a] Based on Livros de Safra for years indicated.

The effects of these changes on the lavradores de cana are difficult to ascertain, but some results may be postulated. First, the planters began to cut back on their need for and dependence on the cane growers; this process, along with a somewhat more conservative planter attitude toward expansion, probably reduced both the number of mill failures and (with the law of 1663 as a control) the rate of ownership turnover. Moreover, as Graph 2 demonstrates, the price of slaves rose sharply in this period while the price of sugar did not, so that the cane growers found it increasingly difficult to finance the original capital investment needed to establish a new mill.[138] Graph 2 demonstrates the movement of the price of fifty arrôbas of white sugar in Bahia through the seventeenth century in comparison with the price of a field slave. We can see a relatively

138. Graph 2 indicates the equivalent value of a field slave in arrôbas of sugar. The sugar price used in an average of the high and low price for each ten-year period.

constant relationship between these prices in the first decades of the seventeenth century. Between 1660 and 1680, a period of fluctuation occurred. After the discovery of gold in Minas Gerais and the demand there for slaves, slave prices began to soar in Bahia. As we have seen in table 5, the purchase of slaves constituted about 85 percent of total lavrador outlay over the course of the seventeenth century. Graph 2 also clearly demonstrates how the rising price of slaves after 1680 led to greatly decreased profitability for the lavradores de cana.

Thus the lavradores de cana found that the traditional paths to the title of senhor de engenho had become more difficult to tread. In a time of sociopolitical change, this important segment of the population discovered that mobility was no longer available to them in the same degree, or at least they perceived the situation in this way. The position of cane grower no longer seemed a step toward mill ownership. At no time in Brazilian history had the conditions for a profound social upheaval been more suitable. In a period of economic crisis and within a sociopolitical vacuum, a potentially powerful element of the population found that its reasons to support traditional patterns no longer existed.

But there was no social upheaval. Two conditions, one social and the other historical, combined to preclude any significant change in the nature of Brazilian society. Within the context of a slave-based economy and great numbers of black slaves, an open clash between the predominantly white barons and squires of King Sugar was unlikely. The constant spectre of a slave uprising which pervaded colonial Brazil reduced the possibility of overt hostility between planters and growers.[139] The risk of unleashing a slave revolt was too great a price for the lavradores de cana to pay. Thus, in a sense they too became captives of a social system built on slavery.

The discovery of gold in Minas Gerais dealt the final blow to the sugar boom, but also assured the survival of the traditional sugar society. The opportunities for new economic enterprises at the gold washings siphoned off large numbers of the free laboring population in and around coastal cities like Bahia.[140] More than one official in Bahia noted that farmers and technicians of all types had set off for the mines. Instances of lavradores de cana selling their slaves to

139. See Stuart Schwartz, "The Mocambo: Slave Resistence in Colonial Bahia," *Journal of Social History*, III (Spring, 1970), 313–333.
140. Sebastião da Rocha Pitta in his *História da America Portugueza* (1724).

the mining district and following after them were by no means isolated.[141] What might have been an explosive situation now disappeared as white men and black streamed toward the washings. At precisely the time that social mobility had decreased for the cane growers, geographical mobility offered new advantages and hopes. Certain patterns that had always existed in the coastal plantations went unchallenged and became dominant. The cane growers turned inland, and in doing so left behind them a lost opportunity for change, and the foundations of the nineteenth-century plantation system of the Brazilian Northeast.

(Lisbon, 1880), 260, 262, noted the rush to the mines but his history merely noted what royal officials had complained of for three decades.

141. Vasco Fernandes Cezar de Meneses to King (Bahia, 5 Oct. 1728), APB, Ordens régias 23, no. 124 complained that farmers no longer tended their crops, but rushed instead toward the mines.

COLIN M. MACLACHLAN:

The Indian Labor Structure in the Portuguese Amazon, 1700-1800

INTRODUCTION

For all practical purposes labor is essential for the creation of wealth. Without the necessary human resources the richest mines as well as the most fertile fields are of little consequence. Hence, the organization of labor is fundamental. Both Iberian powers came to view their American possessions as a means of assuring the economic well-being of the mother countries. The transition from collections of Indian artifacts to more permanent sources of wealth depended on the ability of the conquerors to organize labor to meet European economic needs. Where labor did not exist, or was unsatisfactory, it had to be imported.

In Brazil the Portuguese faced a scarcity of Indian labor and were forced to deal with Indian cultures not easily adaptable to a wage economy. Initial attempts to employ Indians as plantation laborers gave way to the use of the more agriculturally advanced African. Only in the fringe areas did Indian labor continue to be in demand. In the eighteenth century the Amazon basin was one of these marginal areas.

The seminomadic Indian of the Amazon basin possessed only a rudimentary knowledge of agriculture, subsisting by cultivating roots and collecting forest products. In spite of such cultural factors, the efforts of the Portuguese to organize the forest Indian succeeded. During the eighteenth century, the Indian progressed through three stages before arriving at the imposed goal of a free worker in a colonial economy. The first of these stages was the mission period, which had been elaborated in the seventeenth century and continued into the middle of the next. In 1757 the Crown ordered the replacement of the missionaries by secular directors appointed by the governor. The directorate system of 1757–1798 in turn yielded to a semicontrolled labor system. The Indian laborer who emerged almost simultaneously with the independence of Brazil was the result of the process of acculturation so relentlessly forced during the eighteenth century.

This study attempts to trace the evolution of Indian labor through each stage of development. Indigenous slave labor is excluded, because slavery does not evolve in the same fashion as a nonservile labor system. In addition, it is debatable whether Indian slaves constituted a significant proportion of the labor pool. The well publicized attempts of the Crown to restrict Indian slavery, although morally significant, did not reflect the actual number of slaves. In any event, the Crown managed to suppress indigenous slavery in the 1750s. The study is limited territorially to the old captaincy of Pará and the subordinate captaincy of Rio Negro (Amazonas). Maranhão, in spite of having been politically linked to Pará until 1772, is omitted because of its different economic development. In Maranhão, a flourishing cotton culture financed the import and effective use of African labor. Consequently, the province developed a different labor structure based on a plantation economy.

The study of Indian labor in the Amazon is of interest for several reasons. First, it provides a picture of how the European organized the less adaptable forest Indian in contrast to the readily adaptable Mexican and Peruvian Indian. Second, the Amazon region is still a fringe area. Twentieth-century progress has yet to destroy the region's link with its colonial past. The central market of Belém, then as now, is the *Ver o Pêso*. One has but to spend a few morning hours observing the provisioning of the city to grasp some of the intricacies of a centuries-old subsistence economy.

THE MISSION SYSTEM
1700–1755

During the mission period the primary concern of the Crown was not the organization of Indian labor. Portugal placed the main emphasis on the spiritual conversion of the natives to Catholicism, as well as on the task of transforming them into "Portuguese Indians." However, the organization of labor was not forgotten. The Crown recognized that the European settlers required labor and that a labor force was necessary to turn the land into wealth. At the same time, the Crown had no intention of basing the economy of the region on Indian labor. The seventeenth century was truly the "sugar century," and sugar plantations required the introduction of the more

robust and culturally advanced African.[1] The Portuguese believed
that the introduction of African slaves virtually assured the prosperity of a region. The Crown's unwillingness to allow the Portuguese settlers unrestricted access to Indian labor stemmed in part
from the experience gained in the sugar regions to the south, where
the use of Indian labor had not been successful.

Rather than risk an unsuccessful and possibly disastrous attempt
to force the Indian into a plantation economy, Lisbon decided on a
policy of defensive colonization. The Indians, organized under Portuguese supervision, would at least assure future control of the area.
Consequently the task of establishing a network of mission villages
received priority. Not surprisingly, the Crown directed the disposi-
tion of Indian labor in favor of the missionaries responsible for the
preservation and expansion of the mission system. During the mission period Lisbon authorized only marginal concessions to the
settlers in response to their demands for Indian labor.

The Labor Structure Under the Mission System

The regulations of 1680 divided Indian laborers into three groups.[2]
One remained in the village to devote itself to agricultural tasks.
This group bore the responsibility for producing sufficient foodstuffs for the village, as well as a surplus to help sustain Indians
recently placed under missionary supervision. The second group, at
the complete disposal of the missionaries, helped conduct other
Indians down from their jungle homes to designated mission
villages. Thus, the missionaries controlled two-thirds of the Indian
laborers. Only the third group (the remaining Indians) was available
to meet government needs and for distribution among Portuguese
settlers. The government's labor needs quite naturally had priority
over those of the settlers. The Indians who remained could then be
parcelled out to the Europeans for a period of two months at a
time. The proportion of Indians available to private employers was
approximately 20 percent of the total Indian labor force. Obviously
the settlers' labor needs could not be met from such a reduced labor

1. In 1682 the Crown charged the *Companhia do comércio do Maranhão*
with introducing 10,000 African slaves into the Amazon region over a twenty-
year period; however, few if any were imported by the company. Roberto C.
Simonsen, *História econômica do Brasil*, (5th ed. São Paulo, 1967), p. 318.
2. *HCJB*, IV, 318.

pool. In addition, the two-month time limit made little sense in an area where a collecting expedition required a minimum of six months. As a result, the hard-pressed settlers resorted to all types of deceptions in an effort to retain a labor force. In neighboring Maranhão, the general dissatisfaction with the share of labor allotted the settlers caused the Beckman revolt in 1684, and the temporary expulsion of the Jesuits from that area.[3]

As a consequence of the Beckman revolt, the Crown modified the formula for distributing Indians. Lisbon hoped the new regulations of 1686 would avoid any further disputes and at the same time would reserve sufficient laborers to sustain and extend the mission system.[4] The regulations reserved twenty-five Indians in each village over thirty leagues from Belém specifically for use by the missionaries. Within the thirty-league radius the Crown reserved the entire village of Goncares for mission duties. The regulation divided the remaining Indians into two groups. One group remained in the village; the other was theoretically available for private employment. The new procedure also extended the two-month time limit to six months. In order to control the assignment of labor, the government required each missionary to draw up a list of all able-bodied Indians between the ages of thirteen and fifty. In theory, the new regulations greatly expanded the labor pool available to the settlers. Nevertheless, the situation was about as desperate as before. The regulation of 1686 gave the missionaries definite and indisputable temporal power over their Indian charges. It also provided for a *procurador* responsible for assuring that Indian laborers were not illegally retained by their employers. In addition, the governor had to approval all requests for labor. To avoid the possible degeneration of the system or its paralysis in the absence of the governor, the regulations provided an elaborate alternative method. In the absence of the governor, the *capitão-mor* and two members of the municipal council, in conjunction with the superior of the missions and the individual village missionary, could assign Indian labor.[5]

Although cumbersome, this procedure assured continuous royal

3. Simonsen, *História econômica*, p. 319.

4. *Regimento e leis sobre as missões do estado do Maranhão e Pará e sobre a liberdade dos Indios*. Copy of a printed document published in Lisbon in 1724. BNRJ, 11, 2, 34 (Maranhão).

5. *Ibid.*, p. 158.

control of labor even in the absence of the governor. Under the new regulations the missionaries still directly controlled the group that remained in the village as well as the twenty-five Indians specifically reserved for mission use. In addition, the regulation exempted any newly "civilized" Indians from labor drafts for a period of two years.

Private Access to Indian Labor

The net effect of the regulation of 1686 was expansion of the labor pool legally available to the European settlers; at the same time the stricter enforcement of the rules kept the actual number of laborers available at about the old level. Under these circumstances, the settlers continued to petition the court for a freer access to labor. In order to relieve some of the pressure, Lisbon subsequently permitted private individuals or groups to resettle "uncivilized" Indians at their own expense.[6] The Crown emphasized, with doubtful effect, that the Indians should be persuaded to resettle rather than forced out of their jungle camps. Although resettlement entitled the settler to the labor of the Indians, they had to be settled in villages at least half a league from the nearest European settlement. Quite naturally those who financed resettlements tended to treat their charges as their personal property. In 1702 Lisbon clarified the status of the resettlements, ruling that settlers who bore the cost of establishing new villages did not have the right to administer them.[7] The temporal and spiritual government of all Indians remained in the hands of the missionaries. The individual who financed the resettlement of Indians did, however, have the sole right to their labor during his own lifetime.[8] The distribution was made in the same manner as that laid down in the regulations of 1686 with only 50 percent of the labor force being assigned at a time.

6. Carta régia of Sept. 2, 1689, BNRJ, 11, 2, 34, doc. 45 (Maranhão).

7. Carta de S.M. para os ministros da junta estado do Maranhão, anno de 702 (April 21, 1702) BNRJ, 11, 2, 34, doc. 51 (Maranhão).

8. The temporary distribution of labor was similar to the *repartimiento* in Spanish America. However, in the Spanish empire the repartimiento was not the primary method of distributing labor, but strictly a forced labor draft to meet some contingency. The private resettlement of Indians also suggests a comparison with the Spanish *encomienda*. The encomienda had originally included a labor tribute but as early as 1549 the Crown limited the encomendero to tribute in kind or in money. See Charles Gibson, *The Aztecs Under Spanish Rule*, (Stanford, 1964), p. 62.

Such a concession guaranteed a stable supply of labor to settlers with sufficient capital to finance resettlements. For example, the government conceded José Portil de Carvalho, owner of a cacao plantation, the right to resettle twenty Indian families.[9] Cattle rancher Francisco Pereira was similarly permitted to relocate twenty families.[10] José da Cunha d'Eça, owner of an *engenho real de açúcar*, obtained permission to resettle seventy Indian families in the vicinity of his operations. As was customary, he possessed the sole right to their labor during his lifetime.[11] Hilario de Morais Bettancourt, who owned one sugar engenho and was in the process of constructing another, received the privilege of resettling fifty families.[12] It should be borne in mind that the number of Indians actually resettled by an individual depended on his ability to locate a sufficient number of Indians and successfully resettle them. The quest for a stable labor supply accounted for numerous requests to resettle Indians.

Settlers unable to finance resettlement had to rely on the normal method of distribution of labor. Ordinary demands for labor also had to compete with government requirements or the requests of more influential people. The fact that wealthy settlers had privately resettled Indians at their disposal did not exclude them from the regular distribution of labor. In addition, the missionaries tended to divert more than the legal number of Indians to the service of the village and the mission system in general. Although the missionaries were specifically forbidden to use Indians in tobacco fields or in sugar engenhos, the prohibition was largely ignored.[13] The missionaries, as well as being the administrators and conservators of their charges, were privileged users of Indian labor.

In addition to the limited labor pool, another factor acted to restrict the settlers' access to Indian laborers. The regulations of 1686 stipulated a set salary for Indian laborers. The employer also supplied the daily provisions of his employee, a minimal expense

9. Carta régia of March 27, 1702, "Livro Grosso do Maranhão," *ABNRJ*, LXVI (1948), 214.

10. Carta régia of July 4, 1710, "Livro Grosso," *ibid.*, 72.

11. Carta régia of Apr. 17, 1702, *ibid.*, 217.

12. Carta régia of February 16, 1703, *ibid.*, 242.

13. The Crown ordered the governor to put a stop to this practice in 1729 and again in 1731. Cartas régias of Aug. 1, 1729 and Jan. 11, 1731, *Annaes da bibliotheca a archivo publico do Pará* (hereafter cited as *AAP*), IV, 57, 66.

since the Indians traditionally gleaned much of their daily suste-
nance from the rivers and jungles. Of more consequence, the regulations required that private employers pay Indian laborers 50 percent
of their salary at the inception of service and the remainder on
completion.[14] For Indians allotted for a period of six months this
amounted to an advance of three-months' salary. In the case of
forest collecting expeditions, which required at least six months of
labor before any monetary return, the investment proved considerable. Frequent desertion resulted in the loss of the salary advanced
without the slightest return for the luckless settler. Obviously large
collecting expeditions could be financed only by wealthy men.

Although the advance salary requirement posed a problem for
less affluent settlers, the wage scale itself was low. The governor,
in consultation with the religious orders, the municipal council of
Belém, and influential settlers, set the scale. With the possible exception of the religious orders, all sectors of society had a vested
interest in holding down the price of labor. The Crown, while firmly
committed to the principle of salaried labor, did not desire to pay
more than it felt was absolutely necessary. The Amazon region and
its marginal economy already required financial subsidies. Under
such circumstances the government understandably was reluctant
to raise the labor costs of fortification and the general establishment
of the Portuguese presence in the Amazon basin. Needless to say,
the settlers preferred to hold the wages to a minimum. The salary
scale of two yards of rough cotton cloth a month had been fixed in
1655.[15] In terms of money, two yards was roughly equivalent to 200
reis.[16] In 1730 the Crown ordered a salary review because of the
exceedingly low wage scale in the region.[17] In spite of such an order,
this rate remained in effect until 1751, when Governor Francisco
Xavier de Mendonça Furtado adjusted the scale upward to a more
reasonable level.[18] The missionaries, who produced much of the

14. Provisão of Dec. 5, 1710, "Livro Grosso," *ABNRJ*, LXVII, 86.
15. *Regimento e leis sobre as missões*, p. 155.
16. Simonsen, *História econômica*, p. 316.
17. Carta régia of Aug. 17, 1730, *AAP*, III, 313.
18. Mendonça Furtado to court, Dec. 22, 1751, *A Amazônia na era pombalina: Correspondência inédita do governador e capitão-general do estado Grão
Pará e Maranhão Francisco Xavier de Mendonça Furtado, 1751–1759*, ed. Marcos
Carneiro de Mendonça, 3 vols. (Rio de Janeiro, n.d. [ca. 1964]) (hereafter cited
as *C/FXMF*), I, 131.

cotton cloth in villages under their administration, had cost advantage. However, the Crown's insistence on placing Indian labor on a salaried basis conflicted with the essentially communal philosophy of the mission system. As a result, the artificial level of Indian wages did not concern the missionaries.

The economy rested largely on the efforts of the Indians, the only significant source of labor in the Amazon region during the first half of the eighteenth century. Consequently, the method of distributing Indian laborers, as well as the uncertainty of supply, directly influenced the economy. Inevitably, the poorer settlers who were lucky enough to obtain a few Indians used them for the most profitable task. Three or four Indians, while not sufficient to apply to agricultural labor, could collect forest products. An overemphasis on collecting resulted. Settlers frequently requested Indian labor for other purposes and then promptly employed them to collect the natural products of the region.[19] The overconcentration on the collecting industry finally forced the government to attempt to restrict the number of canoes that could be dispatched for this purpose. Overeager collectors had depleted the sources of supply by stripping trees bare, often before the fruit matured.[20] The limited number of Indians available to the average settler also encouraged the use of Indians in such nonproductive positions as domestic servants. Those who applied their allotted Indian laborers to more productive tasks complained of the constant change of personnel. They were required to train each new allotment of labor, in effect serving as a vocational school for village Indians.[21]

Government Use and Control of Labor

Only the government retained the power to intervene and make exceptions to the normal distribution of Indian labor. As has been observed, the government drew its occasional labor requirements from the same labor pool as the settlers. In addition, the government did not hesitate to reserve labor for its exclusive use when necessary

19. Carta régia of Dec. 29, 1705, "Livro Grosso," LXVI, 273.
20. Carta régia of April 20, 1737, "Livro Grosso," LXVII, 263.
21. Even the government found the constant turnover of labor inconvenient. In response to the governor's complaints that the canoe factory on the Moju river suffered as a result of the rotation of its work force, the Crown ordered that the Indians of an entire village be reserved solely for use in that factory. Conselho Ultramarino to Frei Miguel de Bulhões, May 26, 1756, BAPP, cod. 667, 13.

to assure a constant supply. Many Indian groups agreed to come out of the jungle only under the condition that the government exempt them from distribution to local settlers. These Indians were logically selected for royal service. When they were unavailable, the government arbitrarily removed others from the labor pool to meet its needs. For example, the inhabitants of the village of Moriceira were reserved for work on the fortifications of Pará.[22] Official action removed the village of Guoma from the labor pool and reserved its inhabitants for the use of tithe contractors.[23] In response to the pleas of the municipal *câmara* of Belém, the government ordered the removal of the village of Igarape from the general distribution. The câmara had complained that the labor shortage made it impossible to complete the construction of the city jail and municipal buildings. The Indians of Igarape were assigned to such construction work for a period of three years.[24]

Apart from reserving labor for specific tasks, the government assigned Indian villages to primary economic functions. The village of Joannes supplied labor for the salt industry, an important endeavor in a region where dried salt fish formed a significant part of the diet.[25] The government assigned the village of Maracanã exclusively to fishing, even denying the local missionaries their legal allotment of twenty-five Indians.[26] On approving the meat contract for the city of Belém, the Crown ordered that twenty-two Indians be reserved to transport meat to the capital; the village of Cayá supplied the required labor force.[27] The constant petitions of the municipality of Belém for a stable work force to provide normal municipal services resulted in a slightly different approach. The city council had originally asked permission to administer a village. The Crown, not anxious to create a precedent that would destroy the governing monopoly of the missionaries, refused. As a compromise, Lisbon permitted the municipality to resettle one hundred and fifty Indian families at its expense under the same condition granted private individuals.[28]

In spite of innumerable complaints of labor shortages, the gov-

22. Carta régia of Oct. 30, 1702, "Livro Grosso," LXVI, 223.
23. *Ibid.*
24. Carta régia of June 2, 1744, "Livro Grosso," LXVII, 269.
25. Carta régia of April 21, 1702. "Livro Grosso," LXVI, 217.
26. *Ibid.*, p. 217.
27. Carta régia of Oct. 13, 1727, *AAP*, II, 193.
28. Carta régia of March 2, 1726, "Livro Grosso," LXVII, 200.

ernment in Lisbon frequently ignored the fact that a labor problem existed. The Crown allotted the bishop of Pará thirty Indians for his personal use, ignoring complaints that to do so would deprive the settlers of needed labor.[29] Subsequently, requests for Indians to work on the construction of the episcopal palace received priority over requests by settlers.[30]

Diversion of Indians to favored projects also absorbed needed laborers. In response to a proposal to establish an indigo factory, the Crown assigned the promoter twelve Indian families. Subsequently, the government deprived him of his labor force because he failed to produce indigo and illegally diverted his labor force to other more profitable enterprises.[31]

The Labor Pool at the End of the Mission Period

The number of Indians available for labor during the first half of the eighteenth century can not be definitely ascertained. In 1751 Governor Francisco Xavier de Mendonça Furtado stated that there were sixty-three *aldeias* in the bishopric of Belém, varying in size from more than 800 to fewer than 150 inhabitants.[32] The modern historian João Lúcio d'Azevedo concluded that the average Indian village at this time held 475 persons and estimated the total Indian population in the Amazon at 30,000.[33] However, at least one-fourth of these Indians had been settled in remote areas and must be excluded from the actual labor pool. Of the remainder, approximately 60 percent fell between the ages of thirteen and fifty.[34] Thus the total labor pool, including men and women, totalled 13,500. Of this sum only one-half, or 6,750, were available at a time. Hence, at the end of the mission period the effective male labor force was approximately 3,375.

29. Carta régia of Jan. 16, 1725, *AAP*, I, 216.
30. Carta régia of July 5, 1745, "Livro Grosso," LXVII, 269.
31. Carta régia of Nov. 4, 1711, "Livro Grosso," LXVII, 89.
32. Mendonça Furtado to Mesa da Consciência, Dec. 30, 1751, *C/FXMF*, I, 153.
33. João Lúcio d'Azevedo, *Os Jesuítas no Grão Pará* (2nd ed. rev.; Coimbra, 1930), p. 229.
34. A rough percentage breakdown of Indians by age group indicates that 30 percent were under thirteen, 60 percent fell into the labor pool which included those between thirteen and fifty, and 10 percent over fifty. This breakdown must be used with caution. However, it appears to reconcile Azevedo's population estimates with the well-established shortage of Indian labor.

THE DIRECTORY SYSTEM, 1757–1798

During the course of the anti-Jesuit propaganda campaign that preceded the expulsion of the Society of Jesus, the issue of Indian labor became distorted. As often happens in such instances, the propagandists fell victims to their own imaginations. Governor Francisco Xavier de Mendonça Furtado and his brother, the Marquês de Pombal, persuaded themselves that the missionaries, particularly the Jesuits, had made themselves "masters of the *sertão*."[35] The temporal power of the religious orders, as well as their profitable involvement in the forest collecting industry, left them open to such a charge. Inevitably the governor overestimated the productivity of Indian labor and the economic potential of the forest collecting industry. Governor Mendonça Furtado assumed that the missionaries, by directing Indian labor to their advantage, had reaped economic benefits to the detriment of the state and the settlers.[36] This interpretation ignored the fact that the Crown, concerned simply with preserving the region for Portugal, had itself directed the labor of the Indians to the support of the mission system.

Under Pombal's influence the old mission philosophy that emphasized conservation of the Indians gave way to a more dynamic attempt to introduce and eventually incorporate the Indians into Portuguese culture. The new philosophy resulted in the *Diretório*, which replaced the mission system in 1757.[37] The directorate transferred the temporal authority of the missionaries to secular administrators directly responsible to the governor. The governing power of the religious orders, as authorized by the regulations of 1680 and 1686, was abolished. The missionaries no longer stood between the Indian villages and the government. The new system was to last during an indefinite period while the Indians learned to assume normal responsibilities and acquired an appreciation of the material benefits of labor. The Crown hoped that ultimately they would not need direction and would be automatically absorbed into the econ-

35. Mendonça Furtado to Sebastião José de Carvalho e Melo, Feb. 18, 1754, BNRJ, 11, 2, 43, doc. 2 (Pará).

36. *Idem* to *idem*, Nov. 21, 1751, *C/FXMF*, I, 73.

37. A complete copy of the Diretório is included in *Collecção da legislação portuguesa desde a última compilação das ordenações, redegida pelo Desembargador Antonio Delgado da Silva, I, Legislação de 1750 a 1762* (Lisbon, 1830), p. 507.

omy as free and willing laborers. In the meantime, the governor appointed individual directors for each Indian village.

The Labor Structure under the Directorate System

Like the regulations of 1686, the directorate divided the available Indian labor into two equal parts. One-half remained in the village to tend to agricultural duties as well as to supply the government's labor needs. In case of emergency this group was expected to rally to the defense of the state. The other half was divided among the settlers.[38] In theory, the new method reserved 50 percent of the Indian labor force exclusively for the settlers' private use. Individual settlers did not have to compete with the government for labor because the government drew its labor requirement from the group that remained in the village. As before, the Indian received a fixed salary. The revised wage scale of 1751 remained in effect. This scale provided for a monthly salary of 400 reis a month for ordinary labor. River pilots and ruddermen drew 600 reis per month, and skilled craftsmen received 100 reis per day.[39] During the next several decades that wage scale became increasingly unrealistic. Evidence indicates that a competing free pricing system for labor had developed. River pilots obtained double the official salary rate from the settlers who competed for their labor. In an effort to regain control of the wage level, Governor João Pereira Caldas officially revised salaries in 1773.[40] The new scale brought the official and the free wage scales together, at least temporarily. It provided for a monthly salary of 1,200 reis for Indians engaged in heavy labor, which included river navigation, lumbering, field labor, work in engenhos, and forest collecting. Indians employed in domestic service or hunting and fishing received 800 reis, and women in domestic service were entitled to 600 reis. Young boys and girls received 600 and 400 reis respectively. The new wage regulations permitted skilled Indian artisans to seek the same salaries as their European counterparts.

Private Access to Indian Labor

Although theoretically the Diretório expanded the labor pool available to the settlers, it retained one of the most criticized features of the previous system. Under the mission system, half of the

38. Diretório, art. 63.
39. Mendonça Furtado to court, Dec. 22, 1751, C/FXMF, I, 131.
40. Bando of May 30, 1773, BNRJ, 11, 2, 43, doc. 180 (Pará).

workers' salary had been paid in advance. The new system required that the Indians' entire salary be deposited in advance with the director, so that the employer would not lose any money if the Indian deserted.[41] However, this advantage was cancelled by the necessity of depositing such a large amount of money. In terms of the 1773 salary scale, a twenty-man collecting expedition assigned for a period of six months required an initial investment of approximately 144,000 reis in labor alone. Such an investment could not be made by the average settler. The advance deposit requirement acted to limit the settlers' labor demands. Only those with capital could afford to be major consumers of Indian labor. Conversely, the accumulation of capital depended on access to sufficient labor. The system thus helped reinforce the concentration of wealth in the established families.

Bishop João de São José Queiróz observed the combination of labor and wealth in the course of his pastoral tours between 1761 and 1763. The bishop understandably preferred to be entertained by the richest families in the districts he visited. Among others he noted a senhor de engenho whose extended family included over forty European women. They lived in a house built in Portuguese style complete with damask curtains. The senhor's labor force consisted of over two hundred people, a figure that included African slaves as well as Indians.[42] On a formerly Jesuit fazenda, Bishop Queiróz observed over two hundred laborers.[43] A settler who specialized in forest products reportedly collected over 1,500 arrôbas of cacao annually. He possessed his own canoe factory in which he claimed to have built over 800 canoes for the use of his employees.[44] Bishop Queiróz observed that he lived in a magnificent house and had a large number of blacks, mulattoes, and Indians at his disposal. At the opposite end of the scale, the bishop noted the Braga family who lived like forest creatures in vice and laziness. Only occasionally were the Bragas able to obtain some Indians through trickery or deception.[45]

Occasionally the government intervened in the normal distribution of labor to provide Indians for individuals who otherwise could not afford them. The assignment of Indian laborers to assist with

41. Diretório, art. 68.

42. João de São José Queiróz, Visitas Pastorais: Memorias (1761 e 1762–1763) (Rio de Janeiro, 1961), p. 405.

43. Ibid., p. 178.   44. Ibid., pp. 169, 170.   45. Ibid., p. 173.

the Macapá rice harvest was such an instance. This type of labor received the same salary, but the advance deposit was not required. In the same manner the government allotted Indians to industries it wished to encourage. In one of its numerous attempts to encourage the production of indigo, the Crown assigned a settler thirty Indians.[46] To assist the settler, the government authorized the construction of a factory at the expense of the royal treasury. The government assigned four Indian laborers at the customary salary to construct the necessary building.[47] In the case of the holder of a tithe contract, the Crown also intervened to supply the required labor. Since most of the tithes were collected in kind, the contractor required a sizable labor force. The contractors naturally tended to sell the products collected in Belém, where the best price was available. The transporting of such goods depended almost entirely on Indian labor.[48] The fact that the contractor had to satisfy the royal treasury with the full amount of the contract by a certain date often resulted in merciless demands on his labor force. The assignment of Indians to such contractors was singled out by the procurador of Indians of Maranhão as one of the principal factors in depleting the labor supply. Subsequently, in 1803, the Crown prohibited the assignment of Indians to tithe contractors.[49] The government also supplied laborers to holders of less important contracts. The royal fisheries, of which Pará had two in 1792, were occasionally operated by the government and at other times auctioned off to a contractor.[50] The royal fishery on the river Tapajós required a labor force of over eighty.[51] The holder of a salt fish contract received sixty Indians. As was customary in such cases, he paid their salaries every six months.[52] Indian labor directly allotted by the government was subject to the normal six-month rotation. In no event did the state

46. Martinho de Sousa Albuquerque to court, Feb. 16, 1784, ANRJ, cod. 99, V, 28.

47. Idem to idem (?) 1784, ANRJ, cod. 99, V, 31.

48. Copy of a report by Procurador dos Indios Antonio Correa Furtado de Mendonça sent by the Conselho Ultramarino to Governor Francisco de Sousa Coutinho, May 12, 1797, BAPP cod. 897, 57.

49. Carta régia of Aug. 18, 1803, BAAP, cod. 898, 95.

50. Francisco de Sousa Coutinho to court, February 6, 1792, ANRJ, cod. 99 XII, 22 and Martinho de Sousa Albuquerque to court, April 26, 1788, ANRJ, cod. 99, IX, 54.

51. Dist. de Indios para o serviço da Pesqueira R¹ do Rio Tapajoz (Mar. 18, 1774), BAPP, cod. 595, 193A.

52. Fernando da Costa Ataide Teive to court, 1767 (?) ANRJ, cod. 99, I, 127.

assign Indians for periods over the six-month limitation laid down in the Diretório.

Not surprisingly, the European settlers who could not afford to deposit salaries in advance, or who were not fortunate enough to have Indians directly assigned to them by the government, resorted to illegal methods. It was the common practice of many employers to hold Indians beyond the set time limit.[53] Other settlers cajoled or bluffed directors into assigning Indians in violation of the regulations. A number of Europeans obtained Indians by falsely claiming they were for royal service. The government attempted, with little success, to control such practices by requiring signed *portarias*.[54]

In order to relieve some of the pressure on village Indians, the government reinstituted the practice of private resettlement of forest Indians.[55] Individual settlers bore the entire expense of such resettlement. During the first year the settler instructed the Indians in religion and taught them rudimentary agricultural skills. If the *patrão*, treated the Indians well, he could keep them for another year. Only during the second year did they receive the normal wage. This arrangement was similar to that practiced during the mission period. As under the mission system, only those with sufficient capital could avail themselves of this alternative method of securing a labor force.

The Crown vaguely envisioned the development of a plantation culture in the Amazon. Consequently, Lisbon instructed Governor Mendonça Furtado to study the region's products and their commercial possibilities.[56] The governor reported the presence of a total of thirty-nine different products. Of these, sugar, cotton, rice, cacao, and coffee were the principal cultivated crops. The report noted that most of the region's production was collected rather than cultivated. In an effort to deemphasize the collecting industry, the Crown urged the directors of Indian villages to apply their charges to the cultivation of cotton, tobacco, and coffee.[57] Lisbon also noted

53. Bando of May 3, 1764, BAPP, cod. 940, n.p.
54. Diretório, art. 62. Repeated warnings testify to extent of the problem. See Bando of Aug. 12, 1764 which refers to an early one of 1754, BAPP, cod, 940, n.p., Bando of Jan. 20, 1785 and Bando of Aug. 25, 1790, BAPP, cod, 988, 21, 26.
55. *Condiçoens com que são concedidos aos particulares os Indios silvestres dos novos descimentos.* (178?), ANRJ, cod. 99, V, 282.
56. Mendonça Furtado to Diogo de Mendonça Côrte Real, Jan. 24, 1752, C/FXMF, I, 199.
57. Diretório, arts. 24, 25.

the advantages of actually cultivating forest products, rather than relying on natural sources. Of all the forest products, cacao was perhaps best suited to the plantation system. Where cacao existed, such as on the islands near the capital, it grew in relatively concentrated stands. A number of plantations of cacao existed in the subordinate state of Rio Negro.[58] Whether these plantations were actually cultivated is unknown. More than likely such plantations consisted of natural stands. In general the harvesting of wild cacao did not give way to plantations. To bring forest products under cultivation would have required the diversion of a sizable labor force over a considerable period of time without any immediate return. The difficulty of securing a stable work force was the chief obstacle, but other factors should also be noted. Unquestionably the Indians preferred collecting to the less traditional labor involved in the cultivation of crops. Moreover, women and children could be used in the collecting industry. Governor Mendonça Furtado noted the employment of both women and young children to collect wild cotton.[59] Finally, the very existence of natural products tended to seduce even the most ambitious settlers. The investment of the time and labor necessary to establish plantations seemed foolish when such products could be immediately collected. In addition, Pará and its subordinate captaincy of Rio Negro proved only marginally suitable for such nonforest products as sugar and cotton.

Earlier attempts to encourage sugar plantations had been unsuccessful. Most sugar engenhos that still functioned in the region produced *aguardente*, the *bebida divina* of the region.[60] In 1757, the Crown ceased encouraging sugar and tobacco as export crops, noting that the production of Bahia was sufficient and of better quality.[61] The production of aguardente served the local market and formed the basis of much of the illegal trade with the Indians. The government did not approve of the diversion of labor to such a task. It observed that the production of aguardente diverted labor from the more profitable export products with consequent ill effects on

58. *Mapa das plantações de toda capitania de S. José do Rio Negro no anno de 1775, calculado em visita das povoações AAP*, VI, 118, 7.

59. Mendonça Furtado to Diogo de Mendonça Côrte Real, Jan. 24, 1752, C/FXMF, I, 200.

60. Queiróz, p. 268.

61. Manoel Bernardo de Melo e Castro to Mendonça Furtado, Oct. 6, 1761, BNRJ, 11, 2, 43, doc. 13, (Pará).

external trade as well as on the consumption of Portuguese wines.[62]

Similar efforts to stimulate cotton and tobacco plantations met with little success. The abundance of wild cotton and the lack of available labor combined to defeat such efforts.[63] Tobacco suffered from insects which lowered both production and quality. Rice, on the other hand, was a partial success. The settlers of Macapá, mainly industrious islanders, did not hesitate to work in their own fields. Yet, even their success depended on the government's willingness to assign Indian labor for their use. Laborers from as far away as Santarem, 300 miles up the Amazon, were assigned to help the settlers in Macapá.[64]

The government's efforts to encourage what it deemed the most productive use of Indians by the settlers never really succeeded: consequently, the collecting industry dominated the economy. In 1790, the government exerted firmer control of labor by requiring settlers who requested Indian labor to state exactly the economic activity planned, the extent of their holdings, the number of employees, and the type and amount of the preceding year's production. The government then assigned Indian laborers on the basis of the most economically useful tasks.[65]

Collecting in Common

While officially attempting to reduce the dependence of settlers on the collecting industry, the government itself indirectly engaged in harvesting forest products. Under the directorate, the collection of forest products by village inhabitants became virtually mandatory. Rather than assume the burden of maintaining a salaried staff, the state allotted to each director a one-sixth share of the profits of his respective village.[66] Such profits could be derived from crops, but directors tended to engage in the more profitable forest collecting industry. The state encouraged this activity by facilitating credit for collecting expeditions. An average canoe required sufficient supplies for a period of eight months. The cost of outfitting

62. João Pereira Caldas to court, Jan. 26, 1780, IHGB, lata 107, doc. 5, 2.

63. Queiróz, p. 273.

64. Pereira Caldas to commandant of Santarem, Mar. 6, 1779, BAPP, cod. 603, 189.

65. Bando of Aug. 25, 1790, BAPP, cod. 988, 26.

66. Diretório, art. 39.

each expedition amounted to an estimated 329,280 reis.[67] After deducting all expenses, including administrative costs, only about 20 to 30 percent remained to be divided amongst the workers. Governor Sousa Coutinho claimed that the individual Indian received less than could have been earned by working on government projects for a fixed salary.[68]

The percentage of village Indians throughout the region assigned to collecting in common averaged approximately 30 percent of the labor force; however, several villages employed over 40 percent. The villages closest to Belém tended to assign lower percentages. Government demands for labor inevitably fell heaviest on those villages closest to the capital, reducing the number of Indians available for collecting. On at least one occasion the government could not meet its labor requirements because of the number of Indians engaged in forest collecting. In 1780, the governor suspended collecting in common throughout Pará in order to reserve sufficient labor to meet the needs of the state.[69] In Rio Negro, where government demands for labor were lighter, such a drastic measure was never necessary.

Government Labor Requirements

In theory, the labor needs of the Crown did not compete with those of the settlers. The state supposedly drew the Indians necessary for its service from the inhabitants assigned to remain in the villages. However, the expansion of the state demand for Indian labor inevitably had a major impact on the available labor supply. Crown officials did not hesitate to remove Indians from the labor pool and assign them arbitrarily to various state projects. This was especially done during the regime of the Marquês de Pombal, whose Amazon policy made serious demands on the labor supply. The Crown's efforts to establish Portugal's claim to as much of the Amazon basin as possible resulted in the disptach of innumerable military expeditions to the interior, and each required a considerable number of Indian bearers and rowers. For example, a party of seven canoes required eighty-nine Indians as boatmen and bearers of

67. Thezouraria Geral dos Indios (Sept. 19, 1782) AHU, caixa 42 (Pará).
68. Sousa Coutinho to Rodrigo de Sousa Coutinho, Aug. 2, 1797, ANRJ, cod. 101, II, 54.
69. José de Nápoles Telo de Menezes to court, June 9, 1780, IHGB, lata 286, ms. 14803, doc. 2.

supplies.[70] The Portuguese also needed laborers to help provision the expeditions. Often, in the course of a long trip, Indians supplemented rations by hunting and fishing and, when feasible, planting and harvesting manioc. The rate of death and desertion in these expeditions was exceedingly high. A frontier demarkation expedition in 1788 resulted in the death of seventy-three individuals, almost all of them Indians.[71] Expeditions to Mato Grosso during the 1780s reportedly resulted in the death or desertion of 300 Indians. Many Indians simply stayed in Mato Grosso rather than make the return trip to Pará.[72]

Portugal's understandable fear of the territorial ambitions of its more powerful neighbors added to the pressure on Indian labor. Although the diversion of labor to the construction of fortifications was politically necessary, it placed a severe strain on both the economy and the labor supply. The secret instructions that Governor Francisco Xavier de Mendonça Furtado brought with him from Lisbon stressed the need to fortify the region.[73] The Crown directed the governor to rebuild and extend the fortifications of the state. The construction of a fort on the northern shore of the Amazon delta received top priority. Subsequently. Lisbon approved Governor Mendonça Furtado's plans for a major bastion at Macapá. The fortress and settlement of São José de Macapá eventually became an important bulwark against French encroachment. From a military and political standpoint the fortress was a success. However, the assignment of labor to construction duties depleted the labor pool. Indians assigned to heavy construction frequently deserted. In a futile effort to keep Indians on construction tasks in Macapá, the governor suggested they be issued a ration of aguardente at the end of a day's labor.[74] Eventually the government found it necessary to rent 112 African slaves belonging to the municipality of Belém to assist Indian laborers.[75] Governor João Pereira Caldas complained

70. Martinho de Sousa Albuquerque to court, July 23, 1789, ANRJ, cod. 99, X, 82.

71. *Idem* to *idem*, Aug. 16, 1788, BAPP, cod. 700, 142.

72. José de Nápoles Telo de Menezes to Martinho de Melo e Castro, May 31, 1783, ANRJ, cod. 99, IV, 50.

73. *Instruções régias, públicas e secretas para Francisco Xavier de Mendonça Furtado Capitão-General do Estado do Grão Pará e Maranhão* (1751), C/FXMF, I, 26.

74. Fernando da Costa Ataíde Teive to Mestre do Campo of Macapá, July 30, 1770, BAPP, cod. 590, 440.

75. Portaria of Nov. 14, 1771, BAPP, cod. 592, doc. 914.

that the construction of the fortress, coupled with constant expeditions, caused the depletion of the labor pool. Work on the fortifications of Macapá, begun in 1764, continued for eighteen years.

By disregarding economic and physical factors, the government often badly misused the limited population resources available. The establishment of the frontier village of Tabatinga in 1770 is a case in point. It did provide some defense against Spanish encroachment on the western frontier and thereby helped to discourage Spanish expansion. But its support required the services of a considerable number of Indians, and the cost, particularly transportation, of sending its forest products down river to Belém was prohibitively high.[76]

The founding of the Vila of Mazagão provides another example of the Crown's wasteful use of human resources. In 1769, as part of a general consolidation of Portuguese strength, the Marquês de Pombal ordered the abandonment of the tiny African enclave of Mazagão. The Castelo Real de Mazagão had originally been established on the Mauritanian coast in 1506, and had successfully resisted Moorish pressure for over a century and a half; however, it had lost much of its strategic importance. The funds necessary to support the settlement as well as its Christian population could be more effectively utilized elsewhere in the empire. Consequently, in 1769 over one thousand evacuees arrived in Pará, and several hundred resettled in a newly selected district named Vila Nova de Mazagão.[77] The Crown provided a generous transition allowance, including both money and livestock, and Indian labor constructed the necessary dwellings and public buildings. At one time the government employed over 200 Indians in such construction.[78] In 1774 nineteen different villages contributed laborers to construction work in Mazagão.[79] Unfortunately, political necessity dictated the selection of the site; economic or physical factors received scant attention. Situated on the northern side of the Amazon, the new vila was intended to discourage French designs on the delta. The settlement, constructed in a low swampy area, proved a natural breeding ground for tropical diseases which caused an alarming mortality rate among the settlers. In desperation many fled to the relative comforts of

76. Thezouraria Geral dos Indios, Tabatinga (1776) BAPP, cod. 157, 60.

77. Palma Muniz, *Immigração e colonisação do estado do Grão-Pará, 1616–1916* (Belém, 1916), p. 17.

78. *Dist. de Indios para . . . nova vila de Mazagão* (Mar. 18, 1774) BAPP, cod. 595, 193.

79. *Ibid.*

Belém.[80] The cost of the Vila Nova in human lives, labor, and money was considerable. The establishment of villages for political reasons drained both the royal treasury and the labor pool. By 1796, the state clearly could not afford such ventures. Governor Francisco de Sousa Coutinho bluntly called the Crown's attention to the limited finances of the state and noted that the establishment of a proposed defensive village would have to be cancelled because of the lack of resources.[81]

Beside employing Indian labor to fortify the region, the government assigned Indians to a number of strictly economical tasks. The spinning of rough cotton cloth had been an important activity since the mission days. During the directorate period the production of cotton cloth continued to be mainly a village industry. However, the government operated at least one spinning mill to provide cotton material for clothing its troops. Such a factory had been planned before 1750. João V had even ordered the recruitment of skilled cotton dyers from the coast of Coromandel for the factory.[82] In spite of these plans, it was not until 1756 that the government seriously attempted to establish a state cotton mill. How many government cotton mills eventually operated is unknown.

Late in the directorate period, the governor of the state of Rio Negro established a cotton factory to help defray government expenses.[83] A description of this cotton mill provides a glimpse of the state of industry in the Amazon region in the late eighteenth century. According to the official report, the factory consisted of eighteen looms operated by eight men and an equal number of women.[84] Careful segregation of sexes assured undivided attention to work. The preparation of the cotton for spinning occupied another ninety-six Indians. Working hours were from five to eight in the morning; then, after a half-hour break, to noon. After a two-hour rest period the workers then worked until six o'clock. Their total work day was, thus, nine and one-half hours. The workers engaged in spinning received a salary based on their level of productivity. For each roll they received 2,000 reis. Indians employed in other capacities re-

80. Sousa Coutinho to court, Dec. 26, 1797, BAPP, cod. 702, 155.

81. Sousa Coutinho to court, July 1, 1796, ANRJ, cod. 99, XVI, 213.

82. Frei Miguel de Bulhões to court, Nov. 14, 1756, BNRJ, 11, 2, 43, doc. 58 (Pará).

83. Manoel da Gama Lobo Almada to Sousa Coutinho, March 10, 1798, BAPP, cod. 703, 81.

84. Ibid.

ceived 1,200 reis a month. The master spinner who supervised the
workers received 1,600 reis. The mill employed a work force of over
a hundred workers, supposedly all volunteers. The governor of Rio
Negro insisted that he avoided using force or punishment to compel
Indians to work. The factory administration simply returned a re-
calcitrant or reluctant worker to his village. In 1797 the factory
produced 407 rolls of cotton cloth. One half of the net profit was
deposited to the account of the treasury. In 1797 this amounted to
5,727,815 reis.[85]

Two of the most important economic activities of the state were
woodcutting and shipbuilding. The government directly, as well as
indirectly through private contractors, engaged in lumbering operations. The woods of Pará enjoyed an excellent reputation as well
as a constant demand in Lisbon. The heavy work of woodcutting
made it a task to be avoided by the Indians. Periodically the government made efforts to replace Indian woodcutters with African
slaves. However, the relatively high investment necessary to purchase slaves retarded this development. Usually the government
was satisfied with Indians, "well suited for heavy labor."[86] As was
customary, the government drafted Indians from diverse villages
for a period of six months, after which they could expect to be re-
lieved by a fresh assignment of Indians. The difficulty of procuring
labor for woodcutitng sometimes resulted in retention of Indians
beyond their allotted period. The heavy labor had a disastrous effect
on the death and desertion rates. The frequent loss of Indians caused
constant complaints. Occasionally it was necessary to apply militia
units and hired slaves to woodcutting activities.[87] With the deple-
tions of the available lumber close to Belém it became necessary to
go further afield. In the eighteenth century lumbering became steadi-
ly more expensive both in time and labor.

Shipbuilding, a related industry, reached a high point in Pará
during the existence of the Company of Grão Pará e Maranhão
(1755–78). Although some African slaves engaged in shipbuilding,
the Indians made up the bulk of the workers. Indian laborers worked
under the supervision of several European carpenters and tech-

85. *Ibid.*
86. Portaria to the Director of the Lugar de Bemfica, BAPP, cod. 603, 246.
87. Sousa Coutinho to Luis Pinto de Sousa, Aug. 1, 1796, BNRJ, 1–17, 12, 2,
doc. 1 (Pará).

nicians.[88] In 1773 the company laid the keels of four ships. The first completed was the 600 ton *Nossa Senhor de Belém e São João Baptista* at a cost of 41,399,361 reis. Two years later the 660 ton *Grão Pará* slid into the muddy waters of the Amazon. Subsequently, the *Maranhão* and the *Macapá* joined the fleet. The combined tonnage of the four ships exceeded 2,370.[89] In spite of such successes, it became increasingly difficult to keep the shipbuilding force up to the required strength. Occasionally it became necessary to import labor from as far away as São Luís do Maranhão.[90]

In addition to these major government labor requirements, numerous minor demands contributed to the depletion of the labor pool. The state recruited many Indians to fill out the local garrison units. Indian labor built and maintained roads and bridges.[91] Fifty Indians manned the two patrol boats that guarded the mouth of the Amazon.[92]

Except for reasonably detailed figures for 1761, statistics concerning the number of Indians employed in these various activities are fragmentary. However, if we piece together the available information, we can arrive at a rough percentage breakdown of the distribution of Indian labor into three broad categories. Of the total Indian laborers carried on the rolls of each Indian village, 65 percent engaged in forest collecting activities either for private employees or under the supervision of the director. Lumbering, shipbuilding, and related tasks occupied 20 percent. The state employed the remaining 15 percent in government service. The number of village Indians employed by the settlers in tasks other than collecting was insignificant. One should bear in mind that the above percentages deal only with those Indians carried on the labor rolls. Many other Indians were under the permanent supervision of individual settlers, and there was a growing number of "free" laborers living in Belém and its suburbs. Those in this last category provided the manpower for tasks other than forest collecting. The total Indian population under Portuguese

88. *Idem* to court, July 18, 1795, BAPP, cod. 682, 40.

89. List of ships constructed by the Company of Grão Pará e Maranhão, IHGB, lata 278, ms. 14743, 27.

90. Sousa Coutinho to Luis Pinto de Sousa, Aug. 1, 1796, BAPP, cod. 682, 113.

91. *Idem* to court, Feb. 10, 1793, ANRJ, cod. 99, XIV, 92.

92. *Indios . . . canoas de guarda costa . . . na foz do Rio Amazonas* (1773), BNRJ, 21, 2, 10, No. 2 (Pará).

control in 1772 was 19,000. Of this number, only 4,000 were carried on the village rolls.[93]

THE POST DIRECTORATE PERIOD

In the last decade of the eighteenth century the labor problem reached yet another crisis point. The existing labor pool had been so overtaxed that no sector, public or private, was able to meet its labor needs. As a result of government fear of a French invasion from Cayenne, Indians were pressed into military service; the labor supply was depleted and the economy strained still further. In 1796 a large number of Indians were ordered to Belém to reinforce the the garrison; however, the lack of foodstuffs forced the governor to distribute those reinforcements among nearby farmers.[94] The governor noted that the subsistence of the garrison made such a step absolutely necessary. In the following year, the government ordered the release from the light infantry corps of all blacks, mestizos, or Indians who agreed to work as fishermen.[95]

By 1796 only an estimated 4,000 Indians remained in the labor pool. Subtracting the number engaged in collecting forest products under the supervision of the directors, the sick and absent, and those occupied in other tasks, 1,000 remained to meet the government's labor demands.[96] The labor requirements of the government obviously could not be met from such a reduced labor pool. To meet some of its needs, the state resorted to the temporary expedient of renting black slaves from their owners, as well as assigning regular troops to important tasks such as woodcutting and stevedoring.[97] It was subsequently suggested that oxen and mules be introduced to replace and conserve Indian labor.[98] The increasingly difficult situation inevitably forced a reconsideration of the entire organization and distribution of Indians.

93. *Relação das villas e lugares e do numero dos Indios, seus moradores e sua distribuição.* (1761) BNRJ, 11, 2, 43, doc. 126 (Pará); Sousa Coutinho to Luis Pinto de Sousa Aug. 1, 1796; BNRJ, 1–17, 12, 2, doc. 1 (Pará).

94. Editál of Oct. 14, 1796, BAPP, cod. 988, 43.

95. Editál of March 24, 1797, BAPP, cod. 988, 52.

96. Sousa Coutinho to Luis Pinto de Sousa, Aug. 1, 1796, BNRJ, 1–17, 12, 2, doc. 1 (Pará).

97. Editál of Aug. 21, 1771, BAPP, cod. 858, n.p.; Sousa Coutinho to Luis Pinto de Sousa, Aug. 1, 1796, BAPP, cod. 682, 113.

98. Carta régia of Jan. 4, 1798, BAPP, cod. 683, 5.

In 1797, Governor Francisco de Sousa Coutinho carefully analyzed the weakness of the directorate system, concluding that it would have to be abolished in order to relieve the labor shortage.[99] Sousa Coutinho examined the Indians' degree of civilization, as well as the effects of over a century of miscegenation. He concluded that the Indian in Pará had made great progress, thanks to his close contact with European settlers. In Rio Negro the Indian still suffered from relative isolation and therefore was not quite as advanced as his Paraense brother. As proof of the Indians' readiness to assume the responsibilities of free labor, the governor pointed to their excellent response to militia service, an obligation avoided by the European settlers. The governor conceded the fact that the mestizo made a superior worker, but noted that many of the Indians' descendants were mixtures of white or black. The governor voiced the opinion that the Indian and his mixed-blood descendants had arrived at the stage of development where they could be successfully integrated into society. Sousa Coutinho pithily observed that in any event the labor situation could hardly be worse.[100]

The extreme competition between the settlers and the government for the available labor supply had, in fact, already altered the system. In response to the competition for labor, a free market situation had developed. Indians who had previously preferred working for the government to being mercilessly driven by the settlers, now deserted government service for private employment.[101] The demand for labor among the settlers had eventually forced them to offer better working arrangements and a larger share of the profits. The wage scale offered by the government was not sufficiently competitive to hold Indian labor. In addition to the competition of private employers, the directors of Indian villages often refused, on the flimsiest pretexts, to furnish Indians demanded by the government The director who profited from a share of the forest products collected in common by the village understandably was relutcant to divert them to other tasks. Governor Sousa Coutinho noted that one of the greatest obstacles to reorganization of the labor system was the sizable interest group consisting of directors, treasurers,

99. Sousa Coutinho to Rodrigo de Sousa Coutinho, Aug. 2, 1797, ANRJ, cod. 101, II, 54.
100. *Ibid.*, para. 14.
101. *Ibid.*, para. 21.

and others who profited from the directorate system.[102] Such people had a vested interest in the Diretório and did not desire a change.

The Reorganization of Indian Labor

The new system proposed by the governor was primarily designed to meet the labor requirements of the government. The governor proposed that a labor corps be organized consisting of as many blacks and mestizos as possible, although Indians were expected to form the bulk of the corps.[103] Such laborers would be required to serve for a set number of years at the same salary rate as Indians in government service. The governor proposed that the new unit be organized along military lines, complete with uniforms and a set chain of command headed by a *capitão do campo e mato*. Although the corps would form the core of the government's labor force, its existence would not exempt the Indian from labor drafts. Sousa Coutinho suggested that in extreme emergency the militia units could be activated. The militia, which theoretically included all able-bodied males, regardless of race, constituted a large emergency pool.[104] While the governor proposed a controlled labor market to meet royal needs, private employers were to compete in the open market. It was assumed that Indian labor would be attracted to those employers who offered the best conditions. In the event the Indians used their freedom to live in idleness, provisions were made for involuntary labor. A settler unable to hire sufficient hands for sowing and harvesting his crops could petition a village judge for the assignment of involuntary Indian laborers. Only Indians who did not possess their own farms or enterprises could be so assigned. In no event were involuntary laborers to be detailed outside their home district.[105] The governor proposed to retain the practice of assigning newly "civilized" Indians to individual settlers.

With a few modifications, Governor Sousa Coutinho's recommendations were accepted in Lisbon. A *carta régia* dated May 12, 1798, ordered the liquidation of the Diretório and the implementation of the governor's recommendations.[106] Publication of the new laws abolishing the directorate system was delayed until January 1799 to permit the government to make an orderly transition.[107] The

102. *Ibid.*, para. 18.   103. *Ibid.*, para. 24.
104. *Ibid.*   105. *Ibid.*, para. 30.
106. Carta régia of May 12, 1798, ANRJ, cod. 101, II, 44.
107. Editál of Jan. 20, 1799, BAPP, cod, 988, 63.

governor instructed the judges of Santarem, Gurupá, and Portel to assume the responsibilities for assigning Indians to woodcutting operations and to work at the royal arsenal in Belém.[108] The cotton-cloth factories and other industries operated in common in the various villages were turned over to their respective municipal councils.[109] Finally, the governor dispatched orders to various village officials to send recruits for the proposed labor corps.[110] Recruits who came from a distance of five or fewer days from the capital labored for a two-month period with the third month free. Those who lived in more distant villages worked two months followed by two months' exemption from labor. All members of the labor corps were subject to military law and discipline. When engaged in purely military activities, they received their instructions from the governor. For labor service they were at the disposal of the *Intendente da Marinha*.[111]

Private employers were now at liberty to contract with Indian labor. The laborer himself could freely seek the best possible wage as well as the most suitable task. The Indian enjoyed freedom to work but not to withhold his labor. As proposed by the governor, local judges could assign involuntary labor if necessary. The Crown exempted from such involuntary arrangements all Indians whose tithe payment equaled their daily salary.[112] Subsequently the state broadened this exemption to permit Indians engaged in woodcutting operations to be released when their tithe payment exceeded the daily wage.[113] Such an arrangement in effect allowed them to buy their way out of this disagreeable task.

Indian Labor at the Turn of the Century

By 1800 the number of laborers identified as Indians in Pará was estimated at 5,000, of whom 2,000 were engaged in government service.[114] In spite of some improvement, the labor situation re-

---

108. Sousa Coutinho to Dez. Intend. Geral, Jan. 9, 1799.

109. *Ibid.*

110. Sousa Coutinho to various local commandantes, Jan. 5, 1799, ANRJ, cod. 99, XX, 217.

111. *Regimento para o corpo de pedestres que S. M. mandou formar para o expediente de seu real serviço neste estado,* (1799), ANRJ, cod. 101, II, 83.

112. Carta régia of May 12, 1798, ANRJ, cod. 101, II, 44.

113. Bando of April 8, 1799, BAPP, cod. 988, 63A.

114. Sousa Coutinho to Rodrigo de Sousa Coutinho, Sept. 25, 1800, IHGB, lata 281 ms. 14769.

mained critical, at least for the government, a fact the governor blamed on the need to occupy so many individuals in such non-productive tasks as defense. In addition, the low salary available in government service caused a constant loss of laborers who deserted to accept employment on the free labor market. In 1802, the desertion rate had become so alarming that the government required all canoes employing Indians to carry passports proving that the Indians were not deserters from the royal service.[115] The governor also restricted the number of Indian crew members per canoe, allowing only nine Indians to man a canoe of 2,000 or more arrôbas and seven if the craft weighed between 1,000 and 2,000 arrôbas. For canoes with a capacity of less than 1,000 arrôbas, the maximum number of Indians was limited to five.[116] Such limitations excluded African slaves or Indians directly assigned to settlers.

In spite of the difficulties of the government in securing a labor force, the new system was basically a success. The Indian had in fact adapted to the needs of the economy. Such an adaptation had not been easy. Often ripped out of their forest culture and sent hundreds of miles downriver, many did not survive; others assigned to heavy labor tasks quickly perished. Constant expeditions and the frequent desertions of Indian laborers disrupted family life and dispersed the Indian from Mato Grosso to French Cayenne. European diseases, formerly unknown in the region, decimated the Indian population.

The labor supply was limited by epidemics throughout the eighteenth century. Totally defenseless against European disease, the forest Indians of the Amazon basin died by the thousands. Once introduced into the area, epidemic disease swept back and forth through the native population with deadly frequency. Smallpox reached epidemic proportions in the late 1720s, early 1730s, and middle 1740s. The outbreak that began in 1743 carried off thousands of victims.[117] After 1757, with the systematic importation of African slaves by the Company of Grão Pará e Maranhão, the number of epidemics increased markedly. Scarcely a year passed without an outbreak of smallpox, and frequently such outbreaks reached major proportions. Totally inadequate sanitation and ineffectual quaran-

115. Editál of June 6, 1802, ANRJ, cod. 99, XXIII, 138.
116. *Ibid.*
117. Azevedo, p. 229.

tine measures almost insured the constant introduction of pestilence along with African slaves.[118] Although all races suffered the ravages of smallpox, the Indian in particular felt the scourge of the dread disease. It is difficult to estimate the number of Indian victims of epidemic disease. Undoubtedly countless Indians met a horrible death far from the scattered outposts of civilization.

Disease and exploitation by settlers, directors, and the government were facts of life. Understandably, an Indian described Pará as "fit for whites but uninhabitable for Indians."[119] However, even before the abolition of the Diretório, increasing numbers of acculturated Indians and their mixed-blood descendants had abandoned the villages for life in the tidal marshes that served as the suburbs of Belém. There, immune to European diseases which had ravaged their forefathers and free of tyrannical directors, they formed a growing core of free laborers. Their presence was officially noted in 1783, when the formation of a mounted patrol was proposed to put down disturbances between Indians and slaves in the suburbs.[120] After the liquidation of the directorate system, the urbanization of the Indian accelerated. The urban trend was a natural consequence of the collecting economy of the Amazon region. Eventually, the collected forest products had to be brought downriver to Belém for export. Since a vast majority of the Indian population engaged in river transportation, most of them were quite familiar with the trip to the capital. Many who made it stayed there rather than return to their village. The pull of commerce inevitably depopulated smaller villages while swelling the population of Belém and important inland centers. Many isolated villages that had originally been founded by religious orders disappeared. At the turn of the century, the government proposed a general consolidation of underpopulated villages.[121] In 1815 the state made a last futile attempt to reverse the trend away from the villages. Noting the alarming depopulation of many of the villages and the consequent difficulty of meeting the government's labor needs, the governor

118. Arthur Vianna, As epidemias no Pará (Belém, 1906), p. 11.

119. Sousa Coutinho to Rodrigo do Sousa Coutinho, Aug. 2, 1797, ANRJ, cod. 101, II, 54, para. 19, 120.

120. Martinho de Sousa Albuquerque to court, Dec. 5, 1783, ANRJ, cod. 99, IV, 239.

121. Sousa Coutinho to Rodrigo de Sousa Coutinho, Aug. 29, 1800, ARNJ, cod. 99, XXI, 289.

ordered all Indians in the city to return to their place of birth within fifteen days; however, such an order had little effect.[122] Almost a quarter of a century later, Antonio Baena reported that Belém and its surrounding area contained 33,377 inhabitants, equal to over 22 percent of the total population of the province.[123] Six population centers accounted for 44 percent of the population.

The Crown, in spite of being officially dedicated to transforming the Indian into an economically motivated free laborer, was in the end reluctant to accept the evolution of Indian labor. The state did not acknowledge the long range effects of forced acculturation and miscegenation that produced the laborer of the postdirectorate period. It continued to attempt to meet its labor requirements by the old method of forced drafts at low wages. The Indian laborer had advanced more than the government cared to admit. The evolution from a controlled to a free labor market was virtually complete.

SUMMARY

The most important thread that runs through the history of Indian labor in Amazonia is aggressive royal control. At no time, even during the mission period, did the Crown abdicate its power over the utilization of Indian labor. While the mission system theoretically stood between the Crown and its Indian subjects, the royal government decreed modifications it deemed in its interest. Two significant modifications were the assignment of entire Indian villages to meet the state's basic economic needs and the practice of permitting private resettlement of Indians. The mission system operated only at the discretion of the government. When the interests of the missionaries clashed with those of the state, the government adjusted the system in its own favor. In general, the Crown viewed the mission villages as useful to assurance of Portuguese control, but there is no doubt that they served the interests of Portugal or faced modification.

With the rise to power of the Marquês de Pombal, the objectives of the state and the missionaries diverged. The Crown assumed more positive control of the region. The active statism of Pombal resulted in the elimination of any authority that, even weakly, stood between the Crown and its subjects. The directorate symbolized the

122. Bando of Aug. 3, 1815, BAPP, cod. 988, 98.
123. Antonio Ladislau Monteiro Baena, *Ensaio corografico sobre a provincia do Pará* (Belém, 1839), p. 350.

desire of the government to assume fully the "direction" of the state. The government's active intervention in the utilization of Indian labor left little doubt that the interests of the state came before those of the settlers. The needs of the private sector were often neglected, in spite of the Crown's repeatedly stated desire to establish a viable economy in the region. Government policy acted to keep the individual settler in a state of chronic uncertainty. Without a stable labor force, expansion of the Paraense economy was impossible.

Although the average settler was unable to secure a guaranteed access to the labor pool, the government did make an important concession to the more affluent settlers. Even during the mission period the government permitted individual settlers to finance the resettlement of forest Indians. This, in effect, gave the wealthy settler a stable labor supply. At the same time such a concession drained away possible additions to the general labor pool. The concentration of labor and wealth was a natural result of the regulations which allowed resettlement. Those without sufficient capital to resettle Indians privately had to rely on the regular labor pool. Many settlers were unfairly blamed for laziness or going "native." However, without sufficient capital at their disposal, they had little alternative.

The advance salary requirement acted to restrict the settlers' access to Indian labor. The necessity of depositing the entire salary in advance restricted the number of laborers the poorer settler could hire. Only the wealthy could afford to employ a sizable number of village Indians. The fact that government policy favored the more affluent settlers possibly accounted for the lack of pressure to reorganize the labor system. When reforms were finally undertaken in 1799, it was because of government difficulties in securing labor, not because of public pressure. Influential settlers in a position to make their complaints heard, both in Belém do Pará and in Lisbon, were apparently quite satisfied with the labor policy. But other settlers, unable to compete with the labor demands of the government, village directors, and more powerful settlers, were unable to generate capital. Significantly, the relatively small number of slaves imported were purchased by those settlers who already possessed a stable labor force. The less fortunate settlers could not finance the purchase of African slaves. When the average settler did secure temporary labor, he applied it to forest collecting which returned a profit and was not dependent on a constant labor supply. Govern-

ment policy, which officially encouraged agriculture, actually confirmed the natural subsistence economy of the region.

As a result of the active competition for Indian labor, a free labor
pool eventually developed. Indians began deserting their villages
and flocking into the capital and the important inland centers. In
Belém, the Indians, and many of their mixed-blood descendants,
sold their labor under more favorable conditions. The growing urbanization of the region was a natural consequence of the collecting
economy. By the end of the century the evolution of a free labor
system was almost complete.

HAROLD B. JOHNSON, JR.:

A Preliminary Inquiry into Money, Prices, and Wages in Rio de Janeiro, 1763-1823[*]

I

To date few historians of Brazil have paid much attention to price history—certainly not in any systematic sense. There is, of course, Antonil's famous treatise on the exotic products of Brazil which gives us an idea of the astounding price rise which took place in Minas Gerais due to the gold rush;[1] and, more recently, Taunay has provided some price material in his work on the development of the coffee economy in the São Paulo region,[2] as has Myriam Ellis in her article on the provisioning of Minas Gerais in the eighteenth century.[3] But aside from these and other works which present scattered prices collected without much pretense at establishment of a scientific series,[4] the cupboard is bare. Even in the more serious of the previously mentioned works, the prices used have normally been gathered hit-or-miss from a wide variety of sources, scattered among several economic markets, and in reality representing, indiscriminately, various types of transactions: wholesale, retail, official evaluations, and others. Needless to say, this cannot pass as price history in the contemporary sense of the term, nor even as much of a con-

* As the title indicates this is merely a preliminary sketch of the subject; Prof. Eulália Lobo of the University of South Carolina and I are presently engaged in a study of price movements in Rio de Janeiro over a much longer period—from 1760 to 1930.

1. André João Antonil, *Cultura e opulência do Brasil, por suas drogas e minas* (Lisbon, 1711).

2. Afonso de Escragnolle Taunay, *Pequena história do café no Brasil* (Rio de Janeiro, 1945).

3. Myriam Ellis, "Contribuição ao estudo do abastecimento das zonas mineradoras no Brasil no século XVIII," *Revista de História* (São Paulo), XXXVI (1958), 429–467.

4. E.g. Charles R. Boxer, *The Golden Age of Brazil* (Berkeley, 1962), 330–332 (essentially a summary of Antonil); Dauril Alden, *Royal Government in Colonial Brazil* (Berkeley, 1968), 509–511.

tribution to it; for these prices, separated from their milieu, of which few if any traces remain in the final product, are like archaeological artifacts dug up and divorced from any contact with their strata or location: just things—curiosities with little significance for anyone.

Fortunately, the study of price history is now a reasonably scientific enterprise which is being carried on internationally, though at a slow pace, in accordance with generally accepted standards and methods first set down by the International Committee on Price History in 1930. Essential points of its program are that prices should be derived from one market, not from scattered ones; that they should be comparable, that is they should apply to the same quality and quantities of goods, purchased in similar types of transactions; and that there must be enough of them to construct a series of yearly, or nearly yearly, price averages; and, finally, that they must be extracted and organized into tables according to certain established methods.[5]

Needless to say, nothing of this sort exists for any market in colonial Brazil; nor, until recently (when Ruggiero Romano began his investigations into prices in Santiago de Chile and Buenos Aires)[6] did it exist for any part of the South American continent. Certainly only the relative backwardness of Brazilian economic history has permitted such a lack to go unfilled. But until this gap is closed, it is futile to attempt the construction of convincing and nuanced explanations of Brazilian economic development.

What explanations we now have are either sterile burrowings in the documentary sands or else theoretical castles resting mainly on air. Simonsen, for example really does not attempt to say much about Brazilian economic development except in extremely broad terms: he has merely collected the most easily available information and put it into quasi-systematic form. Not to disparage his effort: it is useful, indeed essential, and we are all indebted to him for making such information readily available;[7] but there is now room

5. See the summary in Sir William Beveridge, *Price and Wages in England from the Twelfth to the Nineteenth Century* (London, 1939), xxi-xxxiii.
6. Ruggiero Romano, *Cuestiones de historia económica latino-americana* (Caracas, 1966), *passim*.
7. Roberto Simonsen, *História econômica do Brasil (1500/1820)* (4th ed.; São Paulo, 1962).

for a considerably more sophisticated synthesis. Furtado appears to have met the need; but has not his obvious reluctance to do laborious spadework induced him to make a reckless jump from Simonsen's undigested facts to the most exquisite theoretical models, producing a perfect example of what might be termed *histoire soufflée*? To read him, one would think scarcely any information was left to be uncovered.[8] The informed, however, know full well that Furtado's treatise is essentially a castle in the air; or, at best, one which rests ever so lightly on the shifting sands barely excavated by Simonsen. Until firmer foundations are laid, Brazilian economic history will never attain a level comparable to that of modern Europe. It will thus remain in a kind of intellectual isolation which delights certain historians with Herderian fixations, but is increasingly irritating and frustrating both to those of us who think Brazil deserves something better than to be regarded as a piece of historical exotica and to those Brazilians who know that only a better understanding of their past can provide the necessary guidance out of many of their present dilemmas.

In order to integrate the economic role played by colonial Brazil, first into the Portuguese economic system for which it had an ever-increasing importance, and then into the common experience of the eighteenth-century Atlantic world, it is essential that we establish the price histories of Brazil's key markets—Bahia, Recife, Olinda, Belém, Rio, Minas, Santos, São Paulo, and others. Once these have been investigated and compared, it should be possible to extend the research outward, as far as the documents will permit, into the less monetized areas, a point to which we shall return in the conclusion. Such an undertaking is, of course, a task for a generation of historians working as a group. It is obviously beyond the capacity of any single person, except, perhaps, for an Earl Hamilton, were he to devote his life to the task. But, alas, there are few Hamiltons about these days, and one is perforce reduced to cultivating merely as much of the common garden as time permits. My own investigations are confined to the city of Rio de Janeiro. They did not really begin with the intention of investigating price history per se, but rather as a part of a long-term study of the society and economy of

8. Celso Furtado, *Formação econômica do Brasil* (Rio de Janeiro, 1959), *passim*.

the city of Rio de Janeiro in the eighteenth century. But they may
be of some general interest, and may also help to stimulate others
to do comparable work elsewhere in Brazil.[9]

Sources

A few general comments about the sources for this study and
their elaboration may be useful. Happily or not, the nature of the
sources has already conspired to settle for the investigator the much
debated question about the type of documentation best suited to
the elaboration of a price series: the conflict, that is, between the
"Hamilton" school, which prefers to use institutional prices, arguing
that only they represent true transactions in the market place, and
thus the only really genuine prices; and the "Lamrousse" school,
which prefers the use of official price tables established for supervised markets, objecting that institutional prices can often be
distorted by discounts, long-term contracts, and various other in-
fringements which make them less sensitive to variation than the
official prices of the *Aver do Pêso* or the *Terreiro do Trigo*.[10] Indeed,
one wonders if these preferences do not in reality simply reflect the
type of sources most readily available to the researcher, who has
then elaborated arguments to make the best of what circumstances
dictate. However that may be, no official price series have come to
light in Rio, and thus the "Hamilton" approach has proved ines-
capable.

The prices used[11] in elaborating the graphs presented in this
study have come from four Rio institutions, which are listed in
order of their importance. It is possible that a few sources or archives
were overlooked, but certainly none substantial enough to affect
the result in any serious way.

1. HOSPITAL DOS LÁZAROS. Livros de Receita e Despesa, Nos. 1 e
2 (1762–1795).

9. I should like to acknowledge my debt to Doutor Vitorino Magalhães
Godinho of Lisbon for his encouragement and suggestions with regard to my
research.

10. V. M. Godinho, *Prix et monnaies au Portugal, 1750–1850* (Paris, 1955),
2–7; see also Pierre Vilar, "Histoire des prix, histoire générale," *Annales.
Économies. Sociétés. Civilisation,* IV (1949), 29–32.

11. It might be stated, parenthetically, that a total of approximately 15,000
individual prices, representing an equal number of transactions, were ab-
stracted from the sources, though of course only a part of these were employed
in construction of the final series.

This was the leper hospital, located in São Christóvão, on the outskirts of the city, and its remaining account books (which unfortunately do not extend beyond the year 1795) provide the best, indeed the essential, series for foodstuffs, and also occasionally for other commodities (see list given below). The first volume, unfortunately, has a lacuna in the accounts between 1764 and 1771, but this gap (not terribly serious in itself) can be remedied by turning to the records of the Penitência Hospital (No. 3 below) which are especially good for these very years. Otherwise, the Lázaros accounts furnish an almost monthly series of prices for manioc flour, wheat flour, wax, bacon, wine brandy (imported), cane brandy (local), butter, olive and fish oils, dried meat, beans, corn, rice, wine, and vinegar. No other source is as consistent or useful; it is essential to this study.

2. Santa Casa de Misericórdia. From this institution I have made use of the four Livros de Receita e Despesa covering the years 1768–1780, 1795–1801, 1801–1809, and 1809–1820. Of the once vast documentation kept by this house, these four volumes are almost the only remnants of the colonial period. All the rest—receipts, purchase lists, and so forth—have vanished. According to the provedor, who was kind enough to receive me, this was the result of a fire early in this century. One can, indeed, only marvel at the fire's uncanny sense of chronology, destroying, as it evidently did, so much of the documentation before 1800, so little after. In any event, the fire spared the general account books of the period 1768 to 1820, though the loss of the rest is an intellectual tragedy for the city of Rio.

The Santa Casa's scribes were not entirely consistent in their methods of entry. In the later volumes commodities are often listed without any quantity. At this point, the commodity in question must be dropped from the series. This is the case, for example, with hens and eggs. Salaries, too, are rarer in the earlier volumes and more frequent in the latter; the same, to a lesser degree, holds true for building materials. In spite of these inconsistencies, the Misericórdia volumes constitute the richest source of all, measured by the number of commodities and prices entered, which is hardly surprising considering the size and importance of the institution. For building materials (which are especially rich in the lustrum from 1796 to 1800) this series is unrivalled, furnishing the basic price data for

lime, bricks, tiles, and nails. It is also a prime source for cloth and
clothing prices, which have been omitted from the preliminary study
owing to lack of space as well as to the bewildering variety of types
and qualities of cloth.

3. IRMANDADE DE SÃO FRANCISCO DE PENITÊNCIA. I have made use
of the accounts of the Hospital (1763–1804), as well as of the
books of income and expenditure running from 1762 to 1806 and
from 1806 to 1822. The archives are unusually well housed and
cared for.

The hospital records are especially valuable for determining the
price of foodstuffs, providing the best data after the Lázaros books
for such commodities until the year 1775, when an unfortunate
change in method of making entries, from a monthly to a yearly
basis, makes the record considerably less useful. The other volumes
can be employed from time to time as a supplement to other series.

4. IRMANDADE DE SÃO FRANCISCO DE PAULA. From this institution
two volumes were retrieved and used, running from 1777 to 1798
and from 1801 to 1829. Because of their poor state of preservation,
this series proved the least useful of all: the initial thirty-four folios
of the first volume are so worm-eaten as to be illegible, and only
the remainder, covering the years 1785 to 1798, are readable. Like
the Penitência Hospital records, this source presents the disadvan-
tage of a shift from monthly entries to entries by fiscal year in 1785
which creates uncertainties about which of two calendar years a
given price should be attributed to. Such ambiguous entries have
been employed in this study only in a supplementary fashion, when
no other prices were available. The volumes, nevertheless, are quite
good for salaries, bricks, wax, lime, and fish oil.

Other sources, not utilized in the present study, but which, time
permitting, will be integrated into a later monograph can provide
valuable additional material: import registers with evaluations of
incoming cargos; testamentary inventories which list and evaluate
the property of deceased *Cariocas*; private account books; *fôros* and
other property rents; and slave auction records and other such material. The present study, with its limited sources, has the advantage
of uniformity—all the prices used are of a like nature, produced by
comparable entities, and all are free market prices except where an
institution had a supply contract, a fact generally mentioned. Thus
all are comparable transactions. Furthermore, the series which result are similar in type to those elaborated by E. J. Hamilton, Lord

Beveridge, and N. W. Posthumus, and, except in certain instances, are similar to those presented by Vitorino Magalhães Godinho in his study of Portuguese price history between 1750 and 1850.[12] Thus comparison with Chile, Argentina, Portugal, and Spain, the most interesting non-Brazilian countries, is facilitated.

Commodities

The following list gives the commodities for which reasonably complete series of prices could be found. They were also chosen, as far as possible, to meet the criteria of comparability with series for other countries elaborated under the auspices of the International Committee, and of usefulness for a possible later elaboration of composite indices—that is, a series of commodities important enough to be "representative" of the economy.

beans (*feijão*)
corn (*milho*)
manioc flour (*farinha da terra, f. do norte, f. de mandioca*)
wheat flour (*farinha de trigo, f. do reino, f. americana*)
rice (*arroz*)
sugar (*açúcar*)
  a) white (*branco*)
  b) dark (*mascavo*)
brandy (*agoardente*)
  a) cane (*a. de cana, a. da terra*)
  b) wine (*a. do reino*)
oil (*azeite*)
  a) fish (*a. de peixe*)
  b) olive (*a. doce*)
wine (*vinho*)
vinegar (*vinagre*)
dried meat (*carne seca*)
bacon (*toucinho*)
lime (*cal*)
bricks (*tijolos*)
slaves (*escravos*)
salaries of various types

---

12. Earl J. Hamilton, *War and Prices in Spain, 1650–1800* (Cambridge, Mass., 1947); Nicholas W. Posthumus, *Nederlandsche Prijsgeschiedenis*, II (Leiden, 1945); Sir William Beveridge, *op. cit.*; V. M. Godinho, *op. cit.*

Weights and measures

Before proceeding to an examination of the price series, it may be useful to define the weights and measures used in this study.

ALQUEIRE: see MOIO. A measure of capacity equivalent to 36.27 liters in Rio, and 13.80 liters in Lisbon.[13]

ARRÁTEL: see LIBRA.

ARRÔBA: Throughout the period concerned, this measure of weight was equal to thirty-two pounds (libras), or to 14.75 kilograms in metric terms. It was the standard measure for dried meat and sugar. Depending upon the quantities involved, commodities were sometimes measured in pounds instead, but conversion into arrôbas is always easily made. The Lisbon arrôba weighed the same as that of Rio.[14]

BARRIL: The capacity of the barrel in Rio varied considerably. Thus a conscientious accountant would always specify in his entry "so many barrels containing so many arrôbas." When only barrels of a commodity are given, the prices have been set aside as unquantified, being comparable neither to one another nor to anything else. Fortunately such cases have been few, though not absent.

BARRICA: A "little barrel." Generally the same remarks apply to it as apply to the barrel. Sometimes it appears that the barrica approximated 200 pounds, but such inferences have been used only with due warning since the barrica, like the barrel, was never a precise measure.

CANADA: see MEDIDA.

LIBRA: (POUND) see ARRÔBA. The pound was equal to the arrátel and contained sixteen ounces.

MEDIDA: The usual capacity measurement for liquids purchased in quantities smaller than a pipa (s.v.). Wine, cane brandy, brandy, vinegar, and fish oil as well as olive oil were almost always measured in medidas. The number of medidas in a pipa is not entirely clear; according to the sources used for this study, it varied from 160 to 180. Simonsen defined a medida as 180 pipas, and that practice has been uniformly followed in this paper except where the sources indicate an equivalence of 160.[15] The Rio medida held 2.662

13. V. M. Godinho, op. cit., 75.
14. António de Morais Silva, Diccionário da lingua Portugueza (Lisbon, 1891), s.v. "arrôba"; Simonsen, op. cit., 463.
15. Simonsen, op. cit., 463.

liters, that of Lisbon 1.166. Nevertheless, the Rio medida has been assumed even in the case of imported liquids, since by the time the product reached the institution it had certainly been broken down into lots consonant with local measures. A medida was equal to one canada.

Moio: The standard Portuguese dry measure of capacity since medieval times, the moio was used essentially for grains, flour, and other commodities. In Rio it usually consisted of sixty alqueires (see above), whereas in Portugal it varied greatly from region to region and city to city. In eighteenth-century Lisbon it generally held sixty alqueires of 13.80 liters each.[16]

Pipa: The normal liquid capacity measurement used for large lots of vinegar, oil, and brandy. It was equal to either 160 or 180 medidas; the latter equivalence is employed here unless otherwise noted.[17] See medida.

Saco: Employed alternately with alqueire and moio to measure grains and flour, usually those of lower value. Thus wheat flour was usually measured by the moio or alqueire, and manioc, rice, and corn by the saco. Although the saco appears at times to have been variable in amount, a careful examination of the sources reveals that it almost always amounted to two alqueires and this equivalence has been used throughout this study.[18]

N.B.: Bricks (along with eggs, hens, roosters, tiles, and nails which do not appear), are not measured by any other unit than themselves. Therefore when the price per unit involves sums so small as to require less than one real, these goods have been lumped into lots of ten or one hundred to round out the price to full reis.

Coinage

The question of the coinage and the monetary stock will be treated more fully in the next section. But here it should be pointed out that all prices have been expressed in reis, or fractions thereof, the universal Luso-Brazilian money of account during the eighteenth century, one which was consistent throughout the period. Thus, the researcher's concern about conversion and possible resultant errors is avoided.

16. Simonsen, op. cit., 463.   17. Ibid.

18. See also the "Memórias públicas e econômicas da cidade de São Sebastião do Rio de Janeiro," RIHGB, XLVII:1 (1884), 50, where reference is made to the export of "farinha de guerra em sacos de 2 alqueires."

This is not to say, of course, that the precious metal content of the real was constant during the period. It changed a number of times.[19] Nevertheless, although such changes may be relevant for analyses of the general movement of prices, the main goal of price history, as Lord Beveridge has pointed out, is not the gold or silver equivalents of prices, but rather the changing relationships between commodity prices themselves.[20] Thus the question of devaluation of the coinage in relation to gold or silver is not of the first consequence, and certainly not in the practical matter of setting up a price series.

II

Before attempting to account for the behavior of the various price series which have been established, it will be helpful to choose some sort of conceptual framework to assist us in the analysis. The most useful and logical, I think, is the classic equation of Irving Fisher, which has been fundamental to the analysis of price fluctuations ever since it was first expounded in 1911.[21] His equation is, in a sense, a tautology. It states, simply, that in any market situation:

$$MV = pQ$$

that is to say, the total amount of money and equivalents in circulation (M) multiplied by the velocity of circulation (V) will equal the total quantity of goods and services sold (Q) at the prevailing price level (p). Since we already know, in effect, the values of "p" for our period in Rio, what we wish to know is the manner in which the other variables play upon "p"—the other factors of the equation and their causes, so to speak.[22]

19. A summary of the gold and silver content of Portuguese national and provincial coinage may be had in João Pandiá Calógeras, *A Política monetária do Brasil*, trans. by Thomas Newlands Neto (São Paulo, 1960), 10–12; as well as in the classic work of Augusto Carlos Teixeira de Aragão, *Descripção geral e histórica das moedas cunhadas em nome dos reis, regentes, e governadores de Portugal*, (Lisbon, 1874), II, 242–243.

20. Sir William Beveridge, *op. cit.* (n. 5, above), xlvii.

21. Irving Fisher, *The Purchasing Power of Money* (New Haven, 1911), 14–21, 24–32, 48–53.

22. In his comments on the paper, Prof. Frédéric Mauro (University of Paris-Nanterre) preferred a somewhat more elaborate version of the Fisher equation:

$$P = f \left\{ \frac{mv + m'v' + \ldots\ldots}{Q} \right.$$

where P equals the prevailing price level, Q is goods and services sold, m is money, v equals velocity of circulation of money, m' is credit, and v' equals velocity of circulation of credit.

Let us first take the question of the money in circulation. Although, due to lack of statistical records, we cannot, by any means, know as precisely as we should wish what was the amount of "circulating media" at any given time in Rio, there is nevertheless some evidence which is useful for gaining an idea of the long term trends in the Rio money supply.

Table 1 gives the figures for the total emission of coin by the Rio mint in the period from 1768 to 1796.[23] (See also figure 1.) The trend is clearly downward. These figures, however, do not tell the whole story with regard to the stock of money circulating in Rio at this time. We know, for example, that there was a great demand for, and considerable influx of, silver from Spanish America, especially from La Plata, and that some of this coin was restamped and used to make up for the growing scarcity of "national" coin in Rio.[24] The great demand for silver is also reflected by the relative premium which it enjoyed over gold in official valuations.[25] Thus, silver served to compensate somewhat for the lack of currency felt by the carioca population about which we have a record of persistent complaint.[26]

Even more significant, and having serious social effects, was the relative shortage of smaller coins, the crude copper vellón so important for the retail trades and to the poorer households.[27] Indeed, if we examine the emissions by type and denomination of coin, an interesting pattern can be observed. Within each group there is always a progression from the highest value coin which is invariably minted in the greatest amount, to the lowest value which, with equal regularity, is minted in the smallest. The monetary emissions of the Rio mint between 1768 and 1796 totalled 60,000,180,682 reis,[28] divided as follows:

23. "Mappa de toda a qualidade de moedas que girão nesta capitanía, cunhadas na real Caza da Moeda no Rio de Janeiro do anno de 1768 até 1796." *RIHGB*, XLV:1 (1883), 191–193.

24. Watkin Tench, *A Narrative of the Expedition to Botany-Bay . . .* (London, 1789), 15; Calógeras, *op. cit.*, 12–13; Severino Sombra, *História monetária do Brasil colonial* (Rio de Janeiro, 1938), 257, 267; see also Alden, *op. cit.* (n. 4, above), 118, and other references cited therein; J. K. Tuckey, *Tuckey's Voyage: An Account of a Voyage to Establish a Colony at Port Philip . . .* (London, 1805), 89.

25. Calógeras, *op. cit.*, 12, 22.

26. Sombra, *op. cit.*, 251; Alden, *op. cit.* 118, 286.

27. In fact, *no* copper coins were minted in Rio after 1777 (see table referred to in note 23), although there is evidence of shipments (all before 1777?) of copper coins from Lisbon to Brazil in Sombra, *op. cit.*, 202, 231.

28. Calculated from the document referred to in note 23.

| Denomination | Value (in milreis) | | | |
of Coin (in reis)	"National" Money (gold)	"Provincial" Money (gold)	(silver)	Vellón (copper)
6,400	59,132,893			
4,000		870,712		
3,200	5,005			
2,000		27,986		
1,600	2,771			
1,000		7,444		
640			68,543	
600			60,424	
300			7,708	
150			520	
5				2,675

Thus, what was acutely lacking was precisely the kind of money most necessary for the functioning of the retail trade and the purchases of the poorest classes. We shall return to this subject in the final section of the paper.

Aside from the declining volume of the mintings during the period

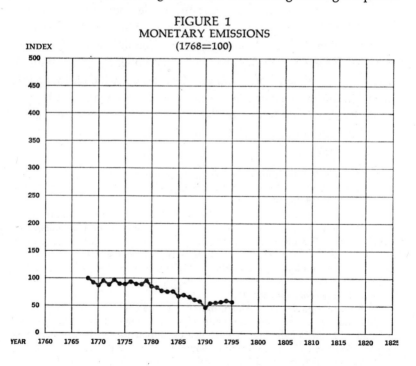

FIGURE 1
MONETARY EMISSIONS
(1768=100)

TABLE 1
Monetary Emissions, 1768–1796

Year	Amount (in milreis)	Index (1768=100)
1768	2,713	100.00
1769	2,550	93.99
1770	2,342	86.33
1771	2,638	97.24
1772	2,422	89.27
1773	2,665	98.23
1774	2,492	91.85
1775	2,388	88.02
1776	2,594	95.61
1777	2,417	89.09
1778	2,431	89.61
1779	2,613	96.31
1780	2,295	84.59
1781	2,302	84.85
1782	2,076	76.52
1783	2,060	75.93
1784	2,093	77.15
1785	1,802	66.42
1786	1,882	69.37
1787	1,769	65.20
1788	1,724	63.55
1789	1,619	59.68
1790	1,350	49.76
1791	1,480	54.55
1792	1,477	54.44
1793	1,530	56.40
1794	1,596	58.83
1795	1,469	54.15
1796	1,399	51.57

1768 to 1796, there is also the factor of specie export to consider. In spite of the drastic decline in the gold production of Minas Gerais and the scarcity of coin in Rio, the Portuguese government insisted upon and received large shipments of coin from Rio.[29] The total amounts cannot be calculated precisely, but they must have been

29. Sombra, op. cit., 203, 270; Tuckey, op. cit., 82; see also the useful discussion of this point in Alden, op. cit., 327–331.

very large. Coupled with this was the tendency of the official under-evaluation of gold to drive it from circulation, either into private hoards or abroad where it enjoyed a considerable premium.[30]

Such, in general terms, was the monetary situation at least up to the year 1809. After the arrival of the Portuguese Court in Rio, it was decided to facilitate royal finances by establishing a bank which would be licensed to issue paper money. These issues were, it would seem, moderate in amount from 1809 until 1813; but beginning in 1814 the temptation to finance government needs with paper money grew apace, and the issues from then on until 1823 were undoubtedly so large as to have an inflationary effect.[31] Here are the total amounts of bank notes in circulation for each of the years from 1809 to 1823.[32] (See also figure 2.)

TABLE 2

Bank Notes in Circulation, 1809–1823
(in milreis)

Year	Amount
1809	000,000
1810	160,000
1811	104,200
1812	60,000
1813	130,000
1814	1,042,500
1815	1,199,700
1816	1,862,280
1817	2,600,350
1818	3,632,350
1819	6,518,350
1820	8,566,450
1821	8,070,920
1822	9,170,920
1823	9,994,320

The inflationary effects of this increase became apparent by 1818, when the Brazilian milreis, until then above parity, began to decline precipitously on the London exchange. By 1823 it had dropped almost 32 percent.[33]

In sum, then, taking the "M" factor of Fisher's equation by itself,

30. Calógeras, *op. cit.* (n. 19, above), 22.
31. *Ibid.*, 30–34.
32. *Ibid.*, 36.   33. *Ibid.*, 33.

FIGURE 2
BANKNOTE EMISSIONS

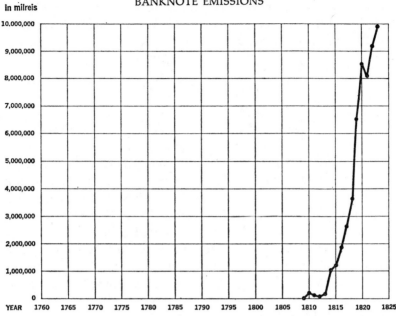

we may say that the pressure on prices was definitely downward, that is, deflationary, from 1763 to 1796 and most likely until 1809. From 1809 until 1814, the banknotes issued may have halted or neutralized the previous tendency; but from 1814 on, the continued issuance of large amounts of paper money had a decidedly infla-tionary effect. Thus, considering the money alone, three periods may be distinguished:

1763–1809	deflationary
1810–1813	neutral
1814–1823	inflationary

We know considerably less about the "V" factor, the velocity of circulation. In fact, we have no way to measure exactly the velocity of circulation, nor the "propensity to spend" of the Carioca popu-lation during our period. One might assume that a considerable amount of hoarding (saving) went on, a tendency that the definite official underevaluation of gold would stimulate. Certainly the hoarding cannot be discounted among the reasons which gave rise to the incessant complaints of a monetary shortage voiced by the citizenry during the period.[34]

34. See note 26.

However, one possible stimulus for increasing circulation of the money stock, a rising population, was present. The population of the city increased more than 200 percent in the period from 1750 to 1821.[35] Here are the figures:

1750	ca. 24,397
1760	30,000 (est.)
1780	38,707
1799	43,376
1808	50,144
1821	79,321

This increase in the population may have produced a more rapid turnover of the money stock, whatever the total amount of the latter may have been. Unfortunately, we have no real means of measuring the turnover. Thus we can only say that from 1763 to 1808 a rise in turnover would have exerted a countervailing tendency to the obvious decline of the monetary stock, though whether this was enough to neutralize the decline is doubtful. In the period 1809 to 1813, the sharp growth in population would likely have exerted a stimulating effect, and from 1814 onward, population growth probably substantially contributed to the general inflationary tendency already present in monetary policy.

If we combine the factors "M" and "V," we might suggest the following scheme for the combined effect of the two on the general price level in Rio:

1763–1808	somewhat downward
1809–1813	slightly upward
1814–1823	strongly upward

Assuming, in general, that the MV factors would behave as suggested, let us now take a look at the various commodities and their price fluctuations to see the possible effects of these factors, as well as that of supply (Q), upon them. Here it will help to clarify the exposition if we group the commodities into categories

35. Data taken from the *Resumo histórico dos inquéritos censitários realizados no Brasil* (Rio de Janeiro, 1951), X, for the years 1750, 1760, 1799, and 1808; from the "Memórias públicas e econômicas da cidade de São Sebastião do Rio de Janeiro," *RIHGB*, XLVII:1 (1884), 46–51 for the year 1780; and from the ANRJ, *Secção de Ministérios*, Commando das Armas no Minístro da Guerra e Estrangeiros, IG¹428 (maço 4), f. 3, for 1821. The existence of this document was kindly called to my attention by Prof. Robert Conrad of the University of Illinois (Chicago).

TABLE 3
Rio de Janeiro:
Trade in Commodities

Market	Imported From		Exported To	
Buenos Aires, Rio Grande do Sul	hides tallow dried meat	silver wheat	sugar cotton cloth slaves cane brandy	tobacco rice manioc
Bahia/ Pernambuco		coin coconuts	manioc beans cane brandy milho Minas cheese	wheat dried meat bacon rice
Portugal		wine olive oil brandy vinegar onions	sugar indigo rice cane brandy hides coffee	fish oil wax woods cotton tallow
Europe (other than Portugal)	woollens cutlery clothing prints (cotton) dairy products	hardware housewares porter		
Africa	wax oil sulphur woods	slaves ivory salt	sugar rice dried meat tobacco cane brandy	manioc gunpowder arms cotton bacon
North America	salted meat wheat furniture	pitch tar		
Asia	silk luxury goods		silver	

depending upon their origin, their principal markets, and their relative sensitivity to foreign or domestic demand. (see table 3.)[36]

36. Table 3 is based on information gathered from the following sources: (a) Tench, *op. cit.* (n. 24, above), 11–15; (b) John Mawe, *Travels in the Interior of Brazil* . . . (Philadelphia, 1816), 103, 108, 109, 110, 281, 325–327, and 331–344; (c) Joaquim de Sousa Leão Filho ed. and trans., *O Rio de Janeiro visto por*

GROUP I: Products produced locally and in the main consumed locally: cane brandy, manioc flour, lime, bricks, fish oil, corn, and beans.

Here we must immediately separate out fish oil, lime, and bricks. Fish oil—which was used mainly for lighting[37]—was produced and sold under royal contract, which explains the unusual character of its price movement (or lack of it) between 1763 and 1795 (appendix, series 1). With one or two exceptions (possibly due to scribal errors in the entries of the account books) the price held steady at 140 reis the medida. Obviously this was not a "market" price.[38]

Lime and bricks (see figures 3 and 4 and appendix, series 2 and 3) are the two commodities which best reflect demand in the building industry, and, as one might expect, their prices behave in a similar fashion. Both show a slow but steady progression upward, with a jump in brick prices in 1802 and 1809, a peak in 1811, and then a decline thereafter. Lime, on the other hand, leaps ahead in 1799, peaks in 1811, tends to fall back in 1813 and then peaks again in 1816 and 1819. In both cases the steady upward trend can be attributed to a steady growth in population and the consequent demand for shelter; the jumps in 1809 and 1810 as well as the peak in 1811 are the obvious results of the extraordinary demands for housing which came with the arrival of the Portuguese Court. Once this boom was over, prices fell back somewhat, but they never dropped to their former levels of the 1770s and 1780s.

The other prices in this group likewise have their own peculiarities. Corn (milho), locally grown (see figure 5 and appendix, series

---

dois Prussianos em 1819 (São Paulo, 1966), 19–20, 48; the two Prussians were Theodor von Leithold and Ludwig von Rango; (d) "Memórias públicas e econômicas . . . ," *RIHGB*, XLVII:1 (1884), 46–51; "Productos exportados da cidade do Rio de Janeiro no anno de 1796," *RIHGB*, XLVI:1 (1883), 197–204; and (f) Sombra, *op. cit.* (n. 24, above), 270, which indicates the silver drain toward Asia.

It will naturally be understood that the commodities received from and exported to Europe and Asia, as well as North America, came largely through Lisbon, though contraband was not negligible, before 1808. After this date, these commodities were traded directly.

37. Alden, *op. cit.* (n. 4, above), 392, n. 20.

38. The average price for each year was calculated as an arithmetical average of the monthly averages (likewise calculated arithmetically). The index numbers are based on the average price for the year 1780.

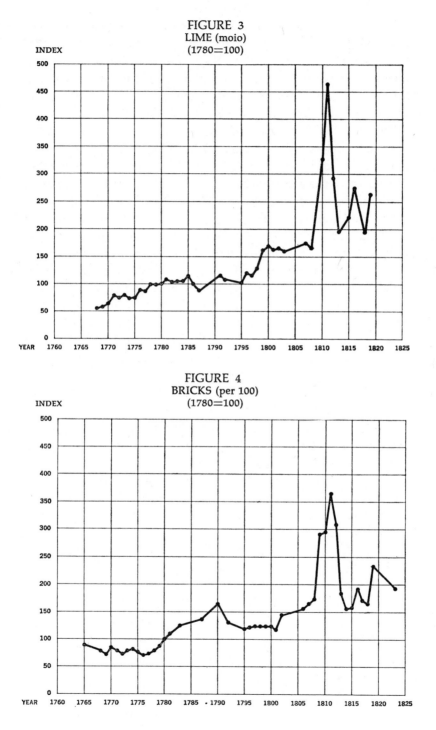

FIGURE 3
LIME (moio)
(1780=100)

FIGURE 4
BRICKS (per 100)
(1780=100)

4), served mainly as animal and chicken feed, although some was exported to Bahia and Pernambuco. Its price fluctuated from 1763 through 1785, with a trough in the years 1780 through 1785, and then a definitely higher level from 1787 through 1795. The reason for this rise after 1785 is obscure, though it may be due to increased exports, both to northern Brazil and to Africa.[39]

The other three foodstuffs—beans, manioc flour, and cane brandy (figures 6, 7, and 8, appendix, series 5, 6, and 7)—shared the characteristic of being the principle staples of the slave population, as well as of the lower classes in general.[40] They also enjoyed a considerable export market to Africa (cane brandy and manioc flour especially), where they were exchanged for the slaves, wax, and gold which were brought back to Rio. Both cane brandy and manioc show indeterminant trends until 1783, when they began a general long-term rise which is particularly accentuated after 1809, especially in the case of cane brandy. The general tendency upward after 1783 may be attributed to the growing slave imports from Africa, which came about as a result of the expanding European market for Brazilian products (rice, cotton, coffee, sugar). That is, the expansion of the export sector brought with it a stimulus for the production of the foodstuffs consumed by and exchanged for that sector's labor force.

GROUP II: The sudden growth in the European markets served by Portugal by the re-export of Brazilian products is clearly evident in the following sequence of rice prices which, along with sugar, may be considered as a second group: products produced and consumed locally, whose price is essentially set by the foreign markets to which the bulk of the production is sold.

After hovering at index numbers in the 70s and 80s, rice (figure 9, appendix, series 8) jumps to an index number of 110 in 1779, and aside from two years (1787 and 1790) which may be years of

39. The lack of published trade statistics (aside from the occasional tables in Simonsen and elsewhere) for the port of Rio de Janeiro is a serious impediment to any full and detailed study of the city's economy in the eighteenth century. It is to be hoped that Senhor Corcino Medeiros dos Santos of the University of Marília (São Paulo) will help to remedy this deficiency in the doctoral dissertation he is preparing on the traffic of Rio during this period. The present author, meanwhile, is engaged in a study of the cabotagem imports (only) of Rio between 1792 and 1823.

40. Tuckey, op. cit. (n. 24, above), 73–74.

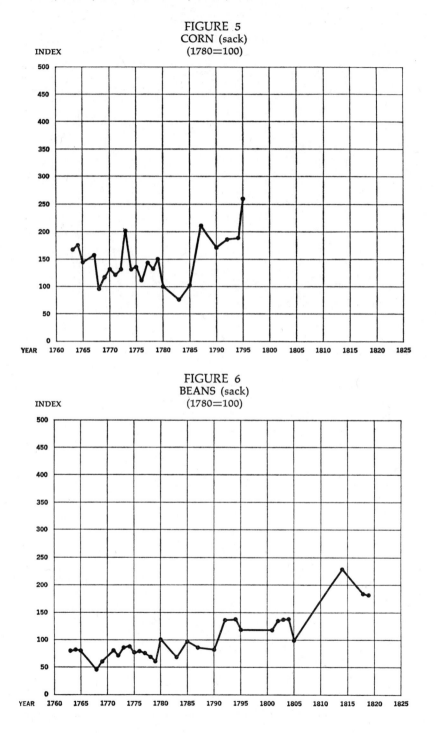

FIGURE 5
CORN (sack)
(1780=100)

FIGURE 6
BEANS (sack)
(1780=100)

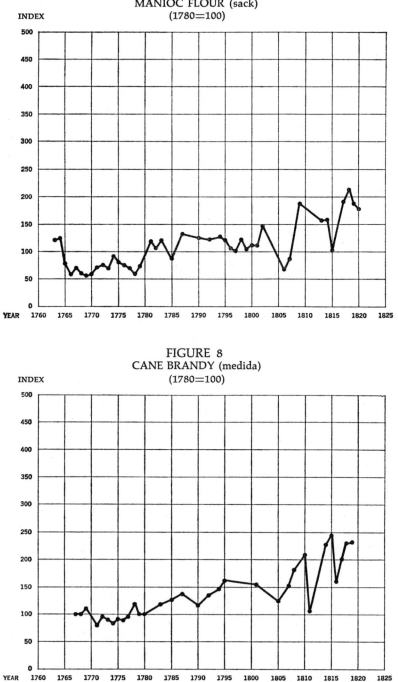

FIGURE 7
MANIOC FLOUR (sack)
(1780=100)

FIGURE 8
CANE BRANDY (medida)
(1780=100)

FIGURE 9
RICE (sack)
(1780=100)

INDEX

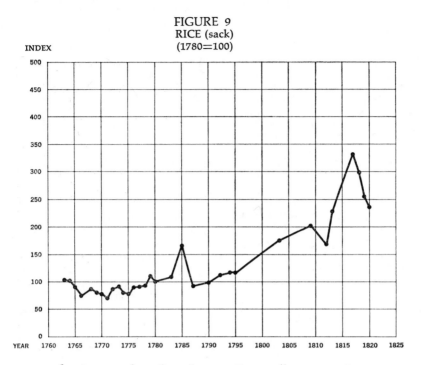

overproduction, or glutted markets in Europe,[41] remains above 100 thereafter. By 1803 the price of rice rose to an index of 175, which constitutes a firm floor thereafter, for its price never drops below that level except during the period of the Napoleonic Wars when markets were generally disturbed in Europe. Patently, it was one of the success products of late eighteenth-century Brazil.[42]

Unlike rice, sugar prices (figures 10 and 11, appendix, series 9 and 10) do not show a boom, due obviously to the fact that demand did not grow in Europe nearly to the degree that it did for rice. One should note, however, the clear rise in sugar prices during the 1790s when production on the island of Haiti collapsed, thus opening the French market to Brazilian exports. Otherwise sugar prices seem to vary, *grosso modo*, in accordance with the fluctuations registered by Posthumus for wholesale prices in Amsterdam. One exception to this, however, is the extremely high price level which prevailed in Europe during the war period (1810–1813), which is

41. The prices of Milanese rice given in Posthumus, *op. cit.* (n. 12, above), I, 40–41, would suggest that the second explanation is the more probable.

42. See D. Alden, "Manoel Luis Vieira: An Enterpreneur in Rio de Janeiro during Brazil's Eighteenth-Century Agricultural Renaissance," *HAHR*, XXXIX (1959), 521–537; also V. M. Godinho, *op. cit.* (n. 10, above), 265.

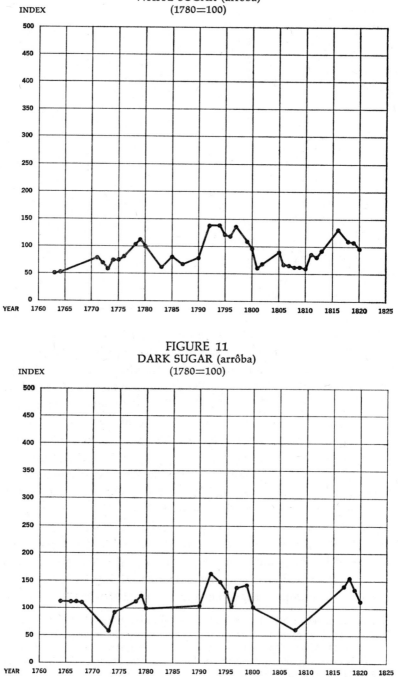

FIGURE 10
WHITE SUGAR (arrôba)
(1780=100)

FIGURE 11
DARK SUGAR (arrôba)
(1780=100)

FIGURE 12
WHITE FLOUR (arrôba)
(1780=100)

INDEX

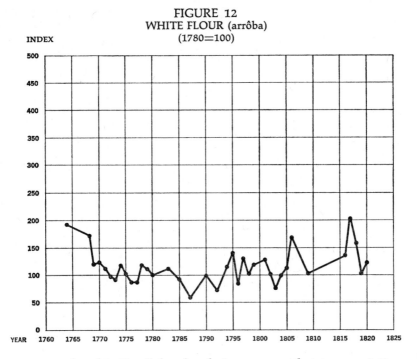

not reproduced in Brazil for the obvious reason that transportation was impeded and consequently local stockpiles grew. Thus Rio prices from 1808 to 1813 are unusually low. Only in 1817 do Rio prices again begin to move in rhythm with those registered in Europe.[43]

GROUP III: A third category of products includes those which, though locally consumed and sometimes re-exported, are largely produced elsewhere in Brazil or in Spanish America: wheat flour, dried meat, and bacon (see figures 12, 13, 14, appendix, series 11, 12, and 13). Two characteristics stand out when one examines these price fluctuations: the seeming irregularity from year to year, with little discernible long-term trend, and the fact that in the case of wheat flour and bacon, the general price level at the end of the period (ca. 1820) is no higher than at the beginning.

The annual irregularity can be explained largely by the vicissitudes of commerce and communication in the Americas. Anyone who has made even the most cursory examination of the records of eighteenth-century American ports can testify to the extreme variation in the volume of shipping, both international and coastal

43. Posthumus, op cit., I, 120–125.

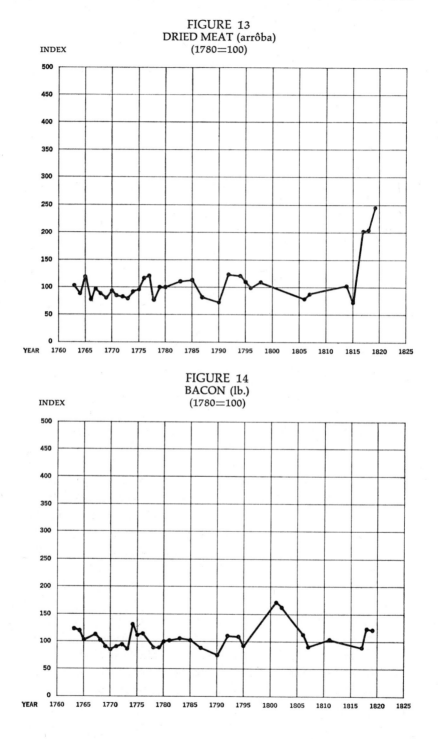

FIGURE 13
DRIED MEAT (arrôba)
(1780=100)

FIGURE 14
BACON (lb.)
(1780=100)

(*cabotagem*).[44] Certain abnormal years (such as 1792, 1801, and 1806 for wheat flour) may be explained by poor harvests or other natural causes. Similar explanations would hold true for bacon and dried meat. The absence of any long-term trend bring up the question of the fundamental nature of the economy (or economies) of eighteenth-century Latin America, a problem recently posed by Ruggiero Romano, and one to which we shall return in the last section of the paper. In this regard, let us note here that all of these products *normally* came from areas of subsistence or quasi-subsistence economy: wheat flour and dried meat from Rio Grande do Sul and the Plate River region, bacon from Minas Gerais and also the Rio hinterland.

GROUP IV. Finally, there is a fourth category of products which Rio largely procured abroad (all but one of them in Europe): wine, brandy, vinegar, olive oil, butter and wax.

With regard to olive oil, vinegar, wine, and brandy (all of which usually came from Portugal), the story is roughly the same (see figures 15 through 18 and appendix, series 14 through 17): a general price stability (aside from single years in which the instability of prices may be attributed to transportation problems or unusual harvests) but an upsurge in the prices of olive oil and wine in 1805, and in vinegar and wine again in 1809. For olive oil, which is the only Portuguese product for which we have a full set of Lisbon price statistics, the correlation between the movement of Portuguese and Rio prices is exceptionally good: a general stability from 1763 to 1790, then a rise in the four years from 1791 to 1794, followed by a leap upward in both Portugal and Rio in 1805 and a high index in both places in the period 1811 to 1818 as well. One would expect the prices for these products to rise after 1809 due to the influx of Portuguese into the city. The failure of prices to decline to prewar levels in 1814 and 1815 is most probably to be attributed to the various inflationary factors already mentioned. The level of Portuguese prices, too, is crucial throughout, especially with regard to olive oil and wine, for even after the opening of the ports, one would expect these luxury commodities to continue to be imported from Portugal irrespective of price.[45]

44. Cf. Romano, *op. cit.*, 40; for Rio de Janeiro see ANRJ, Codex 157: *Fianças de Embarcações*, 1724–1808, *passim*.

45. Indeed, Mawe remarks at the time of his visit (c. 1809) that "the imports of the mother-country consist chiefly in wine and oil." Mawe, *op. cit.*, 110.

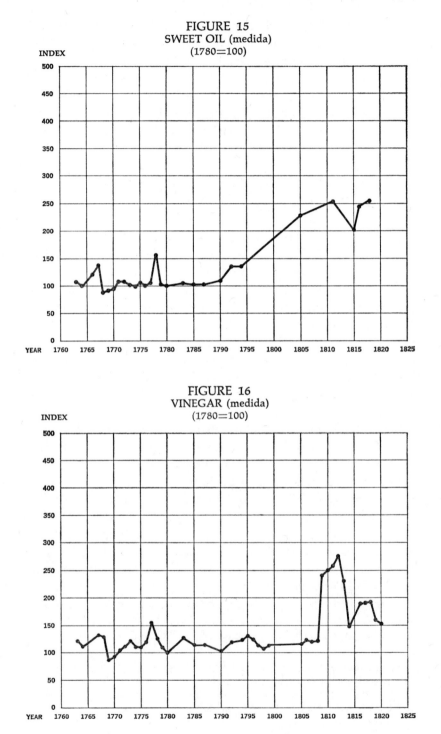

FIGURE 15
SWEET OIL (medida)
(1780=100)

FIGURE 16
VINEGAR (medida)
(1780=100)

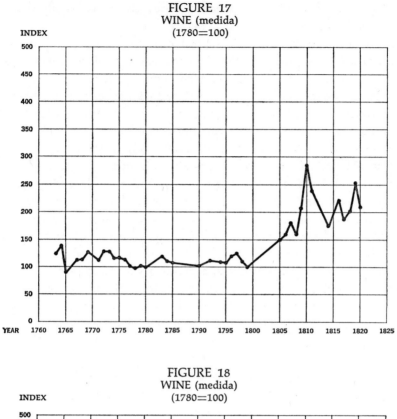

FIGURE 17
WINE (medida)
(1780=100)

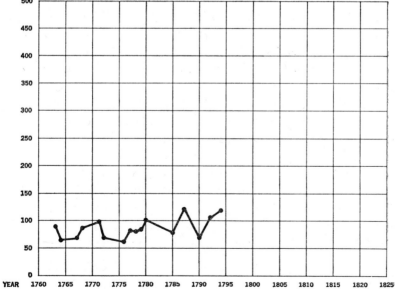

FIGURE 18
WINE (medida)
(1780=100)

Butter (figure 19 and appendix, series 18) came largely from England and the Netherlands. Before 1809 it was imported via Portugal; thereafter it was shipped directly from the producing countries.[46] The price data reveal an erratic record during the period before 1809, as might be expected for a Portuguese re-export. Later, in the four years 1817 through 1820, its price index oscillated between 170 and 243, reflecting not only possible problems of supply, but the decline of the milreis on the London market.

Wax (figure 20 and appendix, series 19), which came mostly from Africa, shows irregular fluctuations in price level throughout the period, bearing in this respect a general resemblance to wheat flour, dried meat, and bacon. Is it irrelevant that wax, too, comes from an area of subsistence economy? These prices (wheat flour, bacon, dried meat, and wax) in fact bring us to the problem of the type of economy which prevailed in South America in the second half of the eighteenth century, a problem which has already been raised by Ruggiero Romano in connection with the price movements which he studied in Chile and Argentina. It is to this question that we must turn our attention in the following section.

III

However useful the equation of Fisher may be in explaining the price movement of certain commodities and some of the long-term trends, there still remains a certain "unexplained" quality in the fluctuations of several commodities (e.g.: wheat flour, bacon, dried meat) which seems immune to the cycles characteristic of European economies, and which raises the problem of the nature of the economy of colonial Rio de Janeiro, as well as of the usefulness of price history as a means for understanding it.

Recently, after studying the price movements in Santiago de Chile and Buenos Aires in the years from 1765 to 1810, Ruggiero Romano suggested some hypotheses regarding the general character of Spanish American economies in the late colonial period. What he found in Santiago was the following: out of a total of sixteen products, the prices of three (chocolate, firewood, and bricks) declined; the prices of twelve (sugar, tobacco, yerba mate, hens, roosters, oil, pork fat, tiles, cordovan leather, ordinary leather, Castillian wax, and coarse cotton cloth) remained at the same

46. Tuckey, *op. cit.* (n. 24, above), 90; Sousa Leão Filho, ed., *op. cit.* (n. 36, above), 19, 143.

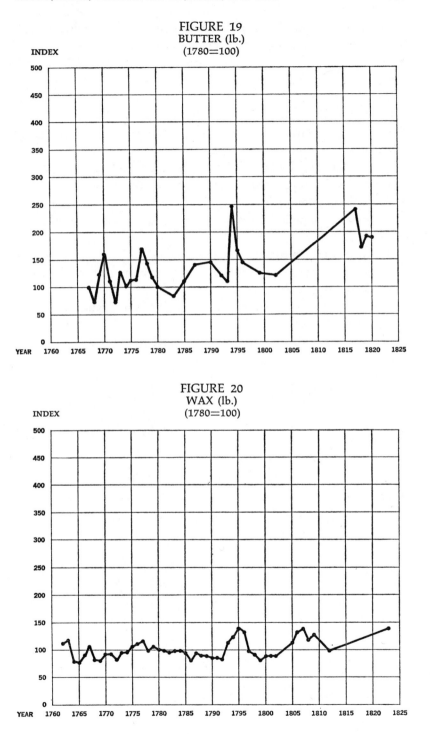

FIGURE 19
BUTTER (lb.)
(1780=100)

FIGURE 20
WAX (lb.)
(1780=100)

level; only the price of sheep tended upward from an index of 100 in 1765 to 133 in 1810.[47] As a result, Romano suggested the following generalizations about the characteristics of the South American economy in the eighteenth century, which he presented as so many points for study:

   a) in spite of increasing mining activity from 1740 on, most of the metal which was produced was either exported to Europe or hoarded;

   b) this flight of bullion and coin to Europe created a situation in which local stocks were not sufficient to stimulate the development of the economy;

   c) monetary emmissions were made up largely of coins of high denomination;

   d) there was, consequently, an absolute lack of small coins;

   e) the result of (d) was the issuance of scrip money which could only be used in certain stores;

   f) a large amount of the money in circulation in Spanish America was of bad "ley" and insufficient weight;

   g) forms of credit were almost non-existent;

   h) most exchanges were by barter;

   i) there was no paper money to speak of;

   j) agricultural production and livestock raising were in constant expansion;

   k) but (j) was a "natural" phenomenon in which human effort had almost no part;

   l) only if there had been substantial inter-American exchanges of goods and a transportation network had been established could this have been a pole of development; and

   m) there was an insufficient growth of exchanges with the metropolis and Europe.

Thus, the general price movement was stationary or descending throughout the eighteenth century despite the fact that the population was continuously growing. In short, he concludes, we are in the presence of a "feudal" or "natural" economy.[48]

To what extent do these hypotheses of Romano apply to Brazil during this period? Can Brazil be fitted into his admittedly rough

47. Romano, *op. cit.* (n. 6, above), 36.
48. *Ibid.,* 24–26.

scheme and characterization? Before addressing ourselves to this question, it seems proper to point out some limiting conditions which Romano tended to ignore in his work.

First, our evidence is confined to Rio (as indeed was his to Santiago and Buenos Aires), and although Rio may tell us some things, indeed *key* things, about the Brazilian economy in the late eighteenth century, it by no means can tell us all. Second, the period of prices discussed here is a bit longer than that used by Romano, beginning in 1762 or 1763 in some cases, and extending in certain instances to 1820 or 1821. Nevertheless, to facilitate comparison of Brazilian prices with his, we shall arbitrarily limit our series to the period before 1809, so that the more chaotic experience of 1809 to 1821 will be excluded.

Taking these qualifications into account, how do Rio prices between 1763 and 1808 compare with those of Santiago de Chile and Buenos Aires? Roughly, one may say that of the commodities chosen for examination, eight (slaves, lime, cane brandy, bricks, rice, wine, olive oil, and beans) show a definite upward climb in price, while five others (corn, manioc, brandy, white sugar, and vinegar) show only a slight upward tendency. Wax and bacon hold steady throughout the period under study; wheat flour and dried meat decline; and butter fluctuated in no clearly discernible long-term trend. The explanations for these movements, which we have offered in part II of this paper, need not be repeated, but they do make it very clear that the economy of Rio, so far as it can be understood from the price behavior of important commodities, had a character and structure decidedly different from those that Romano found in Argentina and Chile.

Assuming that Romano's characterization of the economy of Spanish America is essentially correct, what can explain this variation? Admittedly, Rio's economy had a number of traits in common with the economies to which Romano gave his attention. Much of the bullion which passed through the city was exported to Europe and Asia, and there is also good reason to believe that much of it was hoarded, especially gold.[49] Monetary emissions, likewise, were mainly in large denominations with a consequent shortage of smaller coins.

But in contrast to the situation described by Romano:

49. See note 26.

a) mining activity in Brazil was certainly decreasing, not expanding as in Spanish America;

b) there is no evidence of the widespread use of scrip money;

c) the coins in circulation generally do not seem to have been debased or clipped;

d) credit certainly existed,[50] though to what extent is difficult to determine; but barter was not, as far as can be discovered, the manner of "most" exchanges;

e) there is a clear exchange of products with other parts of Brazil as well as with the Plate river region, and Brazilian exports to Portugal (and through Portugal to Europe) were both large and growing during this period.

Thus it should be obvious that the Brazilian economy, at least in the coastal region, cannot be easily characterized as a "natural" economy. There is little doubt that certain areas and regions were close to that: Minas Gerais, certainly, and probably much of Rio Grande do Sul.[51] The stagnant prices displayed by wheat and dried meat, which came from Rio Grande, as well as by wax, which came from Africa, and by bacon, which originated mainly in the mountains above Rio and in Minas Gerais, testify to this and fit in with Romano's thesis. But the economy of the city of Rio and of the surrounding region was clearly a "market" economy, thoroughly monetized (although coin may have been scarce), and linked by trade (however irregular) with Europe and later North America.

This is not to argue that Rio was an internally *integrated* market, however. In fact, a large percentage of the population remained essentially outside the market. This percentage included the city poor, who were numerous enough, and especially the slave population which made up, if we may believe the various estimates and censuses, about 43 percent of the population in 1789 and about 45 percent in 1821: a group which was both large in proportion to the population as a whole, and on the increase.[52] What was the effect of this group on the character and structure of Rio's economy?

50. This is clear from the structure of the retail trade as revealed by various statistical descriptions of the city (e.g., the "Memórias públicas e econômicas . . . ," *RIHGB*, XLVII:1 (1884), 44–45) as well as travel accounts which confirm the profusion of small shops and the minute quantities purchased at one time by the *frequêses* (Sousa Leão Filho, ed., *op. cit.* [n. 36, above], 18).

51. Furtado, *op. cit.* (n. 8, above), 90–91, 104–106. Also Alden, *op. cit.* (n. 4, above), 80–81 and Mawe, *op. cit.* (n. 36, above), 325–327.

52. See note 35.

First, the most obvious effect was that the slave population tended to hold down wage rates for unskilled or mechanical labor. With such a large force of captive labor available, free labor could hardly hope to secure wages much above those paid to the *escravos de ganho*, or slaves hired out as laborers. And what were these wages? Detailed evidence is lacking, but it seems that from a standard rate of 120 reis per day at the beginning of our period wages, rose by about 166 percent to 320 reis at the close (1821). And the wages of free laborers? Basically the same: they rose by about 150 percent during the same period.

What determined the level of wages paid to the escravos de ganho? Essentially it must be seen as a function of the price of slaves to the buyer. The slaveowner expected a certain rate of return (essentially the prevailing interest rate, or a bit more) from his slaves, considered as a capital investment. He figured the rate taking into account the probable life of the slave, his health, and other such factors.[53] Thus if the basic wage for laborers, both slave and free, rose by about 150 to 166 percent in the period, one would expect a similar rise in the price of slaves. This is exactly the case. From about 50 milreis in 1766, the price of a prime male slave rose to about 140 or 150 milreis in 1821, a rise of approximately 175 percent.[54]

But wages earned by escravos de ganho went, by and large, to the owner and not to the slave, and their wages in turn tended to determine the general wage level in the city. Clearly this sector would not provide any real dynamism for development. With regard to this sector of the population, one may well speak of a quasi-subsistence economy.

Nevertheless, though this sector acted as a brake upon internal demand, the result was not in any way a "natural" economy. For this captive force was employed, and probably quite efficiently, in a capitalist agriculture which produced the various commodities sold in foreign markets. Depending upon the spread between prices for its chief capital investment, slaves, and the prices which it received for its products, this sector was periodically highly profitable.

Unfortunately we do not have for the Rio region the detailed es-

53. Alfred H. Conrad and John R. Meyer, *The Economics of Slavery* (Chicago, 1964), 48–50.
54. Data from the account books of the hospital of the brotherhood of São Francisco de Penitência: 1766, 51,000 reis; 1821, 140,000 reis.

tate accounts which would provide direct evidence of the degree of prosperity of the various agricultural enterprises. Nevertheless, a rough index of profitability can be had through a comparison of the various prices of input and output factors (slaves *vs.* rice, cotton, sugar, etc.). In good times, it is clear, large profits could be made and considerable capital accumulated.

What was done with the accumulated capital? In times of growing foreign demand for various products,[55] capital tended to be channelled into the acquisition of more land for planting, and purchase of more slaves to increase the labor force. But at the same time, almost irrespective of profitability, a large amount of accumulated capital was expended for luxury imports (especially cloth whose variety defies description) and for the slaves who provided lavish service and represented conspicuous consumption. Both of these aspects of Rio society were noted and remarked upon by nearly every traveler of the period.[56] Thus the capital accumulated by the export sector during profitable periods was largely returned to Europe and Africa through the purchase of slaves and luxuries. What else could be done with it? With no internal market to speak of, there was next to no stimulus for manufactures (aside, perhaps, from cheap cotton cloth), and only in times of market expansion was there any alternate use for the capital in investment.

Thus, in contrast to the situation in Argentina or Chile, what prevailed in Rio was essentially a *dual* economy[57] comprising a quasi-subsistence sector, largely outside the market, side by side with a sector of highly capitalized agriculture oriented to export markets whose profitability was largely determined by conditions exterior to the economy.

This brief analysis suggests in conclusion that the price history of South America, as yet in its period of infancy, has revealed to date two clearly distinguishable economic systems:

1. the "feudal" or "natural" system which Romano has found in Chile or Argentina, characterized by prices tending either toward stagnation or decline; and

55. See note 42.
56. For Rio travel accounts in general see the excellent bibliography of Paulo Berger, *O Rio de Janeiro dos viajantes e autores estrangeiros* (Rio de Janeiro, 1964).
57. Cf. J. S. Furnivall, *Netherland's India: A Study of Plural Economy* (Cambridge, 1944), 446–469.

2. the classical *dual* economic system of colonial regions which prevailed in Rio, where prices behaved in more volatile fashion, with a long-term upward tendency except for those commodities which came from subsistence areas.

It would be of interest to study the price histories of Minas Gerais and Rio Grande do Sul in order to test further the hypothesis that each economic system of eighteenth-century South America had a typical or characteristic price behavior. These two areas of Brazil seem to have resembled in type the economies of Chile and Argentina, and might be expected to show a similar behavior in their prices. Such studies would constitute important contributions to an economic typology of the South American continent in the late colonial period and would enable regional nuances and mixtures, as well as their structures and functions, to be more clearly mapped and understood than is presently possible. Certainly the use of price history would be an essential tool in pursuit of that goal.

APPENDIX

(Price Series)*

1. FISH OIL (medida)

Year	Average Price	Index	Year	Average Price	Index
1763	140	100.00	1780	140	100.00
1764	140	100.00	1781	113	80.71
1765	...	.....	1782	...	.....
1766	...	.....	1783	140	100.00
1767	140	100.00	1784	...	.....
1768	140	100.00	1785	140	100.00
1769	140	100.00	1786	...	.....
1770	140	100.00	1787	140	100.00
1771	140	100.00	1788	148	105.71
1772	140	100.00	1789	...	.....
1773	140	100.00	1790	140	100.00
1774	134	95.71	1791	...	.....
1775	140	100.00	1792	140	100.00
1776	137	97.86	1793	...	.....
1777	140	100.00	1794	140	100.00
1778	140	100.00	1795	140	100.00
1779	140	100.00			

2. LIME (moio)

Year	Average Price	Index	Year	Average Price	Index
1768	3,020	54.98	1778	5,465	99.49
1769	3,164	57.60	1779	5,448	99.18
1770	3,520	64.08	1780	5,493	100.00
1771	4,261	77.57	1781	5,863	106.74
1772	4,077	74.22	1782	5,621	102.33
1773	4,213	76.70	1783	5,705	103.86
1774	4,008	72.96	1784	5,750	104.68
1775	4,040	73.55	1785	6,267	114.09
1776	4,780	87.02	1786	5,513	100.34
1777	4,770	86.84	1787	4,916	89.50

* All prices in reis; 1780 is the base year for each series; no data available for missing years.

2. LIME (cont.)

Year	Average Price	Index	Year	Average Price	Index
1788	.....	.....	1804	.....	.....
1789	.....	.....	1805	.....	.....
1790	.....	.....	1806	.....	.....
1791	6,354	115.67	1807	9,667	175.99
1792	5,978	108.83	1808	9,167	166.89
1793	.....	.....	1809	.....	.....
1794	.....	.....	1810	18,000	327.69
1795	5,670	103.22	1811	25,550	465.14
1796	6,498	118.30	1812	16,150	294.01
1797	6,353	115.66	1813	10,750	195.70
1798	6,988	127.22	1814	.....	.....
1799	8,875	161.57	1815	12,195	222.01
1800	9,333	169.91	1816	15,180	276.35
1801	9,000	163.84	1817	.....	.....
1802	9,080	165.30	1818	10,855	197.62
1803	8,875	161.57	1819	14,543	264.76

3. BRICKS (per 100)

Year	Average Price	Index	Year	Average Price	Index
1765	453	88.48	1782	....	.....
1766	....	.....	1783	640	125.00
1767	....	.....	1784	....	.....
1768	400	78.13	1785	....	.....
1769	373	72.85	1786	....	.....
1770	440	85.94	1787	700	136.72
1771	407	79.49	1788	....	.....
1772	365	71.29	1789	....	.....
1773	409	79.88	1790	840	164.06
1774	418	81.64	1791	....	.....
1775	392	76.56	1792	672	131.25
1776	360	70.31	1793	....	.....
1777	368	71.88	1794	....	.....
1778	414	80.86	1795	608	118.75
1779	442	86.33	1796	632	123.44
1780	512	100.00	1797	640	125.00
1781	576	112.50	1798	640	125.00

3. BRICKS (cont.)

Year	Average Price	Index	Year	Average Price	Index
1799	640	125.00	1812	1,588	310.16
1800	645	125.98	1813	950	185.55
1801	606	118.36	1814	800	156.25
1802	750	146.48	1815	810	158.20
1803	....	.....	1816	977	191.21
1804	....	.....	1817	875	170.90
1805	....	.....	1818	850	166.02
1806	800	156.25	1819	1,200	234.38
1807	853	166.60	1820	....	.....
1808	900	175.78	1821	....	.....
1809	1,500	292.97	1822	....	.....
1810	1,521	297.07	1823	1,000	195.31
1811	1,884	367.97			

4. CORN (sack)

Year	Average Price	Index	Year	Average Price	Index
1763	1,000	167.79	1780	596	100.00
1764	1,048	175.84	1781	....	.....
1765	870	145.97	1782	....	.....
1766	....	.....	1783	462	77.52
1767	940	157.72	1784	....	.....
1768	659	95.45	1785	618	103.69
1769	702	117.79	1786	....	.....
1770	788	132.21	1787	1,260	211.41
1771	719	120.64	1788	....	.....
1772	793	133.05	1789	....	.....
1773	1,200	201.34	1790	1,027	172.32
1774	785	131.71	1791	....	.....
1775	818	137.25	1792	1,114	186.91
1776	677	113.59	1793	....	.....
1777	864	144.97	1794	1,138	190.94
1778	786	131.88	1795	1,550	260.07
1779	899	150.84			

5. BEANS (sack)

Year	Average Price	Index	Year	Average Price	Index
1763	1,160	79.18	1792	1,997	136.31
1764	1,215	82.93	1793	....	.....
1765	1,160	79.18	1794	2,039	139.18
1766	....	.....	1795	1,747	119.25
1767	....	.....	1796	....	.....
1768	682	46.55	1797	....	.....
1769	892	60.89	1798	....	.....
1770	....	.....	1799	....	.....
1771	1,207	82.39	1800	....	.....
1772	1,073	73.24	1801	1,750	119.45
1773	1,281	87.44	1802	1,980	135.15
1774	1,300	88.74	1803	2,000	136.52
1775	1,139	77.75	1804	2,040	139.25
1776	1,166	79.69	1805	1,440	98.29
1777	1,120	76.45	1806	....	.....
1778	1,010	68.94	1807	....	.....
1779	883	60.27	1808	....	.....
1780	1,465	100.00	1809	....	.....
1781	....	.....	1810	....	.....
1782	....	.....	1811	....	.....
1783	1,025	69.97	1812	....	.....
1784	....	.....	1813	....	.....
1785	1,444	98.57	1814	3,360	229.35
1786	....	.....	1815	....	.....
1787	1,263	86.21	1816	....	.....
1788	....	.....	1817	....	.....
1789	....	.....	1818	2,705	184.64
1790	1,231	84.03	1819	2,671	182.32
1791	....	.....			

6. MANIOC FLOUR (sack)

Year	Average Price	Index	Year	Average Price	Index
1763	1,254	123.30	1767	720	70.80
1764	1,280	125.86	1768	603	59.29
1765	797	78.37	1769	574	56.44
1766	606	59.59	1770	591	58.11

6. MANIOC FLOUR (cont.)

Year	Average Price	Index	Year	Average Price	Index
1771	733	72.07	1796	1,084	106.59
1772	782	76.89	1797	1,050	103.24
1773	712	70.01	1798	1,261	123.99
1774	928	91.25	1799	1,068	105.01
1775	825	81.12	1800	1,155	113.57
1776	770	75.71	1801	1,152	113.27
1777	729	71.68	1802	1,500	147.49
1778	590	58.01	1803	....	.....
1779	753	74.04	1804	....	.....
1780	1,017	100.00	1805	....	.....
1781	1,216	119.57	1806	700	68.83
1782	1,082	106.39	1807	903	88.79
1783	1,227	120.65	1808	....	.....
1784	....	.....	1809	1,920	188.79
1785	909	89.38	1810	....	.....
1786	....	.....	1811	....	.....
1787	1,358	133.53	1812	....	.....
1788	....	.....	1813	1,600	157.33
1789	....	.....	1814	1,620	159.29
1790	763	75.02	1815	1,067	104.92
1791	....	.....	1816	....	.....
1792	1,255	123.40	1817	1,961	192.82
1793	....	.....	1818	2,180	214.36
1794	1,294	127.24	1819	1,932	189.97
1795	1,222	120.16	1820	1,823	179.25

7. CANE BRANDY (medida)

Year	Average Price	Index	Year	Average Price	Index
1767	160	100.00	1775	148	92.50
1768	160	100.00	1776	142	88.75
1769	177	110.62	1777	152	95.00
1770	...	.....	1778	191	119.38
1771	128	80.00	1779	160	100.00
1772	153	95.63	1780	160	100.00
1773	145	90.63	1781	...	.....
1774	135	84.38	1782	...	.....

7. CANE BRANDY (cont.)

Year	Average Price	Index	Year	Average Price	Index
1783	191	119.38	1802	...	.....
1784	...	.....	1803	...	.....
1785	203	126.88	1804	...	.....
1786	...	.....	1805	200	125.00*
1787	222	138.75	1806	...	.....
1788	...	.....	1807	245	153.13*
1789	...	.....	1808	290	181.25*
1790	188	117.50	1809	...	.....
1791	...	.....	1810	335	209.38*
1792	217	135.63	1811	170(?)	106.25*
1793	...	.....	1812	...	.....
1794	236	147.50	1813	...	.....
1795	260	162.50	1814	364	227.50*
1796	...	.....	1815	393	245.63*
1797	...	.....	1816	264	165.00*
1798	...	.....	1817	320	200.00*
1799	...	.....	1818	370	231.25*
1800	...	.....	1819	375	234.38*
1801	249	155.63*			

8. RICE (sack)

Year	Average Price	Index	Year	Average Price	Index
1763	2,560	103.06	1775	1,940	78.10
1764	2,548	102.58	1776	2,214	89.13
1765	2,240	90.18	1777	2,243	90.30
1766	1,860	74.88	1778	2,328	93.72
1767	....	.....	1779	2,751	110.75
1768	2,112	85.02	1780	2,484	100.00
1769	1,989	80.07	1781	....	.....
1770	1,938	78.02	1782	....	.....
1771	1,733	69.77	1783	2,728	109.82
1772	2,135	85.95	1784	....	.....
1773	2,283	91.91	1785	4,085	164.45
1774	2,004	80.68	1786	....	.....

* These prices have been derived from the price for a pipa assumed to hold 160 medidas.

8. RICE (cont.)

Year	Average Price	Index	Year	Average Price	Index
1787	2,315	93.20	1804	....	.....
1788	....	.....	1805	....	.....
1789	....	.....	1806	....	.....
1790	2,471	99.48	1807	....	.....
1791	....	.....	1808	....	.....
1792	2,826	113.77	1809	5,040	202.90
1793	....	.....	1810	....	.....
1794	2,903	116.87	1811	....	.....
1795	2,900	116.75	1812	4,160	167.47
1796	....	.....	1813	5,700	229.47
1797	....	.....	1814	....	.....
1798	....	.....	1815	....	.....
1799	....	.....	1816	....	.....
1800	....	.....	1817	8,267	332.81
1801	....	.....	1818	7,450	299.92
1802	....	.....	1819	6,376	256.68
1803	4,347	175.00	1820	5,900	237.52

9. WHITE SUGAR (arrôba)

Year	Average Price	Index	Year	Average Price	Index
1763	960(?)	50.03	1779	2,175	113.34
1764	1,000(?)	52.11	1780	1,919	100.00
1765	....	.....	1781	....	.....
1766	....	.....	1782	....	.....
1767	....	.....	1783	1,218	63.47
1768	....	.....	1784	....	.....
1769	....	.....	1785	1,556	81.08
1770	....	.....	1786	....	.....
1771	1,501	78.22	1787	1,287	67.07
1772	1,325	69.05	1788	....	.....
1773	1,121	58.42	1789	....	.....
1774	1,430	74.52	1790	1,506	78.48
1775	1,430	74.52	1791	....	.....
1776	1,555	81.03	1792	2,660	138.61
1777	....	.....	1793	....	.....
1778	2,000	104.22	1794	2,651	138.14

9. WHITE SUGAR (cont.)

Year	Average Price	Index	Year	Average Price	Index
1795	2,316	120.69	1808	1,200	62.53
1796	2,282	118.92	1809	1,200	62.53
1797	2,624	136.74	1810	1,125	58.62
1798	....	.....	1811	1,663	86.66
1799	2,097	109.28	1812	1,567	81.66
1800	1,873	97.60	1813	1,780	92.76
1801	1,208	62.95	1814	....	.....
1802	1,366	71.18	1815	....	.....
1803	....	.....	1816	2,500	130.28
1804	....	.....	1817	....	.....
1805	1,698	88.48	1818	2,118	110.37
1806	1,248	65.03	1819	2,079	108.34
1807	1,230	64.10	1820	1,850	96.40

10. DARK SUGAR (arrôba)

Year	Average Price	Index	Year	Average Price	Index
1764	1,280	111.79	1785	....	.....
1765	....	.....	1786	....	.....
1766	1,280	111.79	1787	....	.....
1767	1,280	111.79	1788	....	.....
1768	1,255	109.61	1789	....	.....
1769	....	.....	1790	1,200	104.80
1770	....	.....	1791	....	.....
1771	....	.....	1792	1,873	163.58
1772	....	.....	1793	....	.....
1773	660	57.64	1794	1,695	148.03
1774	1,045	91.27	1795	1,477	129.00
1775	....	.....	1796	1,200	104.80
1776	....	.....	1797	1,600	139.74
1777	....	.....	1798	....	.....
1778	1,304	113.89	1799	1,620	141.48
1779	1,390	121.40	1800	1,187	103.67
1780	1,145	100.00	1801	....	.....
1781	....	.....	1802	....	.....
1782	....	.....	1803	....	.....
1783	....	.....	1804	....	.....
1784	....	.....	1805	....	.....

10. DARK SUGAR (*cont.*)

Year	Average Price	Index	Year	Average Price	Index
1806	....	.....	1814	....	.....
1807	....	.....	1815	....	.....
1808	720 (?)	62.88	1816	....	.....
1809	....	.....	1817	1,611	140.70
1810	....	.....	1818	1,783	155.72
1811	....	.....	1819	1,553	135.63
1812	....	.....	1820	1,300	113.54
1813	....	.....			

11. WHEAT FLOUR (arrôba)

Year	Average Price	Index	Year	Average Price	Index
1764	3,584	192.69	1789	....	.....
1765	....	.....	1790	1,831	98.44
1766	....	.....	1791	....	.....
1767	....	.....	1792	1,389	74.68
1768	3,215	172.85	1793	....	.....
1769	2,275	122.31	1794	2,168	116.56
1770	2,310	124.19	1795	2,650	142.47
1771	2,068	111.18	1796	1,599	85.97
1772	1,846	99.25	1797	2,458	132.15
1773	1,733	93.17	1798	1,900	102.86
1774	2,205	118.55	1799	2,248	120.86
1775	1,923	103.39	1800	....	.....
1776	1,667	89.62	1801	2,403	129.19
1777	1,668	89.68	1802	1,888	101.51
1778	2,197	118.12	1803	1,428	76.77
1779	2,091	112.42	1804	1,831	98.44
1780	1,860	100.00	1805	2,091	112.42
1781	....	.....	1806	3,138	168.71
1782	....	.....	1807	....	.....
1783	2,112	113.55	1808	....	.....
1784	....	.....	1809	1,920	103.33
1785	1,750	94.09	1810	....	.....
1786	....	.....	1811	....	.....
1787	1,106	59.46	1812	....	.....
1788	....	.....	1813	....	.....

11. WHEAT FLOUR (cont.)

Year	Average Price	Index	Year	Average Price	Index
1814	....	.....	1818	2,950	158.60
1815	....	.....	1819	1,928	103.66
1816	2,563	137.80	1820	2,279	122.53
1817	3,793	203.92			

12. DRIED MEAT (arrôba)

Year	Average Price	Index	Year	Average Price	Index
1763	846	104.32	1792	1,005	123.92
1764	735	90.63	1793	....	.....
1765	960	118.37	1794	983	121.21
1766	640	78.91	1795	889	109.62
1767	800	98.64	1796	800	98.64
1768	710	87.55	1797	....	.....
1769	666	82.12	1798	900	110.97
1770	777	95.81	1799	....	.....
1771	700	86.31	1800	....	.....
1772	692	85.33	1801	....	.....
1773	673	82.98	1802	....	.....
1774	766	94.45	1803	....	.....
1775	788	97.16	1804	....	.....
1776	962	118.62	1805	....	.....
1777	975	120.22	1806	640	78.91
1778	638	78.67	1807	720	88.78
1779	814	100.37	1808	....	.....
1780	811	100.00	1809	....	.....
1781	....	.....	1810	....	.....
1782	....	.....	1811	....	.....
1783	904	111.47	1812	....	.....
1784	....	.....	1813	....	.....
1785	926	114.18	1814	850	104.81
1786	....	.....	1815	600	73.98
1787	666	82.12	1816	....	.....
1788	....	.....	1817	1,650	203.45
1789	....	.....	1818	1,678	206.91
1790	578	71.27	1819	2,000	246.61
1791	....	.....	1820	....	.....

13. BACON (lb.)

Year	Average Price	Index	Year	Average Price	Index
1763	60.00	124.15	1792	54.19	112.12
1764	58.47	120.98	1793	....	.....
1765	50.00	103.46	1794	52.20	108.01
1766	....	.....	1795	45.00	93.11
1767	54.75	113.28	1796	....	.....
1768	49.20	101.80	1797	....	.....
1769	44.14	91.33	1798	....	.....
1770	41.24	85.33	1799	....	.....
1771	44.02	91.08	1800	....	.....
1772	46.00	95.18	1801	82.28	170.25
1773	42.16	87.23	1802	79.12	163.71
1774	63.33	131.04	1803	....	.....
1775	54.21	112.17	1804	....	.....
1776	55.65	115.15	1805	....	.....
1777	....	.....	1806	55.55	114.94
1778	43.59	90.19	1807	44.58	92.24
1779	43.90	90.83	1808	....	.....
1780	48.33	100.00	1809	....	.....
1781	49.95	103.35	1810	....	.....
1782	....	.....	1811	50.00	103.46
1783	50.97	105.46	1812	....	.....
1784	....	.....	1813	....	.....
1785	49.23	101.86	1814	....	.....
1786	....	.....	1815	....	.....
1787	42.53	88.00	1816	....	.....
1788	....	.....	1817	43.75	90.52
1789	....	.....	1818	60.00	124.15
1790	36.58	75.69	1819	59.54	123.19
1791	....	.....	1820	....	.....

14. OLIVE OIL (medida)

Year	Average Price	Index	Year	Average Price	Index
1763	570	109.40	1767	720	138.20
1764	530	101.73	1768	473	90.79
1765	....	.....	1769	486	93.28
1766	640	122.84	1770	499	95.78

14. OLIVE OIL (cont.)

Year	Average Price	Index	Year	Average Price	Index
1771	569	109.21	1796	....	.....
1772	571	109.60	1797	....	.....
1773	528	101.34	1798	....	.....
1774	513	98.46	1799	....	.....
1775	549	105.37	1800	....	.....
1776	528	101.34	1801	....	.....
1777	560	107.49	1802	....	.....
1778	823	157.97	1803	....	.....
1779	532	102.11	1804	....	.....
1780	521	100.00	1805	1,196	229.56
1781	....	.....	1806	....	.....
1782	....	.....	1807	....	.....
1783	551	105.76	1808	....	.....
1784	....	.....	1809	....	.....
1785	538	103.26	1810	....	.....
1786	....	.....	1811	1,320	253.36
1787	538	103.26	1812	....	.....
1788	....	.....	1813	....	.....
1789	....	.....	1814	....	.....
1790	576	110.56	1815	1,056	202.69
1791	....	.....	1816	1,275	244.72
1792	709	136.08	1817	....	.....
1793	....	.....	1818	1,326	254.51
1794	709	136.08	1819	....	.....
1795	....	.....	1820	....	.....

15. VINEGAR (medida)

Year	Average Price	Index	Year	Average Price	Index
1763	220	122.22	1771	186	103.33
1764	200	111.11	1772	204	113.33
1765	...	.....	1773	221	122.78
1766	...	.....	1774	200	111.11
1767	240	133.33	1775	200	111.11
1768	232	128.89	1776	217	120.56
1769	160	88.89	1777	281	156.11
1770	170	94.44	1778	230	127.78

15. VINEGAR (*cont.*)

Year	Average Price	Index	Year	Average Price	Index
1779	200	111.11	1800	...	.....
1780	180	100.00	1801	...	.....
1781	...	.....	1802	...	.....
1782	...	.....	1803	...	.....
1783	232	128.89	1804	...	.....
1784	...	.....	1805	213	118.33
1785	206	114.44	1806	225	125.00
1786	...	.....	1807	219	121.67
1787	206	114.44	1808	400	222.22
1788	...	.....	1809	438	243.33
1789	...	.....	1810	453	251.67
1790	188	104.44	1811	469	260.56
1791	...	.....	1812	500	277.78
1792	220	122.22	1813	419	232.78
1793	...	.....	1814	269	149.44
1794	225	125.00	1815	...	.....
1795	240	133.33	1816	340	188.89
1796	224	124.44	1817	344	191.11
1797	203	112.78	1818	...	169.44
1798	194	107.78	1819	288	160.00
1799	160	88.89	1820	276	153.33

16. WINE (medida)

Year	Average Price	Index	Year	Average Price	Index
1763	410	125.00	1775	385	117.38
1764	453	138.11	1776	372	113.41
1765	219 (?)	66.77	1777	336	102.44
1766	...	.....	1778	330	100.61
1767	369	112.50	1779	341	103.96
1768	373	113.72	1780	328	100.00
1769	416	126.83	1781	...	.....
1770	...	.....	1782	...	.....
1771	375	114.33	1783	390	118.90
1772	423	128.96	1784	...	.....
1773	423	128.96	1785	365	111.28
1774	379	115.55	1786	...	.....

16. WINE (cont.)

Year	Average Price	Index	Year	Average Price	Index
1787	360	109.76	1804	...	.....
1788	...	.....	1805	500	152.44*
1789	...	.....	1806	526	160.37*
1790	342	104.27	1807	600	182.93*
1791	...	.....	1808	530	161.59*
1792	366	111.59	1809	685	208.84*
1793	...	.....	1810	939	286.28*
1794	360	109.76	1811	789	240.55*
1795	360	109.76	1812	...	.....
1796	394	120.12*	1813	...	.....
1797	411	125.30*	1814	575	175.30*
1798	363	110.67*	1815	...	.....
1799	331	100.91*	1816	733	223.48*
1800	...	.....	1817	623	189.94*
1801	...	.....	1818	665	202.74*
1802	...	.....	1819	835	254.57*
1803	...	.....	1820	692	210.98*

17. BRANDY (medida)

Year	Average Price	Index	Year	Average Price	Index
1763	640	89.89	1779	600	84.27
1764	467	65.59	1780	712	100.00
1765	...	.....	1781	...	.....
1766	...	.....	1782	...	.....
1767	480	67.42	1783	...	.....
1768	620	87.08	1784	...	.....
1769	...	.....	1785	560	78.65
1770	...	.....	1786	...	.....
1771	700	98.31	1787	855	120.08
1772	490	68.82	1788	...	.....
1773	...	.....	1789	...	.....
1774	...	.....	1790	501	70.37
1775	...	.....	1791	...	.....
1776	440	61.80	1792	748	105.06
1777	580	81.46	1793	...	.....
1778	574	80.62	1794	853	119.80

* Price derived from a pipa holding 160 medidas.

18. BUTTER (lb.)

Year	Average Price	Index	Year	Average Price	Index
1767	128	100.79	1794	313	246.46
1768	95	74.80	1795	210	165.35
1769	158	124.41	1796	185	145.67
1770	204	160.63	1797	...	.....
1771	142	111.81	1798	...	.....
1772	93	73.23	1799	160	125.98
1773	160	125.98	1800	...	.....
1774	131	103.15	1801	...	.....
1775	143	112.60	1802	153	120.47
1776	145	114.17	1803	...	.....
1777	213	167.72	1804	...	.....
1778	183	144.09	1805	...	.....
1779	148	116.54	1806	...	.....
1780	127	100.00	1807	...	.....
1781	...	.....	1808	...	.....
1782	...	.....	1809	...	.....
1783	107	84.25	1810	...	.....
1784	...	.....	1811	...	.....
1785	143	112.60	1812	...	.....
1786	...	.....	1813	...	.....
1787	178	140.16	1814	...	.....
1788	...	.....	1815	...	.....
1789	...	.....	1816	...	.....
1790	185	145.67	1817	308	242.52
1791	...	.....	1818	217	170.87
1792	155	122.05	1819	244	192.13
1793	140	110.24	1820	240	188.98

19. WAX (lb.)

Year	Average Price	Index	Year	Average Price	Index
1762	450	111.39	1767	425	105.20
1763	480	118.81	1768	339	83.91
1764	320	79.21	1769	334	82.67
1765	313	77.48	1770	370	91.58
1766	373	92.33	1771	373	92.33

19. WAX (cont.)

Year	Average Price	Index	Year	Average Price	Index
1772	359	88.86	1798	369	91.34
1773	387	95.79	1799	332	82.88
1774	395	97.77	1800	360	89.11
1775	426	105.45	1801	361	89.36
1776	449	111.14	1802	360	89.11
1777	470	116.34	1803	...	.....
1778	403	99.75	1804	...	.....
1779	424	104.95	1805	459	113.61
1780	404	100.00	1806	548	133.17
1781	400	99.01	1807	560	138.61
1782	388	96.04	1808	477	118.07
1783	398	98.51	1809	515	127.48
1784	400	99.01	1810	...	.....
1785	381	94.31	1811	...	.....
1786	334	82.67	1812	400	99.01
1787	380	94.06	1813	...	.....
1788	360	89.11	1814	...	.....
1789	360	89.11	1815	...	.....
1790	346	85.64	1816	...	.....
1791	350	86.63	1817	...	.....
1792	338	83.66	1818	...	.....
1793	460	113.86	1819	...	.....
1794	502	124.26	1820	...	.....
1795	560	138.61	1821	...	.....
1796	531	131.44	1822	...	.....
1797	395	97.77	1823	560	138.61

Glossary

Aguardente—Brandy

Alfândega—Customs House

Almoxarife—Receiver of customs

Alferes—Ensign, second-lieutenant

Alqueire—A grain measure, generally 13 liters

Alvará—Royal decree

Aposentador-mor—Chief quartermaster

Arrôba—Unit of weight, normally 32 pounds in the Portuguese empire

Aver do (de) pêso—Public scales for the weight and measurement of commodities

Bandeirante—Explorer, gold-seeker, and Indian slaver

Bando—Proclamation

Câmara (Senado da)—Municipal council

Capitão-mor—Governor, fortress commander, or administrator of an unincorporated settlement

Capitão de campo e mato—Officer charged with capture of runaway Negro slaves

Carioca—Native of the city of Rio de Janeiro

Carta de doação—Royal charter issued to captains-donatary

Carta régia—Royal decree directed to a particular official or official body

Casa de Suplicação—Appeals tribunal in Portugal

Certidão—Certificate or affadavit

Comarca—Judicial district

Consulta—Minute(s) of a council meeting; recommendation by council to king

Corregedor—Royal magistrate

Criado—Dependant or servant

Cruzado—Monetary unit worth 400 reis

Desembargador—Senior royal magistrate

Desembargo do Paço—High Court of Justice in Portugal

Emboabas—"Tenderfeet," a derisive term applied by Paulistadiscoverers of the gold fields of Minas Gerais to those who came after them from Portugal and other parts of Brazil

Engenho—Sugar mill; by extension, the plantation where a mill was situated

Engenho real de açúcar—Large sugar mill and plantation

Entrada—Official exploring party

Estrangeirados—Peninsular Portuguese, especially reform thinkers, influenced by foreign cultural ideas

Fazenda—Landed property: plantation or ranch

Fiscal—Crown attorney

Foral (carta de)—Charter granted to the subjects of an administrative unit defining the sovereign's rights and the settler's responsibilities

Fôros—Rent, sometimes merely symbolic, paid by tenants to estate owner

Freguês—Customer, purchaser

Frota—Fleet of ships

Henriques—Black militia units named after black hero of the Brazilian revolt against the Dutch

Intendente de Marinha—Chief port officer

Irmandade—Religious brotherhood

Juiz das calafates—Ship inspector

Juiz do pôvo—theoretically popular tribune; practically, guilds' spokesman

Juiz ordinário—Justice of the Peace and president of municipal council

Lavradores—Tillers; share tenants

Licenciado—A person trained in civil law

Mascate—Merchant; peddlar

Massapé—Rich, black soil in All Saints Bay, particularly suitable for growing cane sugar

Mecânico—Artisan; manual worker; plebeian

Milreis—1,000 réis or 2.5 cruzados

Mineiro—Native of the interior captaincy of Minas Gerais

Misericórdia (Santa Casa da)—Brotherhood of Our Lady of Mercy; concerned with the alleviation of distress among the sick, jailed, and survivors of the deceased

Moio—Dry measure, generally sixty alqueires (*s.v.*)

Ouvidor—Circuit magistrate and administrative inspector

Ouvidor-general—Senior judicial officer

Pardo—Person of African extraction; often synonymous with mulatto

Parecer—Opinion; a statement by king or council

Patrão—Landlord; dominant socio-economic figure

Patrão da ribeira—Waterfront superintendent

Paulista—Native of the city or captaincy of São Paulo

Peça de Indias—Standard based on age and physical condition for determining the value of Negro slaves

Poderosos da terra (do sertão)—Powerful landowners

Portaria—Administrative order, usually authorizing payment

Procurador da fazenda—Treasury counsel

Procurador dos indios—Indian welfare officer

Prolegômenos—Prefactory comments

Provedor—Custodian of a government facility

Provedor da fazenda—Royal treasurer

Provisão—Royal decree

Real (pl. réis)—Monetary unit which existed only as money of account

Recôncavo—Periphery of All Saints Bay

Regimento—Instructions

Relação—High Court of Appeals

Requerimento—Petition

Residência—Terminal inquiry into the conduct of a public official

Santa Casa—See Misericórdia

Sargento-mor—Sergeant major

Senhor de engenho—"Lord of the mill"; the owner of a large plantation

Sertanista—Pathfinder

Sertão—Backlands

Terreiro do Trigo—Grain market

Trapiche—Primitive sugar mill; also a warehouse for storage of sugar

Várzea—Alluvial lands

Ver o pêso—See Aver do pêso

Vintem (pl. vintens)—Coin worth twenty reis

Index

Abolitionist movement, origins of. *See* Slaves and slavery (Negro)

Aguardente. See Brandy, sugar-cane

Albuquerque, Cristóvão de (uncle of proprietor of Pernambuco), imprisonment of for criticism of royal officials, 31

Albuquerque, Duarte Coelho de (elder son of founder of Pernambuco), 24

Albuquerque, Jerônimo de (*capitão-mor* of Maranhão), 52, 54–55

Albuquerque, Jorge de (third donatary of Pernambuco), 31

Albuquerque, Matias de (viceroy of India and royal councillor), 31–32

Albuquerque, Matias de (brother of fourth donatary of Pernambuco): background of, 41; report of concerning conditions in Pernambuco, 41; conflicts of with Luis de Sousa, 43–48; disputes of with Diogo de Mendonça Furtado, 50; and defense of Northeast against the Dutch, 52; as acting governor-general, 57; death of, 60

Almeida, Manuel José de Novais de (emancipationist), 117

Alvarenga Peixoto. *See* Peixoto, Ignácio José de Alvarenga

Argomosa Ceballos, Francisco (governor of Santa Cruz): searches for Portuguese mining camps, 78; recommends severing of communications between interior and coastal Brazil, 79–80; consequences of warning by, 80

Arrôba, defined, 238

Assumar, Count of, Pedro de Almeida (captain-general of Minas Gerais and later viceroy of India and marquis of Alorna), orders *bandeirantes* to leave disputed territory, 70

Azeredo Coutinho. *See* Coutinho, José Joaquim da Cunha de Azeredo

Azevedo, João de Sousa (merchant-adventurer): first to sail Tapajós river, 98; illicit expedition by, 103

Bacon, price movements of, in Rio de Janeiro, 255, 256, 260, 263, 278

Bahia (captaincy-general): population of in 1790s, 118; trade of with Portugal, 124 n. 68

Bandeirantes (frontier adventurers), 61, 65, 70

Bank of Brazil, paper money issued by, 244

Barbalho, José Joaquim Maia e (Brazilian medical student, alias Vendek), contacts Jefferson, 107

Barbosa, Domingos Vidal (Brazilian student in France), 108

Barrow, John (British scientist and traveler), assessment by of Brazilians' reaction to slave revolt in Saint Domingue, 116

Beans, price movements of, in Rio de Janeiro, 250, 251, 263, 271

Beckman, Manuel, revolt by in Maranhão, 201

Betancourt, José de, escape of from Minas Gerais, 131

Bishoprics of Mariana and São Paulo, creation of, 96

Bonifácio, José. *See* Silva, José Bonifácio de Andrada e

Botelho, Diogo (eighth governor-general of Brazil): arrival of in Pernambuco, 26, 29; investigation of conduct of, 32; instructions issued to, 36

Brandão, Ambrósio Fernandes (author of *Diálogos das grandezas do Brasil*): criticism of royal officials by, 28, 58

Brandy, price movements of, in Rio de Janeiro, 257, 259, 263, 281

Brandy, sugar-cane: production of in the Amazon, 214; price movements of, in Rio de Janeiro, 250, 252, 272–273

Brazil, archival sources for historical study of, 3, 4, 9, 10, 12

Bricks, price movements of, in Rio de Janeiro, 248, 249, 269–270